MODERN CHINESE

现代中文

Workbook 2A
Simplified Characters

BetterChinese

MODERN CHINESE 现代中文

Workbook Volume 2A

First Edition

Project Director:	James P. Lin
Editorial Consultant:	Li-Hsiang Yu Shen, Chi-Kuo Shen
Executive Publisher:	Chi-Kuo Shen
Curriculum Advisors:	Norman Masuda and Rebecca Starr
Editorial Team:	Christopher Peacock, Bin Yin
	Sue-Ann Ma, Cheuk-Yue Fung,
	Lillian Klemp, Lauren Chen,
	Tiantian Gao, and Ying Jin
Illustrations:	Better World Ltd

© 2013 BETTER CHINESE LLC (a Better World LTD company)

Library of Congress Cataloging-in-Publication Data: To be Assigned

ISBN: 978-1-60603-488-0

2 3 4 XLA 17 16 15

ALL RIGHTS RESERVED. No part of this work covered by the copyright hereon may be reproduced or used in any form or by any means – graphic, electronic, or mechanical, including photocopying, recording, taping, web distribution, information storage and retrieval systems, or in any other manner – without the written permission of the publisher.

Photos used with permission from Thinkstock Photos.

For more information about our products, contact us at:
United States
2479 E. Bayshore Rd., Suite 110
Palo Alto, CA 94303
Tel: 888-384-0902
Fax: 888-442-7968
Email: usa@betterchinese.com

Contents 目录

Foreword i

Unit 1 天 Weather

Lesson 1: 天气 Weather 1

Lesson 2: 旅游和气候 Travel and Climate 17

Unit 2 学 Academics

Lesson 1: 申请留学 Applying to Study Abroad 33

Lesson 2: 加入社团 Joining a Student Club 49

Unit 3 住 Housing

Lesson 1: 住校与租房 Living On-Campus vs. Off-Campus 65

Lesson 2: 找公寓 Apartment Hunting 82

Unit 4 买 Shopping

Lesson 1: 网上购物 Shopping Online 98

Lesson 2: 退货 Returning Merchandise 115

Unit 5 娱 Hobbies

Lesson 1: 篮球比赛 At a Basketball Game 132

Lesson 2: 采访 An Interview 149

Unit 6 食 Cuisine

Lesson 1: 学做中国菜 Learning Chinese Cooking 166

Lesson 2: 逛超市 Going to the Supermarket 183

Unit 7 祸 Emergencies

Lesson 1: 交通意外 A Traffic Accident 199

Lesson 2: 自然灾难 Natural Disasters 216

Unit 8 行 Travel

Lesson 1: 在机场 At the Airport 232

Lesson 2: 中国游 Traveling in China 248

Foreword

About the Workbook
The *Modern Chinese* workbook is designed to create opportunities for students to practice individual language skills in targeted settings as well as in holistic and applied ways. For each section in the workbook, there are numerous real-life practices focused on getting students to understand, to speak, and to write Chinese. These exercises are not only useful for achieving the objectives of each lesson, they are also designed to build on top of previous lessons. In this way students are able to establish a strong foundation in the language.

Please visit our website, http://college.betterchinese.com, to access additional resources, such as audio files for listening comprehension practices, audio recording tools, further cultural information, and additional character writing materials. The workbook is comprised of the following sections:

Vocabulary Review
Various exercises aim to help students absorb the new vocabulary introduced in each lesson. Exercises focus on character recognition and pinyin accuracy.

Character Writing Practice
Characters highlighted in the Practice section of the textbook are revisited with ample space for writing practice. Complete stroke-order sequence diagrams and radical information are also included. For further character writing practice, please visit the website to download additional character writing sheets.

Listening Comprehension
This section offers an extra opportunity to gain exposure to Chinese sentences and conversations outside of the classroom. Students answer a variety of comprehension questions after listening to short dialogues and/or narratives in Standard Mandarin. Visit our website to download the audio files for the exercises.

Speaking Practice
To encourage active production of Chinese sentences, this section prompts students to make audio recordings that role-play everyday situations they may encounter. Students can also visit our website to use our online tools to record their compositions and send them to their teacher for review. Alternatively, teachers may want to use this section in the classroom for additional speaking practice.

Structure Review
Each section provides the Structure Note formula introduced in the lesson and also exercises focusing on mastery of the grammar.

Reading Comprehension
Lesson vocabulary and Structure Notes are reviewed in passages, narratives, and other authentic materials. Questions are provided to assess students' comprehension of the material.

Writing Practice
This section provides another opportunity for students to practice writing Chinese using authentic materials. Students must draw from previously learned vocabulary and Structure Notes to compose short essays based on prompts relevant to the theme of the lesson.

祝你学习进步!
Happy Chinese learning!

UNIT 1 – LESSON 1

现代中文 Modern Chinese

天气

VOCABULARY REVIEW 1.1

I. Write down the meanings of the characters below. Use each character to form different vocabulary terms by filling in the boxes with appropriate characters, and include the pinyin and meaning for each phrase.

Example: 气 means _____air_____

 tiānqì   weather

 qìwēn   temperature

1. 游 means _____

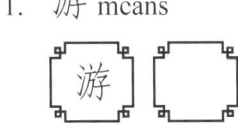 _____

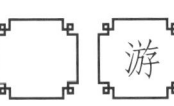 _____

2. 雨 means _____

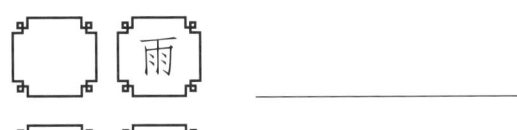 _____

3. 节 means _____

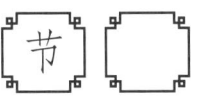 _____

 _____

II. Write down characters with the same radicals provided below and form vocabulary phrases with each character.

Example: Radical 口. Words related to "mouth":

吃(东西), 嘴(巴), 告(诉)

1. Radical 冫. Words related to "cold, cool":

_____

2. Radical 日. Words related to "sun":

_____

3. Radical 雨. Words related to weather:

_____

III. Read the sentence below. Choose a character in each column to form a complete sentence in Chinese that matches the English one.

The average temperature in summer is about 70 degrees.

冬	天	的	比	均	气	活	在	一	干	度	做	右
夏	太	得	别	趣	天	泳	来	七	上	都	作	左
下	大	第	平	裙	亲	游	再	八	十	短	右	又
暑	天	地	半	进	季	温	这	几	千	步	左	有

Unit 1 • Lesson 1 • Weather

CHARACTER WRITING PRACTICE 1.1

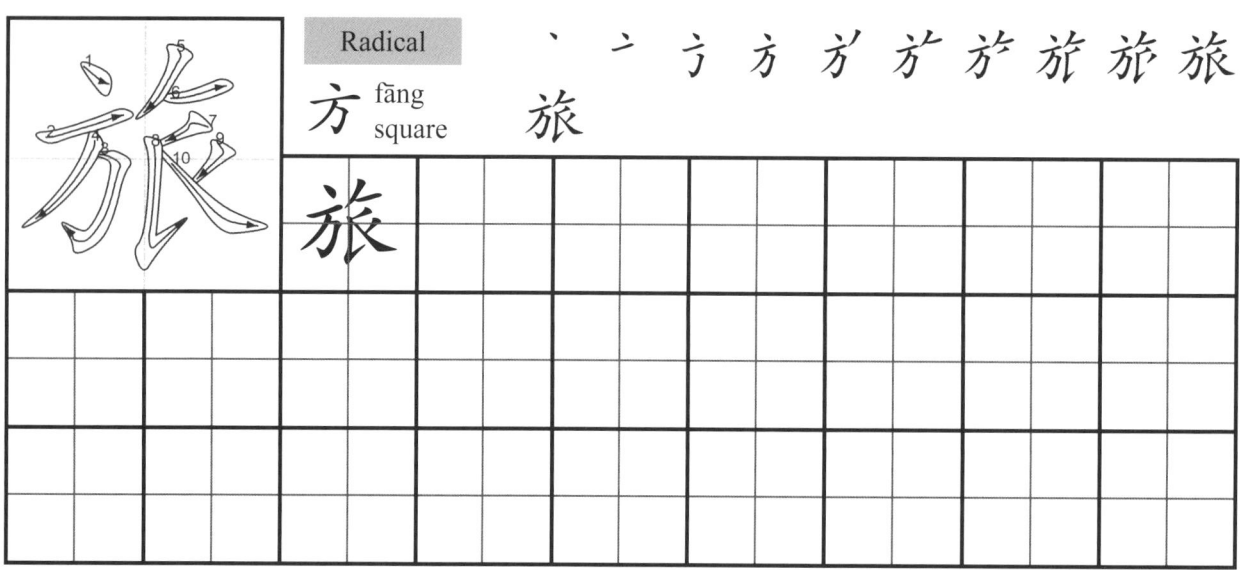

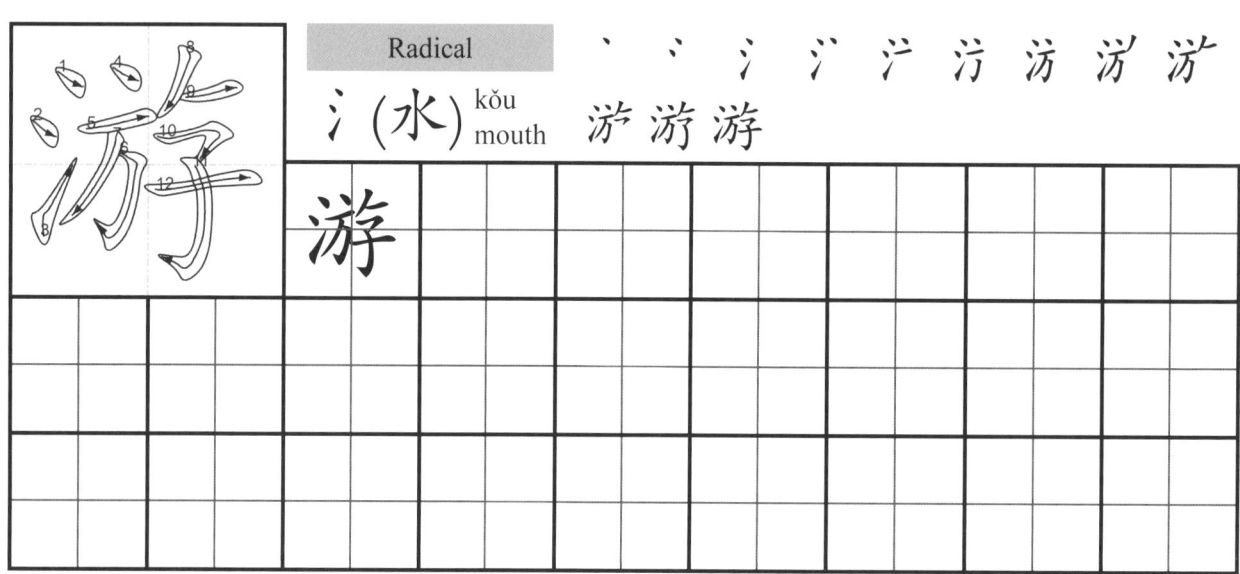

第一单元 · 第一课 · 天

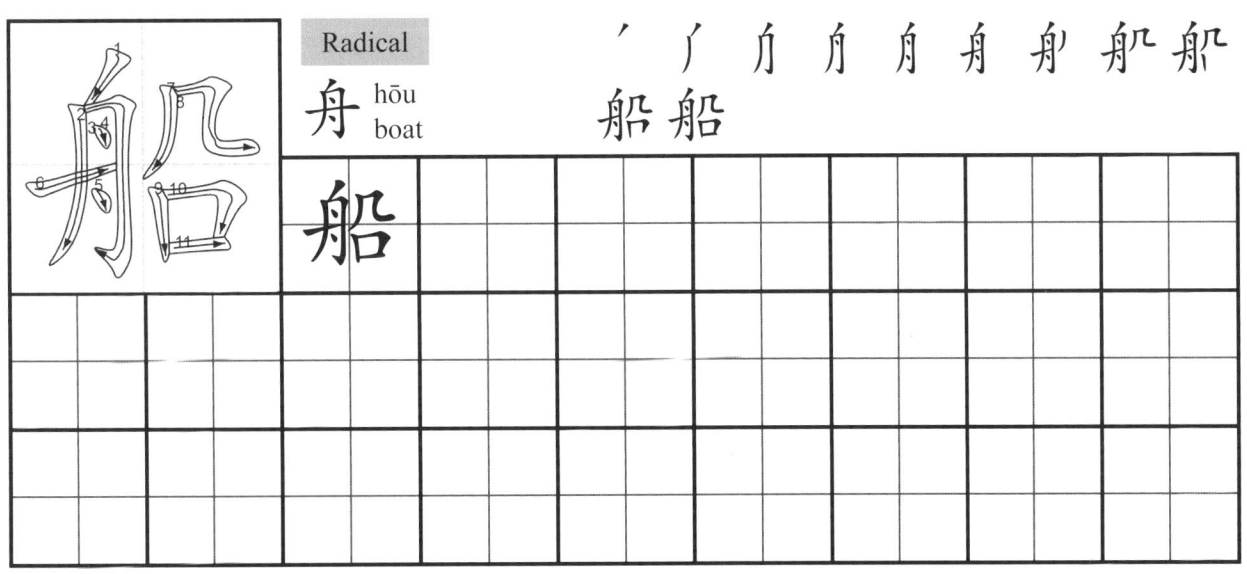

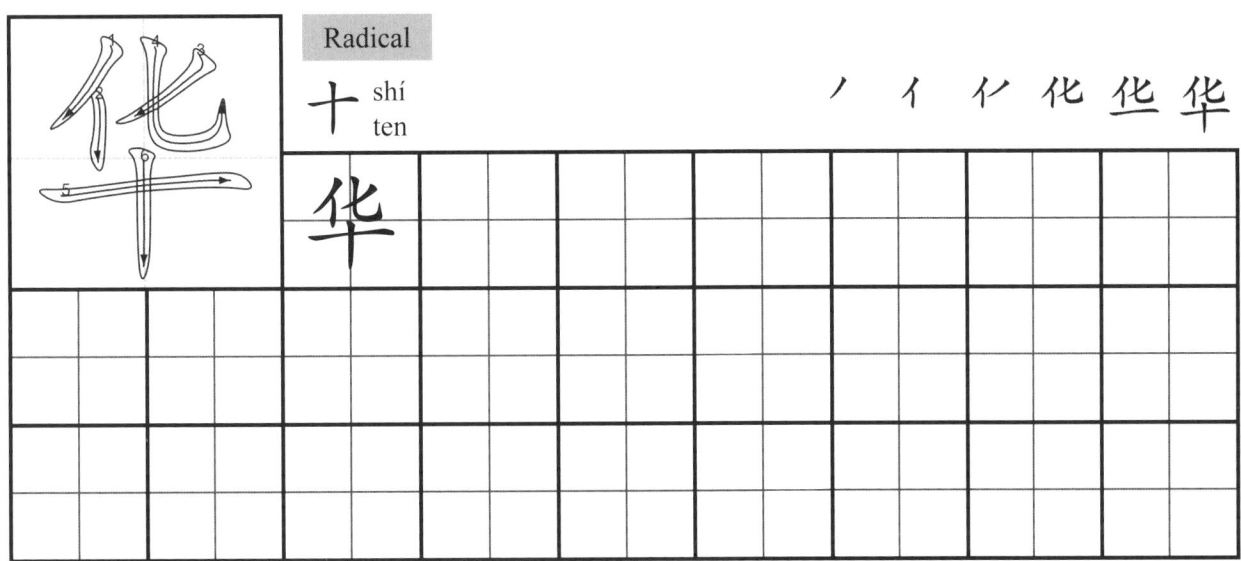

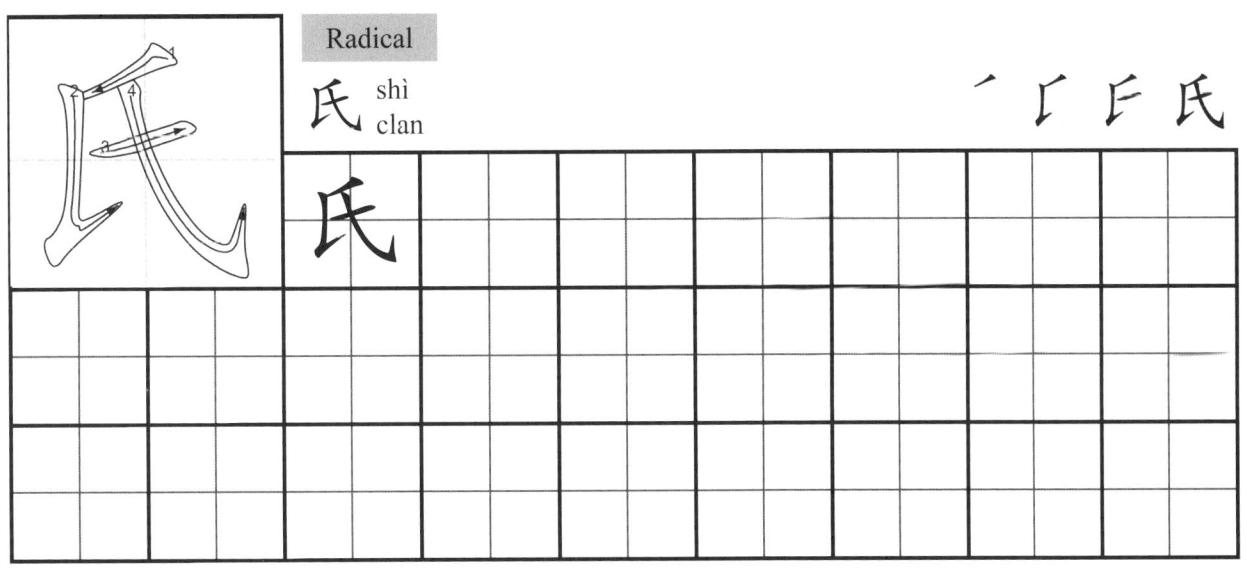

Unit 1 • Lesson 1 • Weather

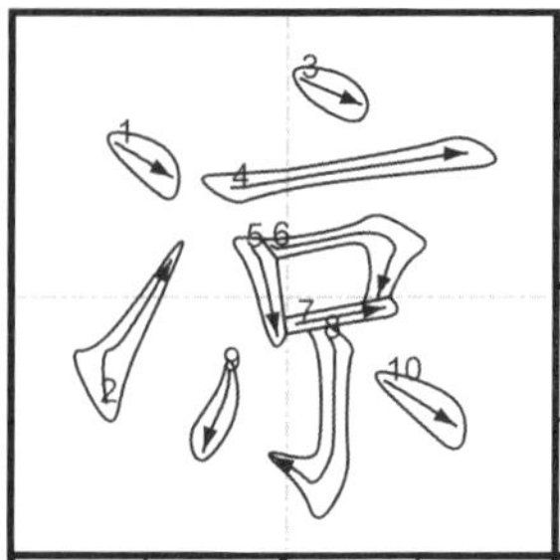

	Radical	、 冫 冫 冫 冫 冫 冫 凉 凉 凉
凉	冫(冰) bīng ice	凉

	Radical	、 丶 丶 丷 丷 米 米 迷 迷
迷	辶 chuò walk	迷

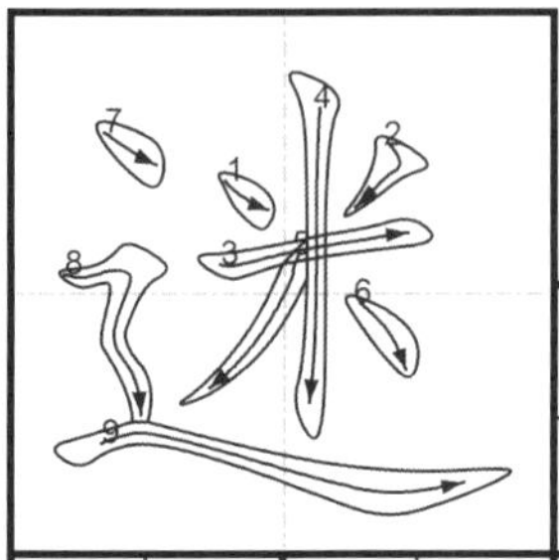

	Radical	⺈ ⺈ ⺈ ⺈ 切 卯 留 留 留
留	田 tián field	留

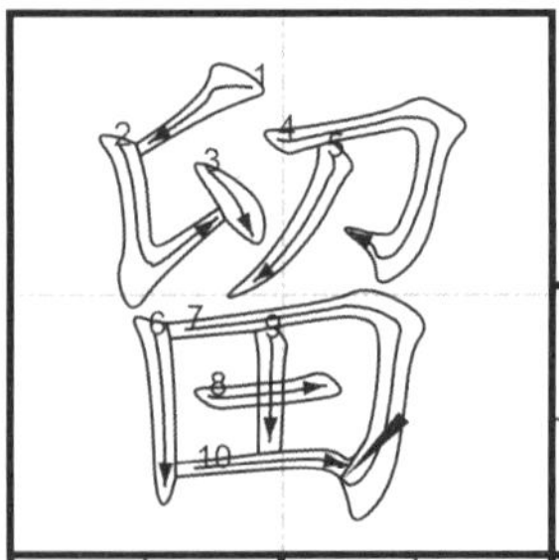

第一单元・第一课・天

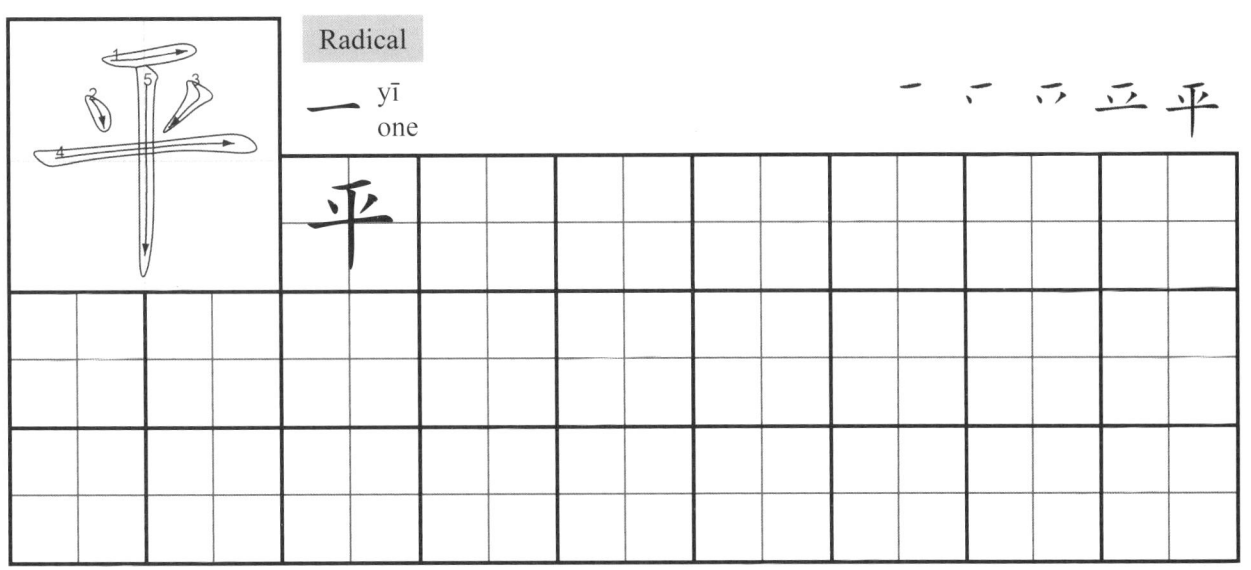

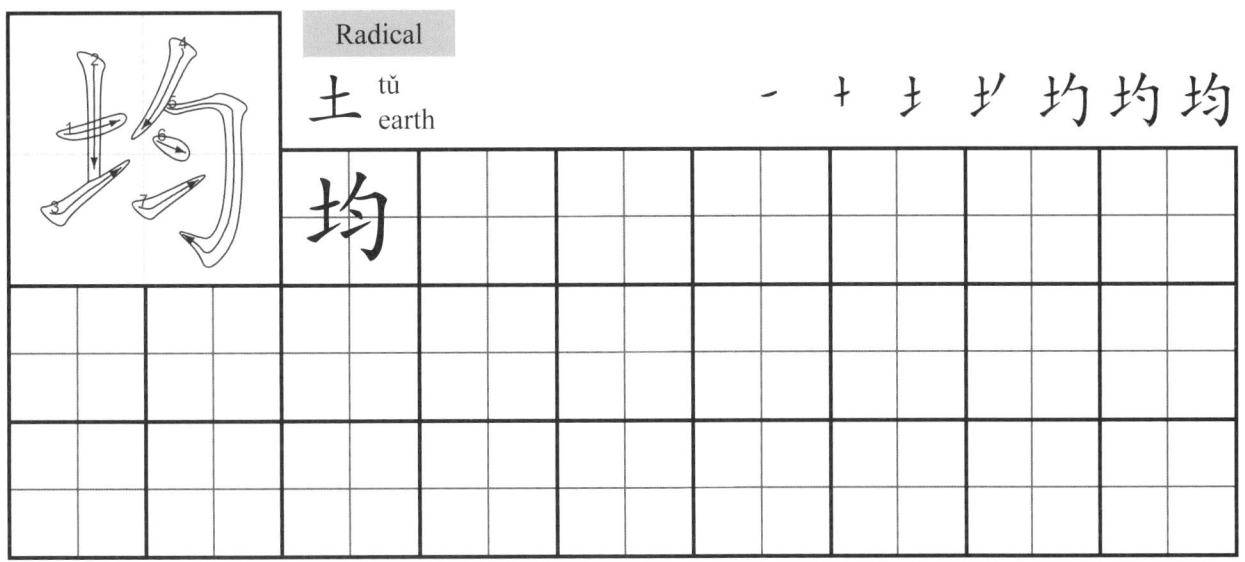

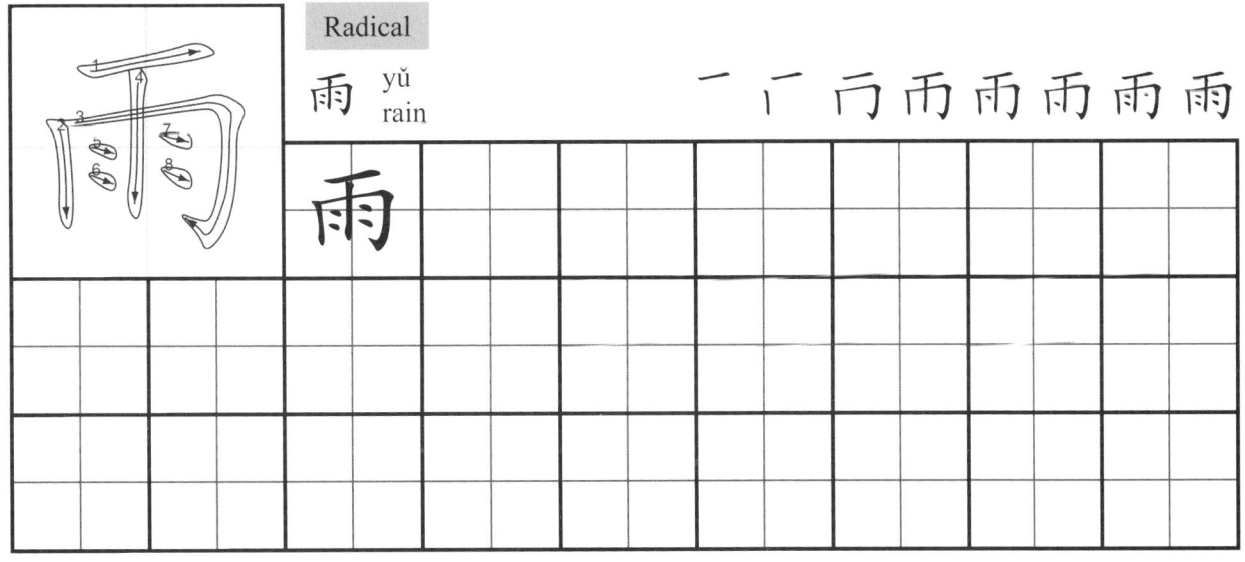

Unit 1 • Lesson 1 • Weather

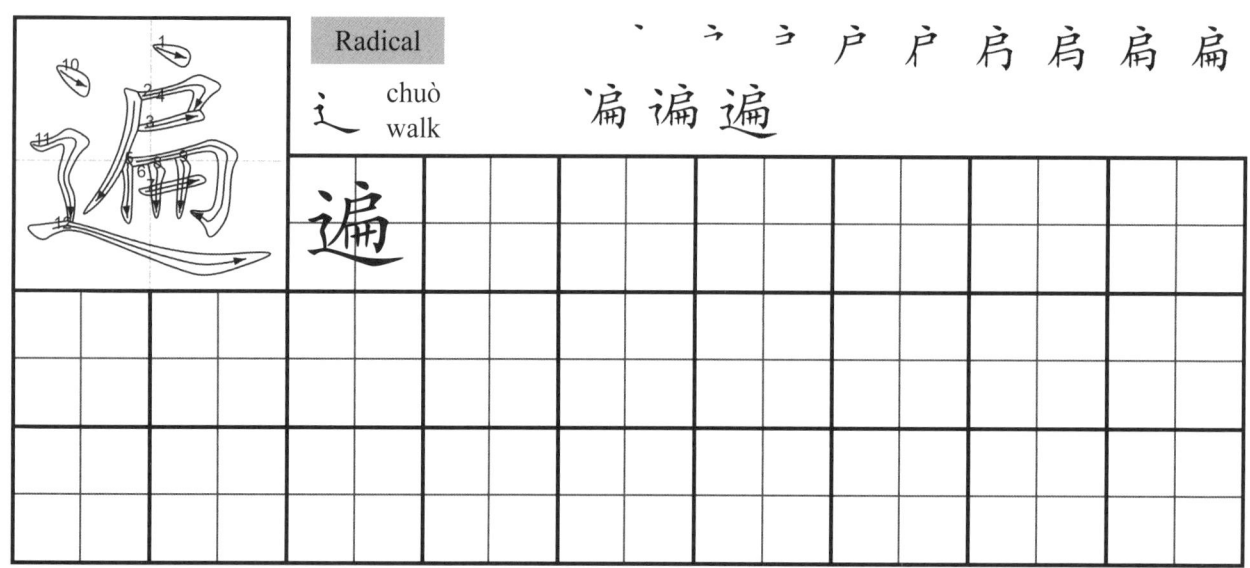

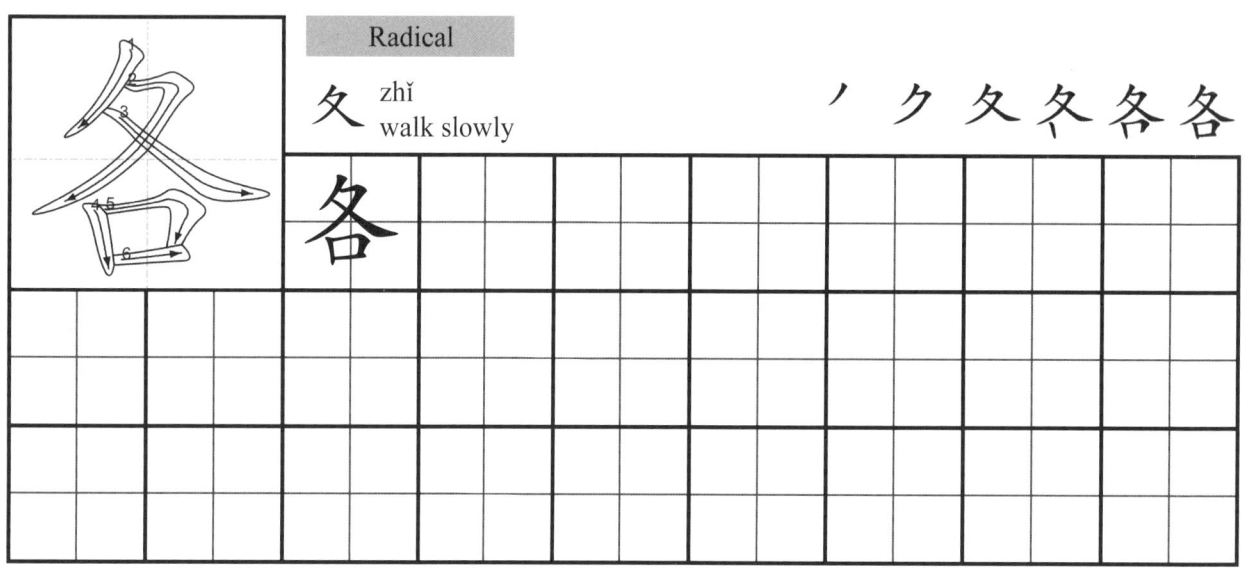

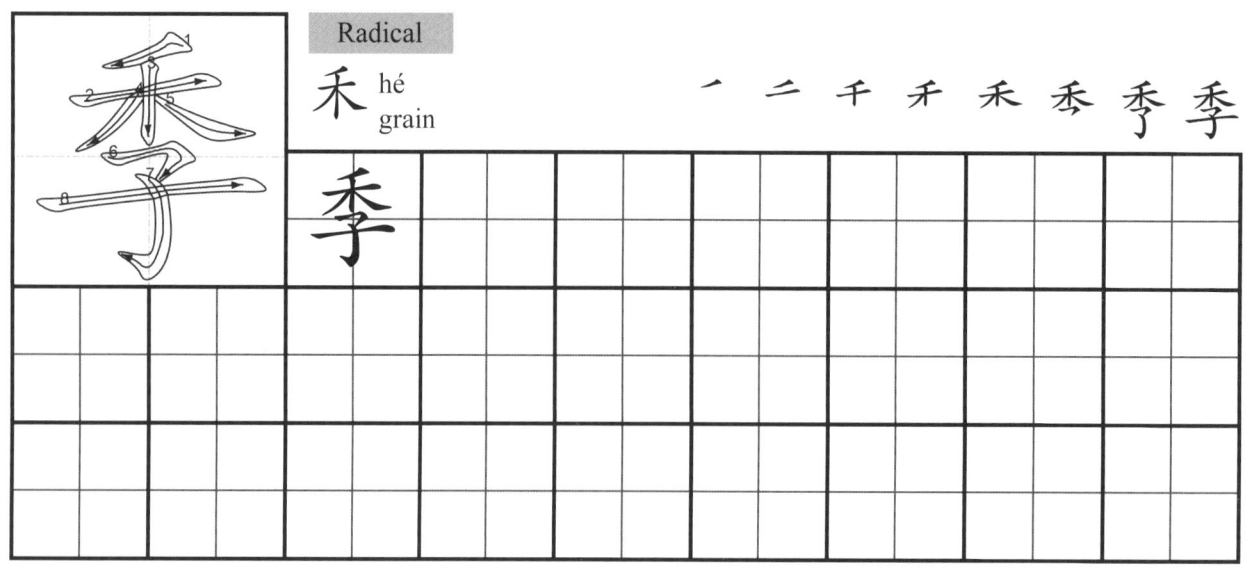

LISTENING COMPREHENSION 1.1

I. **Listen to the recording and select the best response below.**

1. The woman would most likely respond with:

    A. 平均气温很高吗?
    B. 那我得带着雨伞。
    C. 希望我能去别的地方玩。
    D. 对了，说不定可以去逛街。

II. **Listen to the recording and answer the following True or False questions.**

1. (   ) The woman wants to take a trip to Spain during the summer.
2. (   ) The woman wants to take a trip because the weather is going to be good.
3. (   ) One reason the woman wants to go there is because there will not be too many tourists.
4. (   ) The man suggests going there to enjoy the culture and do some shopping.
5. (   ) The man will definitely take a trip to Spain no matter how much it costs.

III. **Listen to the recording and answer the questions in Chinese.**

1. What is the summer weather like?

    _____

2. What is the speaker's general attitude toward the weather condition?

    _____

3. What is the speaker's plan following the summer vacation?

    _____

SPEAKING PRACTICE 1.1

I. Imagine you are traveling in China. Talk about your travel experiences, including the weather, activities, clothing, and items you brought in preparation for the different weather you encountered.

II. Your friend is planning to visit your city. Talk about the best season to visit and what a typical day is like, including the weather, what kind of clothing and items your friend should bring. Also, offer suggestions of different activities your friend can do when he/she comes to visit.

STRUCTURE REVIEW 1.1

I. Complete the following Structure Note practice activities.

Structure Note 1.1: Use 才 after a number to make an estimate.

$$\text{Subject} + 才 + \text{Phrase}$$

A. Your friend asks you some questions about your study abroad experience in Beijing. Answer the questions using 才:

1. 去北京的飞机票多少钱?（一千块）

   _____

2. 北京冬天的平均气温是多少?（零下四度）

   _____

3. 你学校有多少美国留学生?（三十个）

   _____

4. 你学校附近有几家美国餐厅?（两家）

   _____

5. 你参观了几个博物馆?（一个）

   _____

Structure Note 1.2: Use 左右 after a number to make an estimate.

$$\text{Number} + \text{Measure Word} (+ \text{Noun}) + 左右$$

B. After attending a concert yesterday, your friend asks you some questions about it. Answer the questions using 左右:

1. 昨天的音乐会几点开始?（晚上八点）

   _____

2. 音乐会的票多少钱?（五十元）

   _____

3. 这次音乐会里有多少个钢琴表演？（七个）

_____

4. 这次的音乐会有几位小提琴家表演？（四位）

_____

5. 这次的音乐会有多少个学生参加？（一百个）

_____

Take the challenge! 动动脑筋！

祥安刚来中国学中文，他在学校看到一位女同学，想知道她多大，我就告诉他："二十左右吧。"祥安问："二十的左边和右边是什么？"我说："不是，二十左右就是二十上下的意思。"他听了还是不明白，就说："你们汉语怎么上下左右都是一样的意思？"

In the passage, what is the meaning of 上下? Why do 左右 and 上下 share the same meaning?

Structure Note 1.2: Use 说不定 to express possibility or uncertainty.

说不定 + Sentence

Subject + 说不定 + Verb Phrase

C. "关系" is very important in China. See what favors you could receive by matching the phrases in Column A with the appropriate ones in Column B to make complete sentences below.

Column A	Column B
1. 我的朋友是语言大学的学生。	说不定他会让我到那里实习。
2. 我认识这家公司的老板。	说不定到那里去买茶叶会便宜一点。
3. 我妈妈的朋友在故宫博物馆工作。	他说不定能给我们买关于中国文化的书。
4. 我有一个同学在书店打工。	说不定她可以教你汉语。
5. 我表哥在一家茶店工作。	他说不定可以给我们介绍中国的历史。

1. _____

2. _____

3. _____

4. _____

5. _____

Structure Note 1.4: Use 各 to mean each or different.

> 各 + Noun (limited to a specific group)

> 各 + Measure Word

D. Read the radio transcript of an ad for a job opening below. Use the nouns or measure words together with 各 to fill in the blanks.

> Measure Words: 家 门 位 个

_____快要毕业的同学们，除了准备_____课的考试以外，你们开始找工作了吗？还是你们已经开始忙着去_____公司面试了？你们对一份能游遍法国_____城市的工作有兴趣吗？

> Nouns: 地 校 国

我们是一家在法国的电影公司，我们欢迎_____的毕业生来法国实习和工作。实习生不但可以学习欧洲_____的电影文化，还有机会走遍法国_____工作。同学们，快准备好你的简历，然后寄到……

Structure Note 1.5: Use 比较 to strengthen an adjective.

$$\boxed{\text{Subject} + 比较 + \text{Adjective}}$$

E. Fill in the table using 比较 to create four sentences that compare Beijing's average temperatures for each season with those of the city you live in.

	季节	北京 平均气温	我的城市 平均气温	我的城市比较……
1.	春天	45 °F		
2.	夏天	80 °F		
3.	秋天	63 °F		
4.	冬天	25 °F		

II. Below are some questions regarding your experience with learning Chinese. Answer each one and include a comparison of your answer with Li Xiaoli's using 才, 左右, and 比较. An example is provided in the first question.

> 李小丽：我开始学中文的时候才九岁。我每天花差不多两个小时学习中文。我一个星期学习生词学五十个左右。和我一起学中文的同学有三四十个。

1. 你几岁开始学中文？

   Example: 我比较晚开始学中文。我十八岁左右的时候才开始学。

   _____

2. 你一个星期学习多少个生词？

   _____

3. 你每天花多长时间学习中文？

   _____

4. 有多少个同学和你一起上中文课？

   _____

READING COMPREHENSION 1.1

I. Read the passage and answer the following True or False questions.

> 玛丽一个月以前去中国实习了。虽然才过了一个月，但是中平已经很想念她了。中平常常收到玛丽的明信片。玛丽说，来了以后她才知道北京的秋天多美。不但天气很好，风和日丽，而且气温不冷不热，每天都在华氏六十度左右，去逛街很舒服。难怪她来中国以前就听很多人说，北京的秋天是最好的季节，很多人来北京旅游。
>
> 中平问玛丽："你每天都吃中国菜，你已经习惯了吗？"玛丽告诉他，虽然这里各个中国饭馆的饭菜都很不错，可是她这几天比较想吃美国菜。再过两个星期就是玛丽的生日了。说不定下个周末她会跟朋友去一家法国饭馆吃晚饭。

1. (　) 玛丽和中平一起去北京旅游了。
2. (　) 现在北京的天气很凉快。
3. (　) 再过两个月左右，北京就是冬天了。
4. (　) 玛丽觉得北京的中餐饭馆不太好。
5. (　) 因为玛丽的生日快到了，所以她可能去吃西餐。

Take the challenge! 动动脑筋！

In the passage, 不冷不热, is used to describe the temperature as being neither cold nor hot. It follows the pattern 不 + Adjective A + 不 + Adjective B to indicate something is "neither . . . nor . . ." The two adjectives are always a pair of antonyms. For example, you could say 学校离我家不远不近 to express that the school is neither far nor close to your house. Can you come up with at least three other sentences that use this pattern to describe a person, place, thing, or situation?

II. Read the following passage and answer the questions.

今年暑假，我在故宫博物馆做了一个星期左右的**志愿者**。每年夏天的时候都有各国的朋友来旅游，这些朋友当然希望能看看故宫博物馆的中国**艺术品**，他们需要有人用外语给他们做介绍。我英语比较好，大学里学习的专业是**艺术**，所以我就会跟这些外国朋友们聊中国古代的**艺术品**。

在博物馆我还认识了一个美国朋友，他叫大中，他是从加州到中国来学习传统文化的，他不但会说中文，而且还知道很多有关中国艺术的事呢！这个暑假我过得真有意思。虽然我做志愿者才有一个星期，但是我已经迷上了这份工作，说不定我下个暑假会再来博物馆做**志愿者**。

Notes:
志愿者 (zhìyuànzhě): *n.* volunteer
艺术品 (yìshùpǐn): *n.* work of art
艺术 (yìshù): *n.* art

1. 今年夏天我去博物馆做志愿者，因为……
   A. 我喜欢故宫博物馆的艺术品。
   B. 我认识一个美国朋友在博物馆工作。
   C. 在博物馆工作的人需要说中文。
   D. 我会说英文，我也懂艺术。

2. Which statement below is NOT true about Dazhong?
   A. He is American.
   B. He does not know how to speak Chinese.
   C. He is knowledgeable about Chinese art.
   D. He is my new friend.

3. 明年夏天我很可能会做什么？
   A. 我会来故宫博物馆旅游。
   B. 我会再做志愿者。
   C. 我会跟外国的朋友说英文。
   D. 我会和美国朋友一起学中国文化。

III. Read the travel ad and e-mail and answer the questions in Chinese.

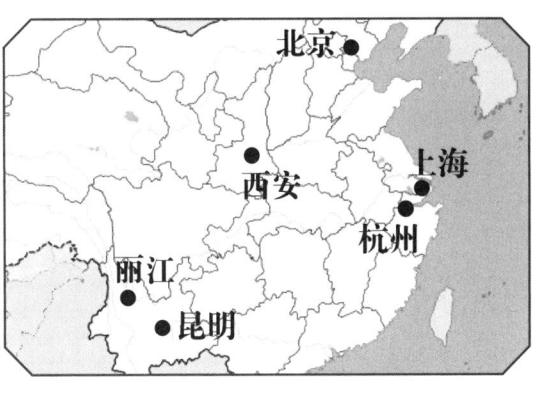

To: 孙玛丽
From: 张安娜
Subject: 去中国旅游

亲爱的玛丽，
　　今年秋天我会去中国旅游。我只有一个星期的时间，而且我中文也不太好，所以我想参加一个**旅游团**。我上网找到了一些**资料**，但是不知道选哪一个好。我听说中国的北方秋天就会凉起来了，所以我想去没那么冷的地方。而且，我想多去几个有**特色**的地方。我的旅游**预算**是2000块左右。你能给我一些建议吗？
安娜

Notes:

旅游团 (lǚyóutuán): n. tour group
资料 (zīliào): n. data, material
特色 (tèsè): n. distinguishing feature/quality, characteristic
预算 (yùsuàn): n. budget

1. Why does Anna want to join a tour group?

2. According to Anna, what places do you think she would be interested in? Circle the places on the ad.

3. Using the travel ad, plan a travel route for Anna while taking into consideration her available time and budget, and describe why she choose those cities. Be sure to include how many days she will be traveling and how much she will spend.

WRITING PRACTICE 1.1

I. While traveling through Asia, you want to send your friend Xiaomei a postcard. On the left side, write about some of the places you visited, what kind of weather you encountered, notable experiences, and your plans for the remainder of the trip. On the right side, draw images illustrating some of things you saw or experienced on your trip.

II. A year has four seasons, but you have been granted by Heaven the right to remove one season. Which season would you remove? Why? What are the advantages and disadvantages of eliminating this season? Please explain.

UNIT 1 – LESSON 2

Modern Chinese 现代中文

旅游和气候

VOCABULARY REVIEW 1.2

I. Write the antonym of each word or phrase below.

1. 高 ⟷ _____   2. 下降 ⟷ _____

3. 潮湿 ⟷ _____   4. 凉快 ⟷ _____

II. Fill in the missing words for each idiom based on the definition and radical provided.

	Idiom:	Definition:	Radical:
Example:	秋高气爽	The autumn sky is clear and the air is bracing.	禾
1.	大____回春	Spring returns to the earth.	土
2.	鸟语____香	Birds sing and flowers give force their fragrance.	艹
3.	春____花开	Spring has come and the flowers are in bloom.	日
4.	冰____雪地	A world of ice and snow.	大

III. Choose one sentence from each of the following pairs that correctly utilizes the lesson vocabulary words.

1. ☐ (A) 小心！这杯水的气温非常高！
   ☐ (B) 今年夏天的平均温度比去年的高多了。

2. ☐ (A) 这里每年秋天都会刮大风，而且非常干燥。
   ☐ (B) 今年的风越刮越多，你们来的时候记得要带件大衣。

3. ☐ (A) 医生建议每个星期去跑跑步、走走山，身体才会健康。
   ☐ (B) 我们爬山的时候要注意安全，特别是雨天的时候。

4. ☐ (A) 今年很少下雨，我都忘了把那件黄色的雨衣放到哪里去了。
   ☐ (B) 天气预报说今天下午会下雨，出门的时候记得穿雨伞。

CHARACTER WRITING PRACTICE 1.2

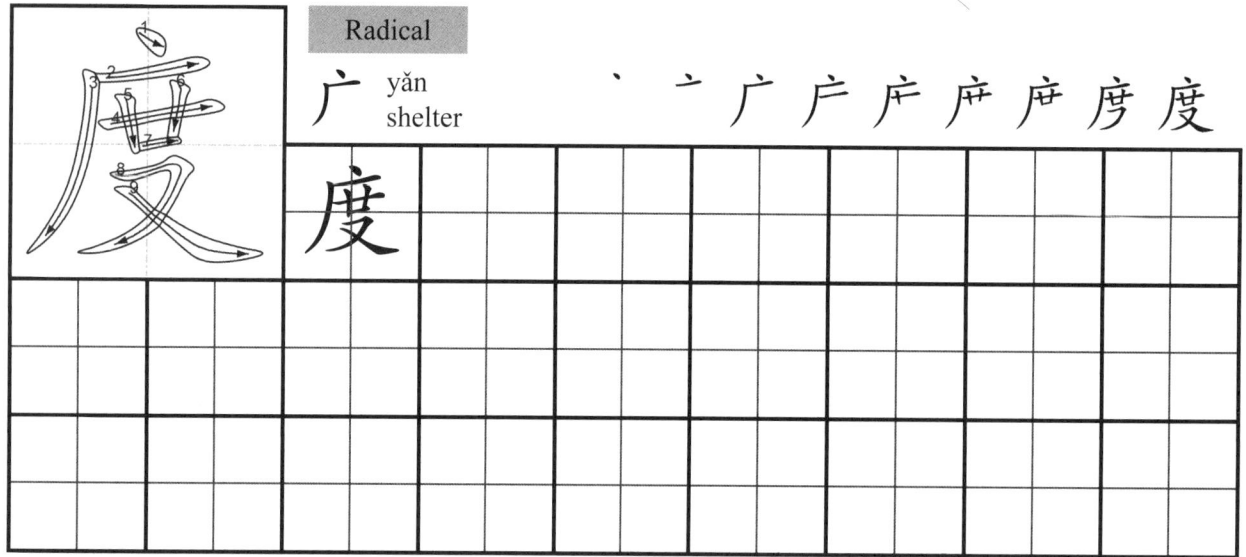

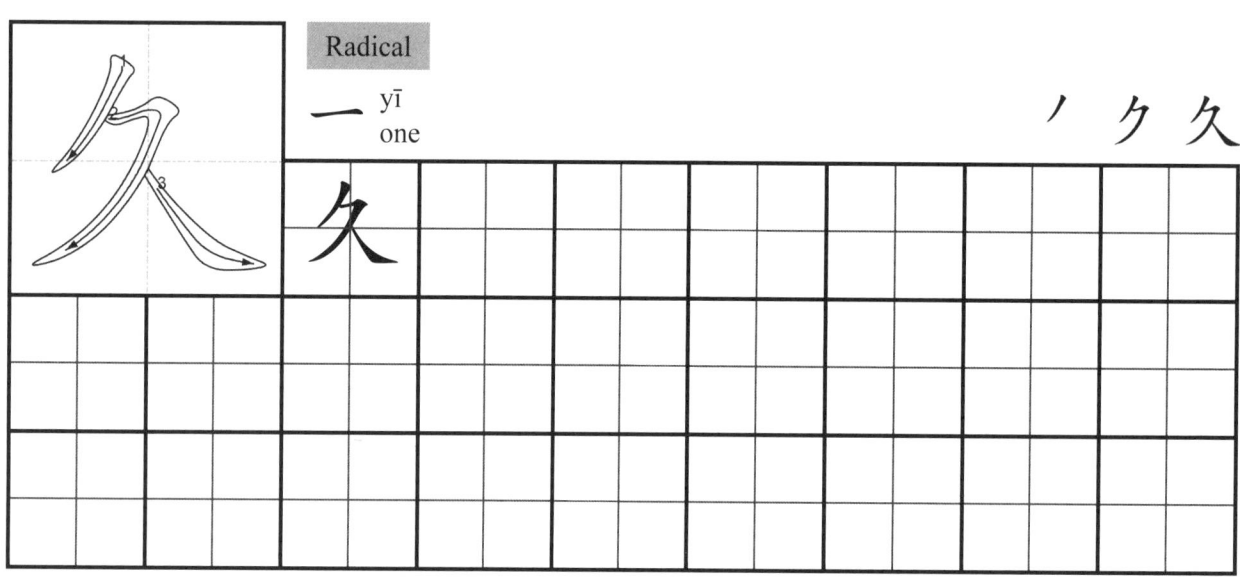

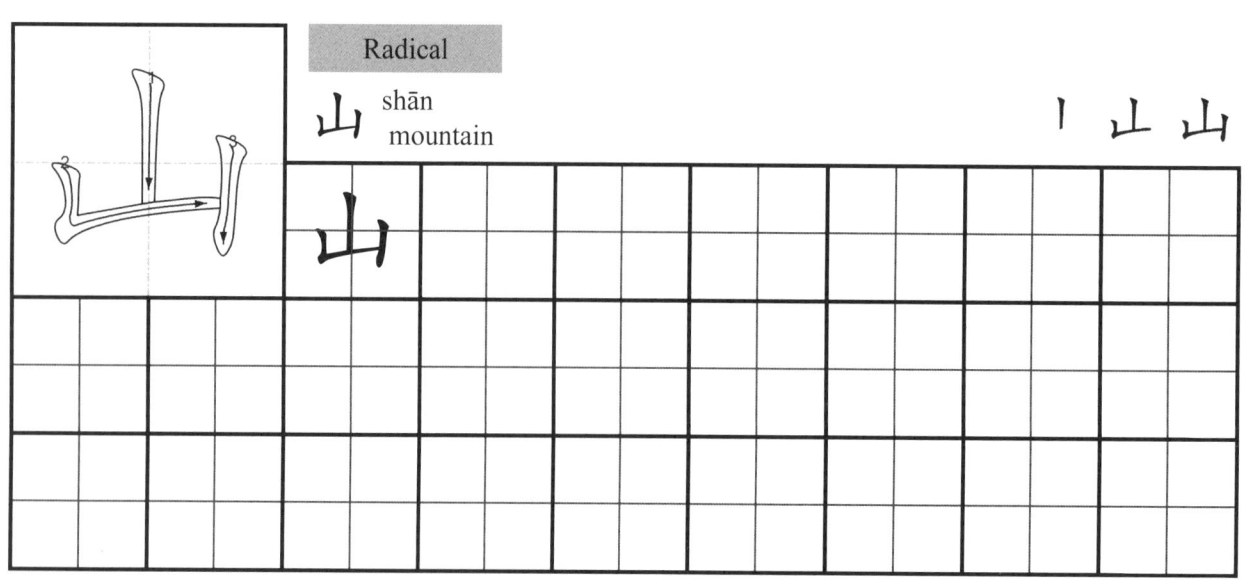

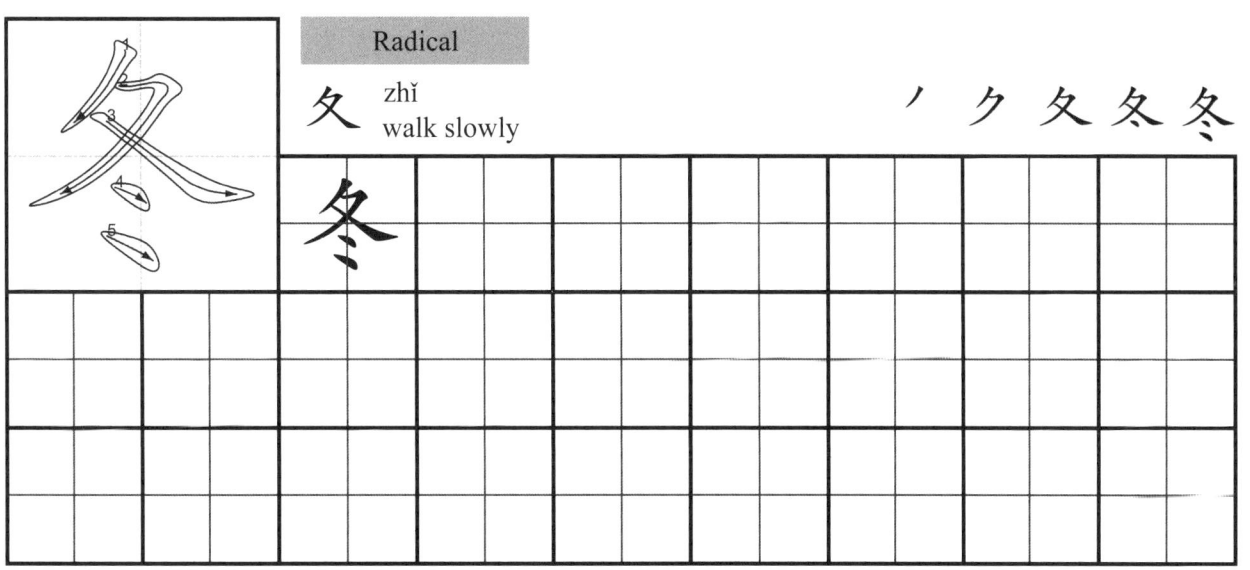

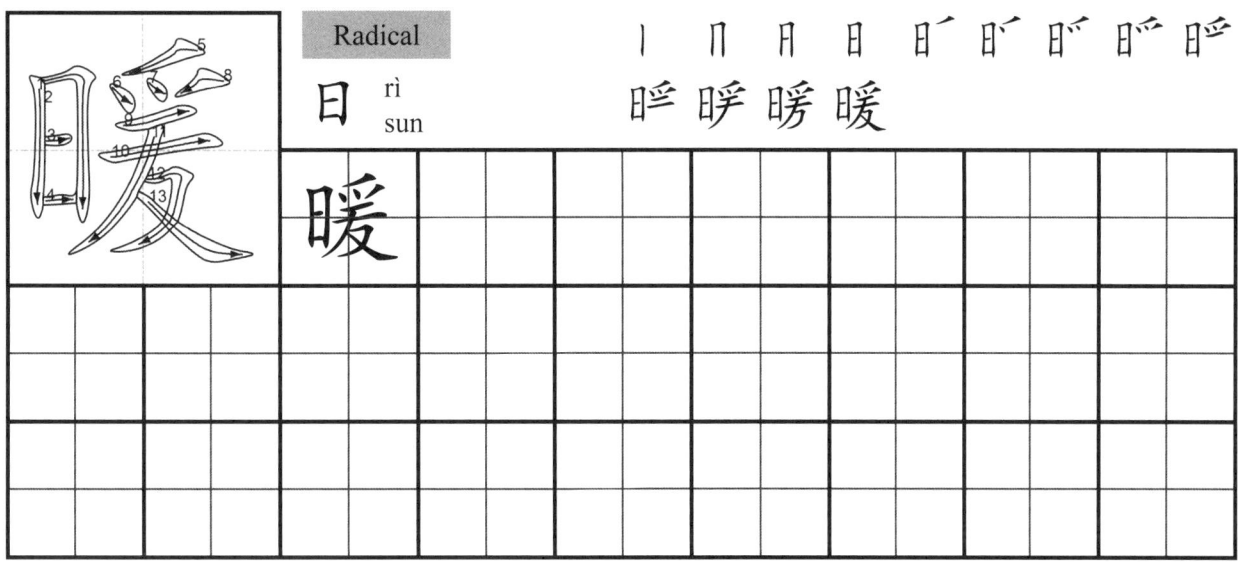

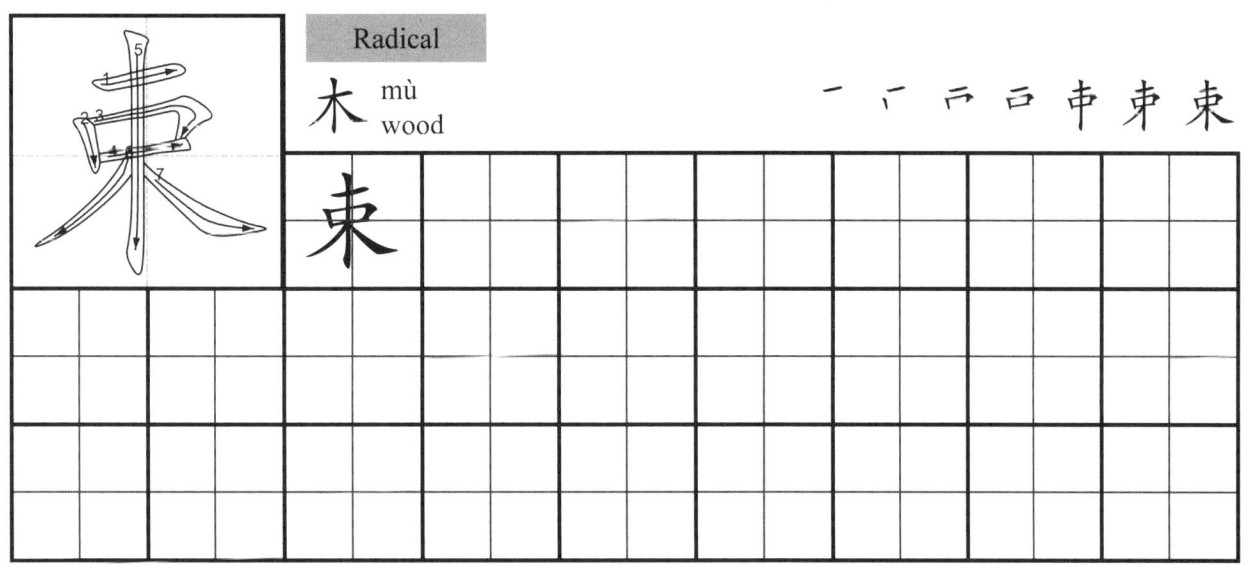

Unit 1 • Lesson 2 • Weather

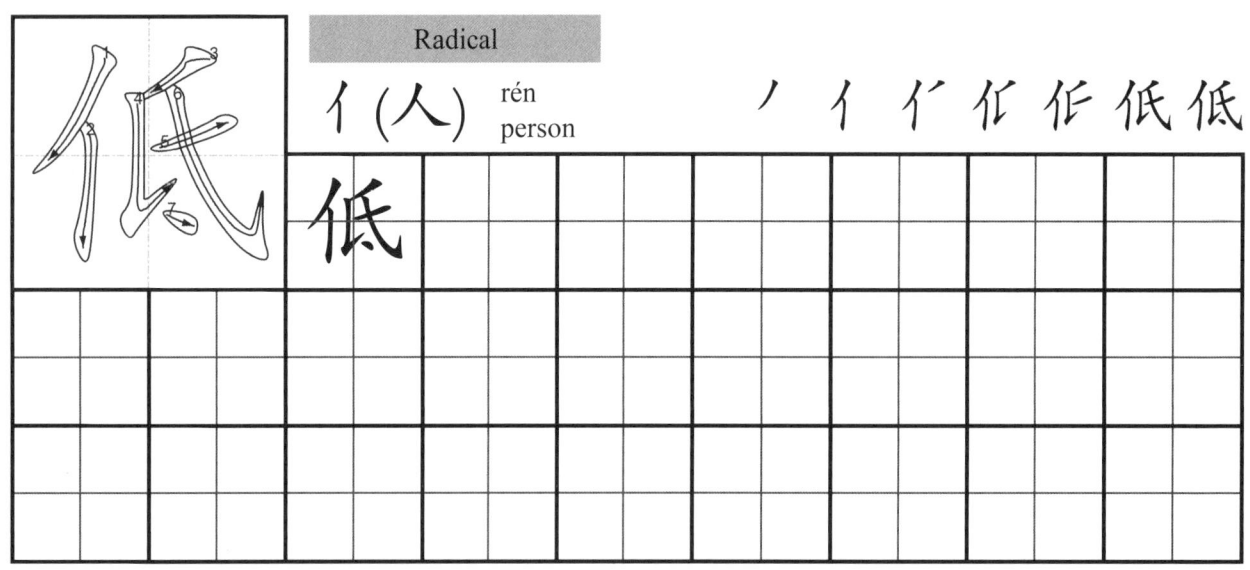

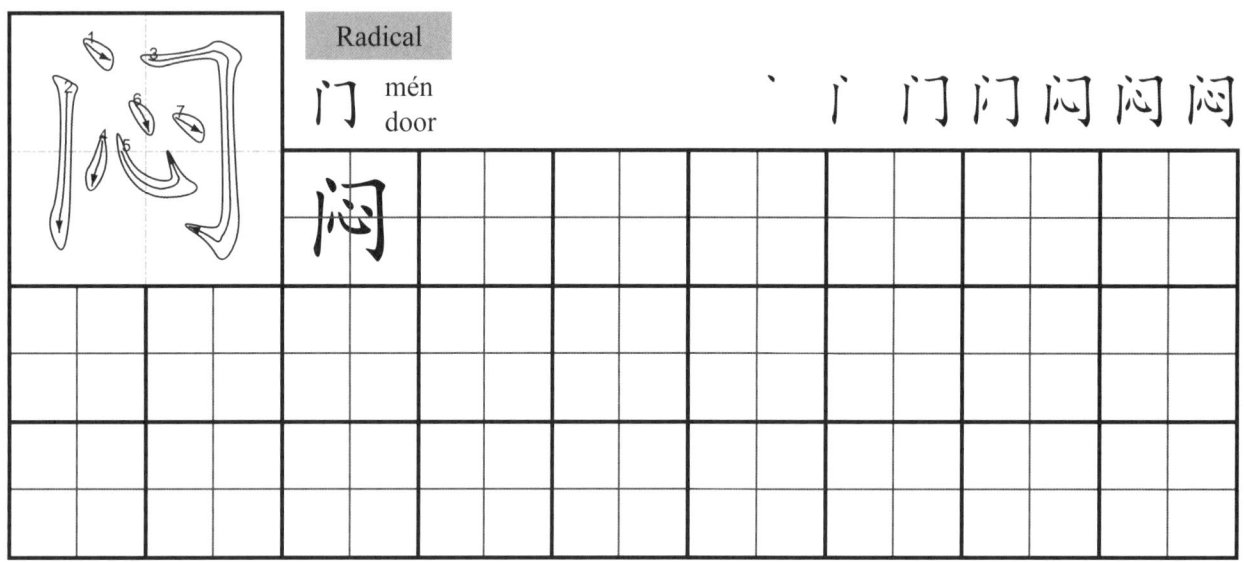

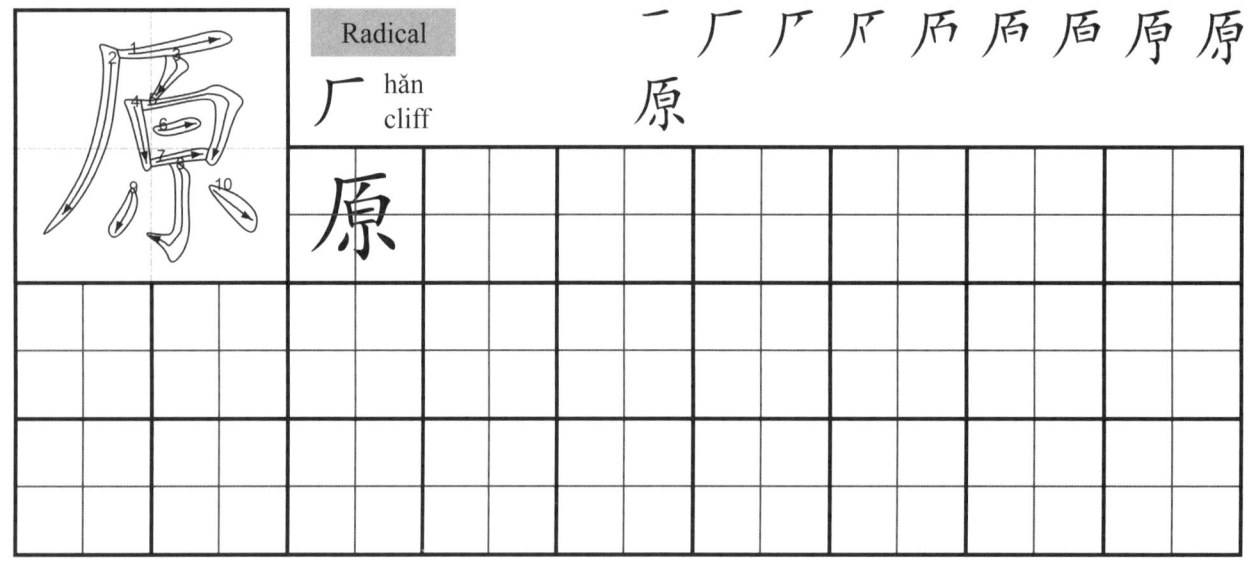

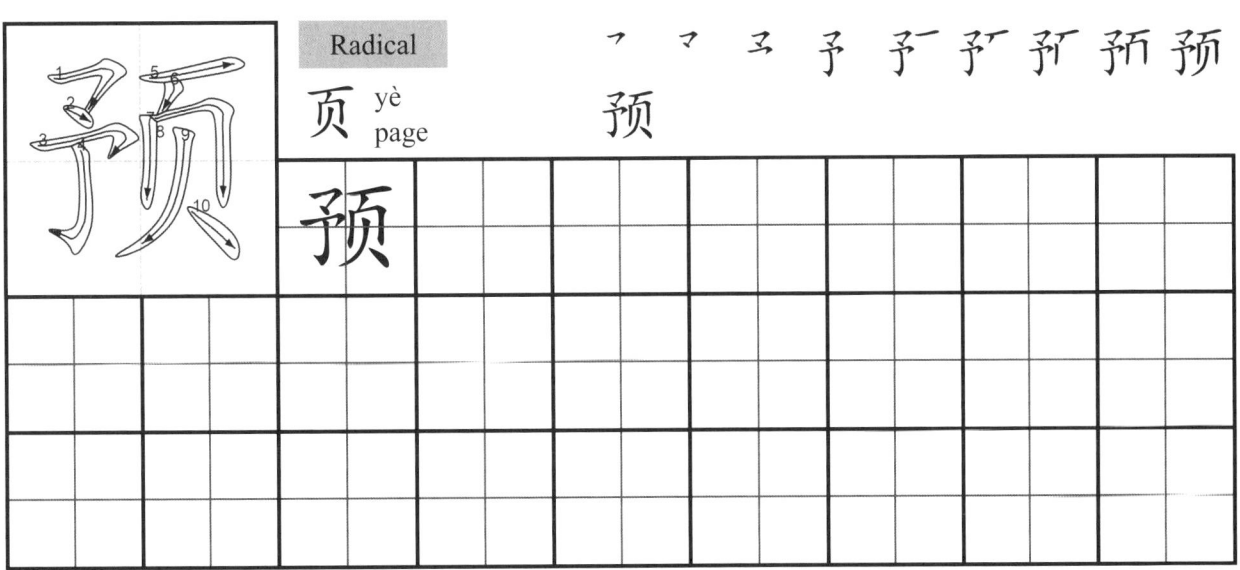

Radical 页 yè page

フ マ ヌ 予 予 予 预 预

预

预

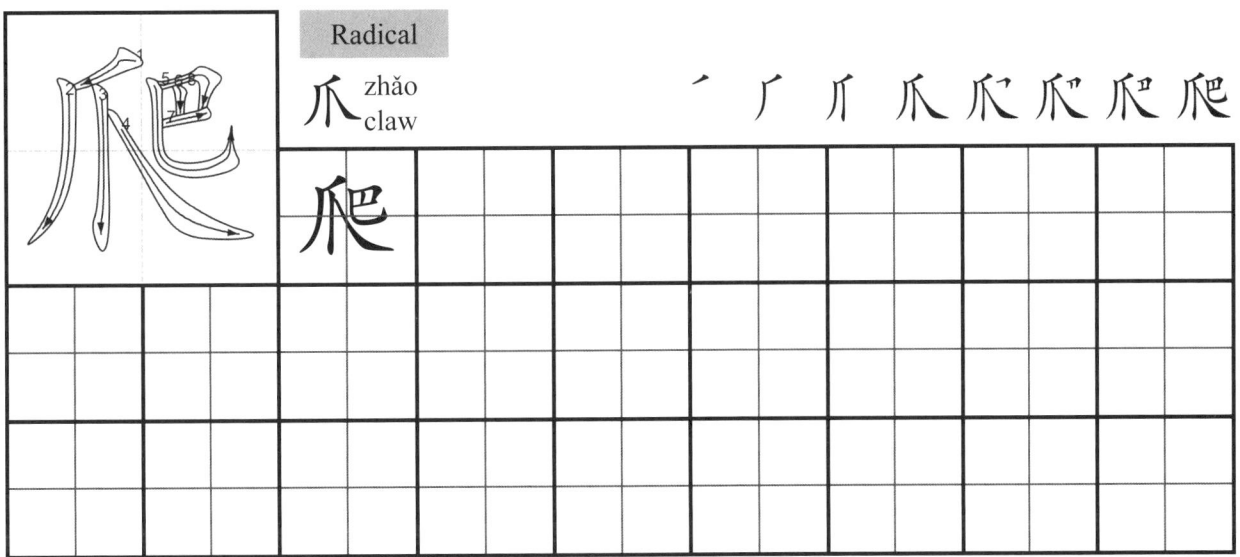

Radical 爪 zhǎo claw

´ ⺁ ⺁ 爪 爫 爫 爬 爬

爬

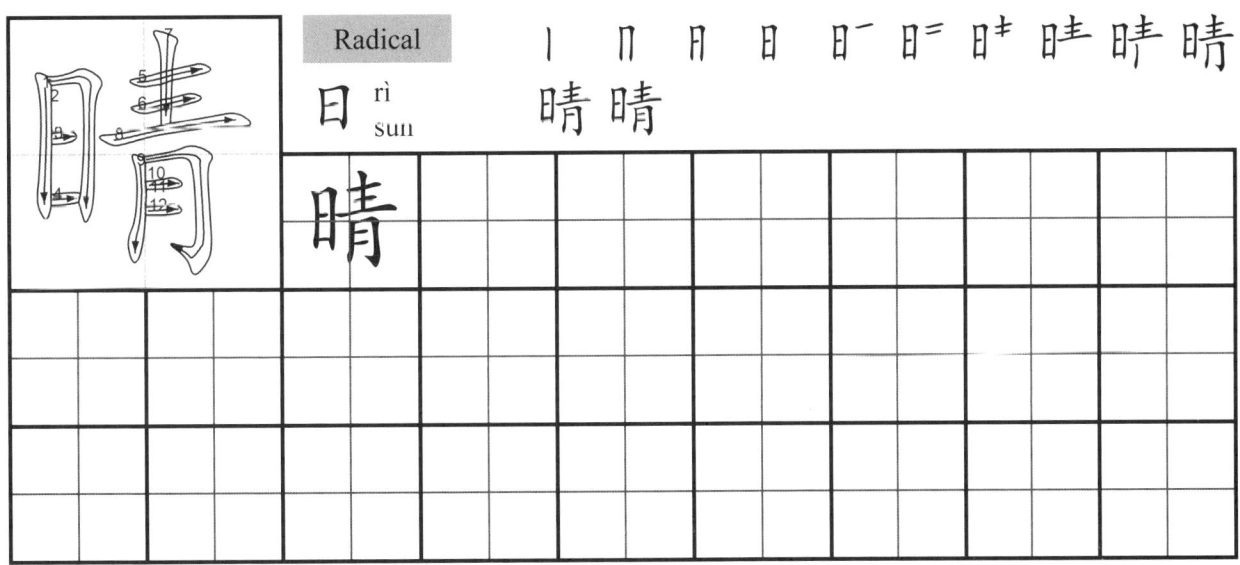

Radical 日 rì sun

丨 冂 冃 日 日´ 日= 旪 晴 晴 晴 晴

晴

Unit 1 · Lesson 2 · Weather

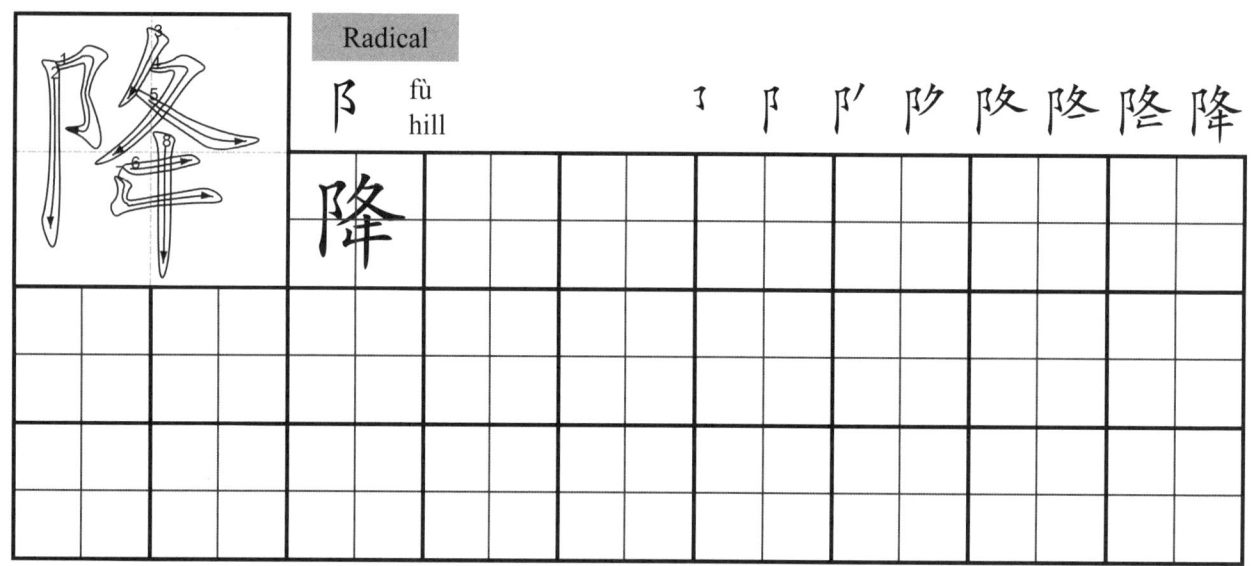

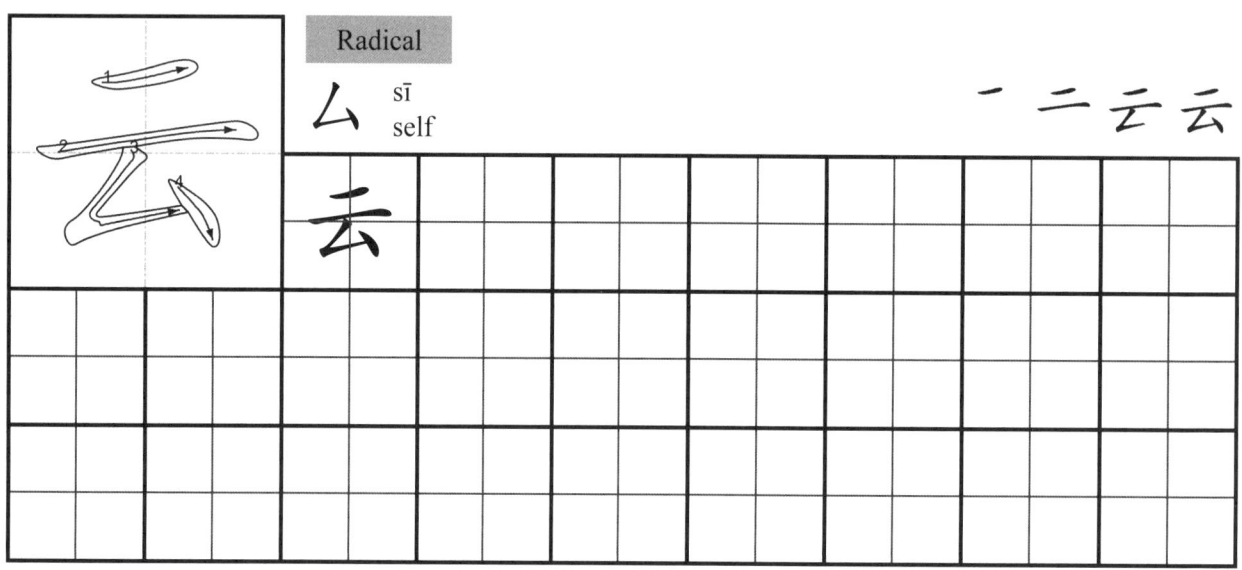

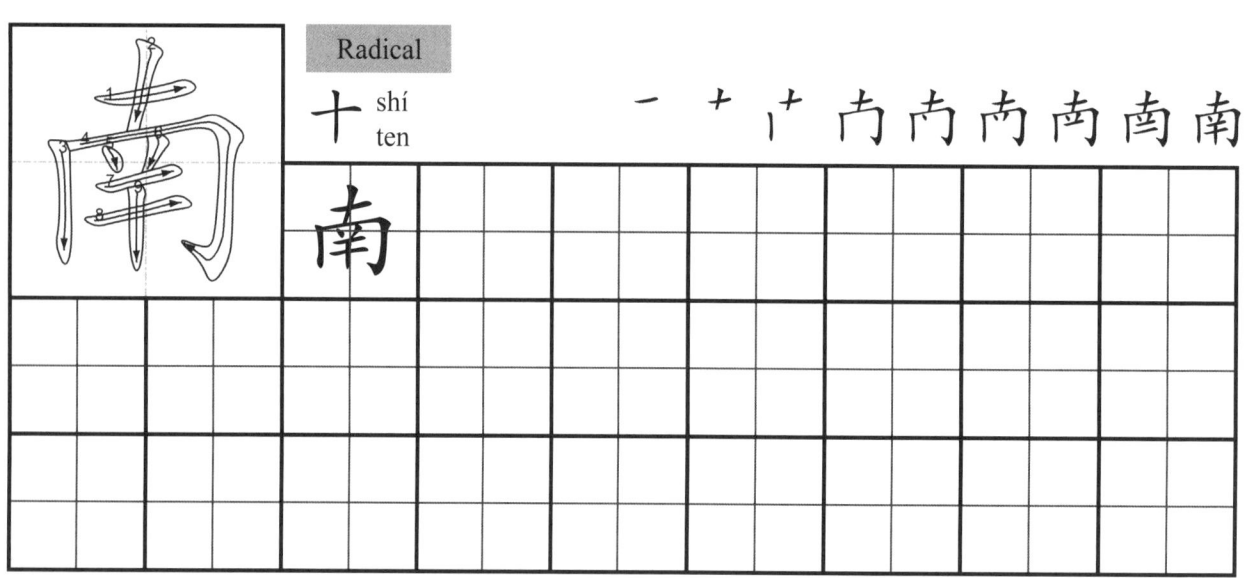

LISTENING COMPREHENSION 1.2

I. Listen to the recording and select the best response below.

1. The woman would most likely respond with:
   A. 我们得早一点出发去爬山。
   B. 听说这里的天气冬暖夏凉。
   C. 中午的气温比昨天高七八度呢。
   D. 晚上气温会不会下降？

II. Listen to the recording and answer the following True or False questions.

1. (   ) The woman and the man took a trip together after the man completed his summer internship.
2. (   ) The man seemed to enjoy his trip very much.
3. (   ) The man will invite the woman to travel with him next time.
4. (   ) The man prefers to travel by himself.
5. (   ) We can tell from the conversation that the man wants to date the woman.

III. Listen to the recording and answer the questions in Chinese.

1. Where did the speaker go and for how long did he travel?

2. What did the speaker bring back as souvenirs for his friends?

3. After the trip, what is the speaker's overall feeling towards buying souvenirs? Why?

SPEAKING PRACTICE 1.2

I. Looking below at the upcoming weather forecasts for Moscow, Johannesburg, and Austin, describe what the weather will be like in these three cities. Include what people should wear and what activities people can do in each city.

莫斯科天气预报			
日期		天气现象	气温
2月10日星期六	白天	阵雪	高温 22°F
	夜间	小雪	低温 9°F

约翰内斯堡天气预报			
日期		天气现象	气温
2月10日星期六	白天	雷阵雨	高温 72°F
	夜间	阴	低温 55°F

奥斯汀天气预报			
日期		天气现象	气温
2月10日星期六	白天	晴	高温 65°F
	夜间	晴	低温 41°F

Notes:

莫斯科 (Mòsīkē): *n.* Moscow
阵雪 (zhènxuě): *n.* snow shower
小雪 (xiǎoxuě): *n.* light shower
约翰内斯堡 (Yuēhànnèisībǎo): *n.* Johannesburg
奥斯汀 (Àosītīng): *n.* Austin

II. If you were given a budget of $2000 and one week winter vacation to go anywhere in the world, where would you go? Be sure to include your reasons for why you chose your particular destination, who you would go with, what the weather would be like, what you would do, what places you would visit, what transportation methods you would take, and what types of clothing you would bring.

STRUCTURE REVIEW 1.2

I. Complete the following Structure Note practices.

Structure Note 1.6: Use 听说 to mean "I've heard that."

> (Subject +) 听说 + Sentence

> Subject + 听说过 + Noun Phrase

A. You hear good reviews about a new Chinese restaurant in town. Your friends want to go to this restaurant and ask you about it. The following are their questions and your statements about what you heard. Use 听说 to write down these sentences.

1. I heard their dumplings are really good. Is that true?

2. I heard that you have to use chopsticks there. Is that correct?

3. I heard they only take cash.

4. I heard there is a very cool waiter working there.

5. Mapo Doufu? I have never heard of this dish. What is it?

Take the challenge! 动动脑筋！

"听说如果在房间里把伞打开的话，个子(gèzi: height)会长不高。"
"听谁说的？"
"妈妈说的。"
"那你在房间里把伞打开过几次？"

听说 is used when you talk about something you heard about. When talking about a superstition, you can use 听说 to start the conversation. Think of some superstitions in your culture.

Unit 1 · Lesson 2 · Weather

Structure Note 1.7: Use A 比 B with an adjective and an amount to specify an amount in comparison.

> A 比 B + Adjective + Number Word + Measure Word

B. Below are various images showing items that were bought for a Chinese New Year celebration you had and showing different activities that took place during the festivity. For each picture, write a caption using 比 to make a comparison of what is shown.

1. _____

2. _____

3. _____

4. _____

Structure Note 1.8: Use 多了 to express much more.

> A + 比 + B + Adjective + 得多 / 多了

C. You just finished your first year in college. Use 得多/多了 to talk about what your school life was like.

1. 中国文学比中国历史_____

2. 学语法比学生词_____

3. 第一个学期的功课比第二个学期的_____

4. 我觉得准备考试比准备见女朋友_____

5. 早上去上课的学生比下午去上课的_____

Structure Note 1.9: Use 原来 to express "as it turns out."

> 原来 + Sentence

D. You will soon graduate from college and you are consulting with your school adviser about job opportunities after graduation. Respond to the information your adviser provides by using 原来 to indicate you have learned tips about job searching that you were previously unaware of.

1. There are a lot of job opportunities for foreigners in China.
   _____

2. You need to prepare a resume.
   _____

3. Many companies are interested in hiring new college graduates with working experience.
   _____

4. Connections are very important in Chinese business culture.
   _____

5. My brother runs a computer company. If you are interested, I can introduce you to him.
   _____

II. The following are some unconfirmed statistics about China. Research or ask others whether these statements are true and rewrite them by using 比 / 多了. If you unable to confirm a statement, add 听说 to express that you heard about the statistics from someone. If you are able to confirm the validity of a statement, add 原来 to express your discovery.

Example: 中国每一百个女生就有一百零七个男生。
→听说中国的女生比男生多。

1. 在中国，人最多的城市是上海，有一千四百多万；北京第二，有一千多万人。

2. 在中国，哈尔滨是冬天最多人去旅游的城市；第二是昆明。

3. 住在中国的美国人有七万多；加拿大人才两万左右。

4. 中国十大最快乐的城市第一是成都；第五是昆明。

5. 在中国，气候最舒服的城市是昆明；北京气候不像昆明四季如春。

READING COMPREHENSION 1.2

I. Read the passage and answer the following True or False questions.

周信是玛丽在北京认识的第一个朋友。玛丽来北京以后，他帮了很多忙，还常常让玛丽做他的"驴友"，到北京很多地方去旅游。

下个周末是长周末，周信听说玛丽没有什么特别的打算，就问玛丽想不想去**承德**看看。玛丽没听说过**承德**这个地方。周信介绍说，**承德**离北京不远，坐汽车只需要三个小时左右。北京夏天常常很闷热，可是**承德**夏天的天气就很凉快，比北京舒服多了。

天气预报说，下个周末那里会是晴天，气温不高，平均温度只有二十二度左右。虽然不像云南那样四季如春，但也还好。而且那里有山有水，可以爬山，去公园，买东西，有很多事情做。玛丽说："原来**承德**是个这么好的地方！那我们下个周末就出发去**承德**玩玩吧！"

Notes:

承德 (Chéngdé): *n.* a place located in Hebei Province

日期		天气现象		气温
8日星期六	白天	☀	晴	高温 29°C
	夜间	☾	晴	低温 16°C
9日星期日	白天	☀	晴	高温 27°C
	夜间	☾	晴	低温 14°C

1. (   ) 玛丽常常和周信一起去旅游。
2. (   ) 北京夏天的气温和承德一样凉快。
3. (   ) 周信觉得承德夏天很舒服。
4. (   ) 周信介绍说承德的天气四季如春。
5. (   ) 下个周末去承德旅行的时候，玛丽得带上雨衣。

II. Read the passage and answer the multiple choice questions below.

　　十月一日是中国的**国庆节**，很多人都会放假。每年这个时候大家都会去各地旅游。以前可以坐火车，坐飞机去，现在也有不少人自己开车出去玩。放假的时候去旅游已经**成为**中国人的习惯。最近有很多的年轻人上网找可以一起旅行的"驴友"，驴友**网站**越来越多。对喜欢旅游的人来说，他们想去的地方不但要气候好，风景美，而且东西便宜也是非常重要的。在驴友**网站**上你可以做很多事，比方说，找需要的**信息**，看别人的建议，或者问有关的问题，联络驴友……难怪这么多人迷上了各式各样的驴友网站呢！

Notes:

国庆节 (Guóqìngjié): *n.* National Day

成为 (chéngwéi): *v.* to become

网站 (wǎngzhàn): *n.* website

信息 (xìnxī): *n.* information

1. 每年十月的时候大家喜欢去旅游，因为……
    A. 这时候很多人不用去工作。
    B. 这时候气候很好。
    C. 这时候有很多驴友网。
    D. 这时候不少人得开车。

2. 为什么驴友网站越来越多？
    A. 年轻人喜欢在网站上找可以一起旅游的人。
    B. 现在很多中国人放假的时候都会出去旅游。
    C. 你可以从这些网站找到很多跟旅游有关的信息。
    D. A, B, 和 C

3. 为什么驴友网站这么受欢迎？
    A. 因为很多人迷上了驴友网站。
    B. 因为现在有很多人开车去旅游。
    C. 因为它可以告诉大家怎么找到便宜的礼物。
    D. 因为它可以帮助大家更好地旅游。

Take the challenge! 动动脑筋！

In *Modern Chinese* Textbook Vol. 1A, Unit 1, Lesson 1, 各 is introduced as meaning each or different. It is usually followed by a noun or measure word. 各式各样 (gèshì gèyàng) is a commonly used fixed expression. Guess what is the meaning of 各式各样, and what kind of things you can use this expression to describe.

III. Read the following weather forecast and e-mail and answer the following questions in Chinese.

日期		天气现象		气温	风向	风力
12日星期五	白天	☀	晴	高温 13°C	西南风	3 - 4级
	夜间	☾	多云	低温 3°C	西南风	微风
13日星期六	白天	⛆	降雨	高温 10°C	西风	3 - 4级
	夜间	⛆	降雨	低温 0°C	西风	3 - 4级
14日星期日	白天	⛆	降雨	高温 5°C	西北风	4 - 5级
	夜间	☾	多云	低温 2°C	西北风	3 - 4级

To: 黄祥安
From: 李中平
Subject: 周末的活动计划

祥安：
　　我觉得我们这个周末不应该去爬山。我看了天气预报，这个周六有雨，而且气温会下降到零度**以下**，会刮风。爬山的话要准备雨衣雨伞，我看还是改天再去吧。要是你想运动一下的话，我们去踢足球，你可以带上你的朋友，我也会打电话叫上大东、小美他们。如果可以的话，我会先去**预订**球场。你觉得怎么样？
中平

Notes:
以下 (yǐxià): *adv.* below
预订 (yùdìng): *v.* to reserve

1. What is the difference between the highest and lowest temperature this Saturday? _____
2. Which day will be a sunny day? _____
3. Why should Xiang'an and Zhongping not go hiking this weekend? _____
4. What does Zhongping suggest he and his friends do this weekend instead? _____

Unit 1 · Lesson 2 · Weather

WRITING PRACTICE 1.2

I. Anna is going home to Moscow to visit her family. She will persuade someone to accompany her on her trip. As Anna, write an e-mail to someone explaining what her plans are and why that person should join her. Use the word box and images below to help you write the e-mail.

博物馆　　　舞蹈表演　　　俄罗斯茶饼　　　俄罗斯饺子　　　俄罗斯帽子

To:
From:
Subject:

II. Based on where you live, choose your favorite season and explain why you selected it. Describe what the weather would normally be like, what clothes you would wear, and what activities you could do.

_____

_____

_____

_____

_____

UNIT 2 – LESSON 1

申请留学

VOCABULARY REVIEW 2.1

I. Circle the vocabulary word or phrase in each box that cannot be paired with the verb.

1. 查 | 资料　　票　　书号　　注意
2. 申请 | 留学　　工作　　成绩　　奖学金
3. 讨论 | 功课　　必须　　报告　　问题
4. 看 | 知识　　小说　　书本　　报告
5. 变 | 冷　　漂亮　　主修　　高

II. The following characters are all missing the same radical. Add the radical and match the characters from Column A with Column B to form a vocabulary phrase.

Column A: 井　寸　司　兑

Column B: 吾　舌　仑　果

Vocabulary:
_____
_____
_____
_____

III. In each of the following sentences, circle the letter of the correct place to insert the phrase.

1. 不见得

    (A) 只看中文书本 (B) 是学习中文的 (C) 最好的办法。

2. 趟

    今年 (A) 春节我打算回 (B) 北京老家一 (C) 。

3. 挺

    这个沙发 (A) 不错的，又 (B) 大又 (C) 舒服。

CHARACTER WRITING PRACTICE 2.1

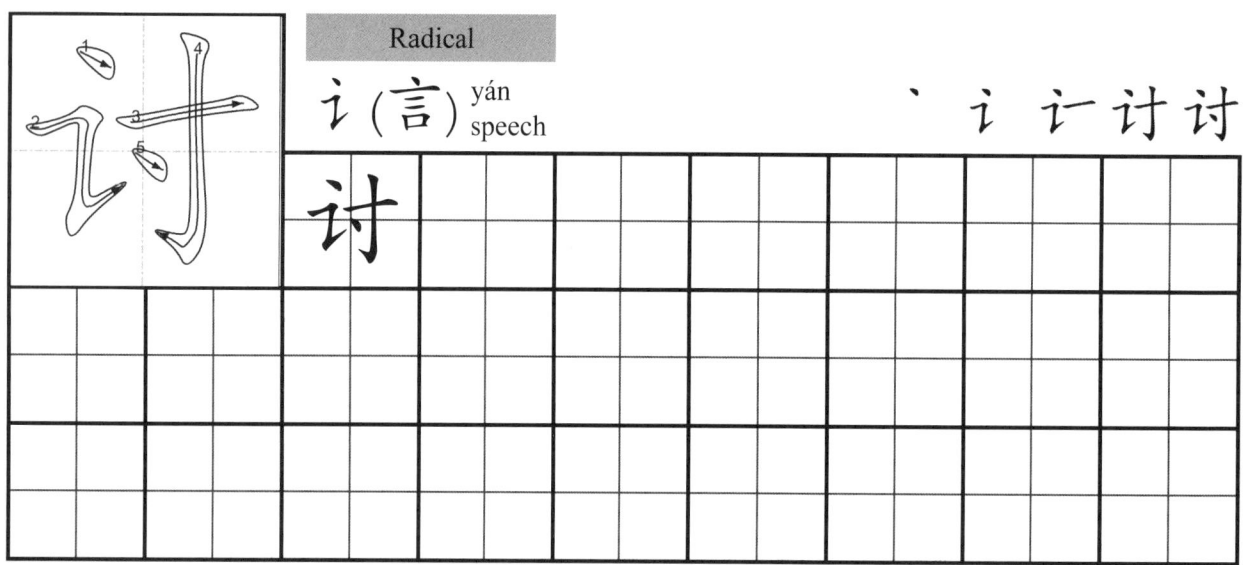

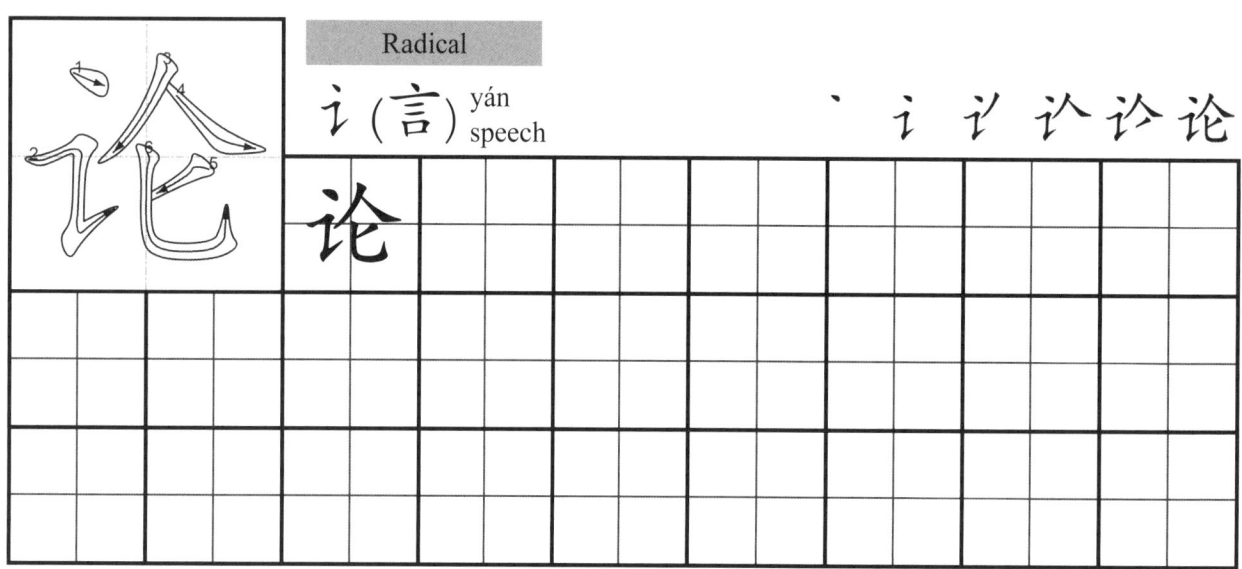

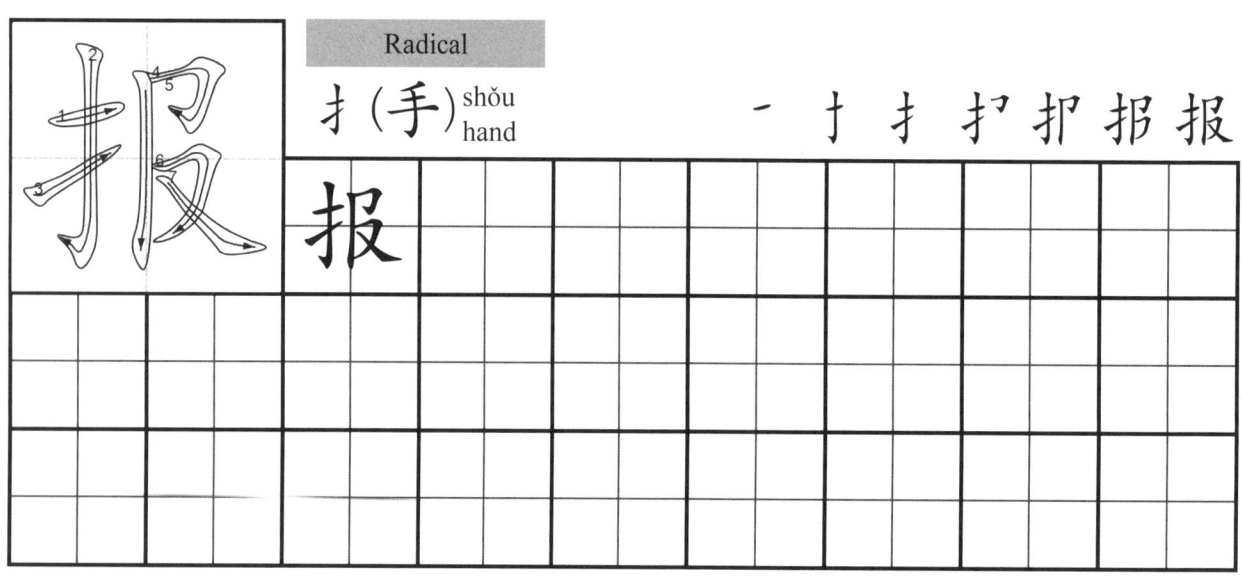

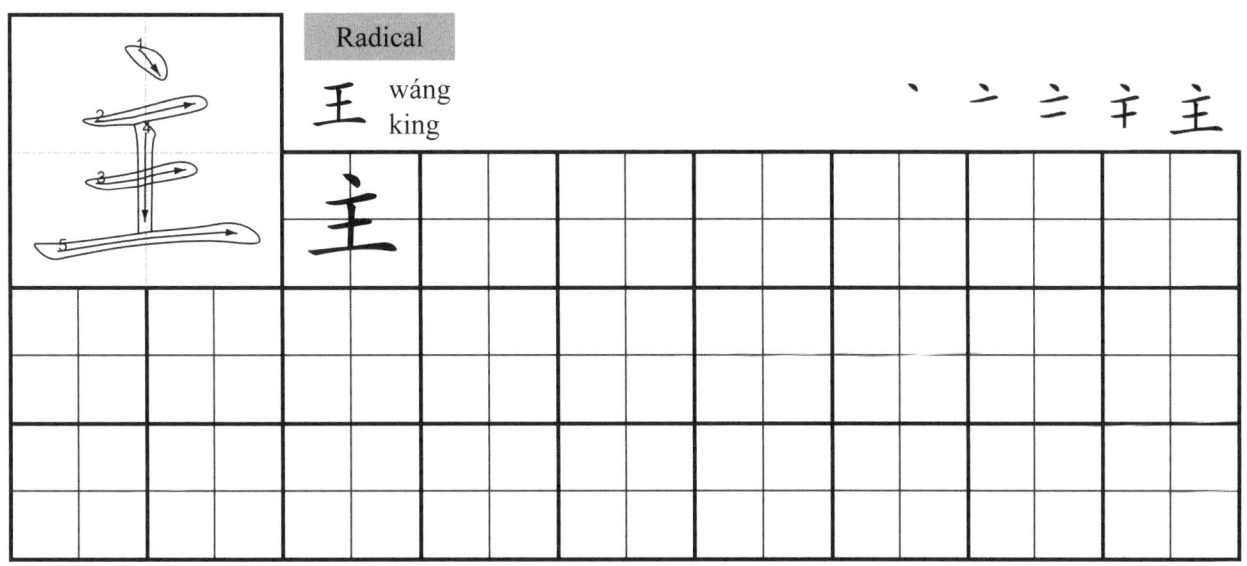

Radical 王 wáng king 丶 亠 二 宁 主

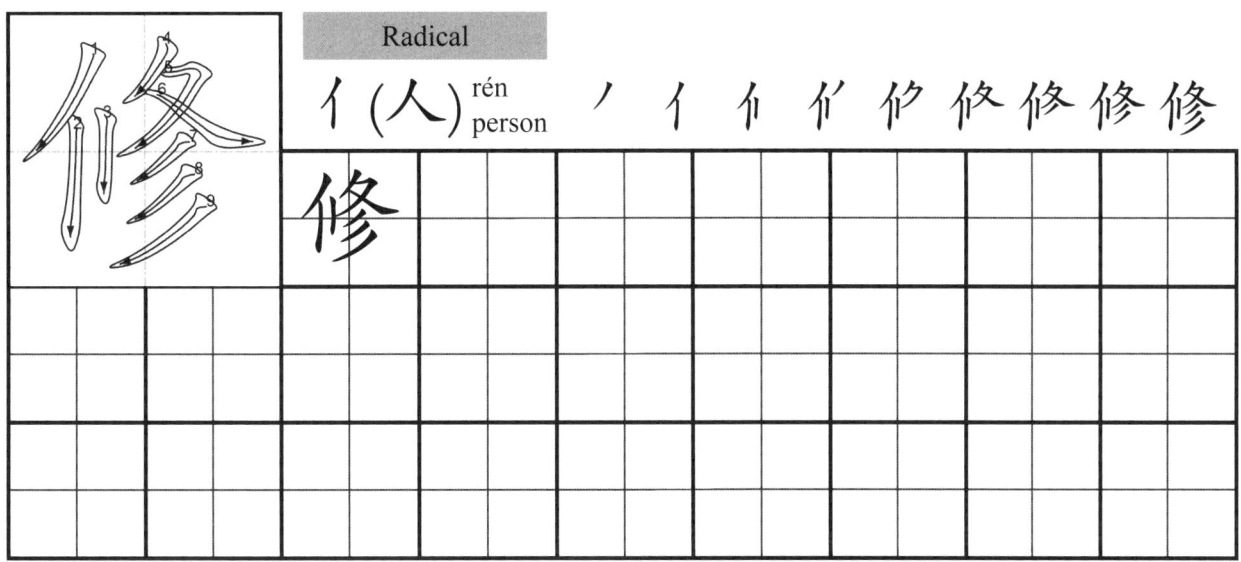

Radical 亻(人) rén person ノ 亻 亻 亻 佟 修 修 修

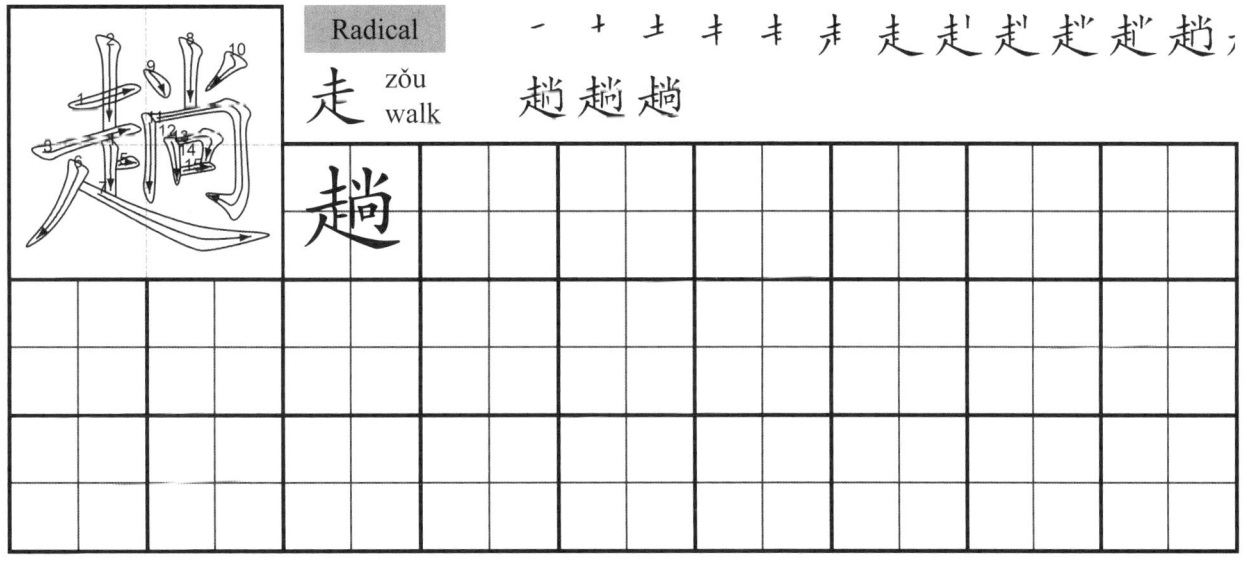

Radical 走 zǒu walk 一 十 土 丰 丰 走 走 赳 赳 赳 赳 赵 赵 赵 赵

Unit 2 ▪ Lesson 1 ▪ Academics 35

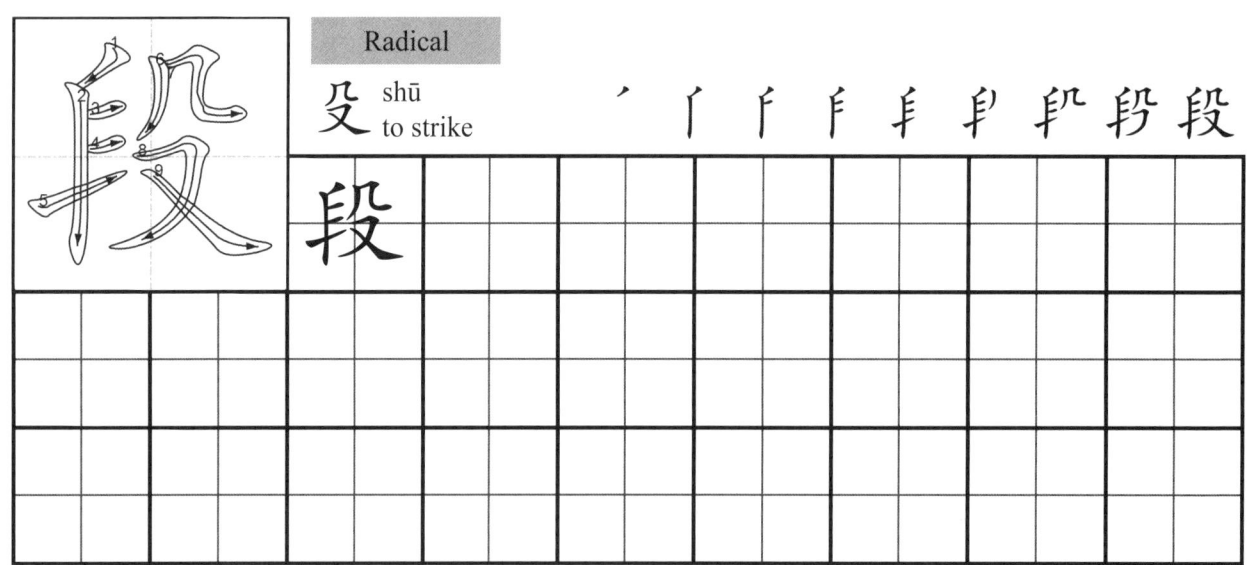

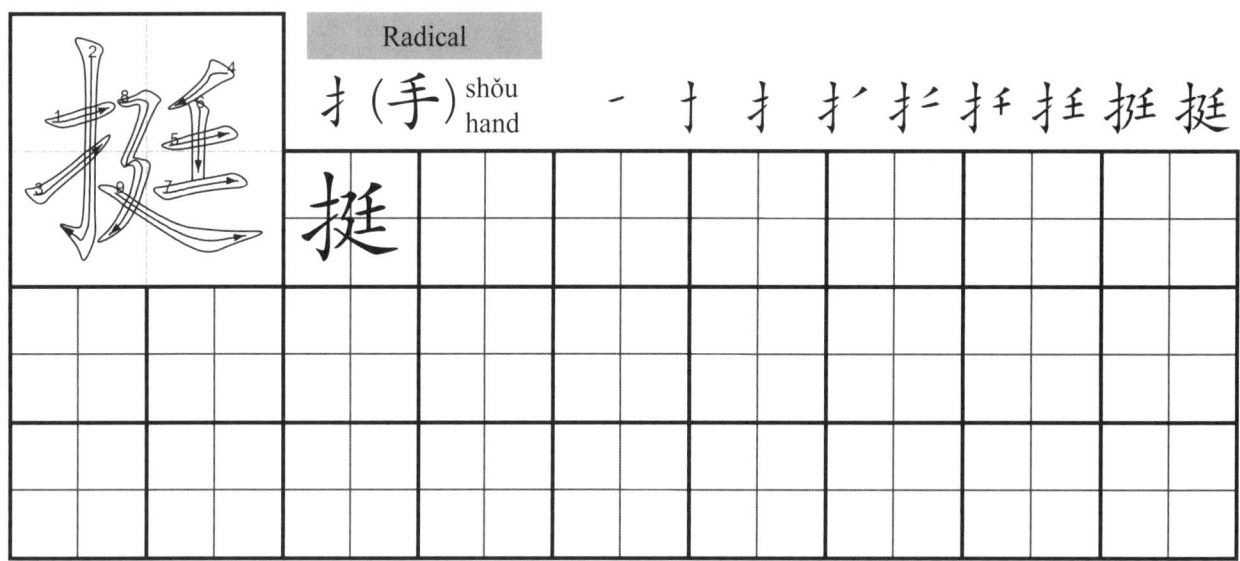

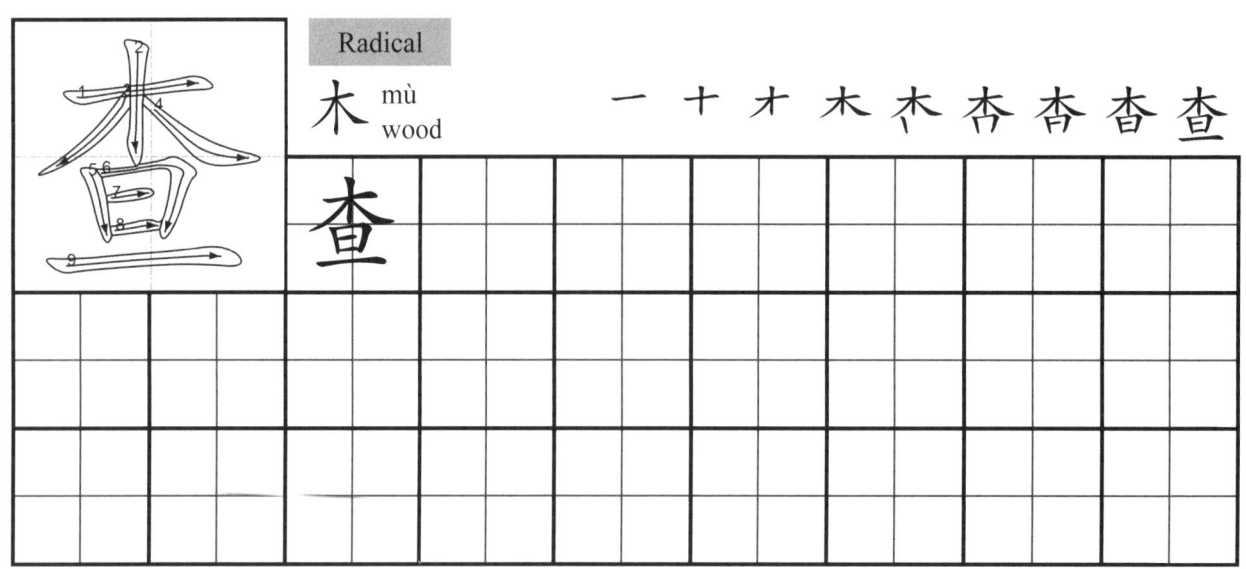

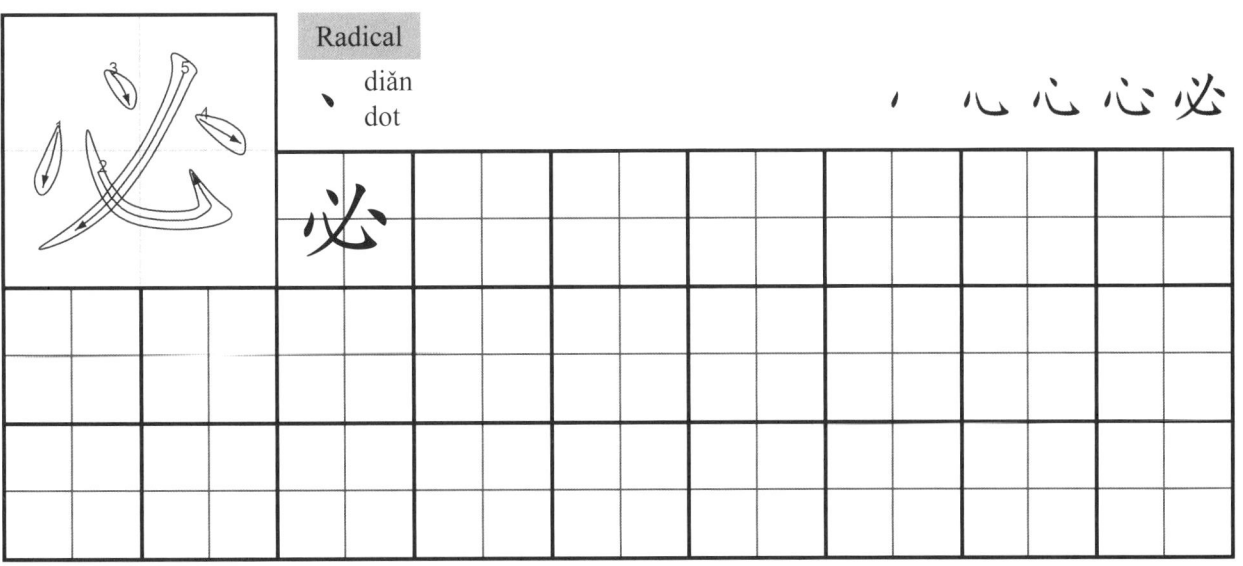

Radical
、 diǎn dot

丶 心 心 心 必

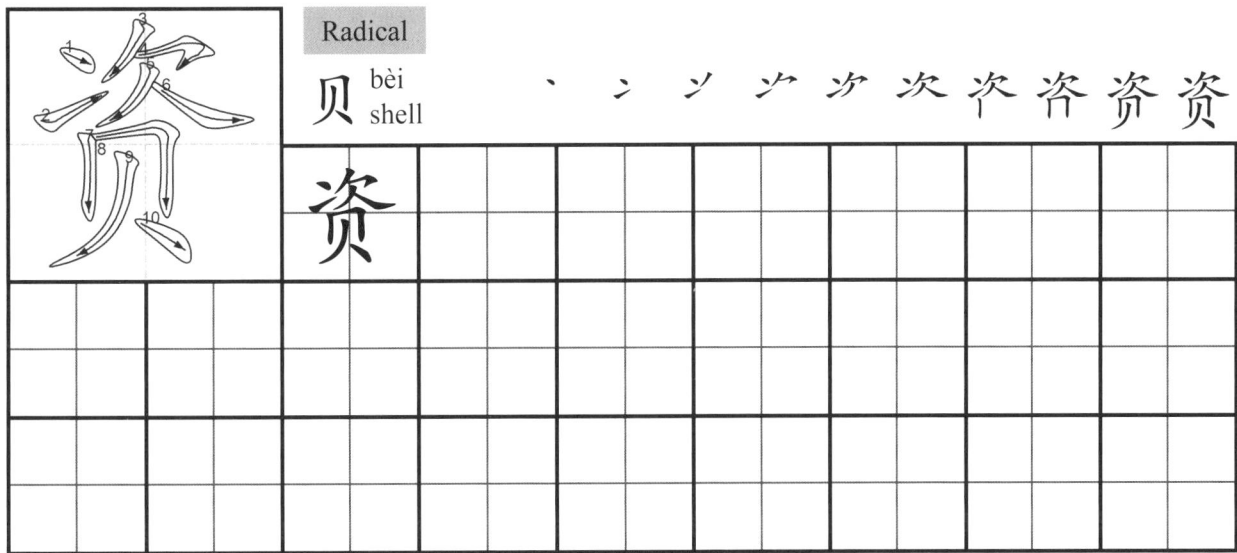

Radical
贝 bèi shell

丶 丷 冫 冫 次 次 咨 资 资

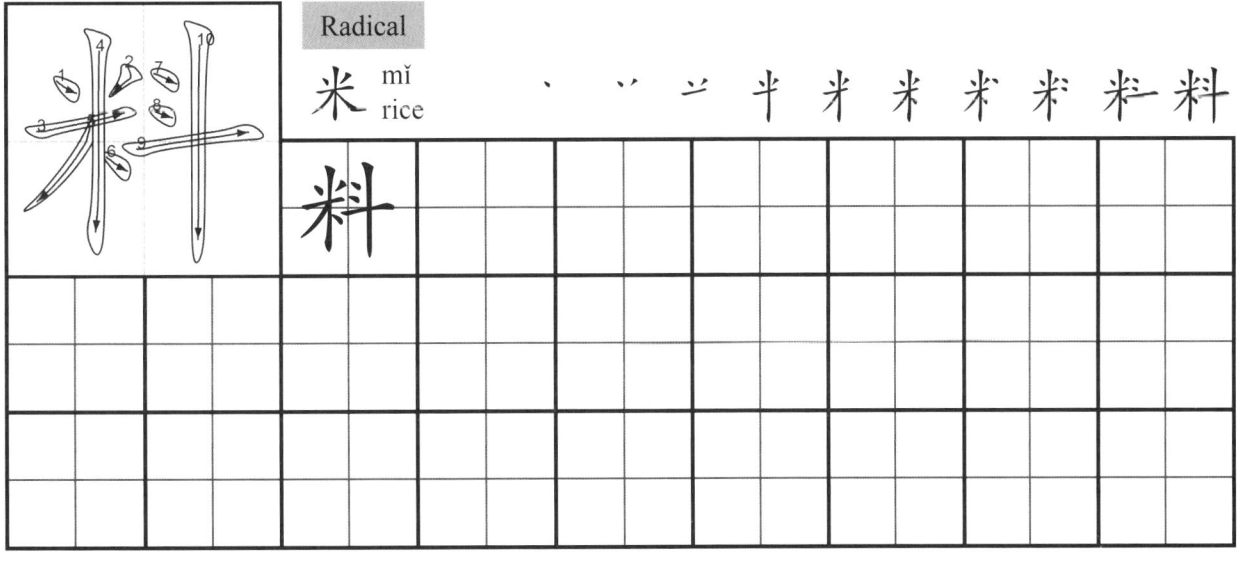

Radical
米 mǐ rice

丶 丷 丷 半 半 米 米 米 料 料

Unit 2 · Lesson 1 · Academics

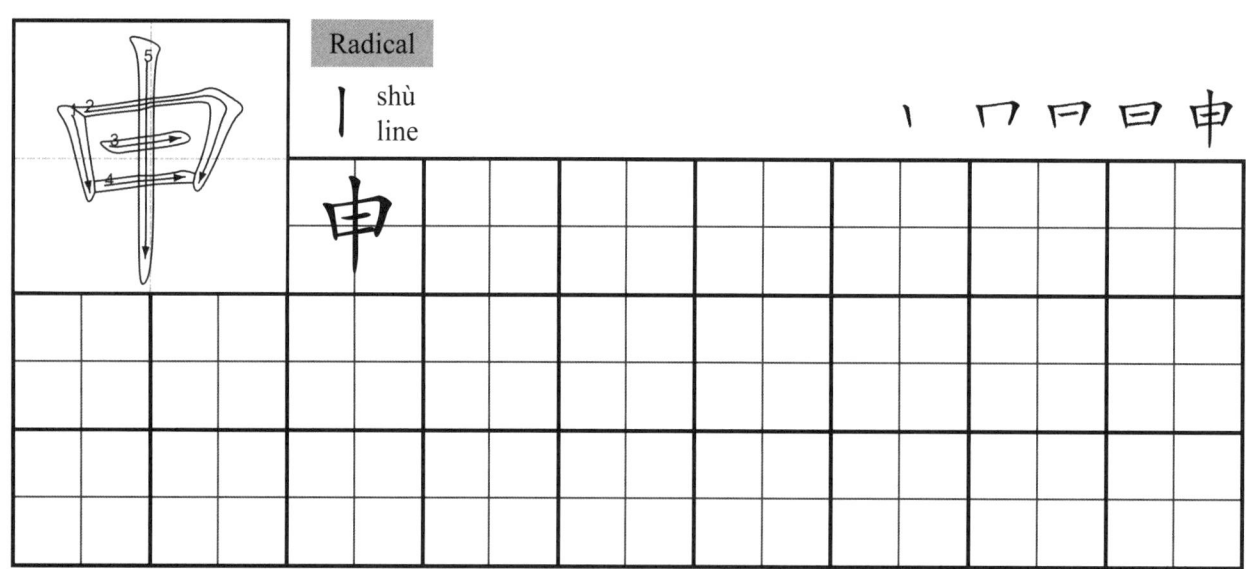

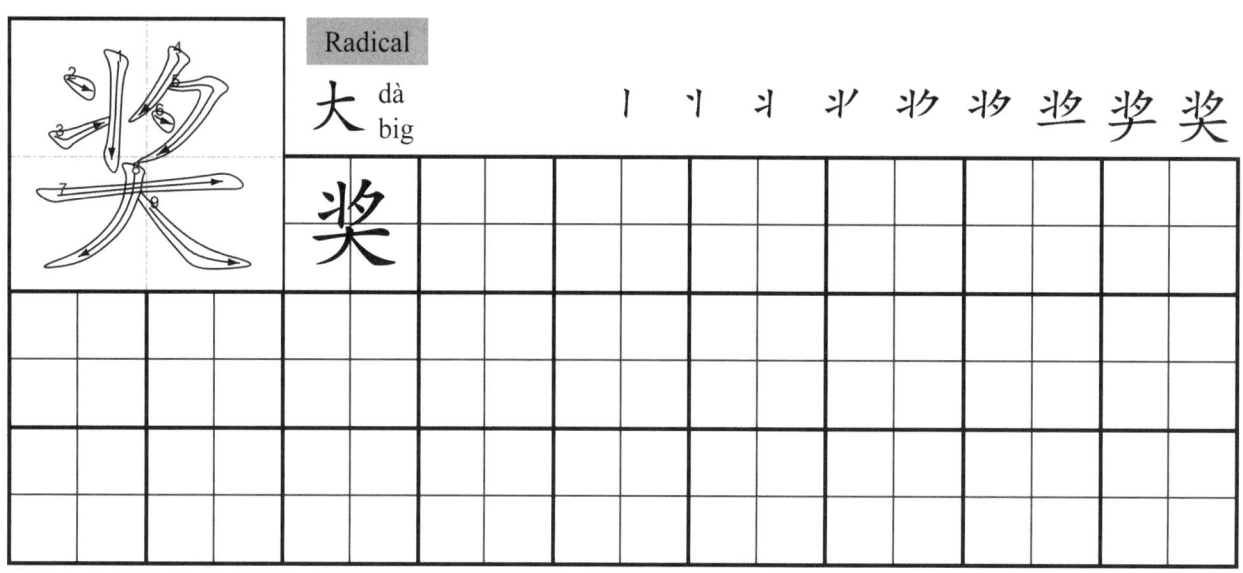

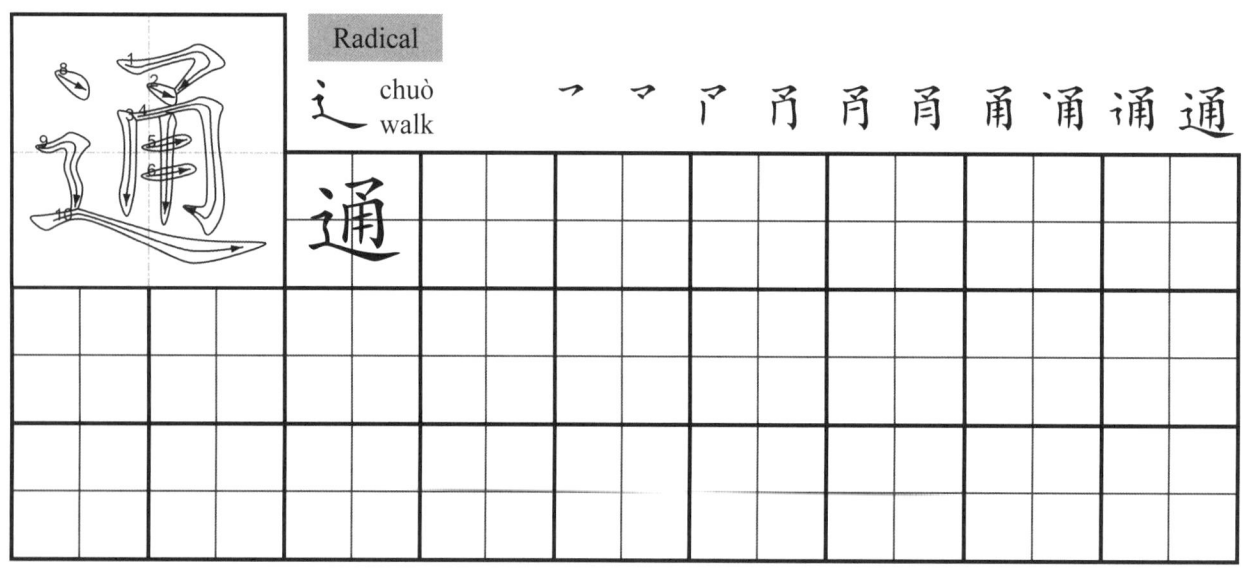

LISTENING COMPREHENSION 2.1

I. Listen to the recording and select the best response below.

1. The woman would most likely respond with:

    A. 你说得对。你觉得奖学金的资料也很重要吗？
    B. 我顺便可以带上历史小说。
    C. 对啊，我希望能去一趟中国学习一段时间。
    D. 为了去留学，我得更好地了解中国文化。

II. Listen to the recording and answer the following True or False questions:

1. (   ) Both the woman and the man were complaining about the tests they have had their classes.
2. (   ) The woman did not like yesterday's quiz because it was long and difficult.
3. (   ) The man wanted the woman to treat him for dinner.
4. (   ) While searching online, the man found a restaurant that teaches people how to make Peking Duck.
5. (   ) From the conversation, we can make the assumption that they will go to a Chinese restaurant.

III. Listen to the recording and answer the questions in Chinese.

1. According to the speaker, what are people's perceptions of majoring in Chinese literature?

   _____

2. What are the pros and cons about studying Chinese literature?

   _____

3. What is the speaker's general attitude toward majoring in Chinese literature?

   _____

SPEAKING PRACTICE 2.1

I. You are a Chinese major and below is your class schedule for the next school term. You have already signed up for three classes and you need to add one more to fill the 11:00 AM - 12:00 PM timeslot. Choose one class from the list below to add to your schedule and provide reasons why you selected that course.

时间表					
时间	星期一	星期二	星期三	星期四	星期五
上午 9:00 - 10:30	中国历史 III		中国历史 III		
上午 11:00 -12:00					
下午 1:00 - 2:30	中国现代文学 I		中国现代文学 I		中国现代文学 I
下午 3:00 - 4:30		中国语言学 I		中国语言学 I	

课程表

星期一、三、五: 上午 11:00 - 12:00
　　中国文化 II
　　欧洲文学 I
星期二、四: 上午 11:00 - 12:00
　　中国哲学 I
星期三、五: 上午 11:00 - 12:00
　　中国艺术 I
　　中国电影的历史 I

Notes:
课程表 (kèchéngbiǎo): *n.* class schedule
语言学 (yǔyánxué): *n.* linguistics

II. You are asked by your teacher about your Chinese language proficiency. Explain what you can do (e.g., order from a Chinese menu, talk about the weather and seasons, discuss hobbies and interests, use Chinese idiomatic expressions in your everyday conversations, etc.) and what else you can do to improve your Chinese.

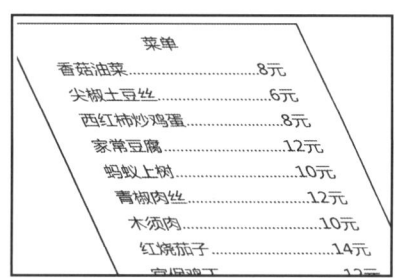

STRUCTURE REVIEW 2.1

I. **Complete the following Structure Note practice activities.**

Structure Note 2.1: Use 只要 A 就 B (了) to indicate A is the only condition necessary for B to occur.

只要 + Condition, (+Subject) + 就 + Result (+了)

A. The following is a list of requirements for applying to study abroad. Write complete sentences using 只要…就 to describe each requirement.

1. 平均成绩2.5或者更高

_____

2. 一年级或二年级的学生

_____

3. 主修或辅修中文

_____

4. 选修跟中国文化有关的课

_____

5. 准备好大学留学的申请表格

_____

Structure Note 2.2: Use 为了 to explain the purpose of doing something.

Action + 是为了 + Reason

Subject + 为了 + Reason + Action

为了 + Reason, + Subject + Action

B. Your friend asks you about your plan for studying abroad in China. Answer your friend's questions below by using 为了.

1. 你为什么想去中国？（学中文）

_____

2. 你为什么想学中文？（找一家中国公司工作）

_____

3. 听说你会去北京，你计划在北京做什么？（看京剧表演）

_____

4. 为什么最近你都睡得比较晚？（准备申请奖学金的资料）

_____

Structure Note 2.3: Use 不过 to say "but" to indicate a contrast to the previous statement.

> 不过 + Sentence

C. You made a list of plans below, but you encountered obstacles for each one. Use 不过 to describe what happened.

1. 我想住学校的留学生宿舍……

_____

2. 我打算选修中国历史课……

_____

3. 我想借一本叫《太极》的小说……

_____

4. 我想去找教授讨论我的报告……

_____

5. 我希望可以多交中国的朋友……

_____

Structure Note 2.4: Use 变得/变成 to describe transformation in state or from one thing to another.

> Subject + 变成 + Noun Phrase
>
> Subject + 变得 + Adjective Phrase

D. After reading about what advice and suggestions the older generation have to offer in the following passage, what changes would you make? Answer by filling in the blanks in the sentences provided and then combine one sentence from one box with a sentence from the second one to make a longer sentence.

长辈说：
什么时候都要对别人有礼貌。
小时候不努力，长大后生活就会过得很苦。
女生都特别喜欢会整理打扫的男生。
常常让别人难过的人，自己也会常常不开心。
认真做事的人，才能找到好工作。

所以从那以后我___更努力了。
所以我现在___一个非常重视礼节的人。
所以我的房间___越来越干净。
所以我想___可以把快乐带给朋友的人。
所以我希望自己做事___越来越认真。

1. _____

2. _____

3. _____

4. _____

5. _____

Take the challenge! 动动脑筋！

"怎样才可以变得聪明一点？"
"只要变成一个聪明的人就可以了。"
"那怎样才可以变成一个聪明的人？"
"变得聪明一点儿不就行了吗？"

Do you know how to differetiate between 变得 and 变成? Using the conversation pattern above, think of additional adjectives and nouns that you can use in place of 聪明 and 聪明的人 to practice this structure.

II. Your teacher asks you the following questions about your progress in learning Chinese. Write your opinions by following the examples and using the same structure patterns.

A. What have you done in order to improve your Chinese?

Example: 为了准备这次的写汉字比赛，我每天都练习两个小时。

_____

_____

B. What is your secret in learning Chinese?

Example: 只要多看中国的电影，就能学到更多的中文生词。

_____

_____

C. What aspect of your Chinese do you want to improve and how well do you hope your Chinese can become?

Example: 我希望我的中文听力能变得越来越好。

_____

_____

READING COMPREHENSION 2.1

I. Read the passage and answer the following True or False questions.

> 玛丽来北京留学已经有两个月左右了。她在美国的大学里主修中文。为了能把中文学得更好、更地道，她来北京上学以后就选修了一些跟中文有关的课，比方说，中国现代小说、中国文学、中国历史……她这段时间挺忙的，一天到晚查资料、写报告。除了准备小考以外，还要跟老师和同学们讨论问题，所以常常很晚才能睡觉。不过玛丽想，只要能学到新知识，心里就很高兴，也就不觉得累了。虽然现在玛丽的中文不见得那么好，但是她希望能在最短的时间里，变成一个中国通。玛丽问她的中国朋友周信，有什么好办法能把中文快快地学好。周信告诉她七个重要的字，"三人行，必有我师"。周信又说："你要把中文学好，我还有一个主意，那就是多跟我在一起，我帮你练习听、说中文。"玛丽说："你是说'两人行，必有我师'，对吗？周老师？"

1. (　) 玛丽和周信都是来北京留学的美国学生。
2. (　) 在美国的大学里，玛丽的专业是中文。
3. (　) 因为要学习中文，所以玛丽每天都很忙。
4. (　) 玛丽的中国朋友给她介绍了一位姓周的老师。
5. (　) 看起来玛丽在北京学中文学得很认真。

Take the challenge! 动动脑筋！

You learned to use 地道 when describing a dish. Guess what it means in the passage when it is used to describe learning Chinese. What else can you describe using 地道?

II. Read the following passage and answer the questions.

> 2012年，在美国留学的中国学生已经有十九万人，中国变成**连续**三年给美国送去留学生最多的国家。最近这几年，中国留学生在美国都是选哪些专业呢？商务、**工程**、电脑是选修的人最多的三大专业，还有很多人对历史、音乐、**艺术**比较有兴趣。
>
> 在越来越多的中国人才去美国留学的同时，也有很多的美国年轻人到中国念书学习。2011年有差不多一万四千多个美国学生留学中国。中国是美国人留学的第五大**目的地**。2009年美国**奥巴马总统**来中国的时候，希望从2010年到2014年，会有十万个美国学生到中国留学，让更多的美国学生学会说地道的中文，给更多的美国学生变成中国通的机会。

Notes:
连续 (liánxù): *v.* to go on without stopping
工程 (gōngchéng): *n.* engineering
奥巴马总统 (Àobāmǎ Zǒngtǒng): *n.* President Obama
艺术 (yìshù): *n.* art
目的地 (mùdìdì): *n.* a destination

1. 这些年去美国学习的中国留学生里面，
   A. 很多人希望买电脑。
   B. 很多人申请了好几个专业，比方说商务和历史。
   C. 有不少人在美国住了三年。
   D. 有不少人学工程师专业。

2. 下面哪一个说法是对的？
   A. 来中国的美国留学生跟去美国留学的中国留学生一样多。
   B. 奥巴马总统希望他能说地道的中文。
   C. 最近来中国学习的美国学生越来越多。
   D. 2014年一定有一万四千名美国学生来中国留学。

3. 因为中国和美国都有更多的学生去留学，所以我们可以相信……
   A. 会有更多的"中国通"和"美国通"。
   B. 会有很多的学生学历史和艺术。
   C. 奥巴马总统会常常来中国。
   D. 中国和美国的商务会越来越好。

III. Read the following form and email and answer the questions in Chinese.

留学生奖学金申请表

申请日期： 年 月 日

姓名：	出生日期：		照片
性别：	联系方式：		
住址：			
身份证号码：			
院系：	年级：		
上学年	第一学期	第二学期	平均
成绩分数			
素质分数			
老师评价：			
自我评价：			
学校盖章：	审核结果：		

Notes:
条件 (tiáojiàn): *n.* condition
评价 (píngjià): *n.* evaluation
办公室 (bàngōngshì): *n.* office
结果 (jiéguǒ): *n.* result

To: 孙玛丽
From: 王老师
Subject: 申请奖学金

玛丽：

好消息！下个学期的留学生奖学金申请已经开始了。你的学习情况很好，而且还参加了很多学校的活动，所以你的条件可以申请留学生奖学金。请你把这张表格**填**好，明天上课的时候，我帮你写上**评价**，然后你在这个周六之前交给学校**办公室**的李老师，下个星期二你就可以知道申请**结果**了。

王老师

1. Why does Teacher Wang encourage Mali to apply for a scholarship?

___

2. What steps does Mali need to take in order to apply for a scholarship?

___

3. How long does the school office need to process and provide the result of the scholarship application?

___

4. Circle the part of the application that Teacher Wang needs to complete.

___

WRITING PRACTICE 2.1

I. Based on your class schedule from the first workbook Speaking Exercise on p. 40, choose one topic you would write about for one of your classes and write a short abstract about what the report would focus on.

Title:

Topic:

Abstract:

II. You applied to study abroad in China with a focus on pre-Han Dynasty Chinese history and made the short list. Now the application panel needs additional information to make their decision. Describe what classes you have taken, what interests related to Chinese culture you have, and what you plan to do after you graduate.

UNIT 2 – LESSON 2

加入社团

VOCABULARY REVIEW 2.2

I. Write the English meaning of each character and the meaning when they combine into one phrase.

Example: 地 earth, ground 球 ball 地球 Earth

1. 碰 _____ 见 _____ 碰见 _____
2. 美 _____ 好 _____ 美好 _____
3. 社 _____ 员 _____ 社员 _____
4. 加 _____ 入 _____ 加入 _____

II. There are some mistakes in the slogans below. Find the mistakes and correct each one by writing the correct character above.

Example: 环

坏保，就从美化校园开始。

1. 录色生活，
   让地球更美好。

2. 保户环境，
   人人有青。

3. 快来当我们的志原者吧！
   环保做得好，不用再烦脑。

III. Substitute the phrases underlined with appropriate vocabulary that you learned in this lesson.

1. 她是一个<u>常常带给大家快乐和希望</u>的女孩。 _____
2. 我一直在烦恼要不要<u>参加</u>舞蹈社。 _____
3. 我在北京<u>见到</u>以前在美国一起念中文的大学同学。 _____
4. 我们虽然认识了才一个月，但我们<u>已经变成</u>好朋友。 _____
5. 你除了踢足球以外还有什么<u>兴趣</u>？ _____

CHARACTER WRITING PRACTICE 2.2

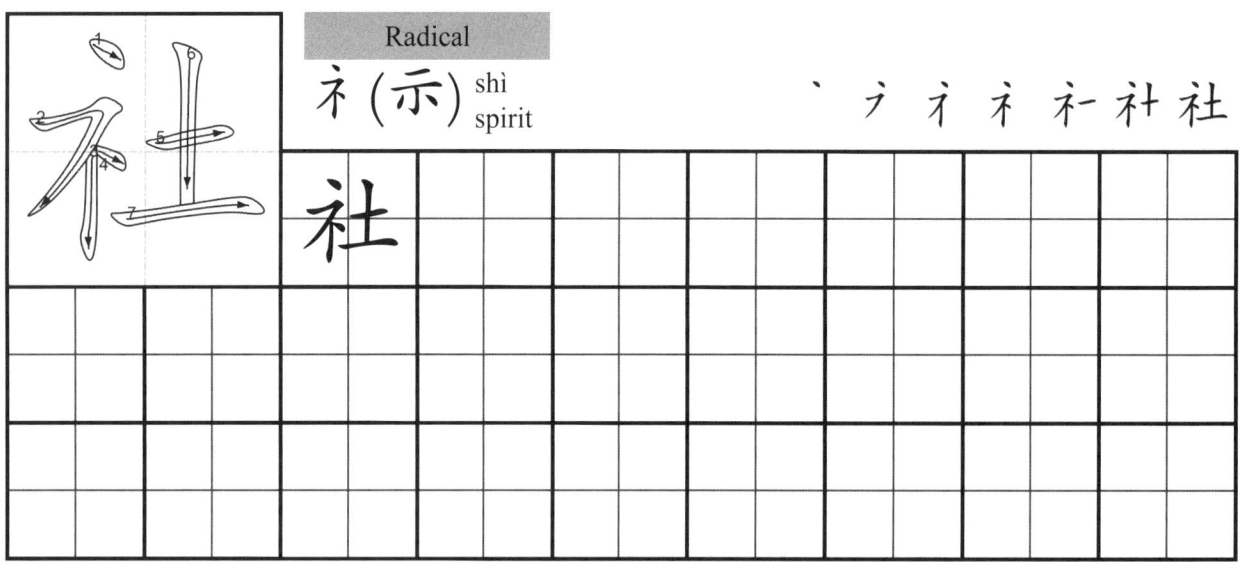

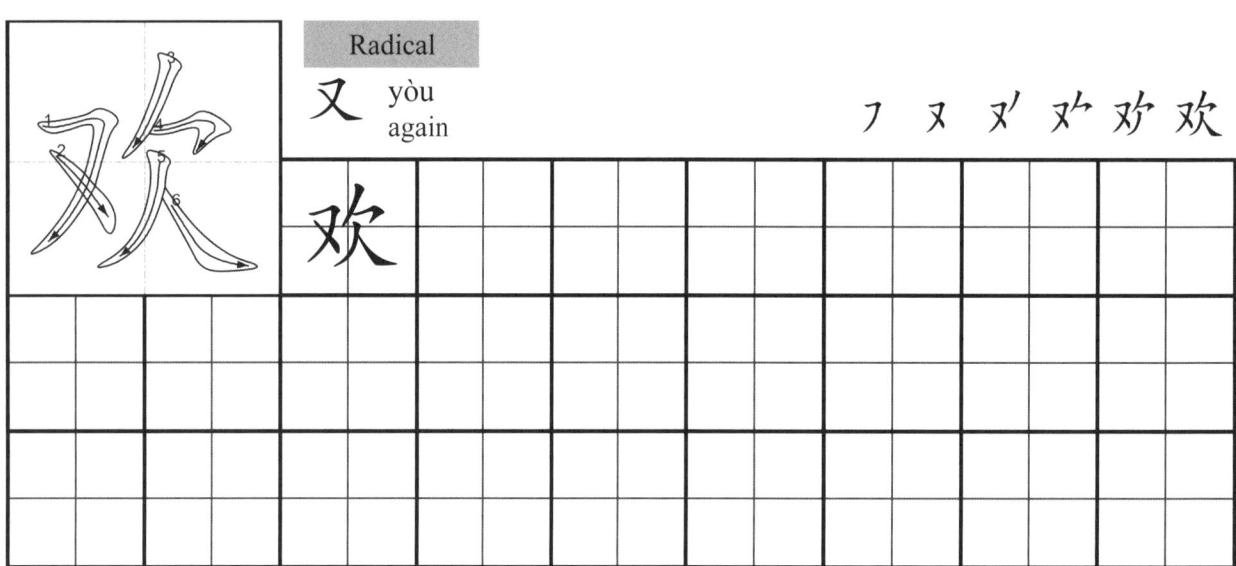

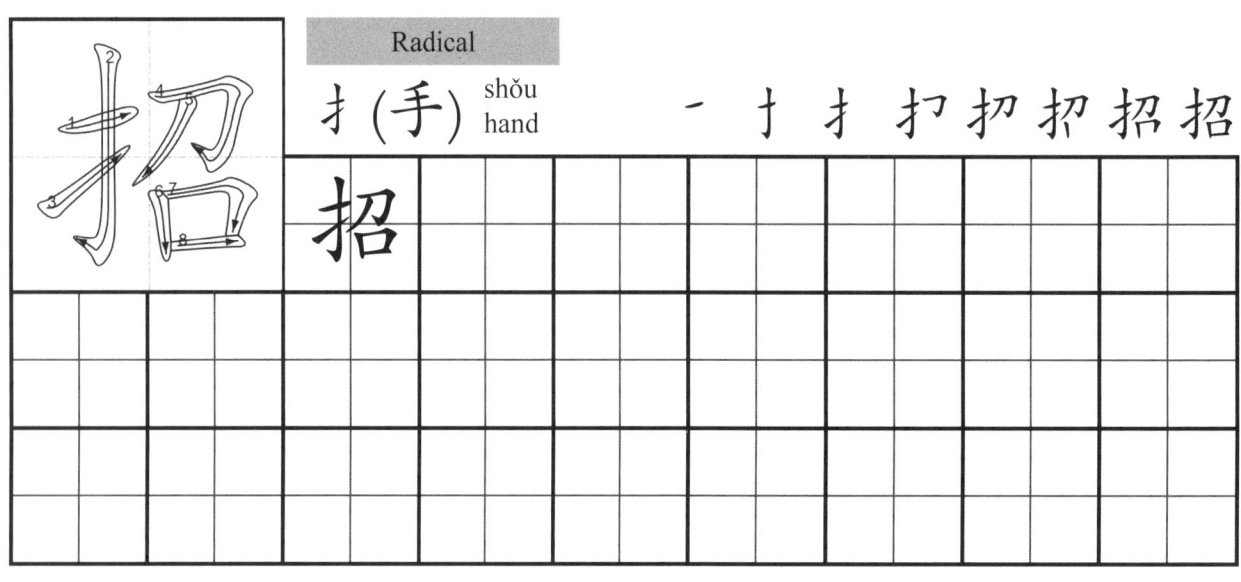

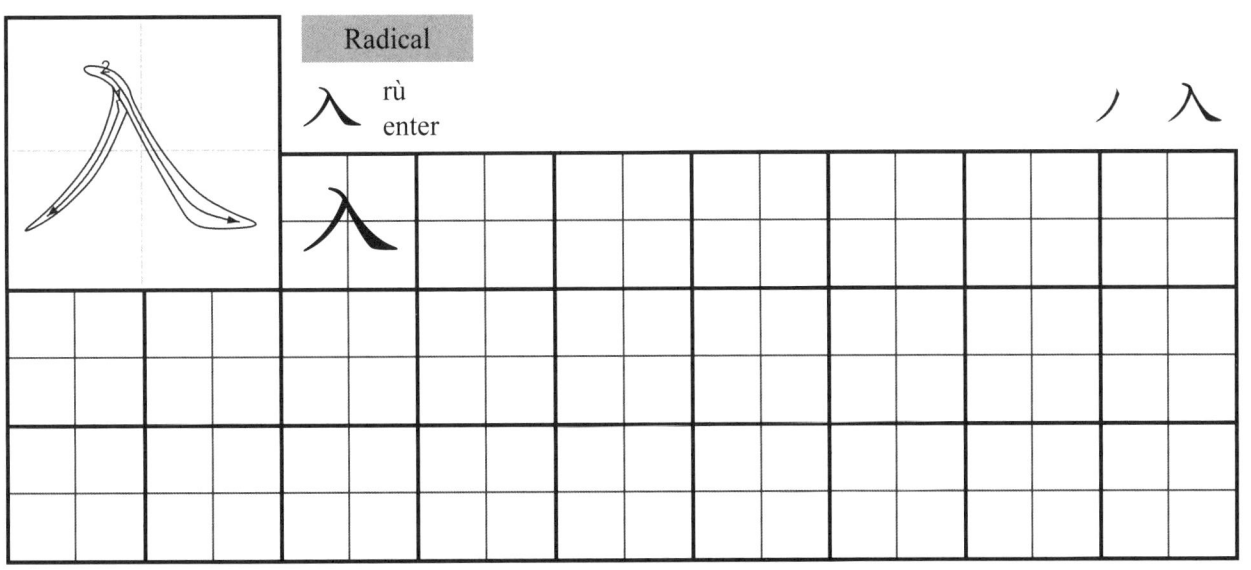

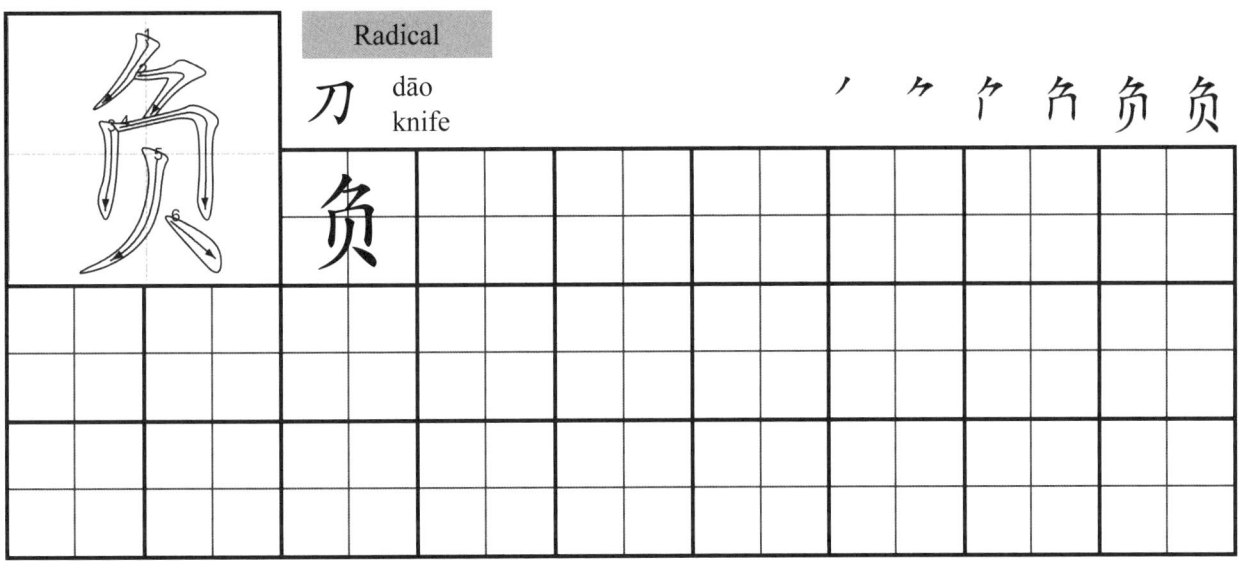

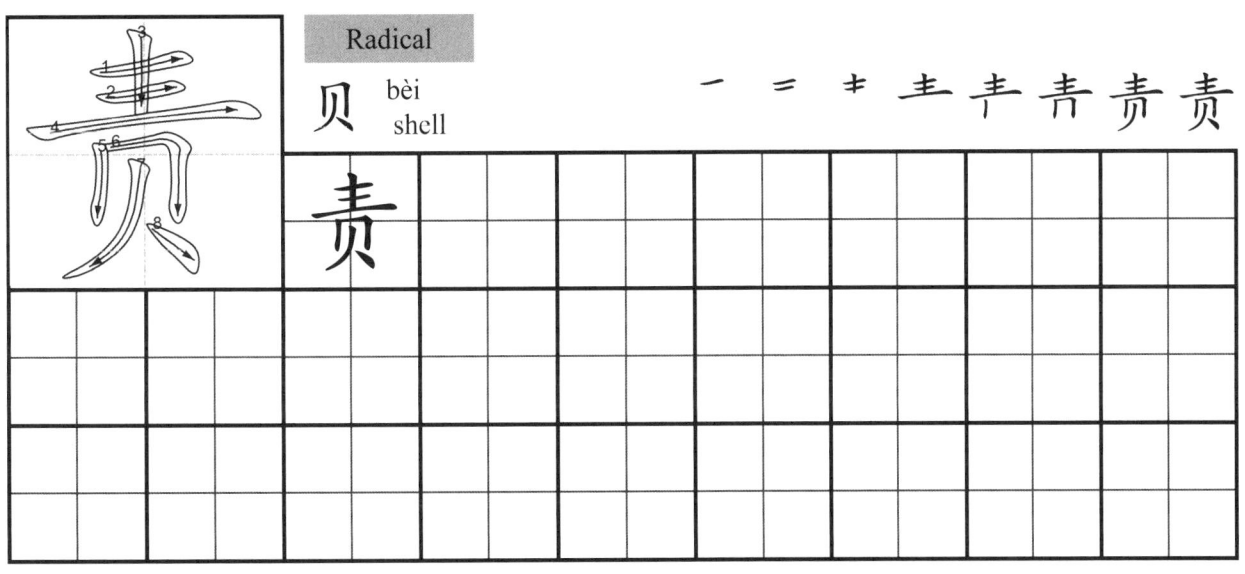

Unit 2 • Lesson 2 • Academics

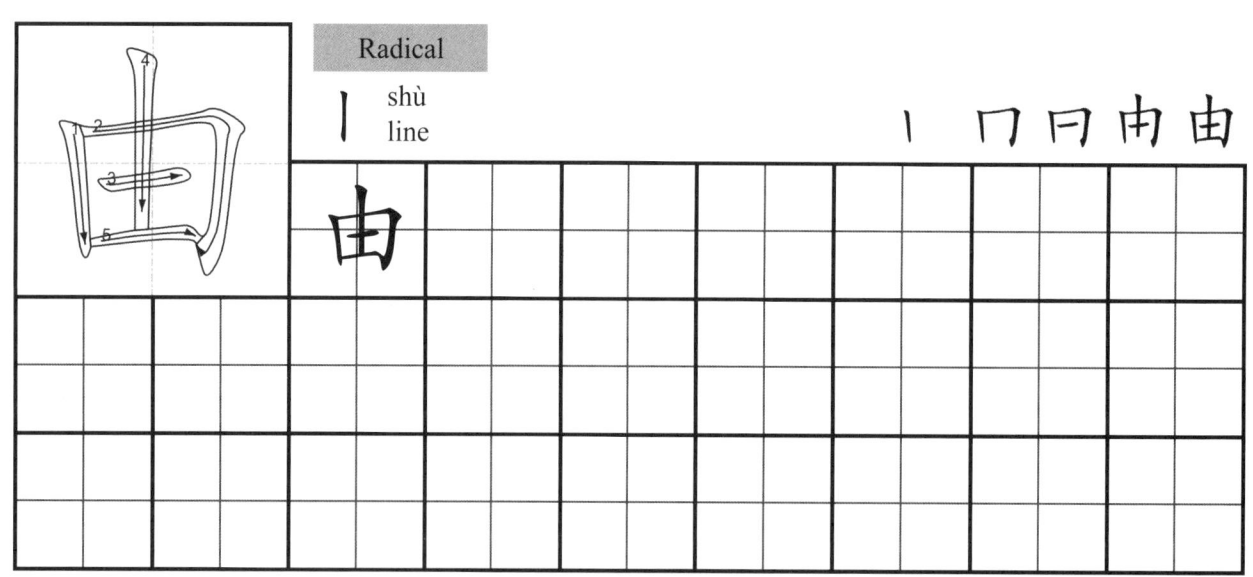

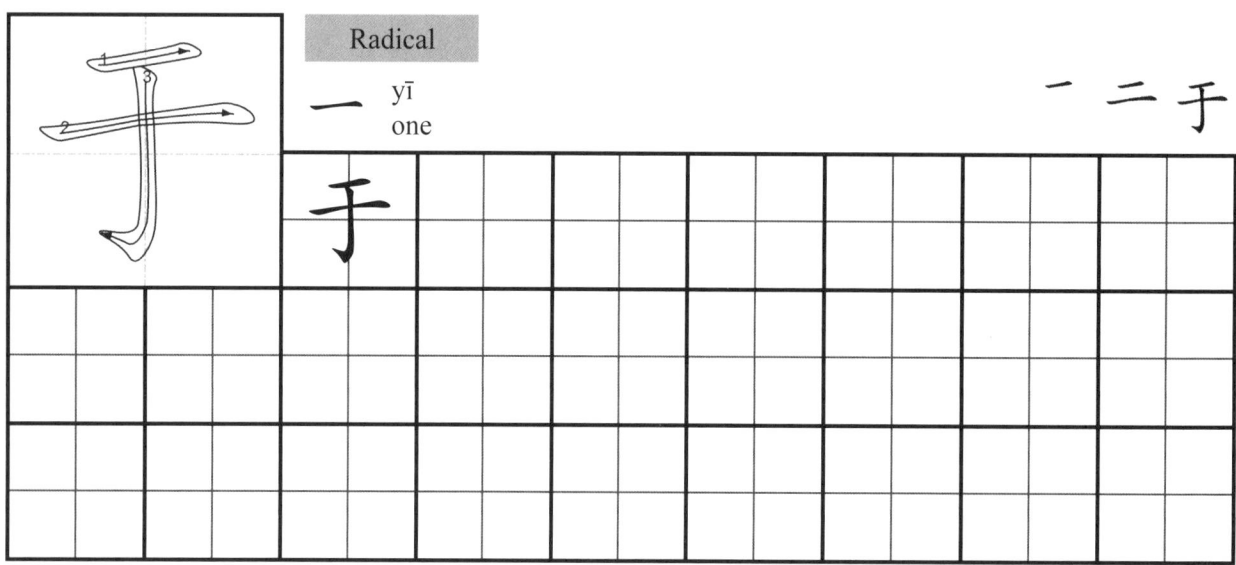

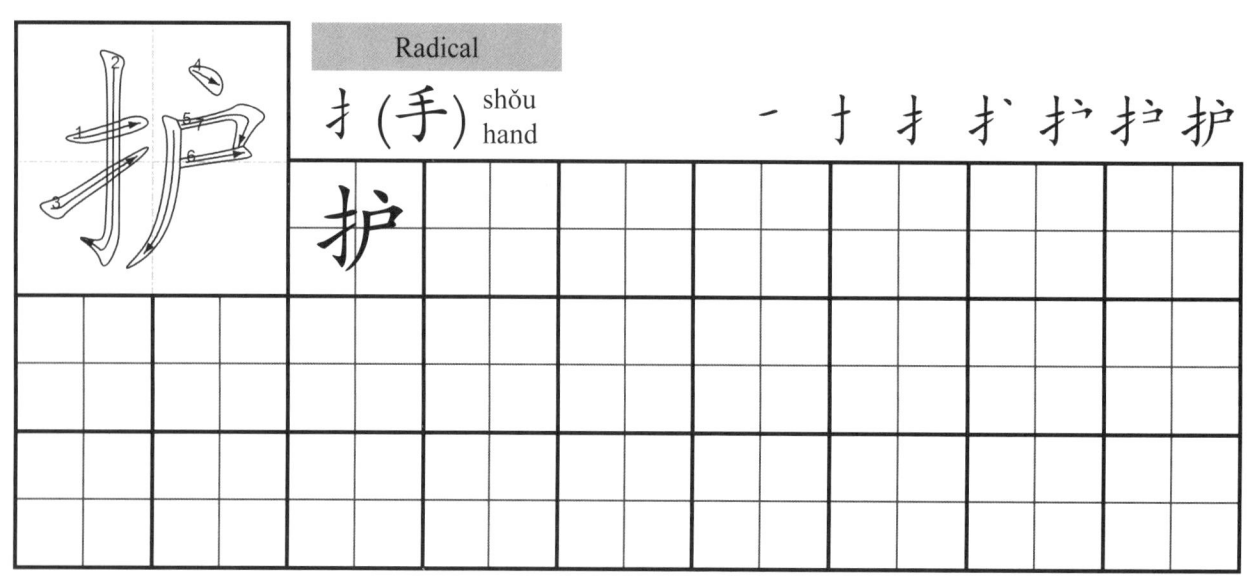

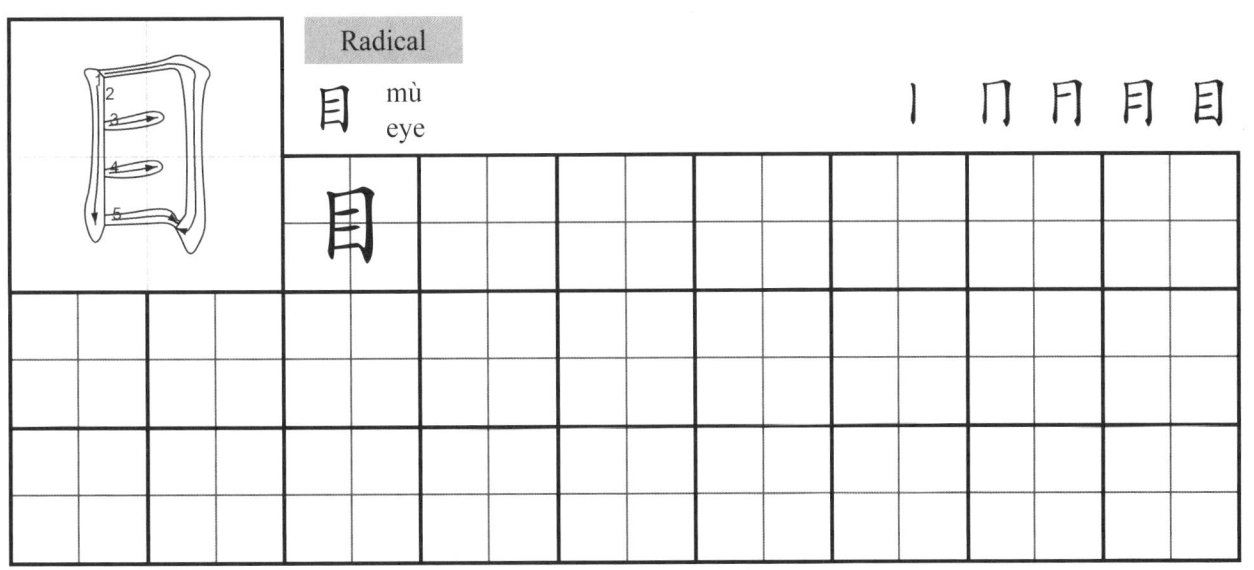

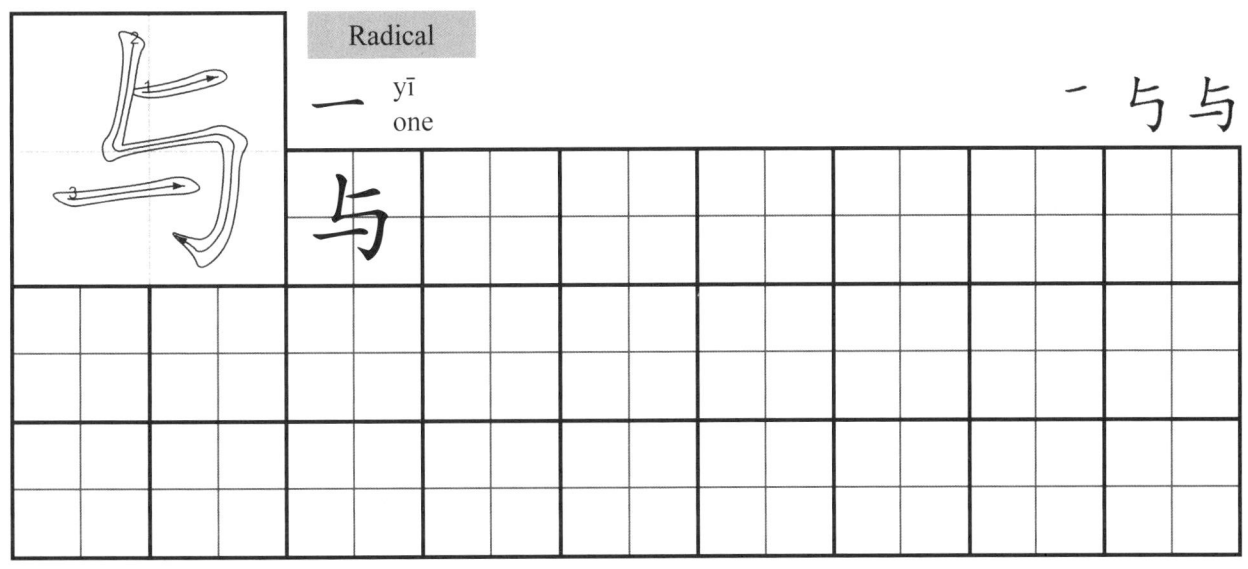

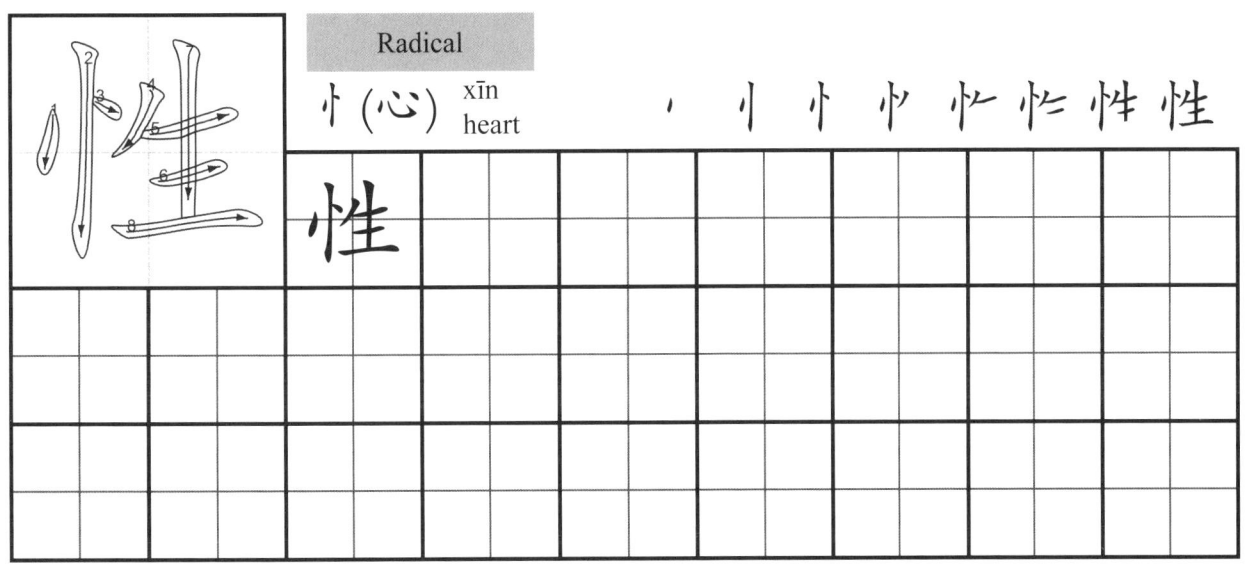

Unit 2 • Lesson 2 • Academics 53

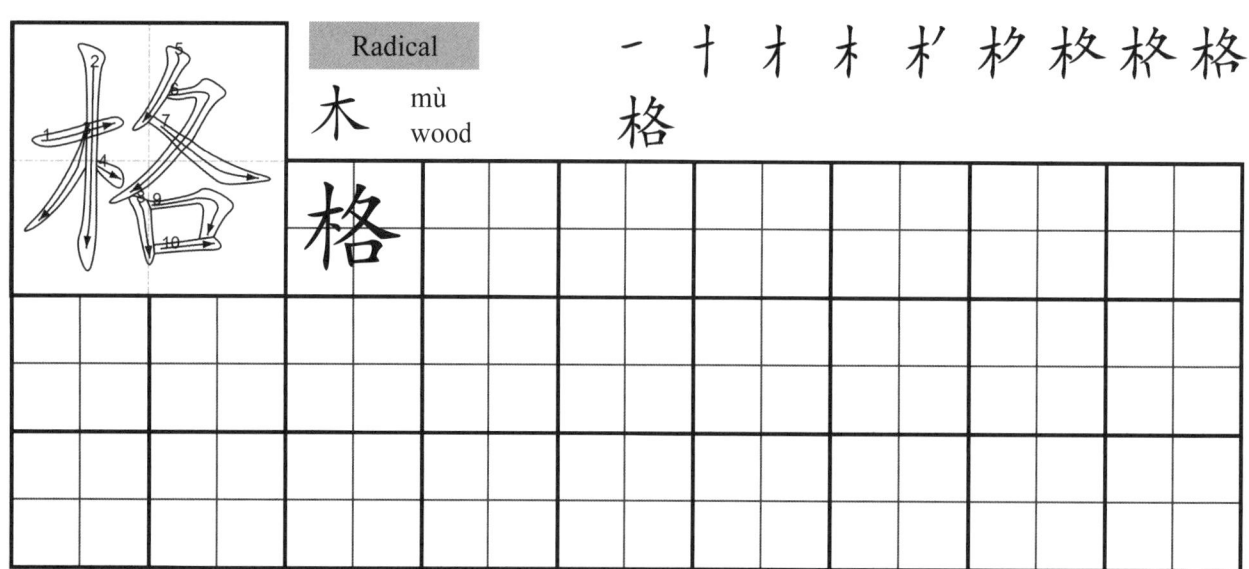

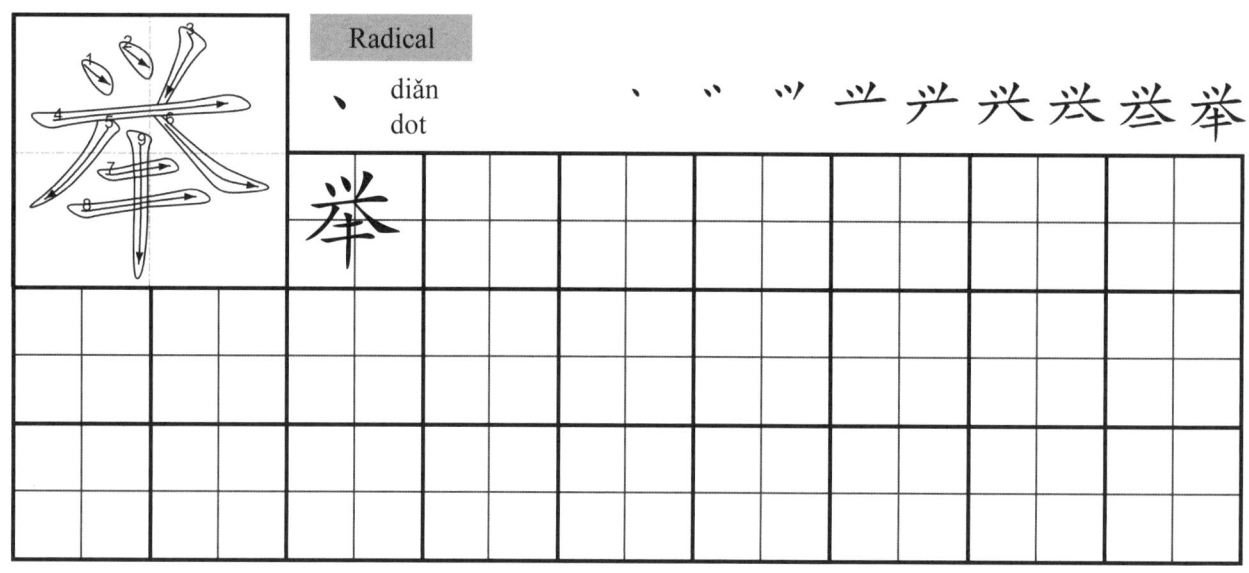

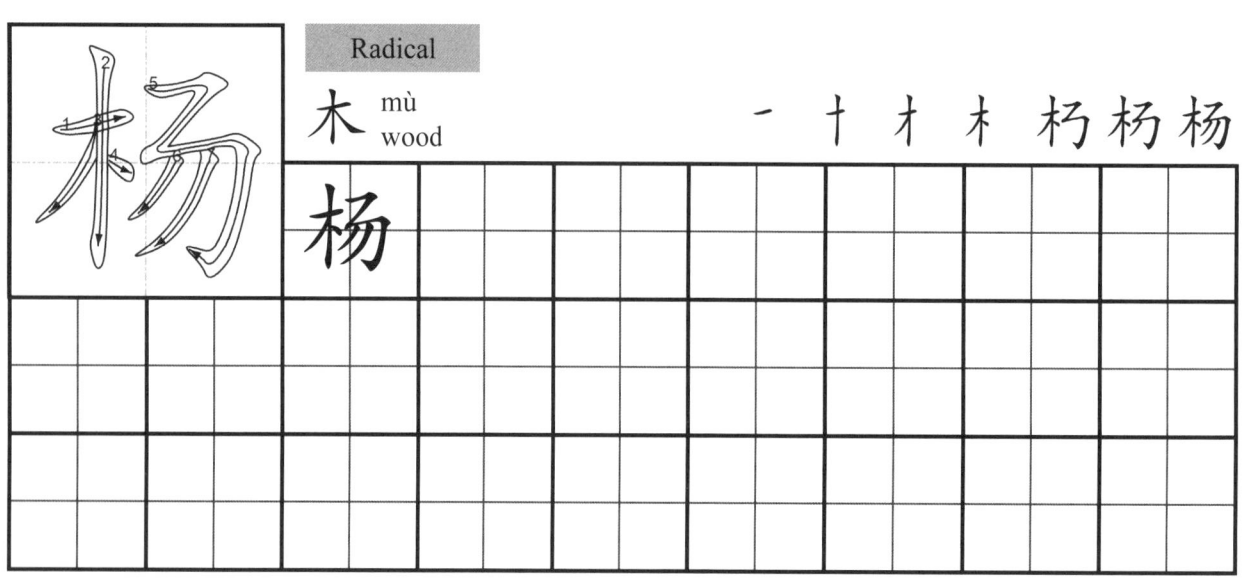

LISTENING COMPREHENSION 2.2

I. Listen to the recording and select the best response below.

1. The woman would most likely respond with:

   A. 那你有空的话就都参加吧！
   B. 我真高兴你能留在这里念书。
   C. 你会参加明天的社团活动吗？
   D. 环保活动很受大家欢迎。

II. Listen to the recording and answer the following True or False questions.

1. (　) Both the woman and the man know Bingbing very well.
2. (　) The woman says that Bingbing is smart and pretty, and speaks Chinese well.
3. (　) The man has met Bingbing a couple of times.
4. (　) The man travels a lot because he is interested in environmental protection.
5. (　) It sounds like Bingbing wants to date the man.

III. Listen to the recording and answer the questions in Chinese.

1. Why is mom against the idea of joining too many clubs?

   _____

2. According to the recording, what will benefit the speaker the most by joining these clubs?

   _____

3. What does the speaker plan to do?

   _____

SPEAKING PRACTICE 2.2

I. Look at the two club posters below and based on the information provided for each, choose which one you will join and give two to three reasons why.

中国艺术社

各位对中国艺术有兴趣的同学，你们想学中国舞、音乐、书法和京剧吗？参加我们活动的同学更有机会在暑假的时候到北京和上海表演。
加入我们吧！

时间：
每个星期五
晚上 6:00 – 7:00
地点：
艺术大楼
602室

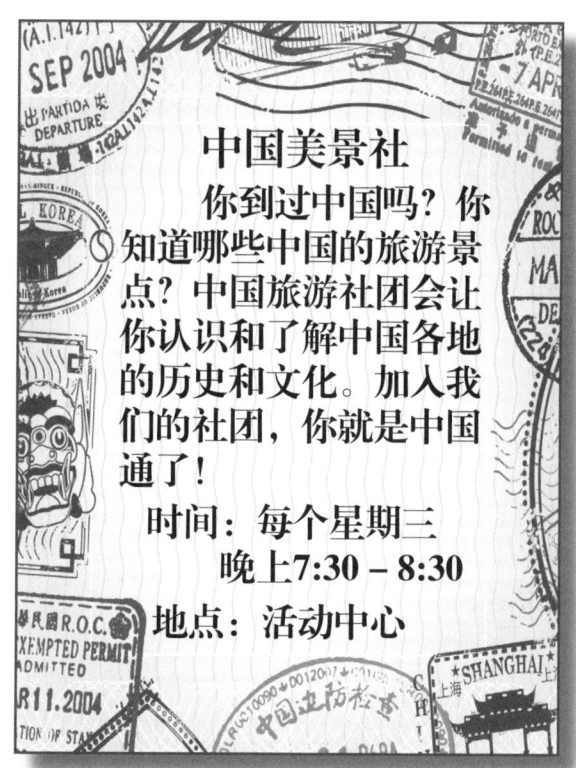

中国美景社

你到过中国吗？你知道哪些中国的旅游景点？中国旅游社团会让你认识和了解中国各地的历史和文化。加入我们的社团，你就是中国通了！

时间：每个星期三
晚上7:30 – 8:30
地点：活动中心

Notes:

艺术 (yìshù): *n.* arts

地点 (dìdiǎn): *n.* place, location

II. You are a representative of a school club and are attending your university's club day to recruit new members. Choose the club you would be a part of — you may choose a club mentioned in the textbook or others that you know of — and convince a potential new recruit to join your club. Explain what your club is about, what activities the club takes part in, and what members will be expected to do. Use the space below to make note of your ideas.

Name:	
Description:	
Number of members:	
Member duties:	
Club activities:	

STRUCTURE REVIEW 2.2

I. Complete the following Structure Note practice activities.

Structure Note 2.5: Use 等等 to indicate "and so on" at the end of a list.

> Item A ＋，＋ Item B ... ＋等等

A. Below is a survey about your hobbies and interests. Answer the following questions using 等等.

1. 你有什么爱好？

   _____

2. 你会什么运动？

   _____

3. 你想学什么乐器？

   _____

4. 你对哪些社团有兴趣？

   _____

5. 你想在社团里负责做什么？

   _____

Structure Note 2.6: Use 当……的时候 to formally indicate when something happened

> 当＋Time Phrase（＋时），＋Sentence

B. The images below show a short story about what happened to a boy. For each picture, write one sentence starting with 当……（的时候）to explain what is happening in each scene.

  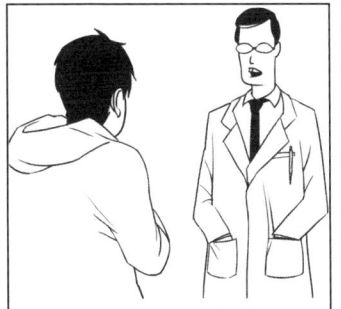 

Structure Note 2.7: Use 由于 to indicate a reason or cause.

$$\text{由于 + Reason, (+ 所以) + Outcome}$$

$$\text{Subject + 由于 + Verb Phrase, (+ 所以) + Outcome}$$

C. A student asks you some questions about your club. Select the best answer from the box below and complete each one by using the pattern 由于……所以.

1. 为什么你们社团叫做"绿色地球社"？

2. 为什么你们社团有这么多社员？

3. 为什么你们要来我们大学招募志愿者？

4. 为什么你们会在中国各地都举办活动？

5. 为什么你们社团的负责人不是学校的学生？

绿色就是环保的颜色，我们是一个保护地球环境的社团，所以……
我们希望中国各地的大学生都有机会认识环保，所以……
我社想请一个比较有经验的人负责招募志愿者，所以……
我们准备和你们学校一起发展一个环保项目，所以……
现在越来越多人重视生活与环境，所以……

Structure Note 2.8: Use 与 to join two nouns in formal writing.

> Noun Phrase + 与 + Noun Phrase

D. You are participating in a competition that tests your knowledge on Chinese culture. For each question, you need to provide two answers. Use 与 to connect your two answers and write a complete sentence.

1. Name two famous scenic spots in Beijing.
   _____

2. Which festivals do Chinese people celebrate with their family?
   _____

3. What traditional foods do people have during Chinese New Year?
   _____

4. If you are going to visit a Chinese friend, what kind of gifts would you bring with you?
   _____

5. Name two famous Chinese philosophers.
   _____

II. In this lesson, you learned about some expressions used in formal settings. Now, read the club poster and replace the words underlined with the structures you learned.

中国文化社---《文化和礼节》

在你的中国朋友送你礼物时，除了谢谢以外，你还知道要怎样做来表示礼貌吗？在你和一位中国长辈吃饭时，你知道为什么要让长辈请客吗？

如果你对中国文化的认识不多，我们欢迎你参加这个星期六中国文化社举办的《文化和礼节》活动。因为越来越多中国学生来我们学校留学念书，我们希望学生们能对中国文化多多了解，也能跟从中国来的同学交个朋友。

这个星期六的活动不但会有老师教大家学习中国礼节，而且还有传统舞蹈表演、书法比赛、京剧历史介绍……不用多想了！大家一起来参加我们的活动吧！

时间：二月二十日（星期六）下午一点

地点：图书馆活动室

READING COMPREHENSION 2.2

I. Read the passage and answer the following True or False questions.

几年前当我大学毕业的时候，朋友介绍我去了一家电脑公司工作。这个工作赚钱不少，工作环境也不错，所以我马上决定加入这家公司。但是在这里工作了两年以后，我开始有了一些烦恼。由于每天都是上班下班，所以没有时间去认识新朋友，做我有兴趣的事。我一直希望做志愿者，认识更多的人。有一次，当我的同屋举办派对的时候，我碰见了几个外国客人，有美国人、欧洲人、日本人等等。我和他们一见如故，特别是那个叫冰冰的女孩子，不但人长得漂亮可爱，而且性格特别开朗，很快就变成了我的好朋友。冰冰在一个社团当负责人，他们的社团已经招募到超过五百名的会员，一直在发展跟环境保护有关的项目，常常举办不同活动。特别是这些年，在他们的努力下，越来越多的人认识到环境保护有多重要。我一听冰冰的介绍，就决定加入他们，与他们一起为环保做点事。我们只有一个美好的地球，每个人都应该爱我们的地球。

1. ( ) 我大学毕业两年左右以后开始在一家电脑公司工作。
2. ( ) 由于我花了很多时间在工作上，所以不能常参加别的活动。
3. ( ) 冰冰是志愿者，不但人很美，而且性格很好。
4. ( ) 我是在一次社团招募的活动上认识冰冰的。
5. ( ) 我对环境保护的社团很有兴趣，会去做环保的志愿者。

Take the challenge! 动动脑筋！

In the passage, 派对 (pàiduì) is borrowed from the English word "party" and has a similar pronouciation to it. There are a lot of other Chinese words like 派对 that are borrowed from foreign languages and generated based on the pronunciation. Can you guess the meaning of the following words by pronouncing them?
Food: 三明治 披萨 汉堡 Sports: 马拉松 保龄球 柔道
Additionally, there are some Chinese terms created by directly translating the words from English. Can you guess the meaning of the following? Food: 热狗 Sport: 冰球

II. Read the following passage and answer the questions:

> 学校今年的社团招募日比去年晚了一点，是由于今年新来了很多留学生，所以我们要等他们先**适应**一下中国的学校生活。我是中国文学社的负责人，这个周末就参加了社团招募日的活动。活动一开始，我就接待了几位留学生。我跟他们好好聊了聊，先给他们来了个简单的中文"小考"。哇，不得了！没想到这几位不但中文都说得挺棒，而且都对我们文学社特别有兴趣，想要加入！其中一位长得很酷的美国**帅哥**还很认真地问我，虽然我们社团的名字是文学社，但是除了文学以外，我们是不是也可以计划举办有关中国历史、书法、**美食**等等的活动。我觉得他的建议挺酷的。看起来不同的文化背景，不同的想法在一起，就会有新的**火花**，我相信今年我们文学社的活动一定会更**精彩**！

1. 为什么今年社团招募日举办得比较晚？
    A. 社团招募日只能在周末。
    B. 学校里有不少的新留学生。
    C. 有很多留学生的中文还不怎么好。
    D. 要参加社团就得先参加小考。

2. Most likely, the club is currently focused on . . .
    A. Literature
    B. History
    C. Calligraphy
    D. All of the above.

3. 下面哪一个说法是不对的？
    A. 我参加招募是因为我是一个社团的负责人。
    B. 跟我聊天的几位同学都希望参加文学社。
    C. 那位美国同学的中国书法写得很棒。
    D. 能有留学生同学参加我们的社团我很高兴。

Notes:
适应 (shìyìng): *v.* to adapt
帅哥 (shuàigē): *n.* a handsome young man
美食 (měishí): *n.* delicious food, fine food
火花 (huǒhuā): *n.* spark
精彩 (jīngcǎi): *adj.* brilliant, splendid, wonderful

III. Read the poster and email below and answer the following questions.

书法社

　　这个学期我社很荣幸邀请到一位从中国北京来的名书法家黄艺兴先生，来我校指导各位有兴趣学写书法的同学。大家想参加的话请到教学楼201室报名。活动详情如下：

活动地点：艺术楼音乐教室
活动时间：九月十五日 星期五下午1:30
指导老师：黄艺兴先生、李京老师

　　参加活动的同学们请自带文房四宝。有任何问题或意见可以向负责人陈健明提问。谢谢！

To: 王小美
From: 孙玛丽
Subject: 书法社

亲爱的小美：
　　你在美国过得好吗？你这学期选了什么课？我在北京学习已经有一个多月了，我的中文进步了很多。为了多了解中国文化，我在学校加入了书法社。书法社的负责人昨天给我发了一张**海报**，是关于下星期的活动，他们邀请了一位书法家来**指导**我们写书法。**海报**上说大家都要准备好自己的**文房四宝**，你知道**文房四宝**是什么吗？
玛丽

Notes:
海报 (hǎibào): *n.* poster
指导 (zhǐdǎo): *v.* to instruct
文房四宝 (wénfángsìbǎo): *n.* The four stationery treasures of Chinese study

1. Whom did the club invite? _____

2. On the poster, circle the location that the activity will take place in.

3. What does Mali ask Xiaomei about in the email? _____

4. If you were Xiaomei, how would you respond to Mali's inquiry? _____

WRITING PRACTICE 2.2

I. You are a member of the Environmental Protection club. There's a contest to help create a new mascot for the club. Write a description of what your mascot would look like and include an image.

II. You want to start a new club at school. As part of the application process, you need to write a short proposal about your club and include the name of your club, the club slogan, the club logo, the focus of the club, the activities club plans to do, what kind of members you want, and how you will recruit them.

Modern Chinese 现代中文

UNIT 3 – LESSON 1

住校与租房

VOCABULARY REVIEW 3.1

I. Each of the underlined phrases below are vocabulary words you have learned. However, a character taken from each pair make up a new phrase — shown within the circle. Determine the correct meaning for each.

Example:

(A) to rent
(B) to save effort
(C) to join force
(D) to borrow

1. 卧室/内外 (室内)
(A) outdoor
(B) indoor
(C) bedroom
(D) bathroom

2.  省心/电费
(A) to save time
(B) to save effort
(C) to save labor
(D) to save power

3.  学校/费用
(A) school fee
(B) utilities
(C) electricity bills
(D) internet charges

4.  隐私/事情
(A) privacy
(B) personal affair
(C) business
(D) troubles

II. In each row, write the English meaning of the radical and the following characters that contain the radical as a component.

Example: 日 sun   晴 clear, fine   春 spring   暖 warm

1. 火 ____   烦 ____   烧 ____   燥 ____
2. 心 ____   想 ____   思 ____   感 ____
3. 宀 ____   家 ____   室 ____   寓 ____
4. 贝 ____   财 ____   资 ____   费 ____

III. Fill in the blanks with the vocabulary term that best completes the phrases below.

坏处   相处   剩   套   平时   隐私   理想

雪丽一直都不喜欢和父母一起住，因为她觉得一点 (1.)_____ 都没有，所以她决定和朋友搬到一 (2.)_____ 两室一厅的公寓，过她 (3.)_____ 的生活。但是雪丽是一个粗心的人，(4.)_____ 也不爱做家务。最后，连室友都没有办法和她继续 (5.)_____。现在 (6.)_____ 雪丽一个人住，她开始想念妈妈做的菜、爸爸对她的照顾。她明白到住外面还是家里都是一样，有好处也有 (7.)_____。

CHARACTER WRITING PRACTICE 3.1

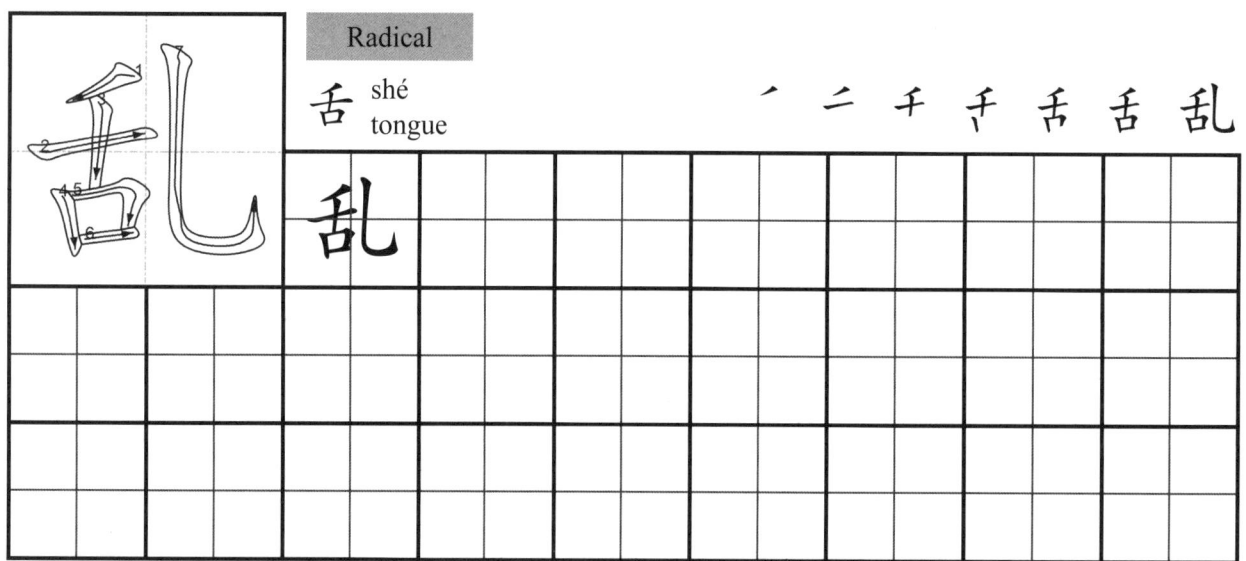

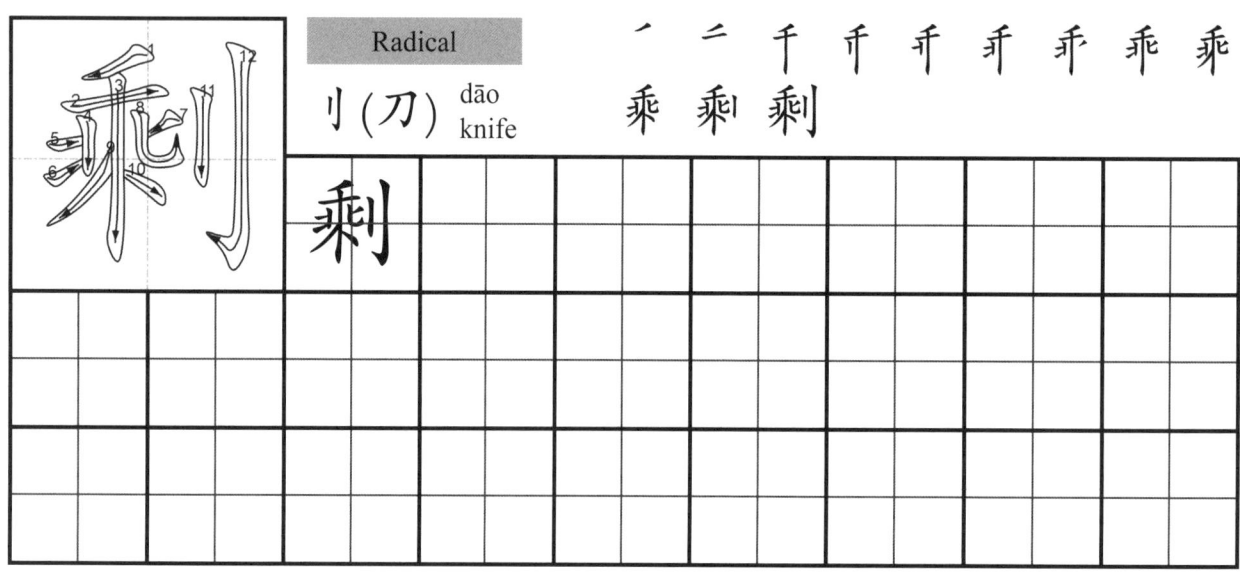

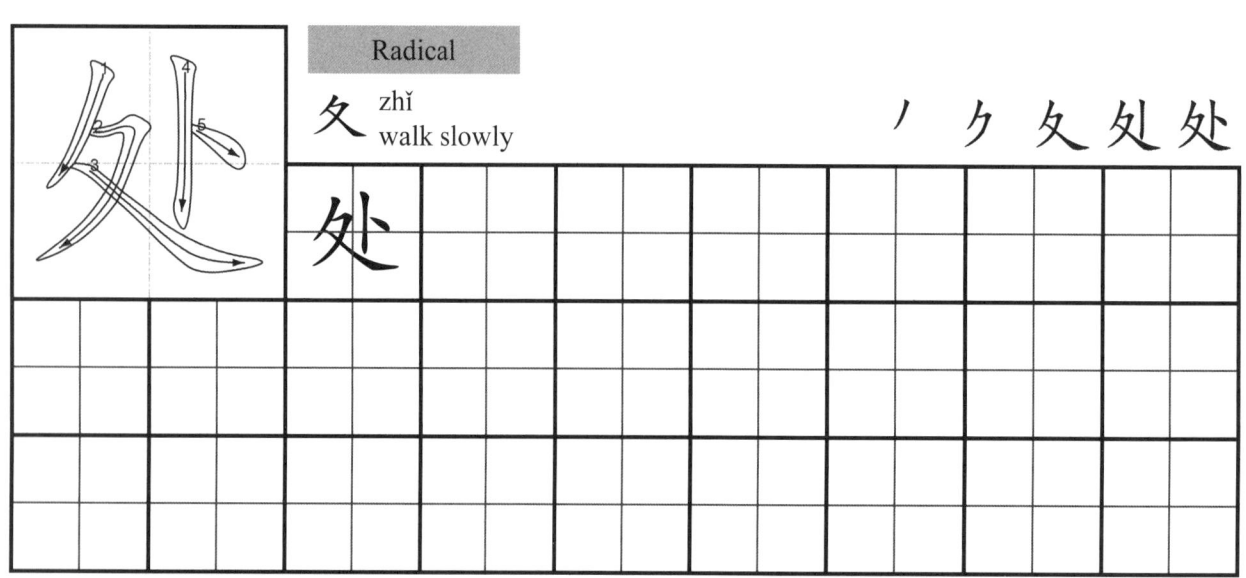

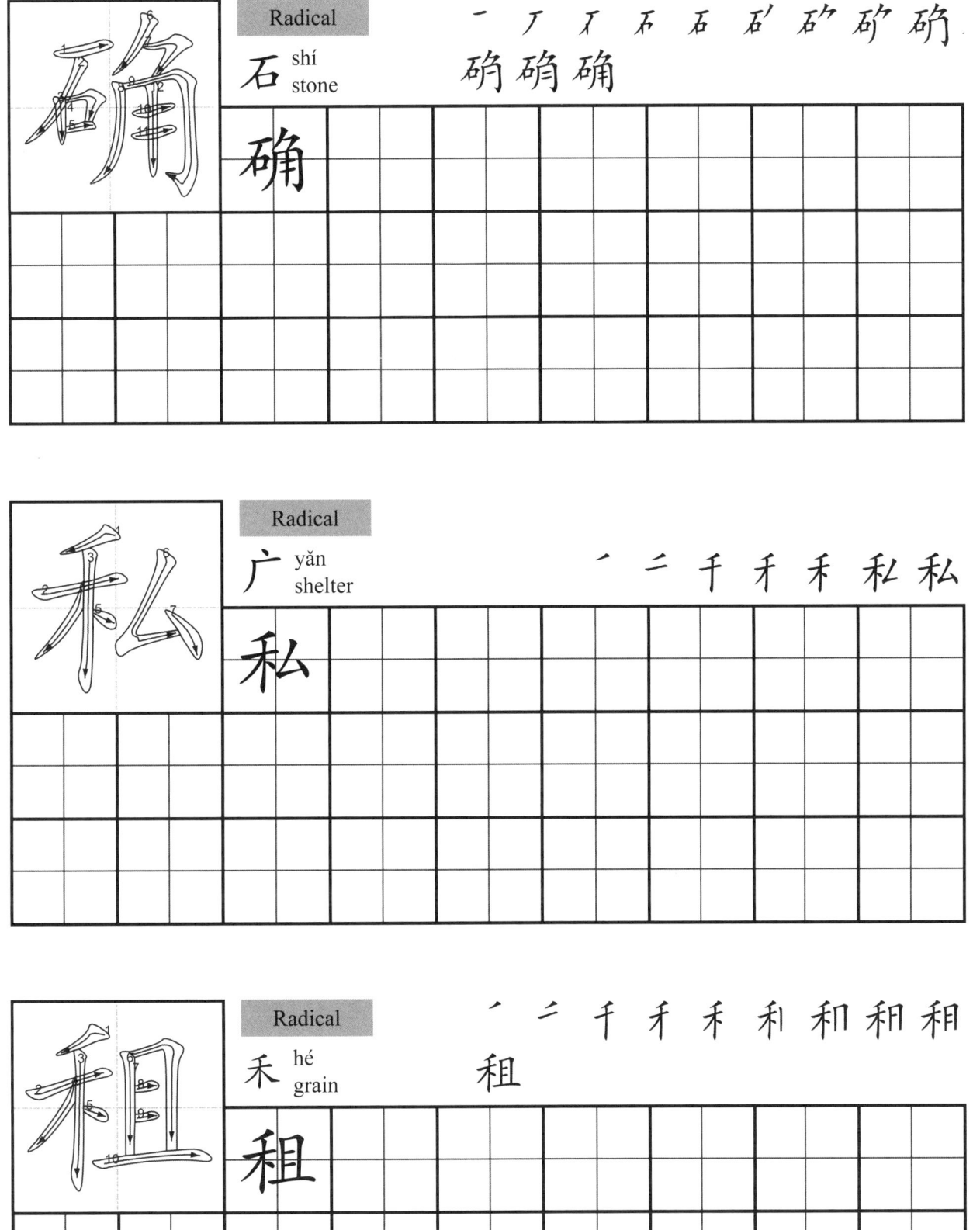

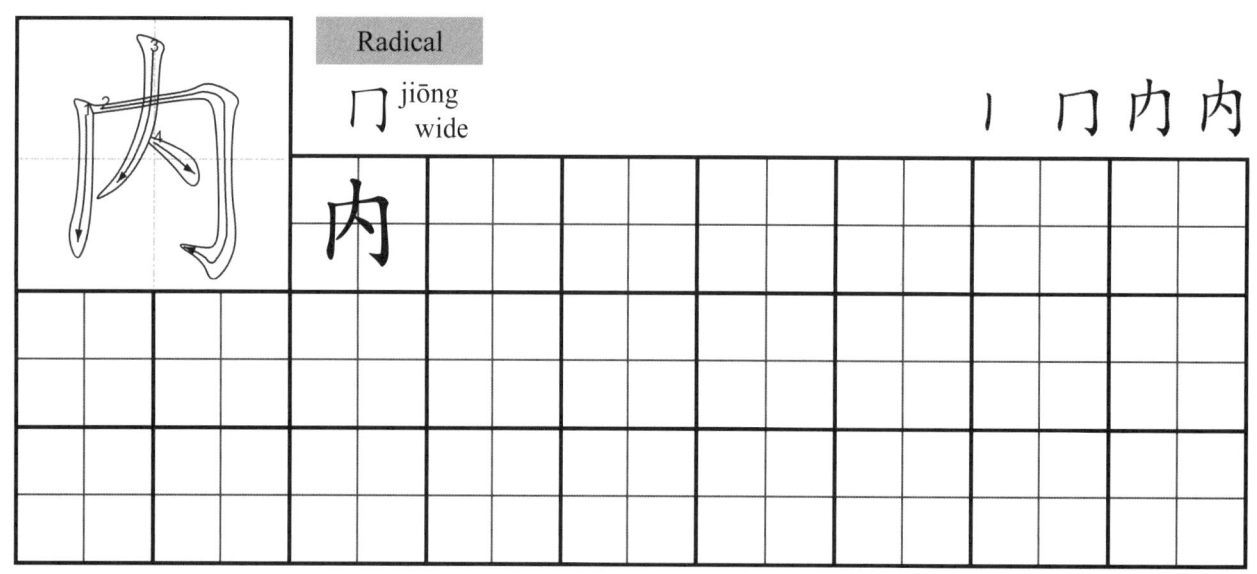

Radical 冂 jiōng wide

丨 冂 内 内

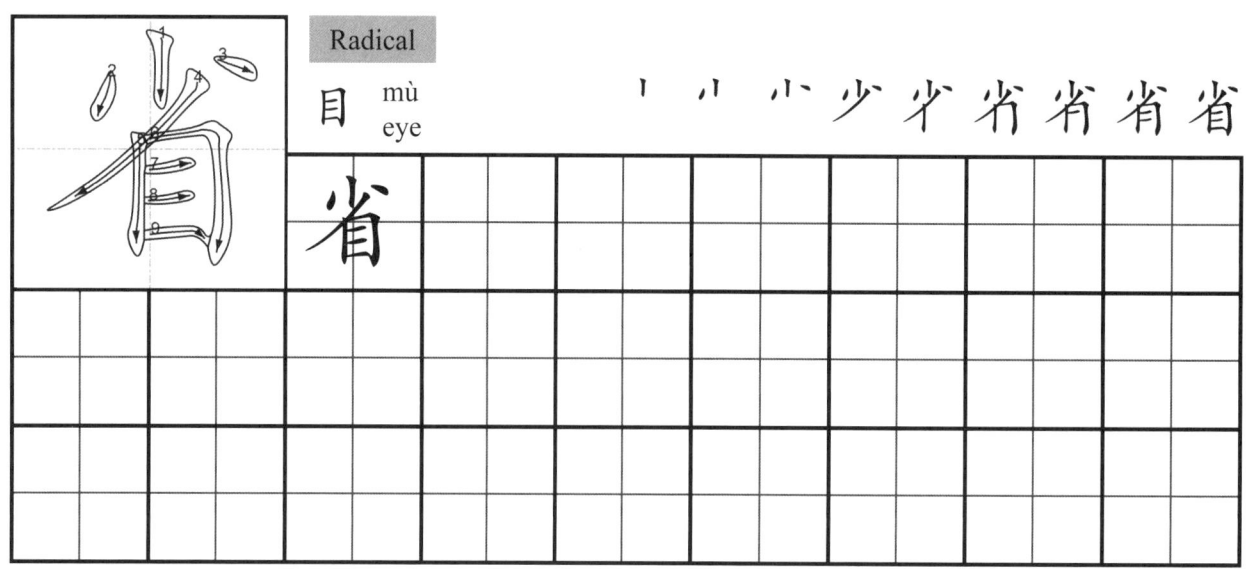

Radical 目 mù eye

丨 丨 小 少 少 尐 省 省 省

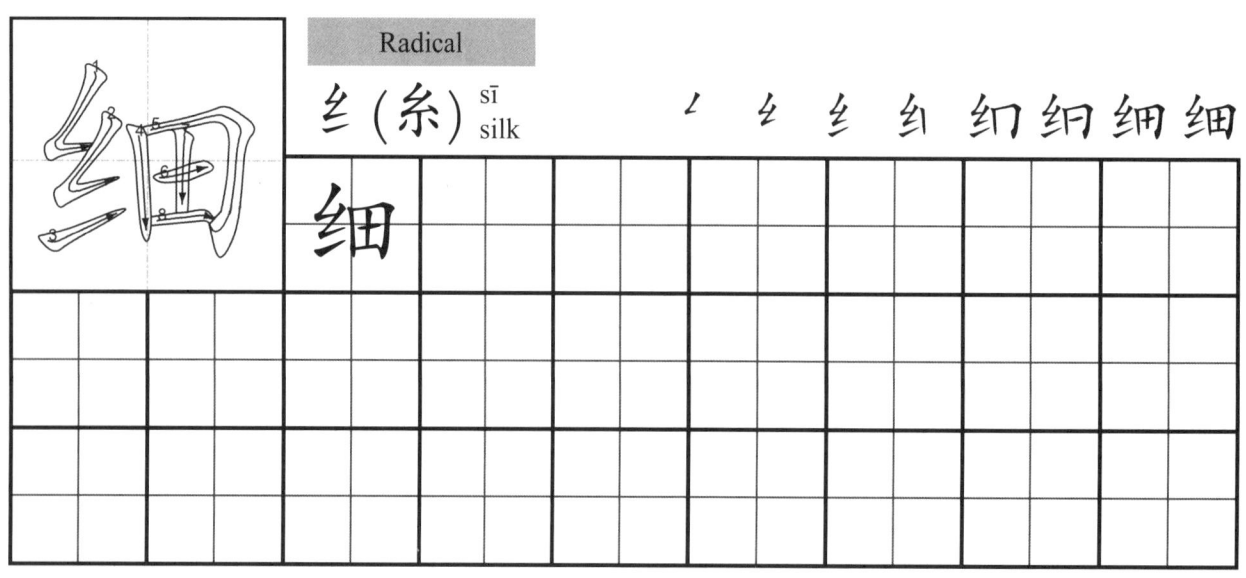

Radical 纟(糸) sī silk

㇀ ㇉ 纟 纟 纠 纠 细 细

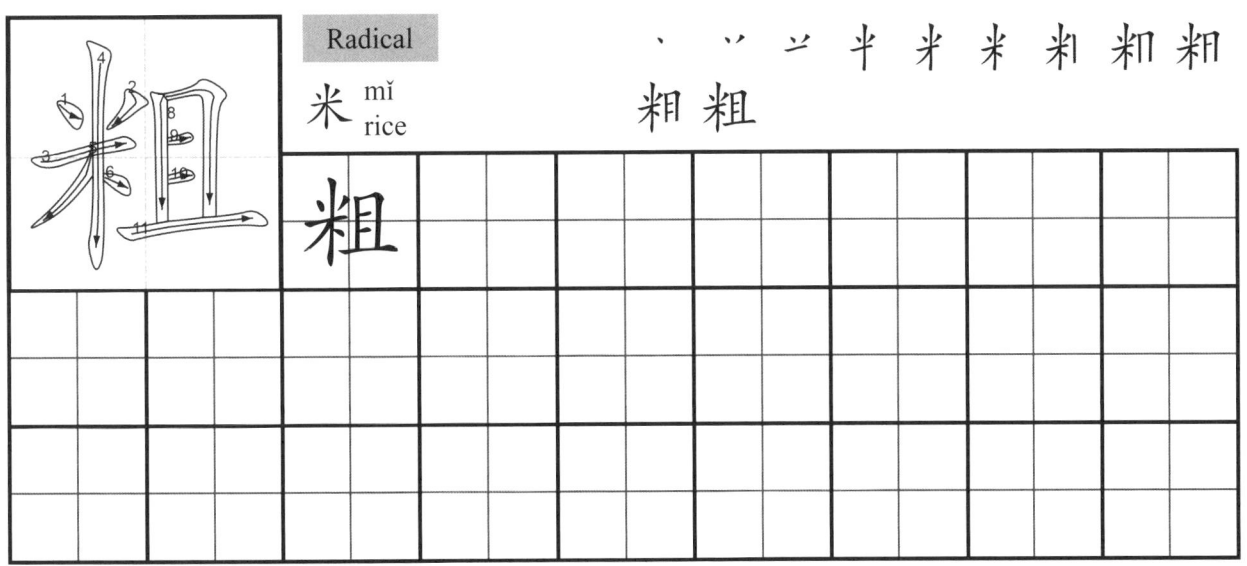

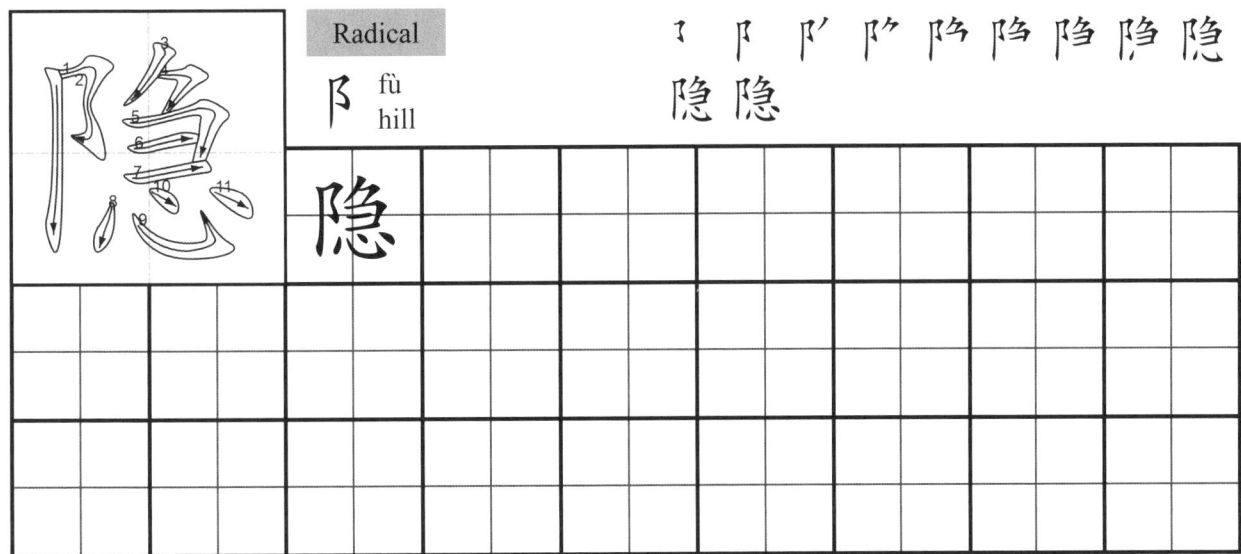

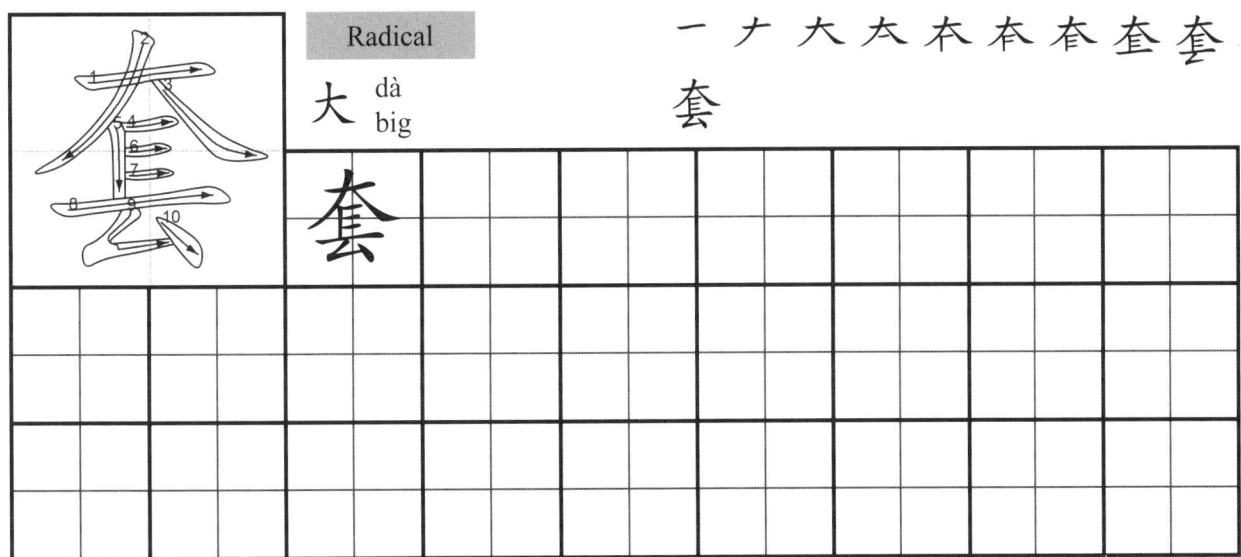

Unit 3 • Lesson 1 • Housing

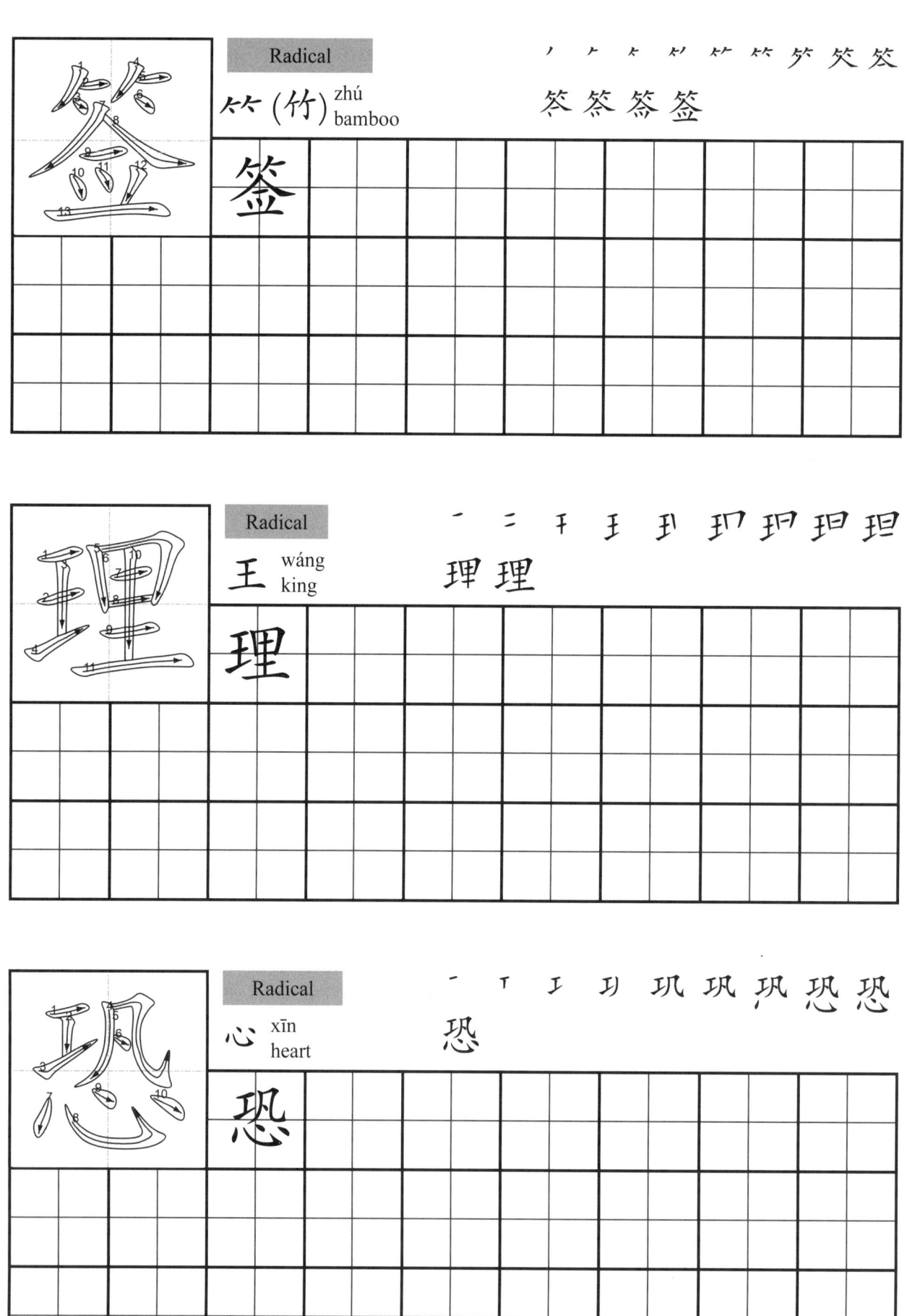

LISTENING COMPREHENSION 3.1

I. **Listen to the recording and select the best response below.**

1. The woman would most likely respond with:

    A. 你的室友会不会照顾人呢？
    B. 住公寓的好处确实挺多的。
    C. 那就签合同吧！
    D. 你别忘了付房租啊。

II. **Listen to the recording and answer the following True or False questions.**

1. (   ) The woman knows whom the man's roommate is.
2. (   ) The man and his roommate do not get along living in the same apartment.
3. (   ) According to the man, shopping is very convenient with a nearby store that carries everything.
4. (   ) The man is renting a furnished apartment.
5. (   ) The woman does not believe there will be any vacant apartments.

III. **Listen to the recording and answer the questions in Chinese.**

1. What problem does the speaker encounter while living in Shanghai?

   _____

2. Provide 1-2 examples of the type of problem the speaker faces.

   _____

3. According to the speaker, what is the cause of the problem?

   _____

SPEAKING PRACTICE 3.1

I. Looking below at the images of two living rooms from separate apartments, explain which you would prefer to live in and why.

公寓1

公寓2

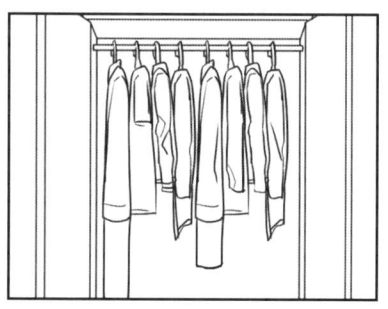

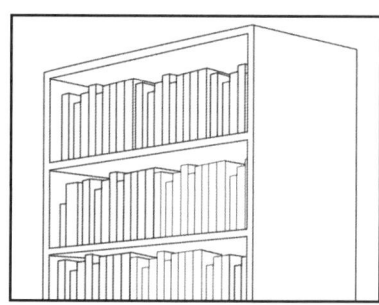

II. You are living off-campus and need to find a new roommate to help share the rent. Persuade a friend to rent the apartment with you. Discuss the advantages of living off-campus versus living on-campus and describe what your apartment is like. Talk about what kind of personality would be compatible with yours.

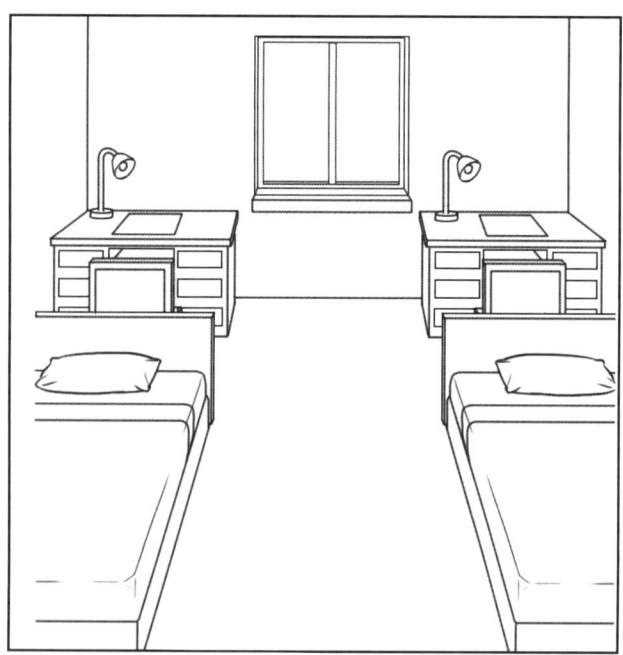

STRUCTURE REVIEW 3.1

I. Complete the following Structure Note practice activities.

Structure Note 3.1: Use 再说 to bring up additional points.

$$\boxed{\text{再说，} + \text{Sentence}}$$

A. Your friend asks you about your new apartment. Answer the questions and bring up additional related points to each answer by using 再说.

1. 客厅大吗？
   _____

2. 公寓干净吗？
   _____

3. 交通方便吗？
   _____

4. 房租贵吗？
   _____

5. 你觉得你的室友怎么样？
   _____

Structure Note 3.2: Use 确实 to say "indeed" or "really."

$$\boxed{\text{Subject} + \text{确实} + \text{Verb/Adjective Phrase}}$$

B. Do you agree with any of the following statements to describe your family? If you agree, use 确实 to explain each one you agree with.

> 家里的事都是长辈决定的。
> 长辈会照顾晚辈，晚辈会尊敬长辈。
> 长辈很重视家里的礼节。
> 父母非常了解自己孩子的想法。
> 小孩子都得帮忙做家务。
> 每个人都得负责打扫自己的房间。
> 每个人都非常好相处。
> 每次过节的时候全家都会坐在一起吃饭。

1. _____

2. _____

3. _____

4. _____

Structure Note 3.3: Use 一点(儿)都没/不 to emphasize "not at all."

> Subject + 一点(儿) + 都 + 没/不 + Adjective / Verb Phrase

> Subject + 一点(儿) + Noun Phrase + 都 + 没/不 + Adjective / Verb Phrase

C. Describe the following pictures using 一点(儿)都没/不.

1. _____

2. _____

3. _____

4. _____

Structure Note 3.4: Use 恐怕 to express doubt over an unfortunate situation.

> 恐怕 + Sentence

> Subject + 恐怕 + Verb Phrase

74　第三单元 · 第一课 · 住

D. You work in a customer service position at a hotel. Respond to the customers' inquiries in a polite manner by using 恐怕.

1. 请问，从这里到机场要花多长时间？
   _____

2. 请问，对面那家饭馆有什么好吃的？
   _____

3. 请问，到了北京后会有旅游团的负责人来接我们吗？
   _____

4. 请问，今天会有人来打扫房间吗？
   _____

5. 请问，哪里能买到长城的纪念品？
   _____

Take the challenge! 动动脑筋！

"李护士，以后你负责帮病人打针。"
"可是我怕针。"
"好吧，不打针，那你负责开药。"
"我怕药的味道。"
"好吧，不开药，那你要负责打扫吗？"
"不好意思，我也怕脏……"
"你什么都怕，恐怕我们这家医院也怕了你了。"

How to differentiate between 怕 and 恐怕?

怕 and 恐怕 share the same definition, "to be afraid." But the meaning behind and usage for each is different. 恐怕 is similar to "I'm afraid" in English. As a conjunction, 恐怕 is always used to show one's opinion, speculation or attitute on one thing. Thus, it can be defined as "perhaps." Furthermore, the phrase can be inserted before a sentence or after the subject of a sentence. Even if this conjunction is taken out, a sentence can still make sense and function without it.

On the other hand, 怕 can only be defined as "to be afraid." It also cannot be omitted as it acts as the main verb in a sentence. Test this out with the passage above.

II. Look at the pictures and read the reviews about the apartment. Respond to the reviews by using the structure patterns you learned in this lesson. Describe whether or not you agree with them and would consider moving into this apartment.

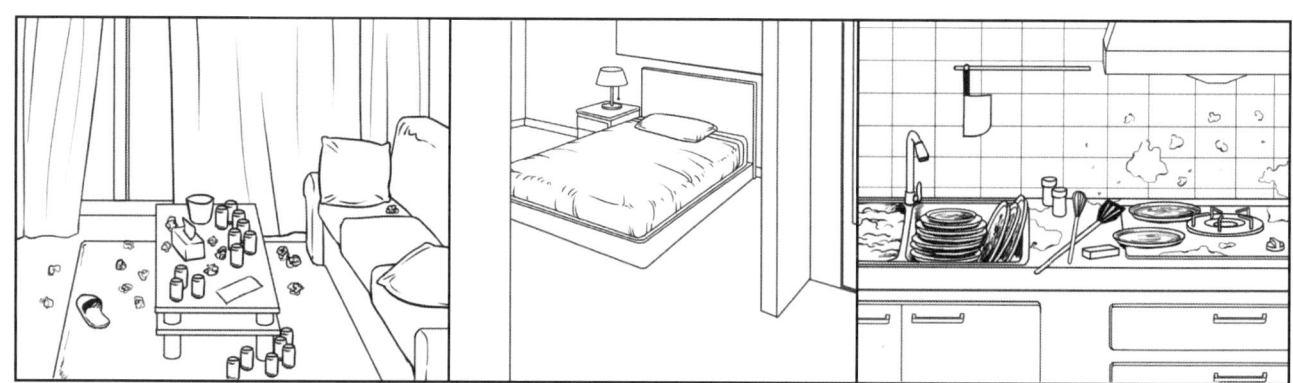

🧑‍🦱 这套两室一厅的公寓还不错，只是卧室都太小了。

　🧑 小不是问题，问题是两间卧室也没门……

　　🧑 卧室怎么可能没有门？

　　　👩 _____

🧑‍🦰 我觉得这套公寓的房租挺便宜的，一个月才三千多块。

　🧑 房租虽然便宜，但不包水电费！

　　👩 _____

🧑 厨房不太干净，客厅也有点乱。

　👩 _____

🧑‍💼 这套公寓离语言学校太远了，非常不方便！

　👩 _____

READING COMPREHENSION 3.1

I. Read the passage and answer the following True or False questions.

> 我上大学第一年的时候住在学校的宿舍，好处是离教室和图书馆都很近，餐厅就在宿舍的对面，而且宿舍里健身房、活动中心等等一应俱全。但是坏处是我们的宿舍里住了三百个左右的学生，平时一天到晚都很吵、很乱。特别是要考试的时候，很多学生很晚还在复习，宿舍里"热闹"极了，我一点都不能睡觉。我这个人喜欢比较安静的环境，所以一放暑假，我就开始找公寓了。玛丽问我希望一个人住还是想合租，我说我喜欢干净，恐怕自己住比较好。玛丽陪我去看了几个地方，我很快就找到了一套很理想的公寓。除了环境和地点非常好以外，想不到房间也是又大又舒服。可是房租不便宜，还不包水电费，再说也没有家具。我还没有想好要不要签合同，玛丽建议我应该找一个爱干净的室友，这样费用就不会那么高了。我真头疼，要怎么做呢？

1. (　) 我已经上了三年大学了。
2. (　) 我非常喜欢我的宿舍因为宿舍很热闹。
3. (　) 我希望住在一个不太乱，不太吵的地方。
4. (　) 我找到的那个公寓环境，地点和费用我都觉得不错。
5. (　) 我应该找一个会做家务的同屋。

Take the challenge! 动动脑筋！

In the passage, the writer uses 热闹 to describe the dorm. 热闹 usually has a positive connotation, referring to a situation that is very lively and full of excitement. However, the writer uses the term in a negative sense. Just like in English, quotation marks can be placed around a phrase to indicate irony — that the person may describe something as x, y, or z, but in reality he/she does not mean it. (See the Lesson Text from *Modern Chinese* Textbook Vol. 2A, Unit 3 Lesson 1 for another example. Quotes around 理想 are used to imply that Xiaomei's description of an ideal roommate is not really ideal to Dadong.)

Can you guess what the sentence below means?
他做的中国菜太"地道"了，连中国人都尝不出来是什么菜。

II. Read the following passage and answer the questions.

谈一谈**收入**和**支出**

这个月才过了一半,没想到我钱包里的钱已经剩下不多了。我的好朋友小美问我钱是怎么花的,我都忘了。她建议我把各个月的费用认真地看一看,这样我就能知道每个月的钱都花在哪里了。

收入		支出	
父母	1,550 元	房租	600 元
做家教	400 元	水电费	65 元
在咖啡店做服务员	1,550 元	手机和上网费	120 元
在学校图书馆打工	200 元	吃饭	200 元
		车费	80 元
		健身房月费	100 元
		买衣服	250 元
		买玫瑰花	100 元
		玛丽的生日礼物	50 元
		看电影、听音乐会	75 元
		看病	80 元
	3,700 元		1,720 元

我的天啊!没想到因为我从来不知道怎样计划,所以不少钱都是乱花的。比如说,学校里有**免费**的健身房,可是我觉得学校的健身房人多,就在公寓对面的健身房买了**月票**。最近功课比较忙,我上个月只去了健身房两次。再说,从我的公寓到校园有公共汽车,车站就在公寓的后边。可是我晚上睡觉睡得晚,早上起床也晚,所以我就得坐出租车去学校了,一个月下来车费也不便宜。还有就是以后我一定要多在家做饭,少去饭馆吃。父母赚钱不容易,我自己打工赚钱也不容易,恐怕我以后要好好计划我每个月的**收入**和**支出**了。

Notes:
收入 (shōurù): *n.* income
支出 (zhīchū): *n.* expenditure
免费 (miǎnfèi): *adj.* free
月票 (yuèpiào): *n.* monthly pass

1. 为什么小美建议我看看我的钱是怎么花的?

   A. 因为我上个月只去了健身房两次。
   B. 因为现在才是16号，但是我已经花了很多的钱了。
   C. 因为我上个月花钱花得很快。
   D. 因为小美很会计划每个月的收入和支出。

2. Every month I will have to spend at least . . .

   A. less than 1,000 kuai.
   B. more than 1,000 kuai.
   C. between 1,000 and 1,500 kuai.
   D. between 3,700 and 1,720 kuai.

3. I can save some money by . . .

   A. taking public transportation to school.
   B. using the school gym.
   C. cooking at home more often.
   D. All of the above.

III. Read the following policy notice and e-mail, and answer the questions.

学生宿舍规则

1. 遵守宿舍作息时间。宿舍大门每天晚上十一点整关门。午休时间不能吵闹，不能影响他人。
2. 外宿需要提前请假。如有校外人员来宿舍探望，需登记才能进入学生宿舍。学校宿舍不能留他人住宿。
3. 宿舍虽包水电费，但请各位节省用水用电，还有注意用电安全。
4. 保持宿舍内以及卫生间干净整洁。每个宿舍制定轮流卫生值日表。

学校宿舍管理处
九月一日

To: 李忠平
From: 李元
Subject: 中国的学生宿舍

Notes:
规则 (guīzé): *n.* rule, regulation
关门 (guānmén): *vo.* to close the door
同意 (tóngyì): *v.* to agree, to consent
请假 (qǐngjià): *vo.* to ask for leave
食堂 (shítáng): *n.* dining room

中平：
　　这个学期我第一次住中国的大学宿舍。宿舍的老师给我发了一张学生宿舍的住宿**规则**。这里的住宿**规则**和美国的不太一样。每天宿舍会有**关门**时间，学生们都要在宿舍**关门**前回来。如果晚上不能回宿舍，需要老师**同意**才能**请假**。真的太麻烦了，所以我一次都没请过假。宿舍里面也没有厨房，所以我们不能自己做饭。但是，这里**食堂**做的菜真的很好吃，这是我最喜欢的地方了。我在这里每天都过得很快乐。你呢？
　　祝天天开心！
李元

1. According to the dorm policy, what do students need to do if they are not coming back at night to sleep?

   _____

2. Circle the utilities that the dorm includes on the dorm policy handout.

3. Which place does Li Yuan like most in the dorm? Why? _____

4. What did Li Yuan mention about the difference between the dorm in China and America?

   _____

WRITING PRACTICE 3.1

I. You are emailing your friend to update him/her about your current living situation. Describe your apartment and also what your new roommate is like (e.g., personality, background, living habits, likes and dislikes, hobbies, etc.).

II. Write a notice for your roommates, outlining the various chores that need to be done and include a time schedule. You have five different roommates, including yourself. First, decide which chores people need to be responsible for and then create a timetable for everyone.

UNIT 3 – LESSON 2

Modern Chinese 现代中文

找公寓

VOCABULARY REVIEW 3.2

I. Match the following furniture and household electrical appliances with the correct location each would be placed.

<u>家具</u>　　　　　　<u>房</u>　　　　　　<u>家电</u>

1. 餐桌　•　　　•　客厅　•　　　•　电视
2. 书桌　•　　　•　厨房　•　　　•　空调
3. 椅子　•　　　•　饭厅　•　　　•　洗衣机
4. 沙发　•　　　•　卧室　•　　　•　干衣机
5. 床　　•　　　•　厕所　•　　　•　冰箱

II. Add a stroke(s) or component(s) to form a different character and include the pinyin.

Example: 未 → ____来____ (lái)

1. 心 → _____
2. 云 → _____
3. 父 → _____
4. 厂 → _____

5. 日 → _____
6. 舌 → _____
7. 氏 → _____
8. 其 → _____
9. 般 → _____

III. The following notes list the advantages and disadvantages of an apartment. Fill in the blanks with appropriate vocabulary words.

好处

- 有(1.)_____空调和洗衣机在内的家电。
- 包桌子、椅子、沙发等等(2.)_____。
- 环境(3.)_____，(4.)_____有两三个公园。
- 交通(5.)_____，而且离学校不远。

坏处

- (6.)_____贵。
- 不包(7.)_____费。
- 必须签两年(8.)_____。
- (9.)_____很脏很乱。
- 家具都非常(10.)_____。
- 近(11.)_____，所以车声非常吵。

82　第三单元 • 第二课 • 住

CHARACTER WRITING PRACTICE 3.2

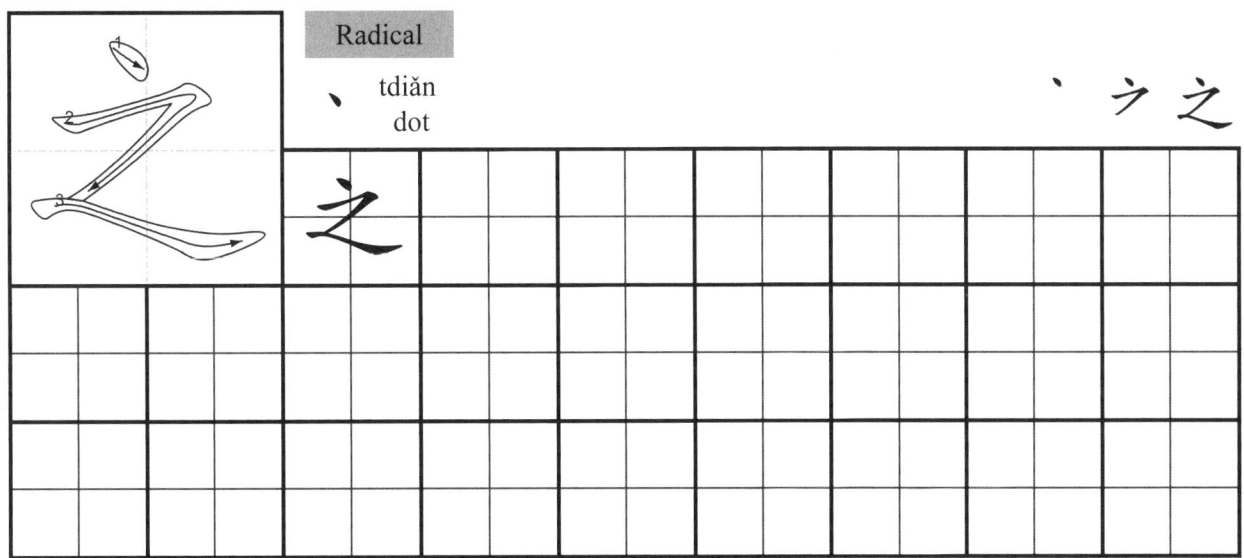

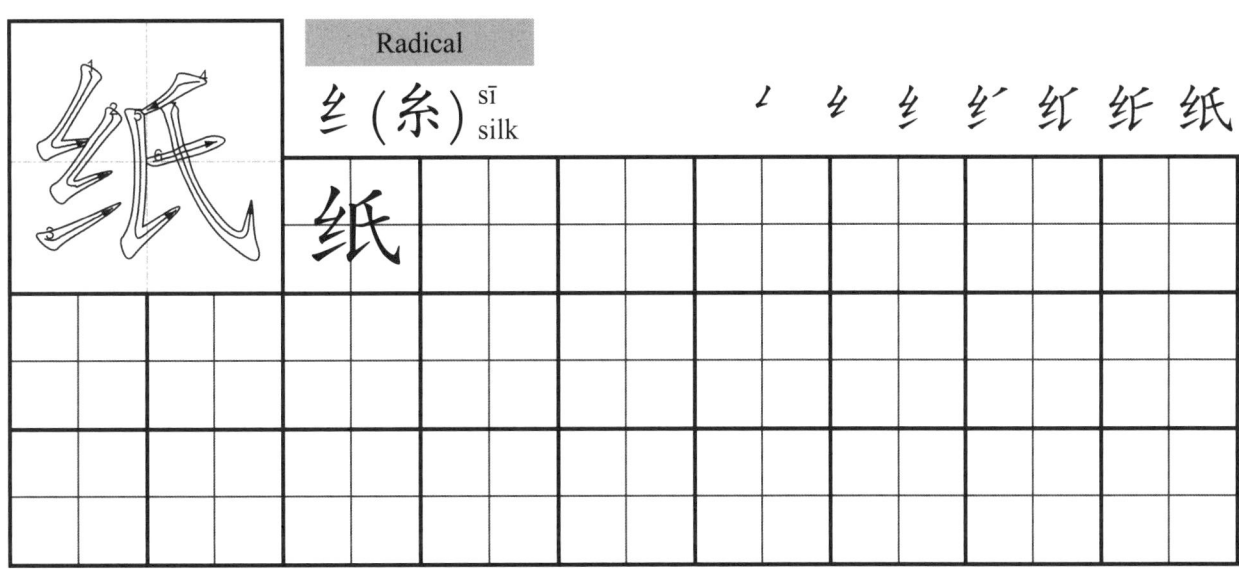

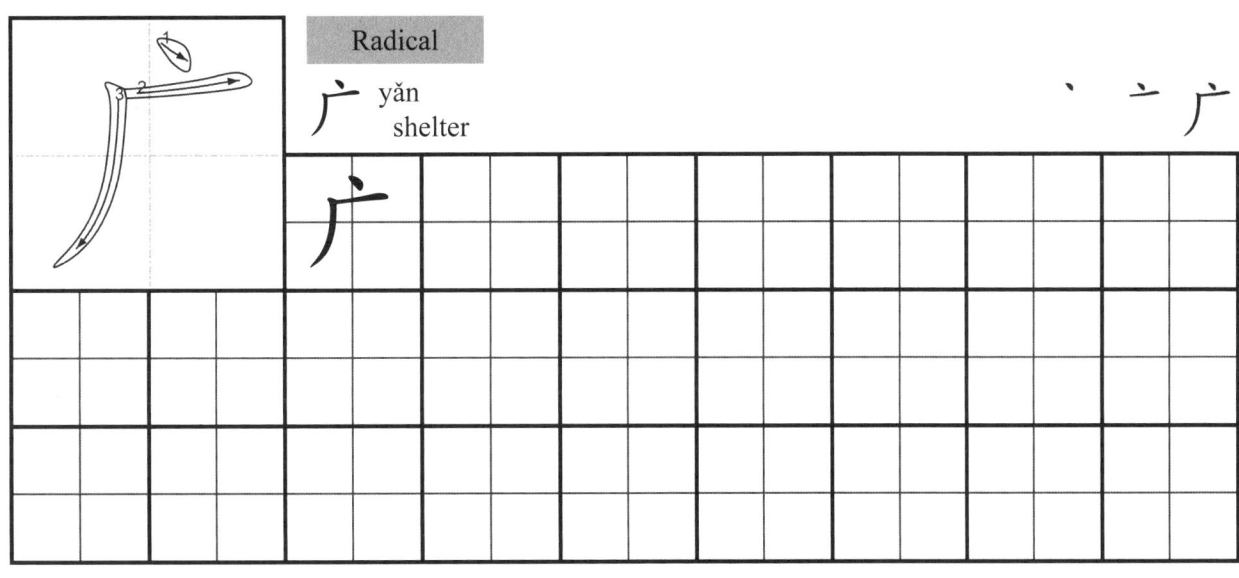

Unit 3 • Lesson 2 • Housing

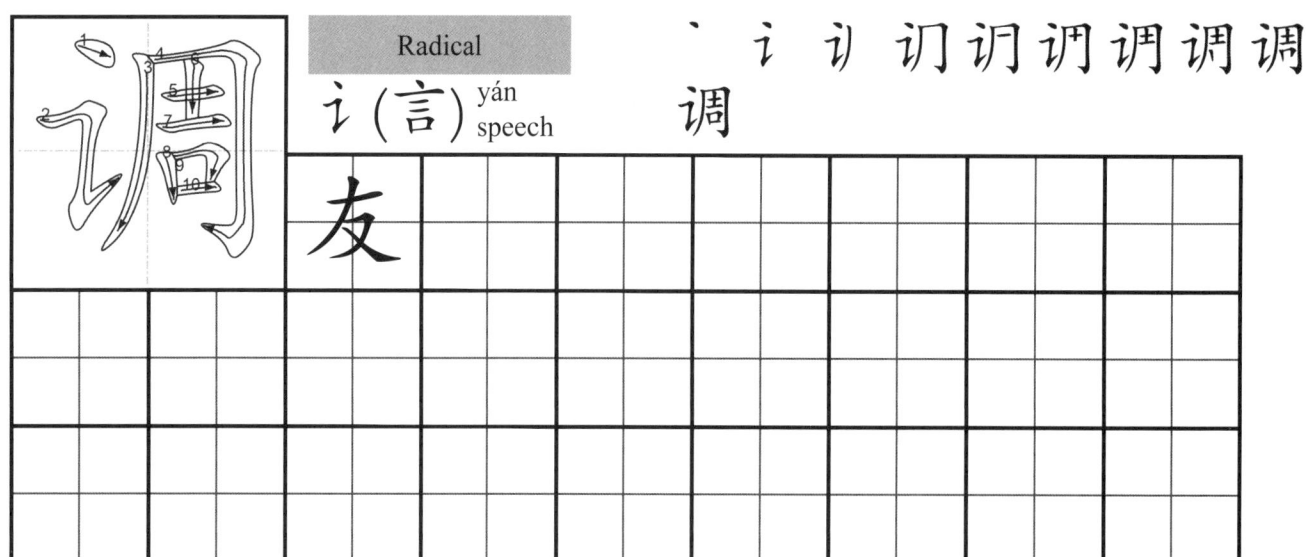

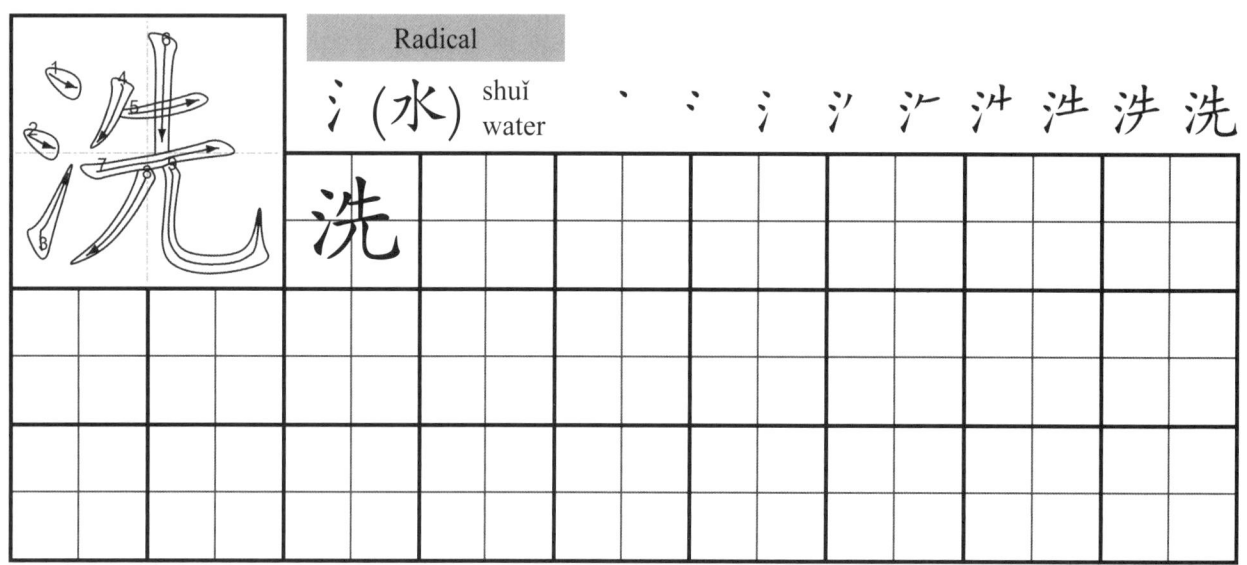

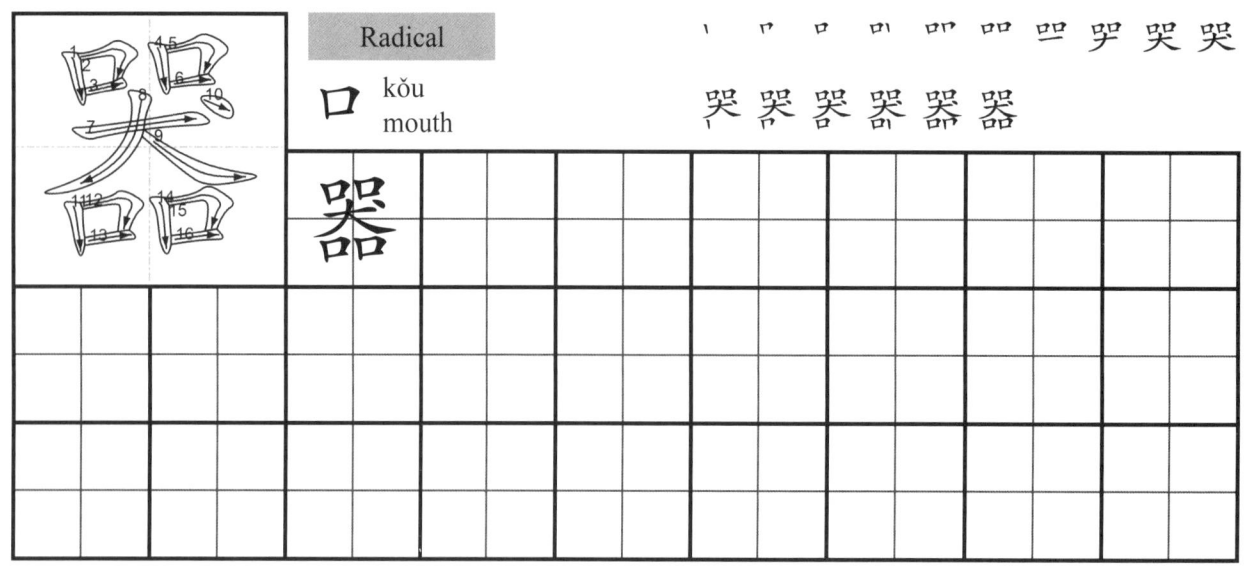

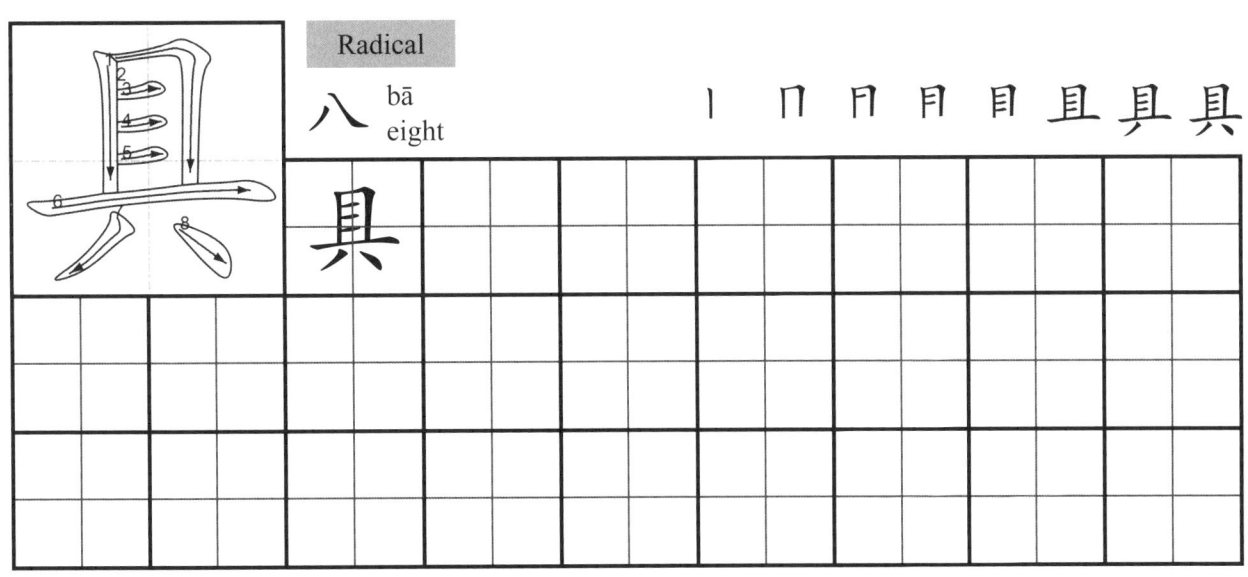

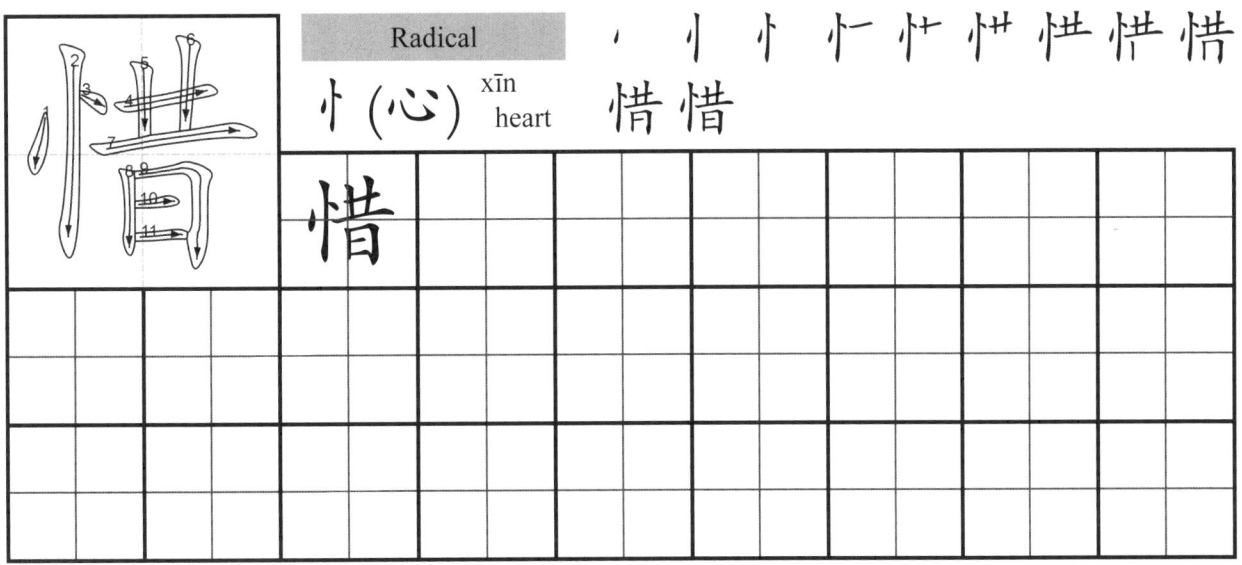

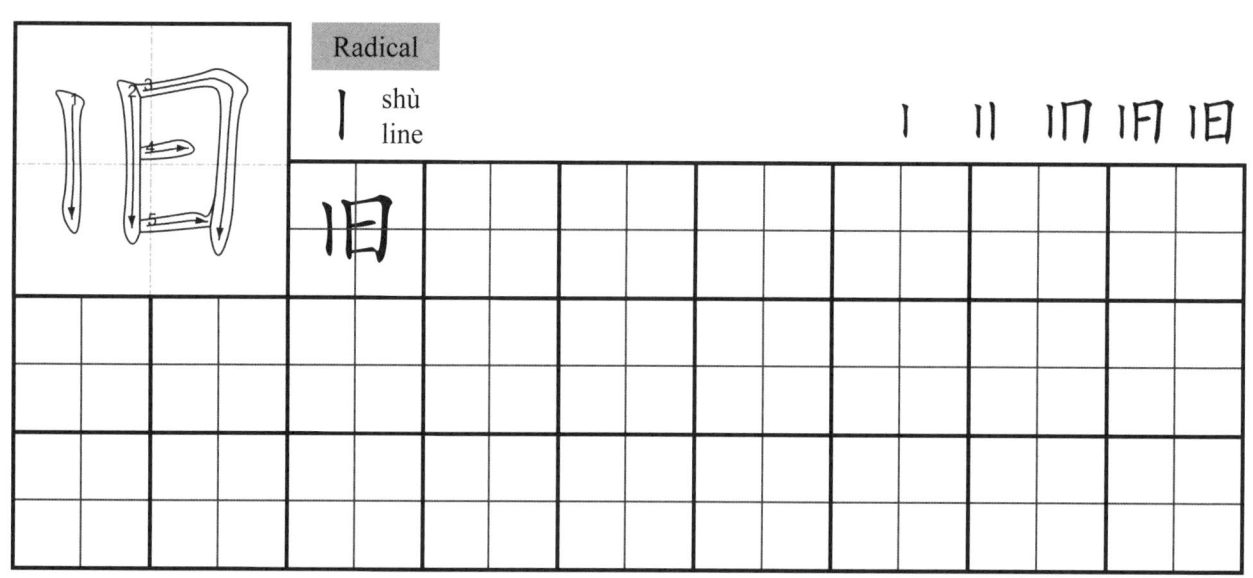

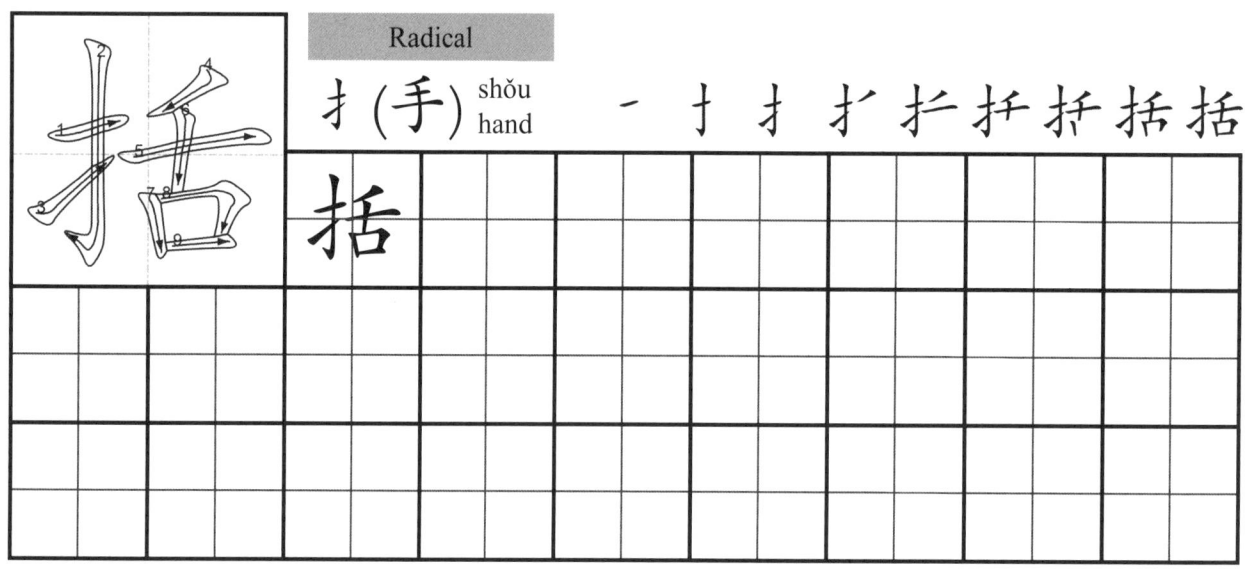

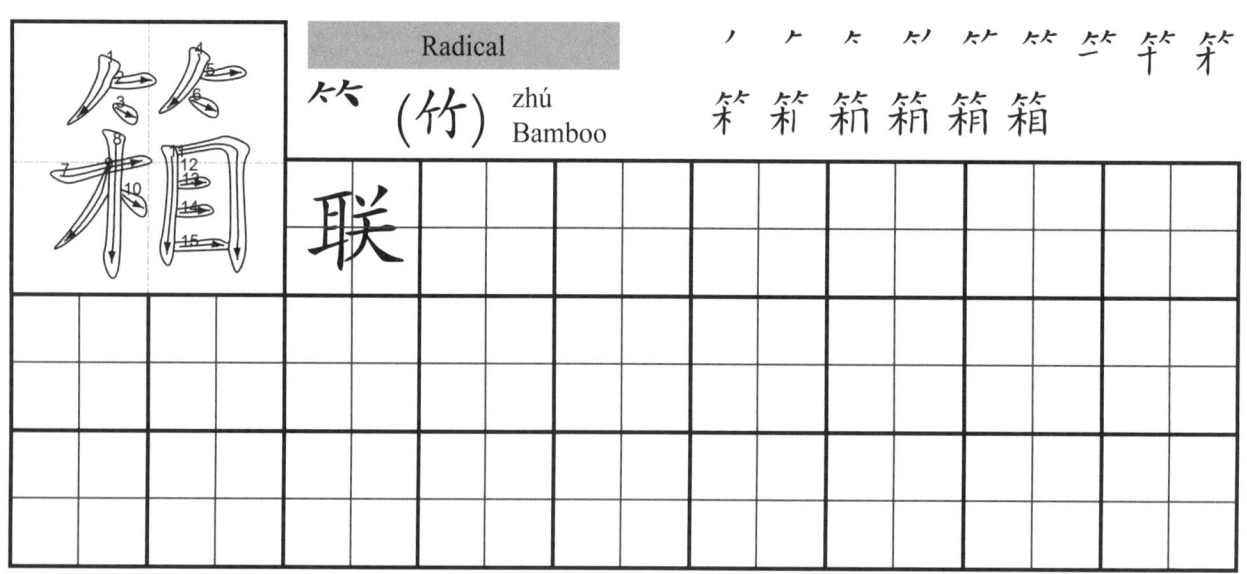

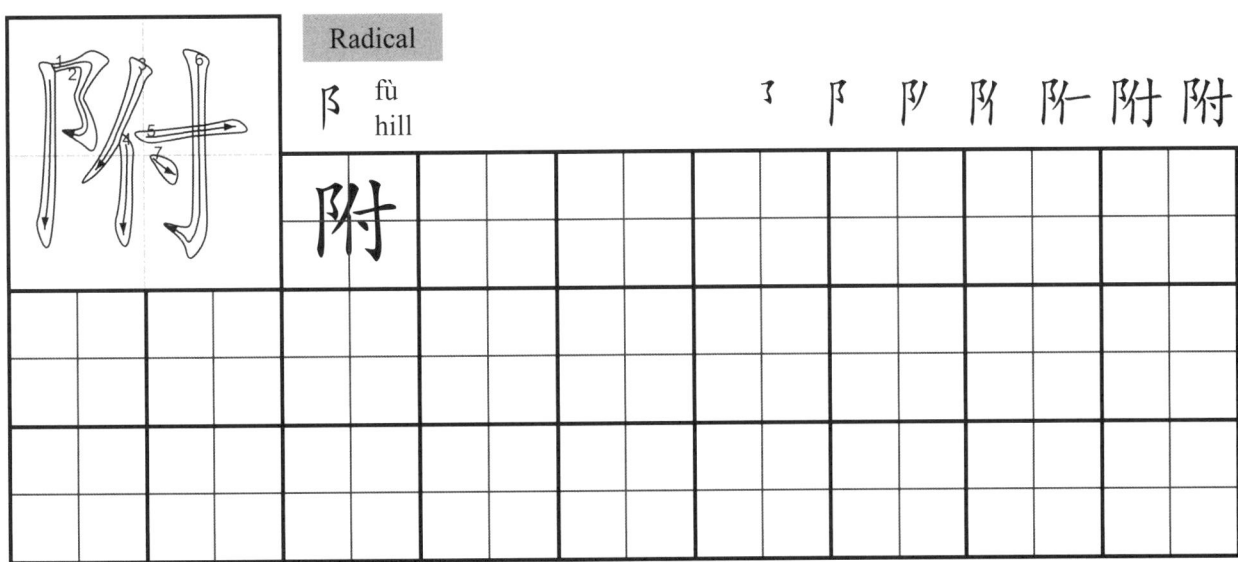

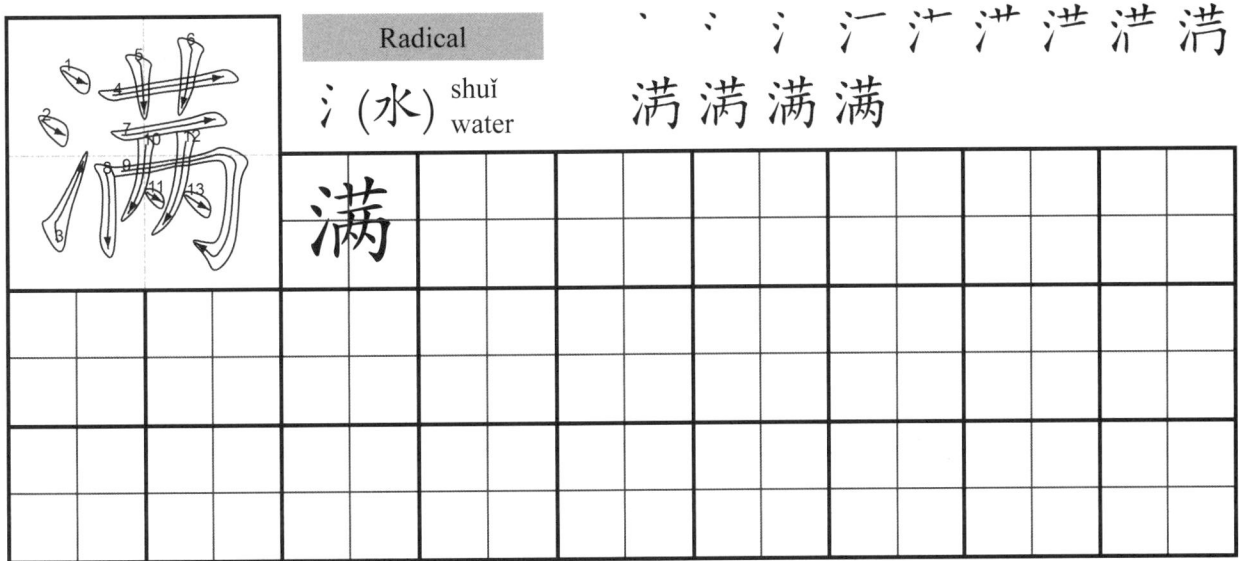

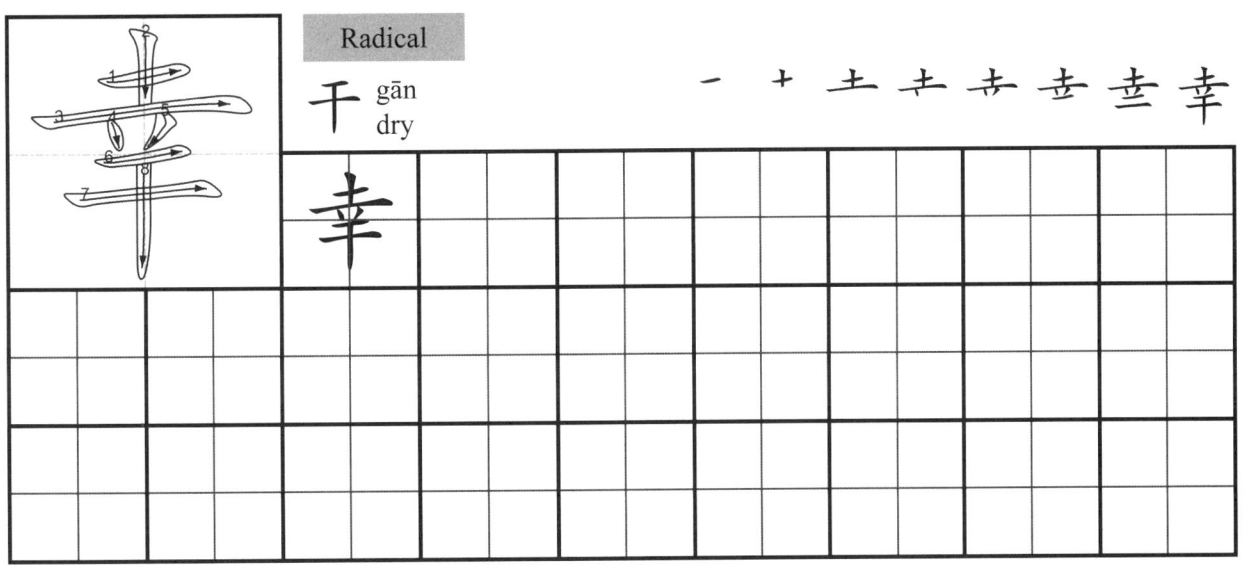

Unit 3 • Lesson 2 • Housing

LISTENING COMPREHENSION 3.2

I. Listen to the recording and select the best response below.

1. The woman would most likely respond with:

   A. 我的房东说有公寓出租，你想不想来看看？
   B. 你的公寓有没有空调和洗衣机？
   C. 家庭电器和家具是不是包括在内呢？
   D. 我觉得你能搬家真幸运，不是吗？

II. Listen to the recording and answer the following True or False questions.

1. (　) The woman's landlord told her that there was an apartment rental ad.
2. (　) The man is currently looking for a new place to live.
3. (　) The man feels the monthly rental price is fine but wants to see if he can get a cheaper price.
4. (　) The woman is willing to help the man get in touch with the landlord.
5. (　) It sounds like the woman is getting frustrated because the man is asking too many questions.

III. Listen to the recording and answer the questions in Chinese.

1. When did the speaker come to the US? Why did she come?

2. According to the speaker, what kind of problems did she encounter while searching for a house?

3. How did the speaker finally find a new place to rent?

SPEAKING PRACTICE 3.2

I. You are about to call a rental agent about available apartments for rent. Make a list of five things you want for an apartment.

Number of rooms:	
Furniture:	
Environment:	
Transportation:	
Lease length & rental price:	

II. Look at the newspaper rental ad below. Call the owner and leave a voicemail to briefly introduce yourself and your background. Explain your interest in obtaining more details about the place, such as rental price, whether pets are allowed, what public transportation is nearby, whether air-conditioning is available, what amenities are included, etc.

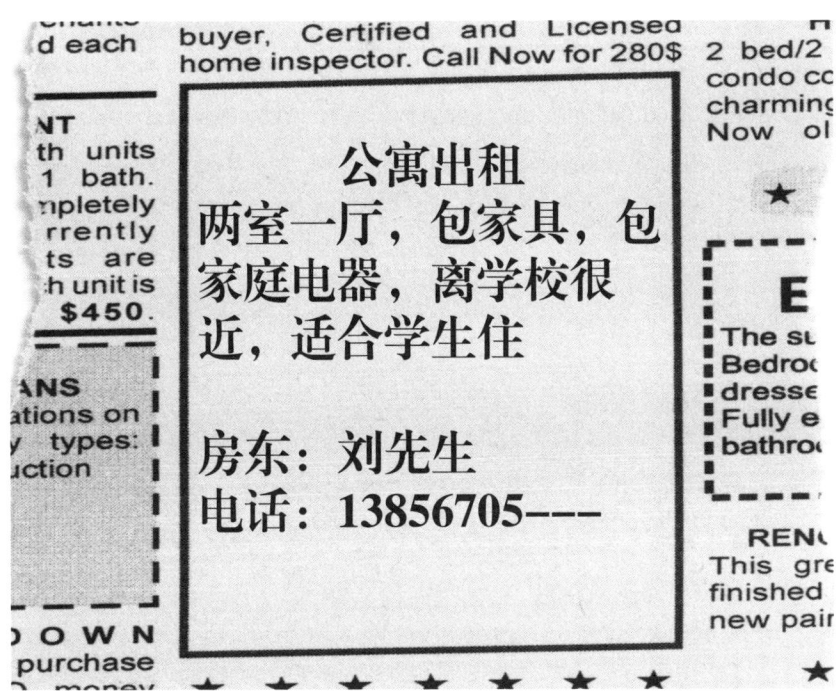

STRUCTURE REVIEW 3.2

I. Complete the following Structure Note practice activities.

Structure Note 3.5: Use 之内/外/前/后 to indicate that things are within or outside of scope.

$$\boxed{\text{Noun Phrase} + 之内/外/前/后}$$

A. The following passage contains homework instructions. Fill in the blanks using 之内/外/前/后.

> 首先，从课本里选一段课文来念。一开始慢慢地读，每个字都要读得清楚，练习完____就可以准备录音。给老师的录音不可以超过五分钟，所以同学最好能在五分钟____把课文念完。练习____记得要先把每个生词的读音都查好。除了读音____，读的时候还要注意感情，这样别人才会有兴趣继续听下去。把录音录完____，请在十月七日____用电邮发给你的中文老师。

Structure Note 3.6: Use 可惜 to express pity at an unfortunate situation.

$$\boxed{可惜 + \text{Sentence}}$$

$$\boxed{只可惜 + \text{Sentence}}$$

B. You just finished traveling through China and you have some regrettable experiences. Complete the following sentences using 可惜 to express "unfortunately."

1. 我们计划好要去长城……

   _____

2. 我们元宵节的时候去看了花灯……

   _____

3. 我们打算去看京剧表演……

   _____

4. 我们想买云南茶叶当纪念品……

5. 我们坐了两个小时的火车去一家很有名的饭馆……

Take the challenge! 动动脑筋！

同学A："老师，我想上厕所，可以吗？"
老师："可是现在是上课时间，刚刚下课的时候怎么不去？"
同学A："我下课的时候去了，可惜人太多了，没办法上。"
同学B："老师，是因为用下课的时间来上厕所多可惜啊！"

The word 可是 means "but" and 可惜 means "unfortunately." While you can use 可是 to replace 可惜 in any sentence such as "可是人太多了" where 可惜 is being used as an adverb, this does not work vice versa, unless you are describing an unfortunate situation.

可惜 can be also act as an adjective to express the meaning "what a pity" by saying "真可惜" or "多可惜。" Can you guess why Student B would say what a pity in the last sentence?

Structure Note 3.7: Use 包括……(在内) to list included items or examples within a category.

$$包括 + A, + B \ldots + (在内)$$

C. Below are some statements describing the department store in your neighbourhood. Rewrite the sentence using the pattern 包括……(在内).

1. 这里的书店除了卖语法书之外，也有生词复习、汉字练习本等等学习汉语的书本。

2. 每到春节前，这家店衣服、帽子和袜子等东西的价钱都会下降。

3. 每年圣诞节这里都会举办音乐表演，比如小提琴、钢琴表演等等。

4. 这里卖的家电像冰箱和洗衣机，都是全国最好的。

_____

5. 这里的电影院里不可以用手机、电脑这样电子用品。

_____

Structure Note 3.8: Use 对……(不)满意 to express satisfaction or dissatisfaction with something.

> Subject + 对 + Object (+ 不) + 满意

D. Read the following passage. Using 对……(不)满意, write four sentences to describe whether the boss is satisfied with the interns and provide reasons why or why not.

> 公司最近来了十几位刚大学毕业的实习生，所以陈老板去看了看他们工作的情况。这些实习生都非常年轻，陈老板喜欢他们给公司带来了很多新的想法。虽然他们做事非常快，可惜他们有时候工作不太认真。陈老板知道实习生经验不多，所以对客人说话的时候常常没有注意到礼节的重要。但是，陈老板还是相信这些实习生只要继续努力，以后一定能变成人才。

_____

_____

_____

Take the challenge! 动动脑筋！

In *Modern Chinese* Textbook Vol. 1A, Unit 10, Lesson 1, Structure Notes 10.5, you learned the pattern 对……（没）有兴趣, and in this lesson we have a similar pattern 对……（不）满意. Both follow the general pattern "Subject + 对 + Object" and the phrase following it can be replaced by different ones to express different meanings. Think of some examples of how you will use the following patterns.

对……（不）感兴趣
对……（不）认真
对……（不）尊敬
对……（没）有礼貌

II. You are filling out your school restaurant's customer survey. Write your comments using the structure patterns you learned to express whether you are satisfied with the restaurant or not. List examples and make suggestions.

Example: 我对你们餐厅食物的价钱很不满意。素菜味道挺不错的，可惜太贵了。我觉得包括素饺子和豆腐在内的素菜应该便宜一点。

餐厅满意度调查问卷

1: 你对我们餐厅的食物满意吗？

☐ 非常满意　☐ 很满意　☐ 还可以　☐ 很不满意　☐ 非常不满意

_____

2: 你对我们餐厅的价钱满意吗？

☐ 非常满意　☐ 很满意　☐ 还可以　☐ 很不满意　☐ 非常不满意

_____

3: 你对我们餐厅的环境满意吗？

☐ 非常满意　☐ 很满意　☐ 还可以　☐ 很不满意　☐ 非常不满意

_____

4: 你对我们餐厅的服务满意吗？

☐ 非常满意　☐ 很满意　☐ 还可以　☐ 很不满意　☐ 非常不满意

_____

5: 你对我们餐厅的地点满意吗？

☐ 非常满意　☐ 很满意　☐ 还可以　☐ 很不满意　☐ 非常不满意

_____

READING COMPREHENSION 3.2

I. Read the passage and answer the following True or False questions.

周信最近忙得不得了也急得不得了。一个月之后就要放暑假了，学校通知他宿舍的合同到期了，他必须搬家。他一边要准备考试，一边要找实习的工作，一边还得找暑假住的地方。以前他觉得找房子很简单，看到报纸上房子出租的广告多极了。谁知道找了几天以后他才发现，要找到一个合适的公寓是这么不容易。学校附近出租的房子不少，过了马路就有好几家公寓空着等人去租，可惜房子太旧，而且房租都挺贵的。后来有一个朋友介绍他去看了一套公寓，离学校不太远，坐公共汽车只要五站。这家公寓是有家具的，房租很便宜。房东说，洗衣机、电视、冰箱、空调等等家电也包括在内，只可惜环境不太好，很脏很吵，周信对这个公寓也不太满意。周信说，如果他在一个月之内还找不到地方安家落户的话，他恐怕就只能住到马路上去了！

1. (　) 暑假的时候周信打算一边实习一边找房子。
2. (　) 因为周信要毕业了，所以学校要收回周信的宿舍。
3. (　) 周信对学校附近的公寓不满意，因为房子老，而且费用高。
4. (　) 朋友给他介绍的公寓包家具和家电。
5. (　) 周信很烦恼，因为他没想到找房子的事情这么难。

Take the challenge! 动动脑筋！

谁知道 is defined as "who knows." For example, you could say 谁知道这个问题？ to ask "who knows this question?" However, like in English, you can also use 谁知道 to express "nobody knows" or uncertainty in a situation. For example, 谁知道！别问了！ or 谁知道呢，说不定明年我就可以去中国了. Additionally, 谁知道 is often used to describe a turning point or an unexpected situation, as in "who knew?" This is equivalent to 没想到, 想不到, 哪想到. For example, 谁知道学费会这么贵.

According to the passage above, what does the writer mean by 谁知道?

II. Read the following passage and answer the questions.

　　每年的十月一日是中国的**国庆节**。**国庆节**的时候，中国的公司，学校都会放一个星期左右的长假。人们都正好用这个机会来旅游，有的人出国旅行，有的人去中国各地看看，去各个大城市玩的人都特别多。2012年过节的时候，来北京旅游的差不多有1,500万人。那个时候，**酒店**房间很快就满了。租不到**酒店**怎么办呢？有很多人就在旅游的时间之内短租房，选短租房的人越来越多。短租房的好处是家具和家电等等都包括在内，有的短租房，还有跟**酒店**一样的**免费**打扫，很受欢迎。不过，短租房的房租在长假的时候就高多了，今年就比去年高了不少，短租房十天的租金和平时一个月的租金一样。比方说，一个卧室的房间在**国庆节**长假的时候，租一天需要付150元，而平时住一个月可能才1,500元。由于看到短租房能赚钱，很多房东都把长租房变成了短租房，出租的时间也从去年的最少三天变成了最少五天。

Notes:
国庆节 (Guóqìngjié): *n.* National Day
酒店 (jiǔdiàn): *n.* hotel
免费 (miǎnfèi): *adj.* free

1. Why do so many Chinese people travel in early October?

    A. Because the weather is good.

    B. Because it is a good time to travel overseas.

    C. Because a lot of people like to visit big cities at this time.

    D. Because it is a big holiday season and a lot of people take time off.

2. What is the major disadvantage of a "short-term rental"?

    A. A lot of people book "short-term rentals."

    B. The prices of "short-term rentals" are higher during extended breaks.

    C. "Short-term rentals" do not provide the same services as big hotels.

    D. There is an extra charge for appliances in "short-term rentals."

3. 下面哪一个说法是不对的？

    A. 短租房的房东喜欢国庆节的长假。
    B. 越来越多的房东开始做短租房。
    C. 短租房房东不希望你只租两天的房子。
    D. 长假的时候，短租房房东就会很紧张。

III. Read the following map and rental ad and answer the questions.

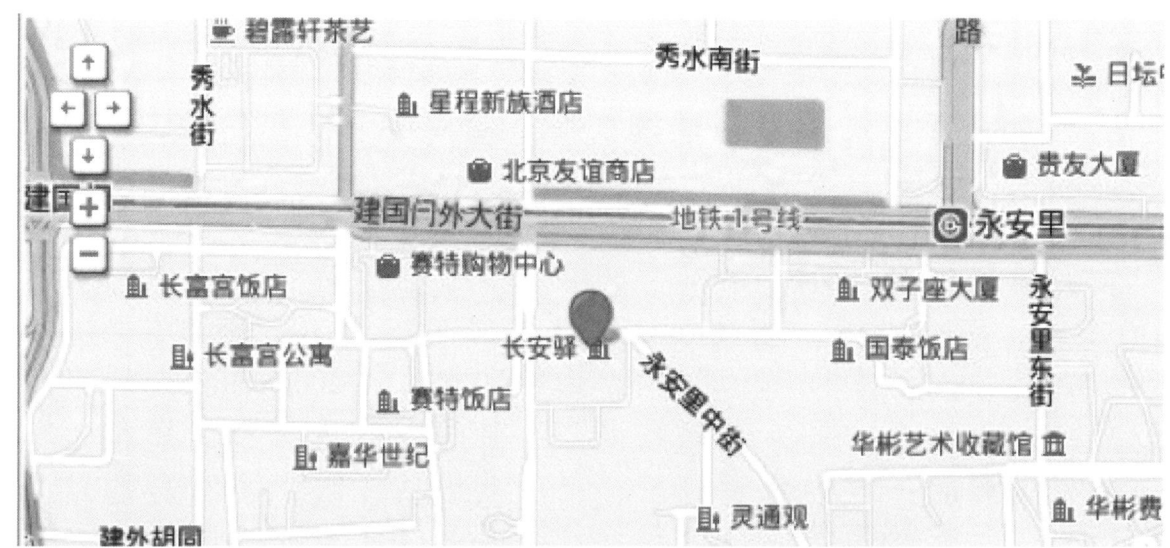

Notes:

卫 (wèi): *n.* short for bathrooms

面积 (miànjī): *n.* surface area

平 (píng): *n.* short for square meters

层 (céng): *n.* floor

朝 (cháo): *v.* to face

1. Fill out the table below based on the rental ad.

Number of rooms:		Environment:	
Area:		Amenities:	
Floor:		Reason for renting out:	
Orientation:			
Transportation:		Contact information:	

2. Assume you are in 赛特饭店, describe how you would walk to the apartment.

3. Which description about the apartment listed above is the most appealing to you? Why?

WRITING PRACTICE 3.2

I. You have an extra room available to rent out. Write a short ad to be placed in your school newspaper and posted on the bulletin boards of your student union. Be sure to include the following items: rental price, location, number of rooms and roommates, what amenities are included, and contact information.

II. You have a friend who will be moving to your area and is interested in finding housing. Write an e-mail explaining the housing situation in your area and give advice on what to look for and avoid (e.g., environment, location, shopping, transportation, pricing of different places, safe areas, weather, etc.).

To:
From:
Subject:

UNIT 4 – LESSON 1

VOCABULARY REVIEW 4.1

I. Fill in each circle with a character to form a two-word vocabulary phrase.

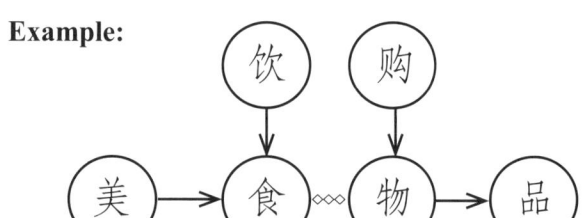

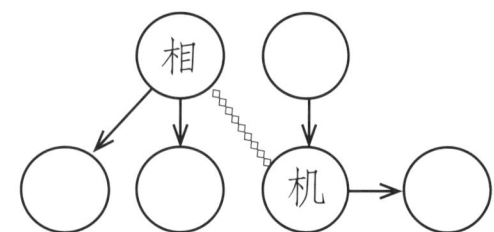

II. In the passage, five characters are written incorrectly. Determine which ones are wrong and write the correct character above the incorrect ones.

祥安的博客：

喜欢慑影的朋友，如果你打算在华东商店的网站购买数码相机，请看下面网友分享的经验：

提醒一、虽然网上产品的价格都会打析，但是要注意在华东的网站购物是不能用优惠券的，并且不包送货。

提醒二、如果你对产品不满意，最好打电话到商店投拆，因为商店的负责人是不会管网站上写的投拆的。

III. Fill in the blanks using the vocabulary from the passage above in question #2.

现在只要在你的博客上，与朋友们(1.)_____我们商店最新款的电子(2.)_____，就有机会拿到我们每星期送出的七(3.)_____优惠券。优惠券可以用来(4.)_____包括电视和相机等等电子商品，并且免费(5.)_____。还在等什么？现在就马上到我们公司的(6.)_____，选一台你最喜欢的电器或电子用品，然后发到你的博客上吧！

CHARACTER WRITING PRACTICE 4.1

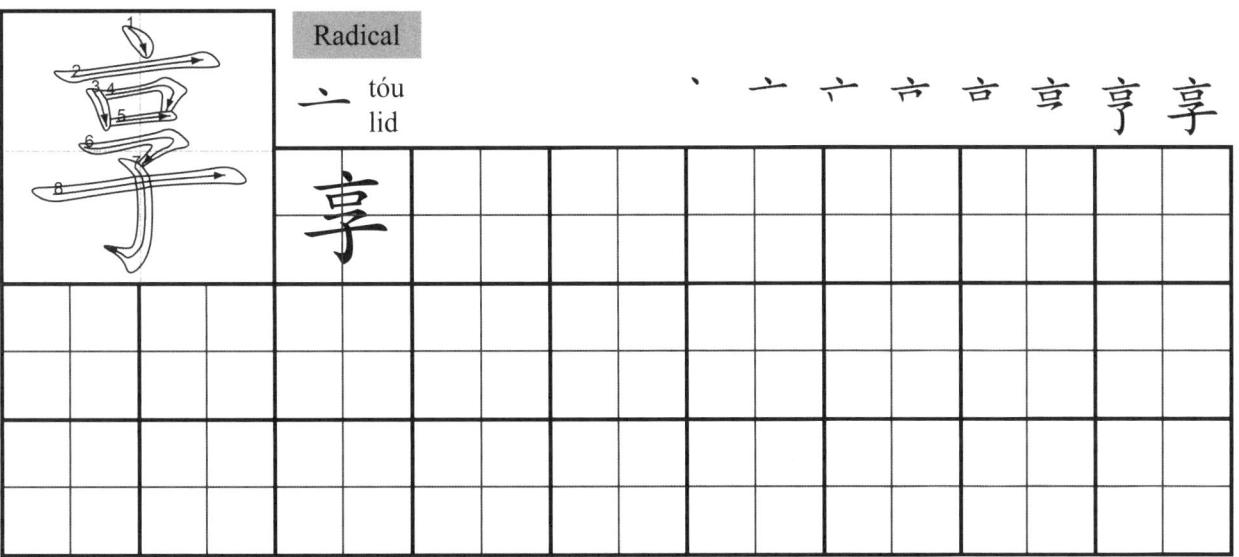

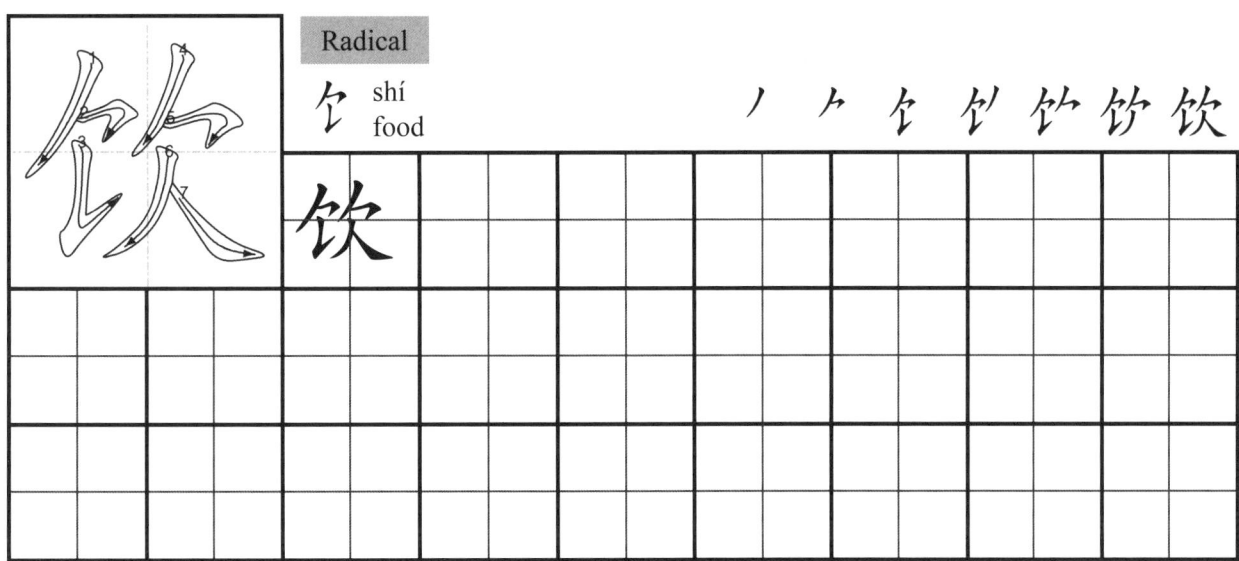

Unit 4 • Lesson 1 • Shopping

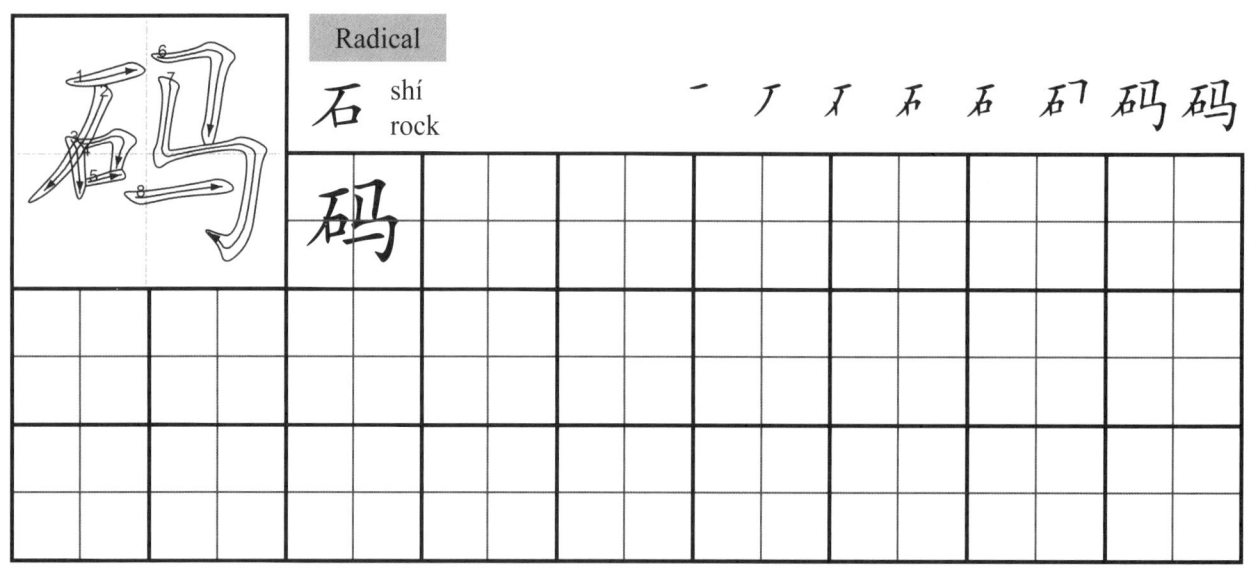

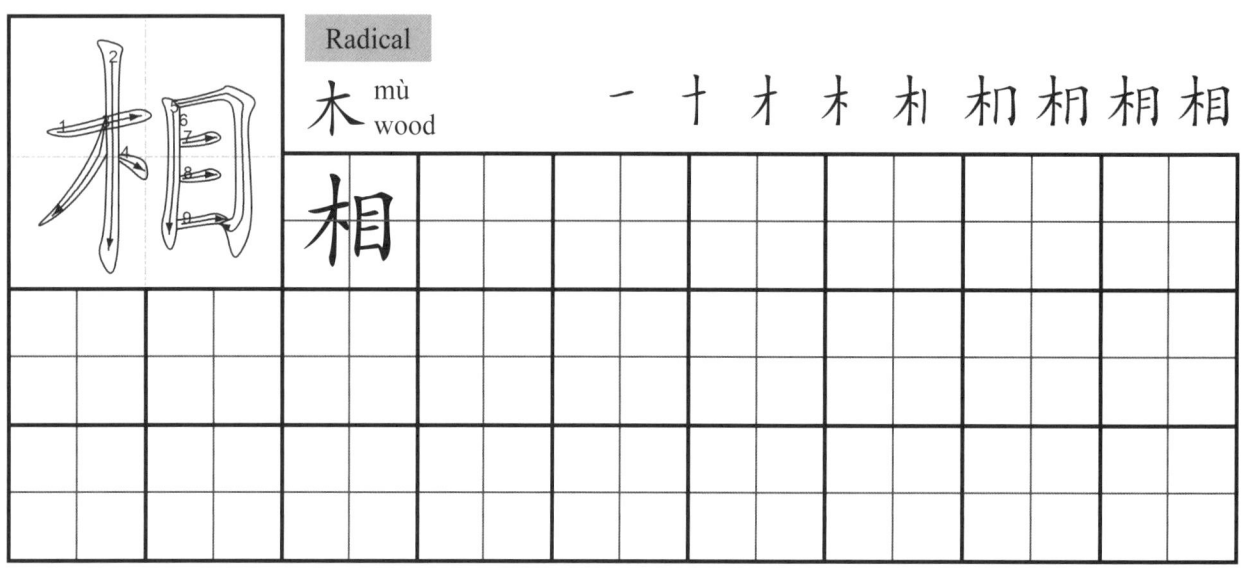

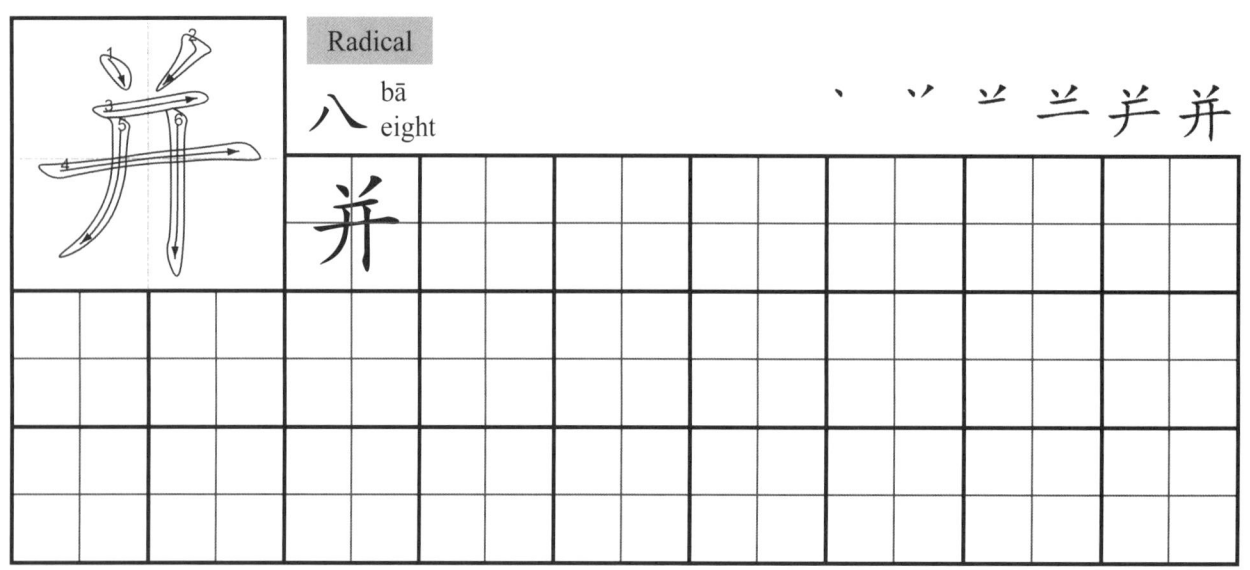

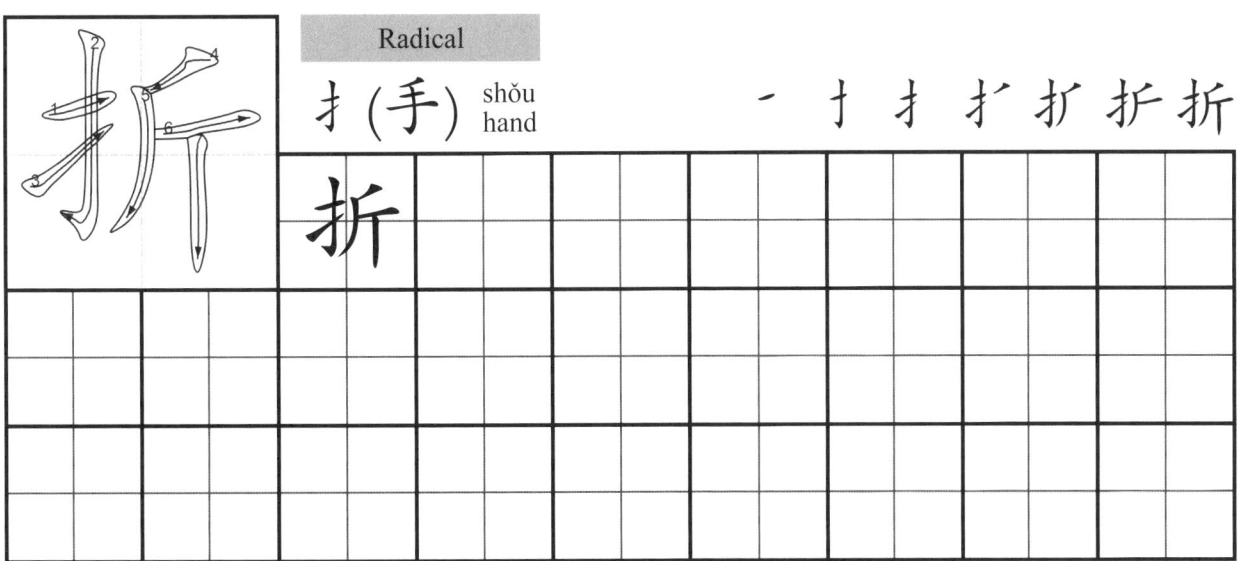

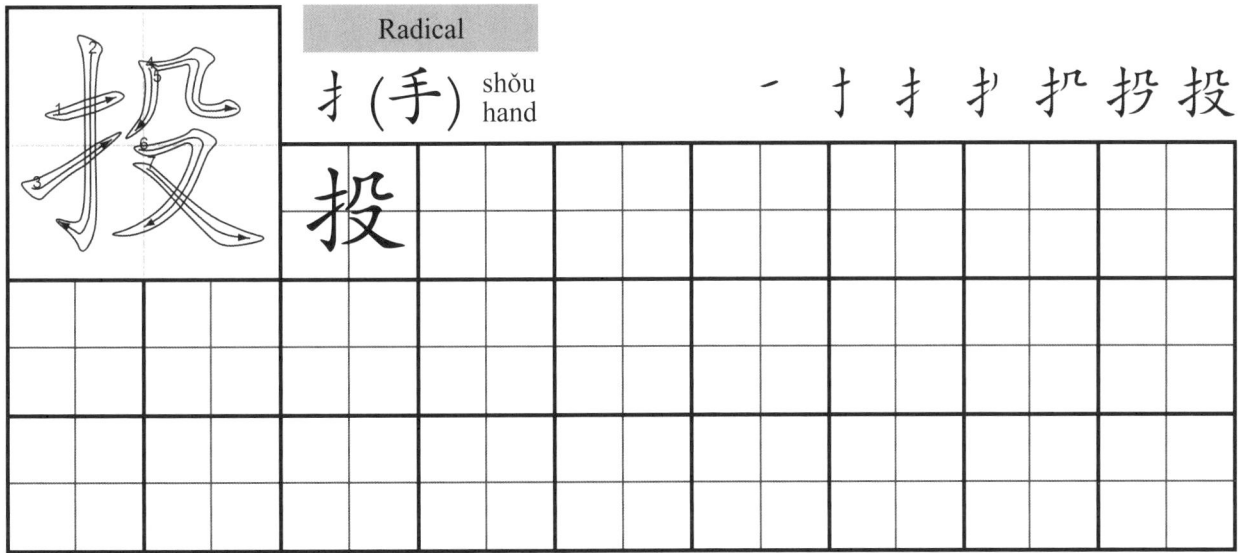

Unit 4 · Lesson 1 · Shopping

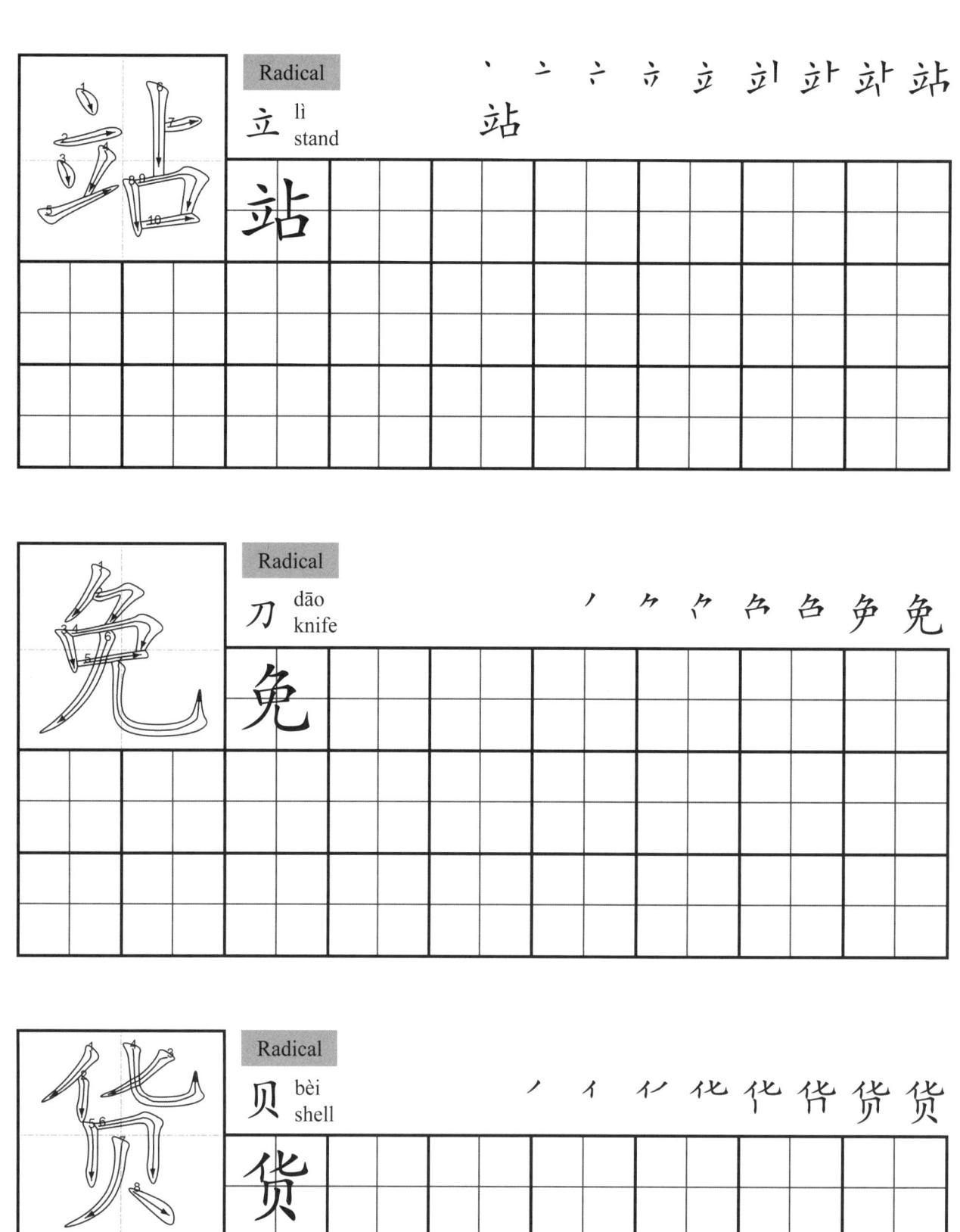

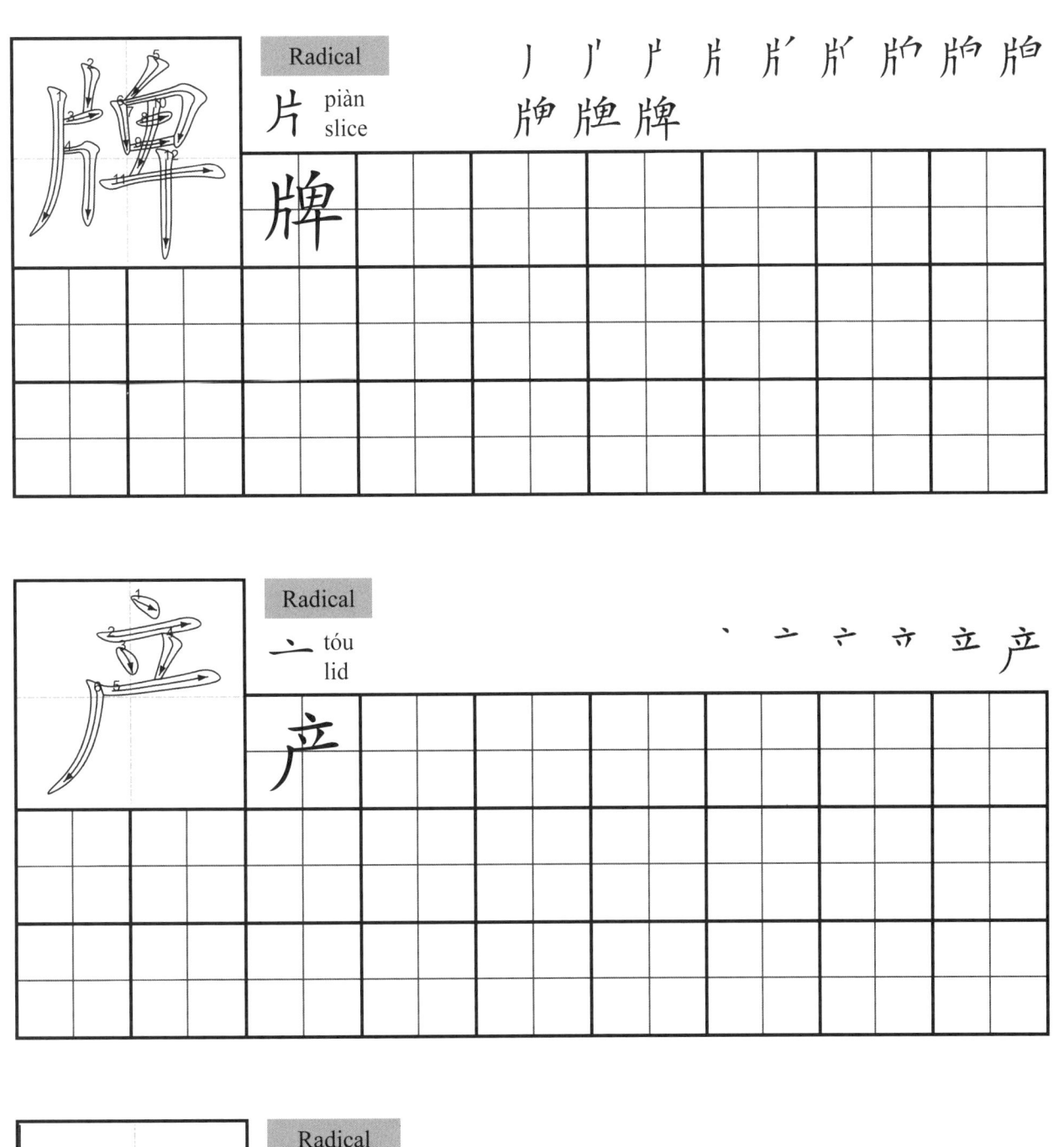

LISTENING COMPREHENSION 4.1

I. Listen to the recording and select the best response below.

1. The woman would most likely respond with:

    A. 那一定是介绍欧洲的饮食文化了，对吗？
    B. 你觉得他们会给优惠券吗？
    C. 太好了！欧洲的名牌产品我最喜欢不过了！
    D. 那我们现在去欧洲旅行要带雨伞吗？

II. Listen to the recording and answer the following True or False questions.

1. (　) It sounds like the woman is very excited about the new sweater.
2. (　) At first, the man did not think it was a good idea to have pandas on a sweater.
3. (　) The woman is planning to go to China this fall.
4. (　) The man thought the sweater was bought in a store.
5. (　) The sweater was discounted at 50% off.

III. Listen to the recording and answer the questions in Chinese.

1. Why did the speaker purchase too many items from the Internet?

    _____

2. What is the major difference, in terms of shopping habits, between the speaker and the speaker's boyfriend?

    _____

3. Do you agree with the speaker's approach to shopping or the boyfriend's approach? Why?

    _____

SPEAKING PRACTICE 4.1

I. Below are two promotions for an electronics store — one for its online website and one for in-store shopping. Compare the two promotions and explain which one you would choose and why.

II. Describe an experience in which you bought something at a store that enables customers to shop in-store and online. Be sure to include whether you shopped online or in-store and why, what you bought and the price of your item, whether there were any promotions, whether the store offered any warranties, and whether there were any shipping fees. Also discuss any tips about shopping at this store.

Online or in-store:	
Item & price:	
Promotions:	
Warrantees:	
Shipping Fees:	

STRUCTURE REVIEW 4.1

I. Complete the following Structure Note practices.

Structure Note 4.1: Use A 不如 B to indicate A is not as good as B.

$$A + 不如 + B\ (+ Adjective)$$

A. Complete the short survey below and and provide a reason using 不如 to explain why you made your selection.

1. 你比较喜欢哪个节日？为什么？ ☐ 中秋节 ☐ 春节

   _____

2. 你比较喜欢哪门课？为什么？ ☐ 中国文化 ☐ 中国历史

   _____

3. 你比较喜欢哪个地方？为什么？ ☐ 上海 ☐ 昆明

   _____

4. 你比较喜欢住哪里？为什么？ ☐ 校内 ☐ 校外

   _____

5. 你比较喜欢吃什么？为什么？ ☐ 北京烤鸭 ☐ 北京饺子

   _____

Structure Note 4.2: Use 并且 to mean "also" to connect words or clauses in formal contexts.

$$\text{Noun / Adjective / Verb Phrase} + 并且 + \text{Noun / Adjective / Verb Phrase}$$

$$\text{Clause,} + 并且 + \text{Clause}$$

B. The following are some examples of Chinese traditional customs. Take a sentence from each box and combine them into one by using 并且.

中国人过春节会穿红色的衣服。
中国人会用两只手来接礼物。
中国人觉得传统礼节很重要。
中国人去朋友家一定会先约好。

中国人接到礼物后不会马上打开。
中国人很重视孔子的思想。
中国人去做客会带上礼物。
中国人过春节会用红色来装饰房子。

1. _____

2. _____

3. _____

4. _____

Take the challenge! 动动脑筋!

并且 and 而且 are usually interchangeable, but there is a slight difference in how you apply them. 而且 is usually used in spoken language, and it emphasizes the latter clause. 并且 is usually used in written language and made to connect two coordinate clauses or similar things.

Examples:
他不但喜欢喝茶,而且对茶文化也非常有研究。

中国的茶非常有名,所以他开始研究中国的茶文化,并且有了喝茶的习惯。

Following the examples above, try to create two sentences — one with 而且 and the other with 并且.

Structure Note 4.3: Use 既 A 又 B as a formal way to express "both A and B."

> Subject + 既 + Adjective / Verb Phrase + 又 + Adjective / Verb Phrase

C. Imagine that you are studying abroad in Beijing for three months. Your friend asks you some questions about your life in Beijing. Answer the questions by using 既⋯⋯又⋯⋯ and the word boxes below.

> 好吃 闷热 安全 干燥
>
> 开朗 辣 干净 细心 好相处 潮湿
>
> 安静 凉快 特别 划算 聪明 便宜
>
> 吵 脏 舒服 贵 漂亮

1. 北京的天气怎么样?

2. 北京的美食怎么样?

3. 你的公寓怎么样?

4. 你的室友怎么样?

Structure Note 4.4: Use 最⋯⋯不过了 to emphasize superlatives.

> 最 + Adjective + 不过了

D. In the following table, there is a list of statements about China in the first column. Using these sentences as a guide, fill in the table using 最不过……了 to create four statements about your country.

		中国	我的国家
1.	动物	四川的大熊猫最可爱不过了。	
2.	菜	湖南菜最辣不过了。	
3.	天气	哈尔滨的冬天最冷不过了。	
4.	城市	上海这城市最现代化不过了。	

II. Read the ads below and answer the following questions using the structure notes you learned in this lesson.

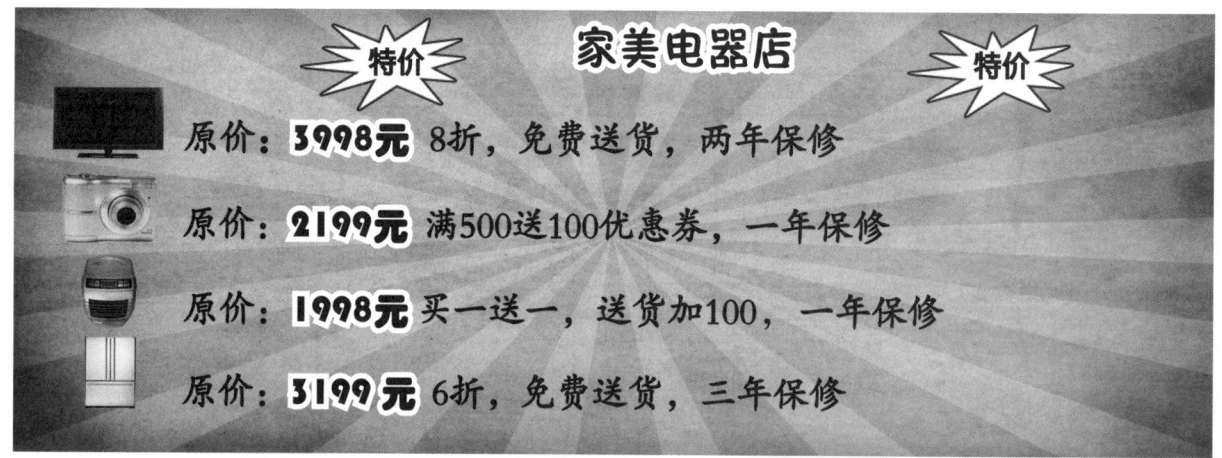

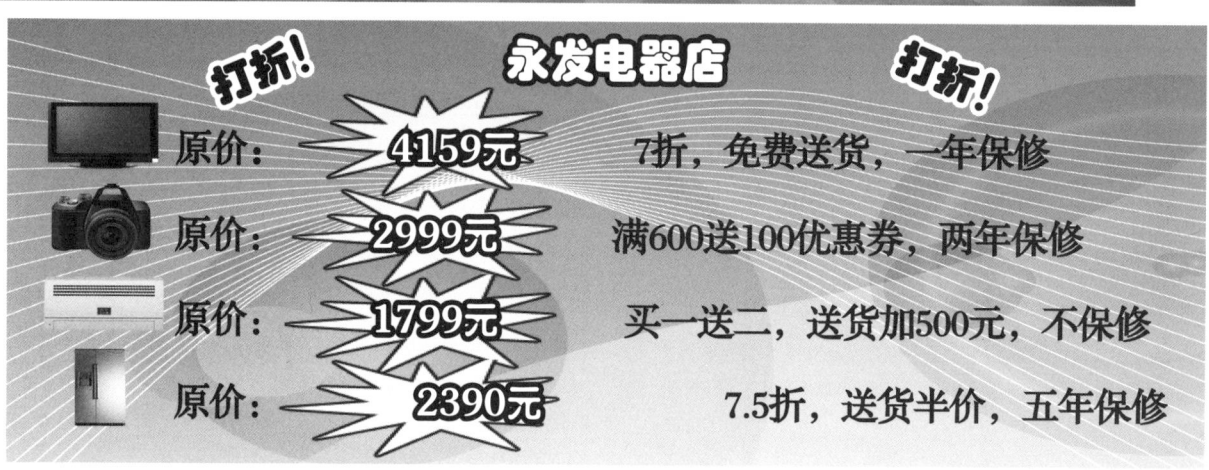

1. 如果你要买一台电视，你会去哪家电器店买？为什么？

2. 你觉得哪家商店卖的数码相机比较划算？

3. 你觉得家美电器还是永发电器的空调比较好？为什么？

4. 你觉得买冰箱最重要的是什么？那你会选哪一款冰箱？

READING COMPREHENSION 4.1

I. Read the passage and answer the following True or False questions.

> 小美一向喜欢买东西，最近又迷上了网上购物。她发现很多购物网站的东西很划算，特别是一些名牌产品，价格既合适样子又好看。她上个月在商店里看中了一款法国的鞋子，小美喜欢得不得了，说正好可以配她最喜欢的那条裙子。玛丽对她说："这双鞋漂亮是漂亮，可惜不便宜啊！比你一个月的房租还要贵两百块呢！你真的要买吗？" 小美一看也觉得太贵了，但她真的非常喜欢这双鞋，她就说："一分钱一分货啊！"玛丽建议小美去购物网站找找看有没有同一款的鞋子卖。小美很幸运，她在网上真的找到了一样的鞋子，并且那家网站正在打折，比原价还要便宜一半。更让小美高兴的是，这家网站还给了她一张优惠券。她下一次再来这里买东西的时候，用这张优惠券他们会免费送货。小美说新鞋送到了以后，她一定会把鞋子的照片放到她的博客上跟大家分享。

1. ( ) 小美既喜欢在商店里买东西又喜欢在网上买东西。
2. ( ) 为了买这双鞋，小美就带了数码相机。
3. ( ) 玛丽觉得在商店里买鞋的费用太高了。
4. ( ) 小美在网上买的鞋不但价格好，而且网站免费把鞋寄给她。
5. ( ) 如果你现在去看小美的博客，你可以看到她的新鞋的照片。

Take the challenge! 动动脑筋！

"Adjective +是+ Adjective, 可是/但是/可惜" is a structure pattern equivalent to "虽然 + Clause, 可是/但是/可惜." For example, 这台手机便宜是便宜，但是质量不好 means "this cell phone is cheap, but the quality is bad." This phrase can also be expressed in the other pattern: 虽然这台手机很便宜，但是质量不好. In the passage, can you guess what Mali means when she says 这双鞋漂亮是漂亮，可惜不便宜啊 and how to convert it to the second pattern structure?

II. Read the following passage and answer the questions:

> 我叫王文文,刚刚三十岁,在一家电子公司上班,月**收入**12,000元左右。我五年以前结婚了,我的先生是商人,**收入**也不错。我非常喜欢在网上购物,朋友们叫我"**网购达人**"。为什么呢?因为我觉得上网买东西最好不过了。除了自己住的房子以外,我一年的吃、穿、用等等,**大部分**都是在网上买的。最多的一次是有一年我一共网购了1,300多次,网购**支出**有26万多块钱。我一向喜欢美食,在网上可以找到不少好吃的东西,价格很划算。再说,网购既可以刷卡,也可以送货的时候付现金,确实很方便。我也喜欢摄影。网上常常可以找到新款的摄影产品,并且还可能有打折的优惠券。我的五台数码相机全部都是在网上买的,价格既便宜,保修期又长,产品的质量又好。由于我有很多有关网购的经验,我很了解哪些网站可以找到让人安心的好东西,也知道有问题的时候怎么跟**商家**联络,特别是去投诉的时候应该准备哪些必需的资料,所以我很希望把我的经验在这个博客里与大家分享。

Notes:
收入 (shōurù): *n.* income
网购达人 (wǎnggòu dárén): *n.* online shopping expert
大部分 (dàbùfen): *adj.* most
支出 (zhīchū): *n.* expenditure
商家 (shāngjiā): *n.* dealer

1. 王文文……

    A. 三十岁左右,还没有结婚。
    B. 每年网购都要花26万块钱。
    C. 喜欢网购因为不用投诉。
    D. 喜欢美食,所以常常在网上买吃的东西。

2. 下面的哪个说法是不对的?

    A. 王文文的朋友们觉得她很懂网购。
    B. 由于王文文是商人,所以她的收入很好。
    C. 除了网购以外,王文文也喜欢摄影。
    D. 王文文知道网购的时候怎么做投诉。

3. Most likely, we would see this passage in . . .

    A. an article about rating websites.
    B. a personal blog.
    C. a diary.
    D. a newspaper interview article.

III. Read the following e-mail and voucher and answer the questions.

To: 陈大东
From: 黄祥安
Subject: 一起去吃火锅吧！

大东，
　　最近我一直忙着出去拍照片、写博客，宿舍都是你在帮忙整理打扫，所以我想今晚请你去一家很好吃的中国饭馆吃饭。你不是一直很想吃我拍那些美食吗？这家饭馆的美食一定让你满意。我知道你喜欢吃辣，所以我会带你去一家特别有名的**火锅**店。这家店客人非常多，而且这两天他们店正在做优惠活动，**消费**满100元就可以**使用**30元的优惠券。我拍了优惠券的照片一起发给你看看。晚上六点在宿舍等你喔！
祥安

Notes:
火锅 (huǒguō): *n.* hotpot
消费 (xiāofèi): *v.* to consume
使用 (shǐyòng): *v.* to use

幸运牛肉美食火锅城

优惠券　　新鲜牛肉 火锅美食

欢迎光临　顾客至上　￥30元

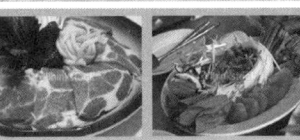

优惠条件
① 消费每满100元，即可使用本券一张。
② 本券限单桌使用，使用本券结算时，不再享有其它优惠。
③ 本券只适用于周一至周五（12:00–17:00）。
④ 本券不可兑现现金。
⑤ 请于13年8月8日前使用本券，过期无效。

地址：XXXXXXXXXXXXXXXX　　电话：XXXXXXXXXXX

1. Why does Xiang'an want to invite Dadong to dinner? _____

2. Assume Xiang'an has two coupons, how much do they need to order in order to use both coupons? _____

3. According to the time Xiang'an suggests to meet up for dinner, will they be able to use the coupon? Why or why not? _____

4. Circle the expiration date on the coupon.

WRITING PRACTICE 4.1

I. You purchased a TV online after seeing the promotion below, and you had a very good experience making your purchase. Write a review on your blog about your transaction and why you decided to buy the TV.

II. You are creating an online store to sell your company's products. Decide what items your company sells and create a special promotion for an upcoming holiday. Be sure to include the promotional period, what special discounts, warranties, and shipping discounts will be offered, etc.

UNIT 4 – LESSON 2

退货

VOCABULARY REVIEW 4.2

I. Write the English definition for each character and reorder the words in each row to form a vocabulary phrase.

Example: 食 eat   文化 culture   饮 drink   →   饮食文化 cuisine culture

1. 暖 _____   电 _____   器 _____   → _____
2. 洗 _____   机 _____   衣 _____   → _____
3. 品 _____   日 _____   用 _____   → _____
4. 公司 _____   货 _____   百 _____   → _____
5. 货 _____   退 _____   须知 _____   → _____

II. Combine the radical with the appropriate characters to make two new characters. Write a vocabulary phrase using each new character below and include the pinyin.

Example:

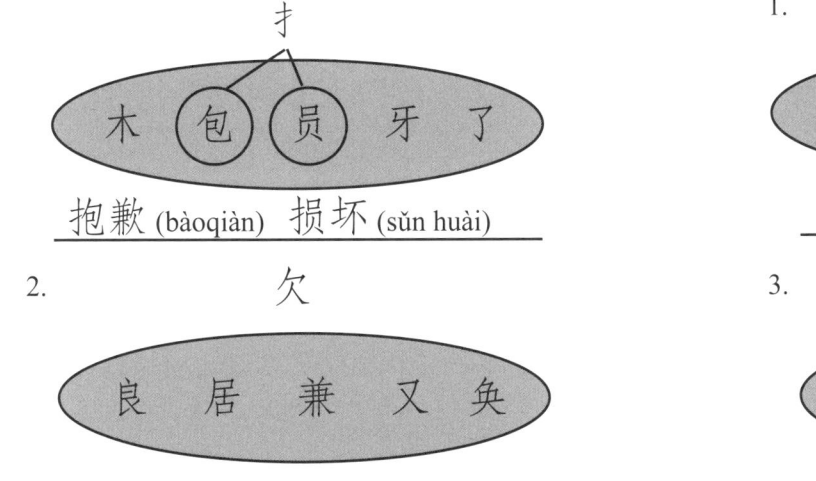

抱歉 (bàoqiàn)   损坏 (sǔn huài)

2. 欠
   良 居 兼 又 免
   _____

1.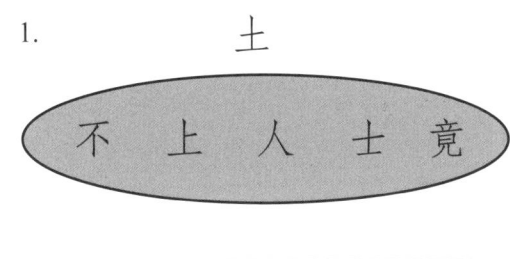
   _____

3.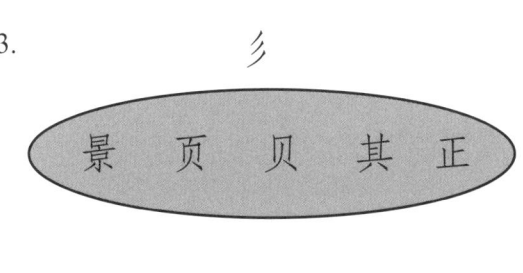
   _____

III. Replace the underlined phrases with appropriate vocabulary words from this lesson.

我们是一家新开的生活家具店。除了家具以外，我们还卖像(1.)<u>洗脸的巾</u>这样的日用品。我们所有商品都是欧洲有名的品牌，(2.)<u>一定</u>没有产品(3.)<u>用不了</u>的问题。(4.)<u>如果</u>你对商品有什么不满意，只要(5.)<u>拿出</u>收据，我们都会帮你退换。如果你对退货(6.)<u>情况</u>不清楚，欢迎与我们的店员联系，我们会给(7.)<u>客人</u>最好的服务。

CHARACTER WRITING PRACTICE 4.2

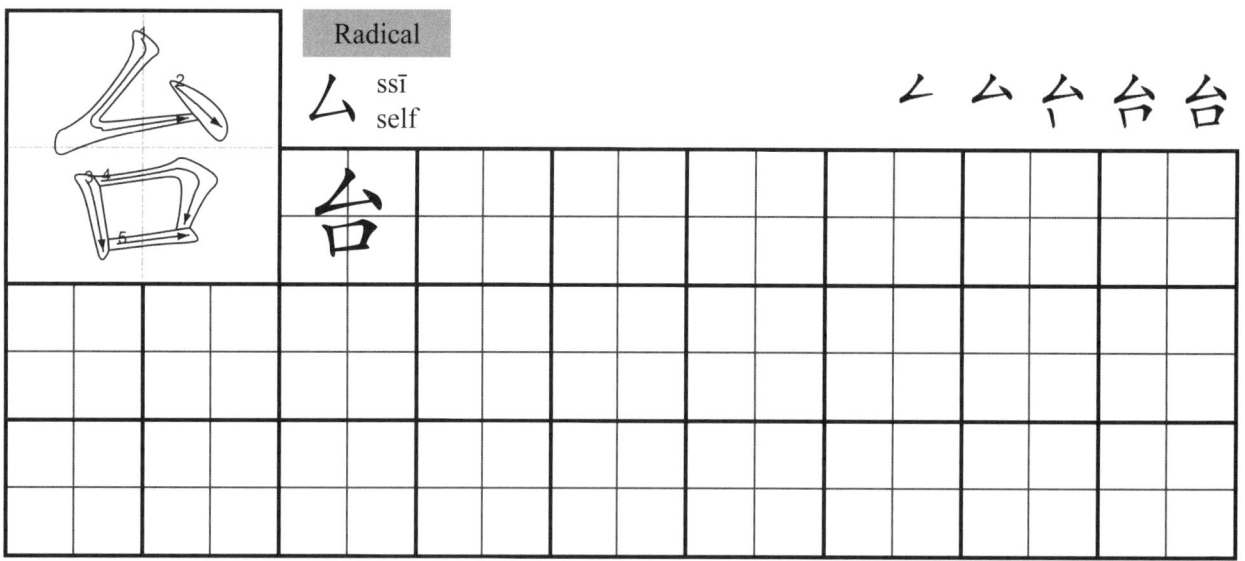

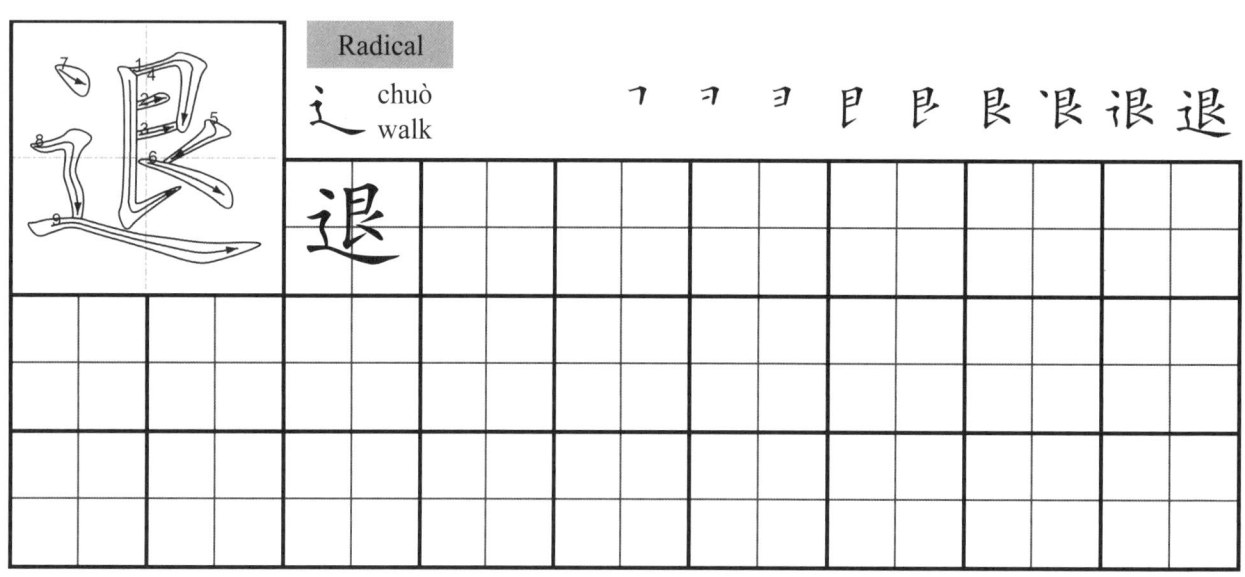

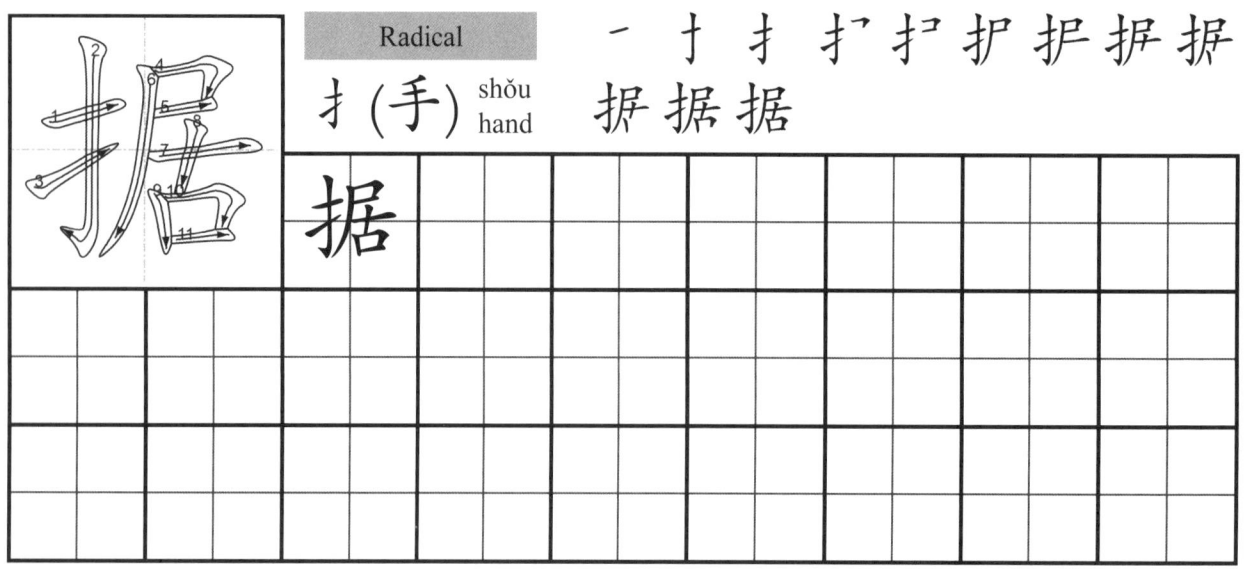

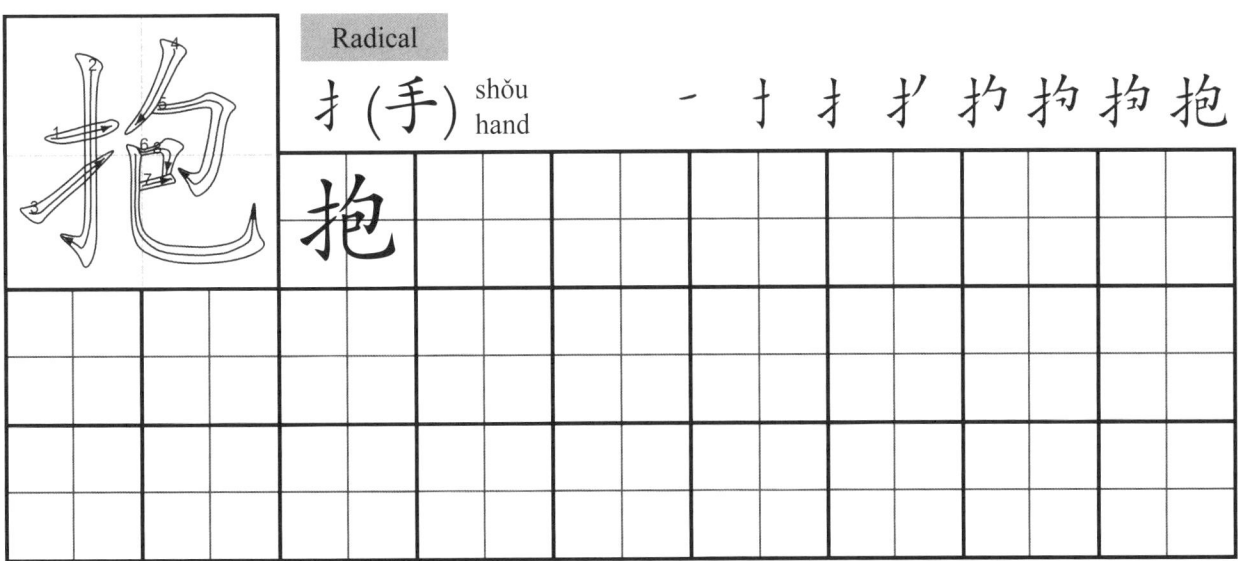

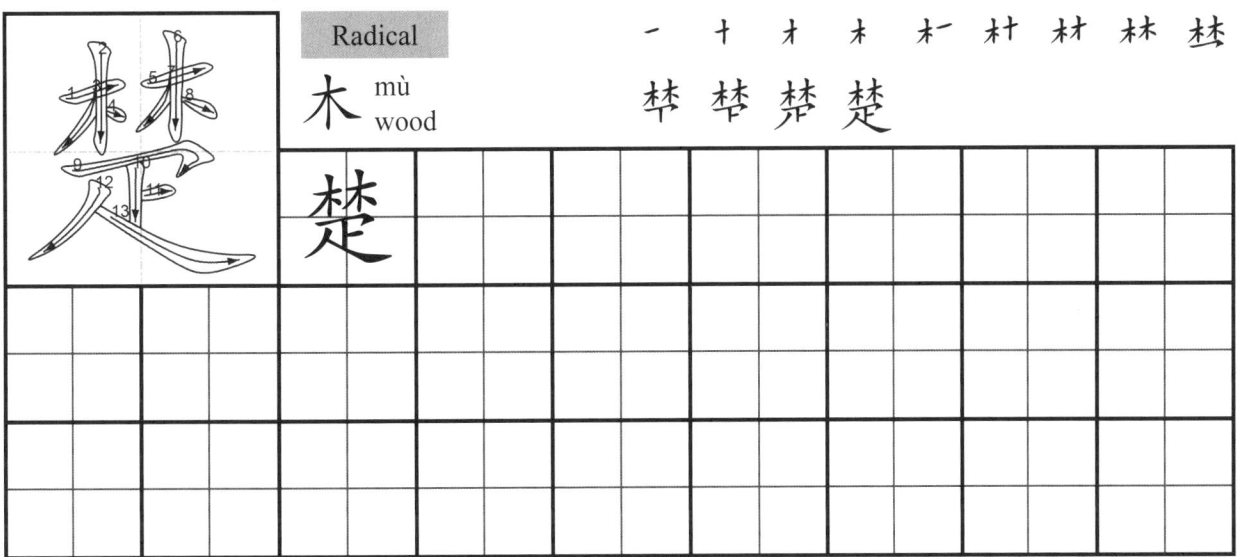

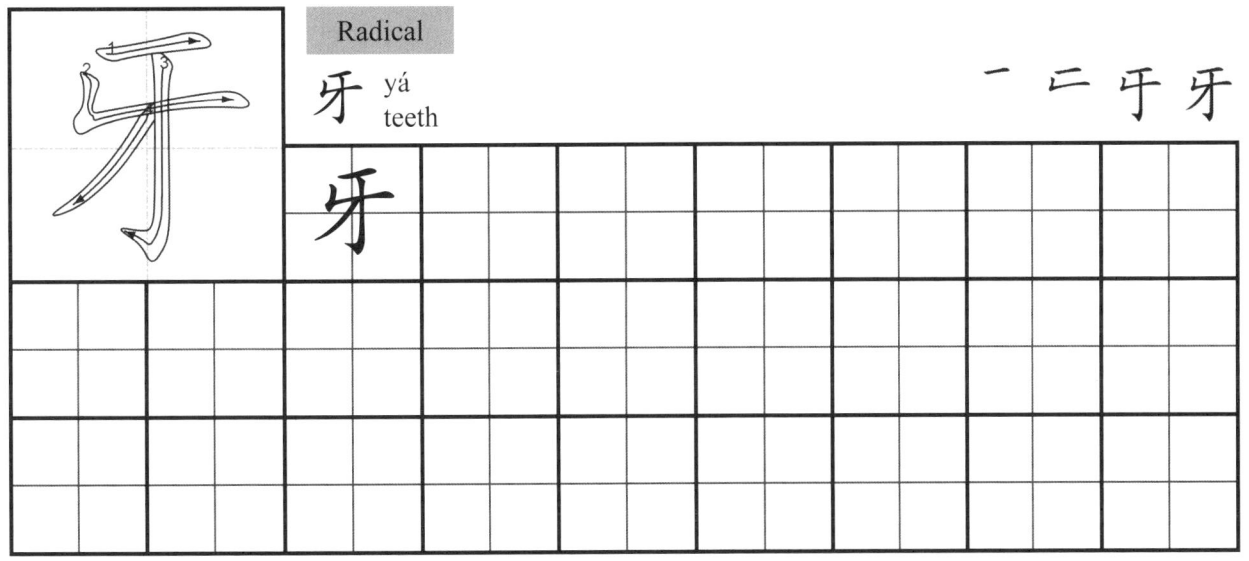

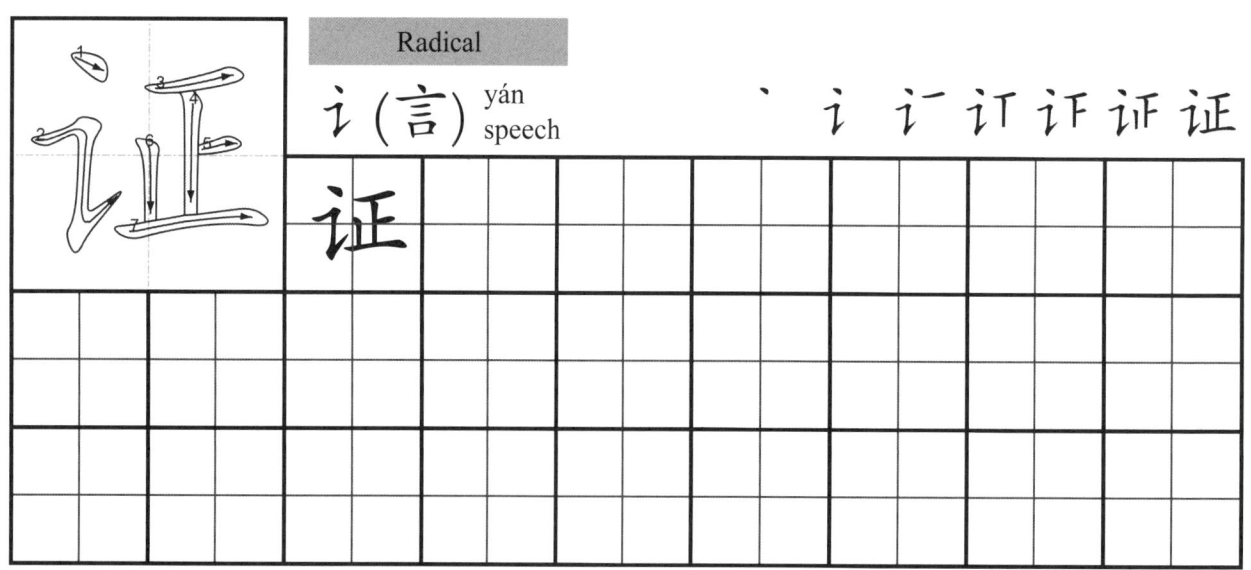

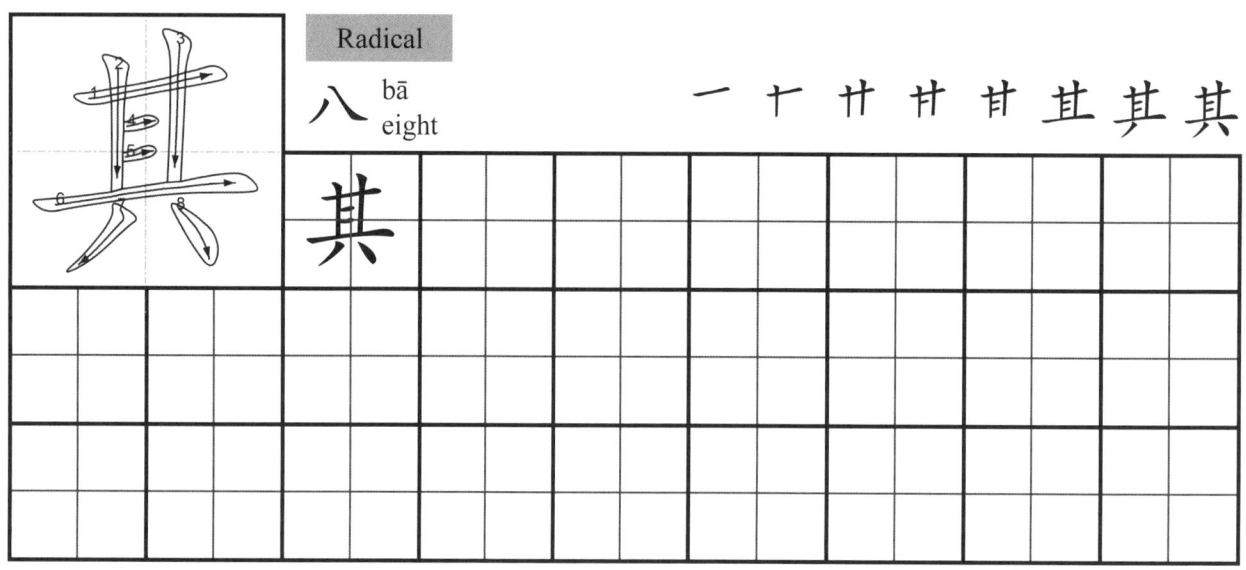

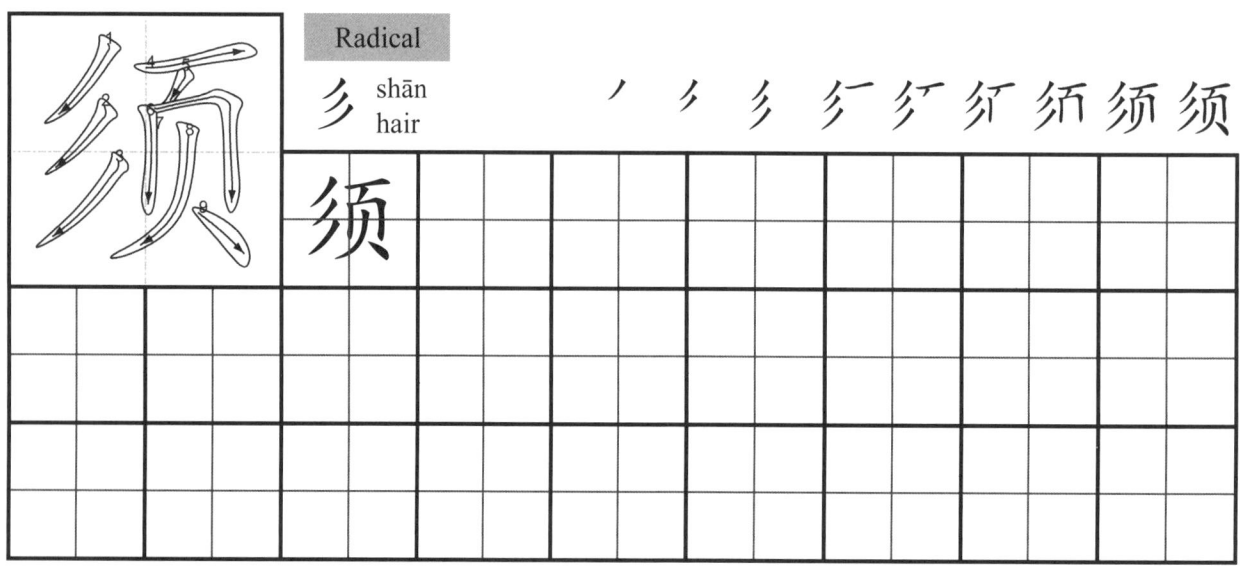

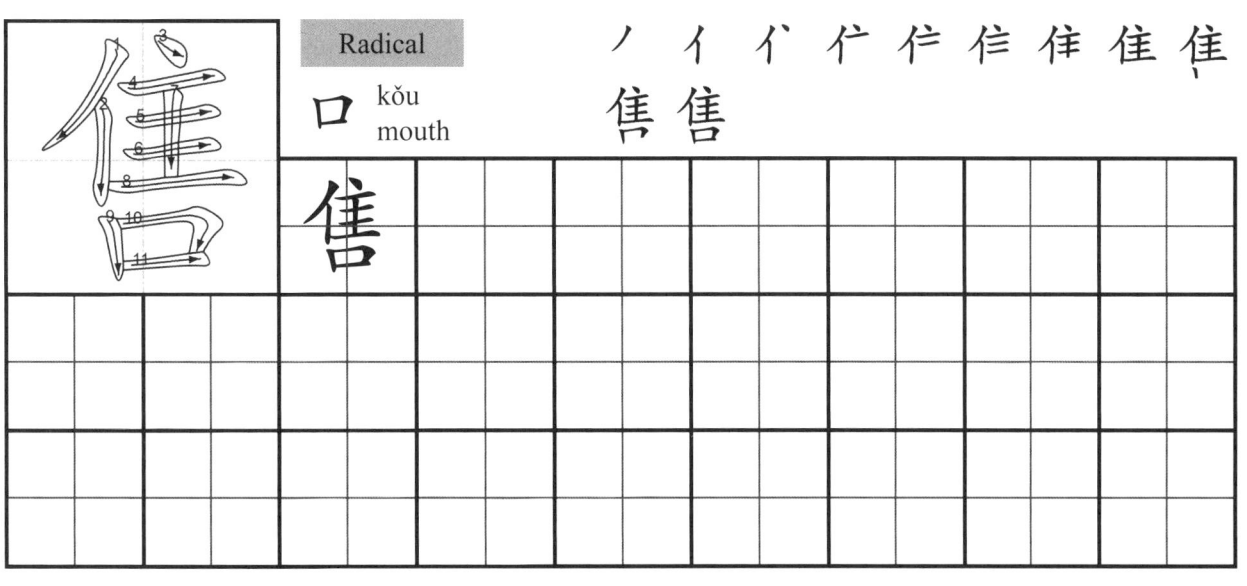

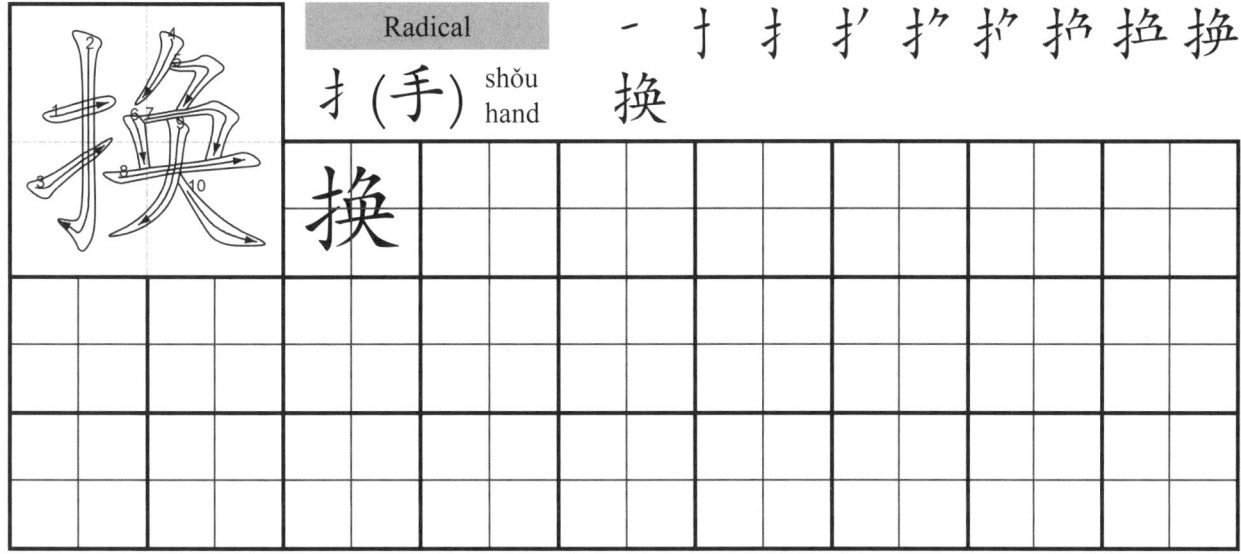

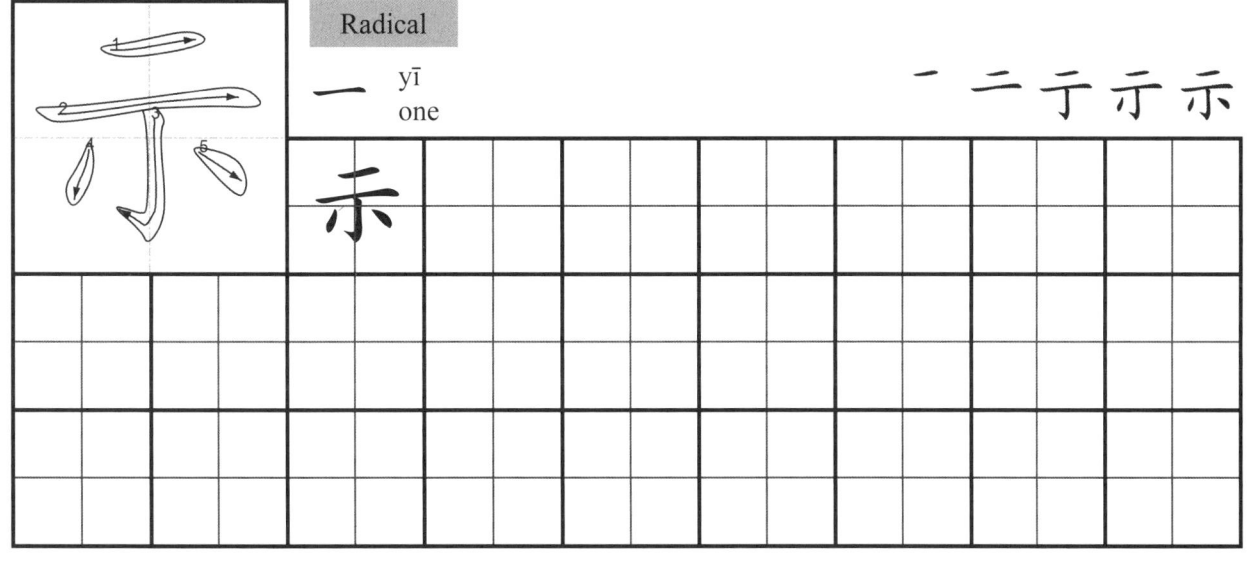

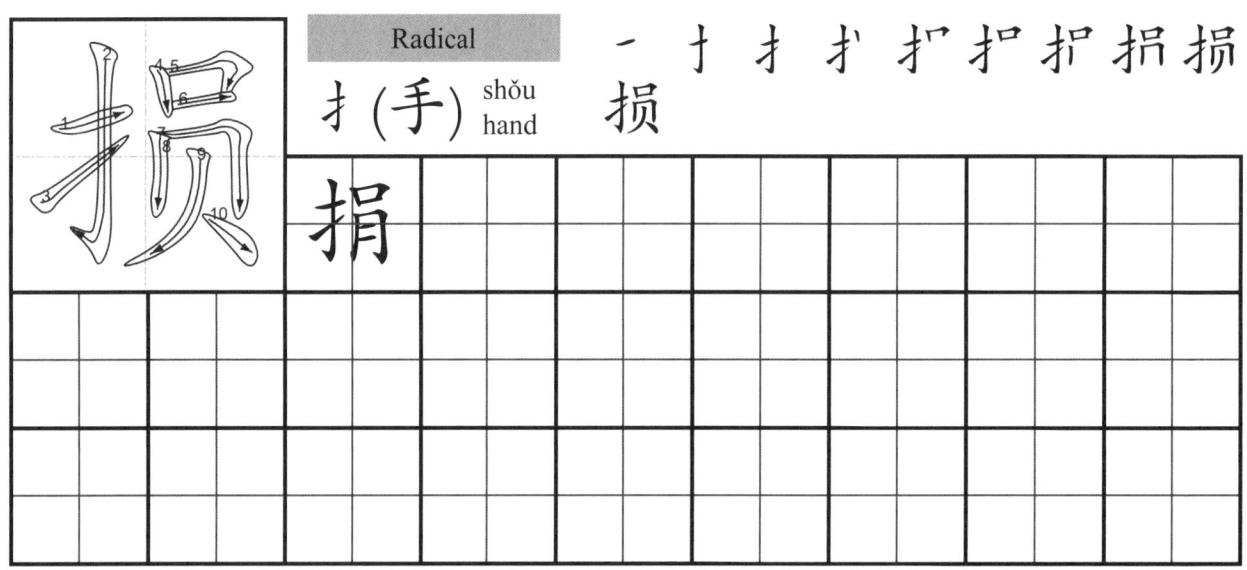

Radical: 扌(手) shǒu hand

一 十 扌 扌 扩 护 护 捐 损 损

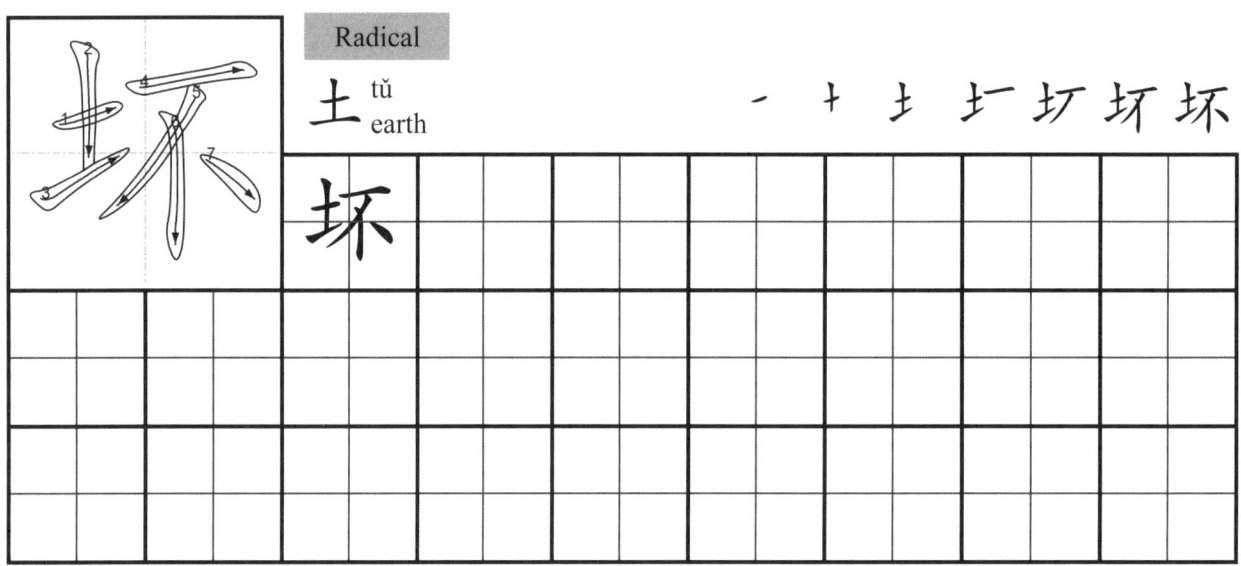

Radical: 土 tǔ earth

一 十 土 ±´ 圹 坏 坏

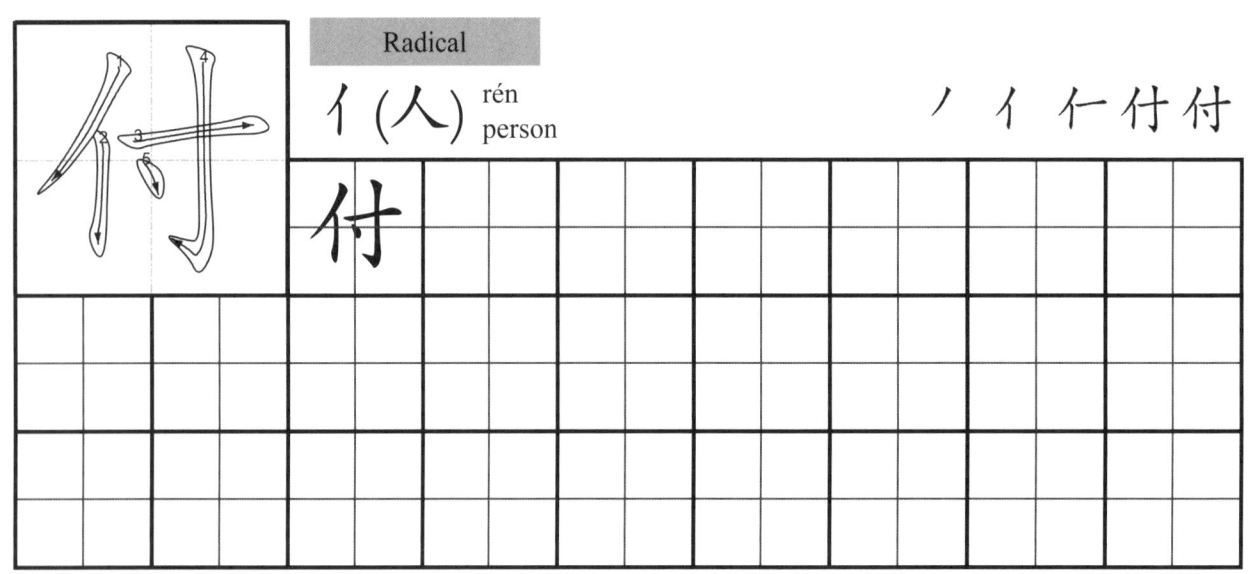

Radical: 亻(人) rén person

丿 亻 亻 付 付

LISTENING COMPREHENSION 4.2

I. Listen to the recording and select the best response below.

1. The woman would most likely respond with:

   A. 哪家的售后服务好一点？
   B. 你不认为价格很重要吗？
   C. 这家的退货条件写得清楚吗？
   D. 我们学校附近有三家百货公司。

II. Listen to the recording and answer the following True or False questions.

1. (   ) The man is looking for a birthday gift for his mom.
2. (   ) The woman praises the man for being considerate to his mom.
3. (   ) The heater, which the woman recommends, does not come with packaging.
4. (   ) Free shipping is very important to the man's mom.
5. (   ) Most likely the man is not going to buy the heater.

III. Listen to the recording and answer the questions in Chinese.

1. Why did the speaker decide to buy a cell phone last month?

   _____

2. What kind of problems did the speaker encounter with the cell phone?

   _____

3. Describe how the speaker was able to obtain a new cell phone.

   _____

SPEAKING PRACTICE 4.2

I. You are a clerk at a store and a customer comes in on February 22 trying to return some items purchased there earlier this year (see the images of the products below). Using the store's return policy, explain to the customer why or why not each item can or cannot be returned. Be sure to express apologies for items that the customer cannot return.

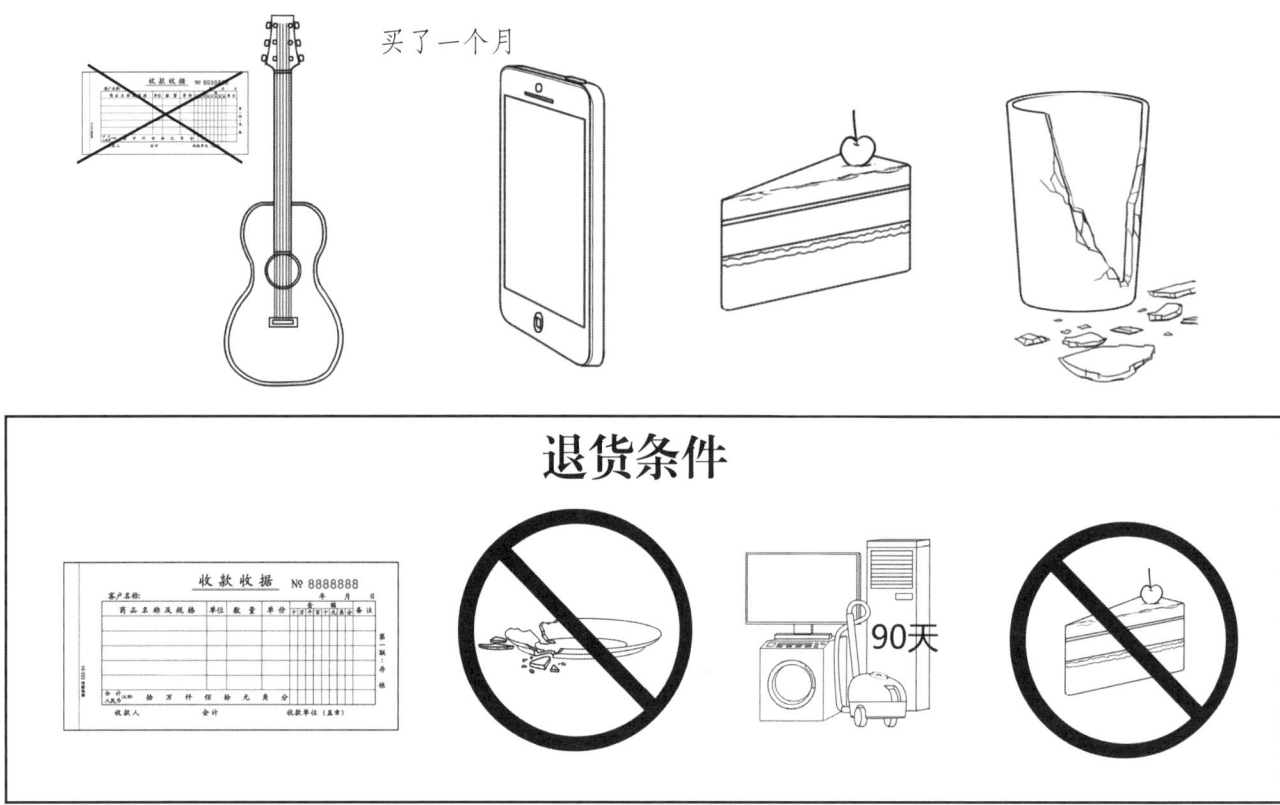

II. You are moving to an unfurnished apartment and need to purchase new household items. With a budget of $2500, determine what you need, what you can buy, and whether you will buy the items in a small store, department store, online, or a combination of the three.

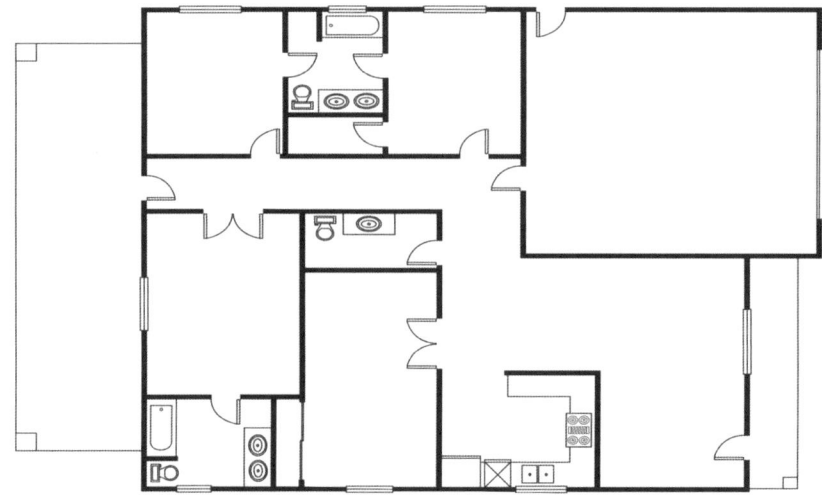

第四单元 · 第二课 · 买

STRUCTURE REVIEW 4.2

I. Complete the following Structure Note practice activities.

Structure Note 4.5: Use 得了/不了 to express ability or inability to complete certain actions.

$$\text{Verb} + 得/不 + 了 \ (+ \text{Object})$$

A. Answer the following questions with your own opinion using 得了/不了.

1. 孔子的思想那么复杂，你认为外国人明白得了吗？

   _____

2. 你认为中国的老年人会习惯得了西方的饮食文化吗？

   _____

3. 你认为现在的年轻人没钱没房子还结得了婚吗？

   _____

Take the challenge! 动动脑筋！

"他房间那么脏谁受得了啊！"
"对啊，所以他的室友全都受不了搬走了。"
"受得了的应该就只有他自己吧。"

受 is usually defined as "to receive or accept," but in this example, it means "to tolerate or endure." Put together with 得了 or 不了, 受得了 means "to be able to tolerate," while 受不了 means "not able to tolerate."

For the phrase 谁受得了, while it is in a question format, it is not really asking for an answer. Rather, it is a common expression that people use to emphasize "no one can tolerate this."

Can you guess the meaning of the following commonly used expressions?
现在这情况管不了那么多了。
你觉得现在的年轻人都吃得了苦吗？

Structure Note 4.6: Use 像…这/那样的… to describe categories using comparisons.

$$像 + \text{Noun Phrase} + 这/那样的 + \text{Noun Phrase}$$

B. You are looking for an apartment and made a list of requirements you would like for your new place. Ask the agency questions based on the list below using 像…这 / 那样的….

家具：桌子、床
家电：洗衣机、冰箱、空调
费用：水电费、网费
商场：货美百货、实惠商场
租房条件：签一年合同

Example: 这个公寓有没有像桌子、床这样的家具？

1. _____

2. _____

3. _____

4. _____

Structure Note 4.7: Use 其实 to say "actually."

其实 + Sentences

C. Your friend has some misconceptions about China. Answer each of his questions below using 其实.

1. 在中国是不是只有中国饭馆？
   _____

2. 在中国是不是所有商店都不能退货？
   _____

3. 是不是每个中国人都喜欢请客？
   _____

4. 是不是所有中国人都会功夫？
   _____

Structure Note 4.8: Use 不管…都 / 还… to express that something does not matter.

$$\text{不管} + \text{Question} + , + \text{Subject} + \text{都} / \text{还} + \text{Verb Phrase}$$

D. The following are some mottos. Rewrite the four mottos using 不管…都 / 还…, and then write one motto of your using this structure.

> 如果你要去一个国家旅行，你要先学习那个地方的礼节。
> 你有烦恼的话一定要说出来和家人一起讨论。
> 虽然你认为老师说的事情不重要，你也要细心注意听。
> 与长辈或者比你大的人讲话的时候一定要有礼貌。

1. _____

2. _____

3. _____

4. _____

5. 我认为 _____

II. Do you agree with the statements below? If yes, check 同意 (tóngyì) to express your agreement. If not, check 不同意 (bù tóngyì) to express your disagreement and provide a reason using the structure notes you learned in this lesson.

1.	便宜的东西质量一定没保证。 ☐ 同意 ☐ 不同意_____
2.	买东西最重要就是看它的牌子。 ☐ 同意 ☐ 不同意_____
3.	所有打折的货品都是卖得不好的东西。 ☐ 同意 ☐ 不同意_____
4.	商品包装越漂亮，价钱就会越贵。 ☐ 同意 ☐ 不同意_____
5.	每家百货公司的退货条件都是差不多。 ☐ 同意 ☐ 不同意_____

READING COMPREHENSION 4.2

I. Read the passage and answer the following True or False questions.

今年夏天大东找到了一个实习的机会。这是一家买日用品的百货公司，他们卖的商品都是每天人们必需用的东西，比如衣服、毛巾、牙膏、电暖器等等。这家商场的东西价格不错，很多商品的牌子都很好，售后服务也有保证，难怪很受大家的欢迎。大东来这里打工的第一个星期是管收银。客人们买好商品以后，就到大东这里来付款。他必须看清楚价钱，要是没有问题的话，就给客人开一张收据。第三个星期，大东开始管退货。他每天要接待差不多三十位来退货的客人。他得跟每一个客人介绍退货条件和退货须知，请他们出示收据，检查商品的包装有没有损坏，再问他们要不要换别的商品。其实在这些客人中，大部分都是因为货品坏了才来退货的，但是也有一些客人是想货比三家，所以买了东西以后又来退货。不管怎么样，大东都非常认真、非常礼貌地接待他们。大东认为，这份工作虽然有时候比较麻烦，但是像这样的经验对以后的工作是非常有用的。

1. (　) 大东今年夏天在一家百货公司打工。
2. (　) 大东实习的时候首先做的是跟退货有关的工作。
3. (　) 由于这家百货公司的商品又好又便宜、服务也好，所以来买东西的客人很多。
4. (　) 要是你想要退货的话，你必须要有发票。
5. (　) 大东认为那些想货比三家，买了东西又来退货的客人很麻烦。

II. Read the following passage and answer the questions.

网上购买月饼的 "九大注意"

大家好！我是王娜。今天是星期三，我们的电视节目 "网上购物你我他" 又跟大家见面了！

下个星期就是中秋节了，不要忘记买月饼哦！今年有不少朋友在网上买月饼。网上购物跟在商场购物很不一样，虽然方便，但是也有很多需要注意的地方。我们今天就跟大家聊聊网上购买月饼的 "九大注意"。

第一、要看牌子。不管是自己吃还是送礼，买月饼都必须要看牌子，一定要选有保证的牌子。

第二、要看**信誉**。买像月饼这样的食物，一定得去**信誉**比较好的商店，这样才比较放心。

第三、要看**日期**。买月饼一定要注意**制造日期**和**保质期**。

第四、要看价格。价钱好当然重要，但是不要只因为便宜而买到坏月饼。

第五、要看包装。月饼送到你手上以后，要看清楚收到的月饼包装有没有损坏的地方。

第六、要看收据。在网上**下单**以后一定要**保留**付款的收据，有问题的时候可能会需要。

第七、要问时间。买月饼以前，最好跟网站联络一下，要知道送货需要多长时间。

第八、要问退货。买东西容易，退换难。问一问如果不满意货品，退货条件是什么。

第九、要货比三家。其实不管是在网上还是在百货公司里买东西，不管是买日用品还是食物，货比三家才能买到自己满意的商品。

希望大家都能高高兴兴地过一个中秋节！我们下星期三再见！

Notes:

信誉 (xìnyù): *n.* reputation
下单 (xià dān): *v.* to place the order
保留 (bǎoliú): *v.* to keep
制造日期 (zhì zào rì qī): *n.* manufacturing date
保质期 (bǎozhìqī): *n.* quality guarantee period

1. 现在应该是……

   A. 春天。
   B. 夏天。
   C. 秋天。
   D. 冬天。

2. Which one below was not mentioned in Wang Na's list?

   A. You need to present the receipt when you make a return.
   B. Brand is a key factor when purchasing moon cakes.
   C. It is very important to check the package when you receive the moon cakes.
   D. You should ask about the return policy before you place an order.

3. "网上购物你我他"……

   A. 是一个卖电视的网站。
   B. 是王娜的网站，你可以在这个网站上买月饼。
   C. 是王娜的节目，她认为货比三家非常重要。
   D. 介绍中秋节和中秋节的时候怎么找到价格好的月饼。

Take the challenge! 动动脑筋！

地方 can be used in two ways. It can be a concrete noun, indicating an actual place or a part of a space. For example, 这个地方有很多中国饭馆. The phrase can also be an abstract noun, indicating an intangible "part" or "aspect" of something. For example, 我与她有很多相同的地方. In this passage above, find the places where 地方 appears. Can you guess what each 地方 means?

III. Read the following two emails and answer the questions.

> To: 周信
> From: 孙玛丽
> Subject: 电暖器的收据
>
> 周信，
> 　　上个星期你陪我去电器商店买的那台电暖器，我记得当时让店员给我写了收据，可是我现在怎么找都找不到那张收据。我在想，要是这台电暖器坏了的话，没有收据是不是不可以换货也不保修啊？怎么办？
> 玛丽

> To: 孙玛丽
> From: 周信
> Subject: RE: 电暖器的收据
>
> 玛丽，
> 　　别着急。当时我们确实是让店员写了收据，可能是回家之前已经不见了。找不到就别找了，我们再去一趟电器商店，让那天给我们写收据的店员再写一次，这样就算电暖器坏了你也不用担心了。
> 周信

1. True or False: (　　) Mali is worried because she cannot find the receipt for the heater.
2. True or False: (　　) Zhou Xin believes that they lost the receipt on the way home the day they bought the heater.
3. True or False: (　　) Zhou Xin and Mali plan to go to the electronics store to find someone to write up a new receipt.
4. You are a clerk at the electronics store where Mali purchased the heater, which she bought for $143. Using the blank receipt below, write a new receipt for Mali.

Notes:
佰 (bǎi): *n.* hundred
拾 (shí): *n.* an elaborate form of "ten" used in writing checks, etc.
仟 (qiān): *n.* an elaborate form of "thousand" used in writing checks, etc.

WRITING PRACTICE 4.2

I. You are starting a new online electronics store. Create a return policy, including conditions about proof of purchase, how long you have to return items, what items cannot be returned, damaged items, and who pays the shipping costs for returned items.

_____

_____

_____

_____

_____

_____

_____

II. Below is an email a customer wrote to your store asking to return an item. Respond to the email based on your return policy you created for the question above.

To: （商店的名字）
From: 刘小红
Subject: 退货

（商店的名字），

　　您好！我两个星期以前在你们的网站上买了一台数码相机和一台小冰箱。货送来以后，我发现送来的数码相机不是我看中的那款。我想应该是我在网上买的时候选错了，不好意思。还有小冰箱也有问题，我在网上选的是白色，但是送来的是灰色，可能是你们出错货了。

　　请问，我应该怎样做呢？希望你们告诉我怎样换货。把相机寄回去的邮费需要我来付吗？还有那个小冰箱我不想要了，请告诉我你们的退货条件是什么？怎么退？

　　希望快一点跟我联络。谢谢！

刘小红

To:	刘小红
From:	（你商店的名字）
Subject:	RE: 退货

UNIT 5 – LESSON 1

篮球比赛

VOCABULARY REVIEW 5.1

I. Fill in the circles with a character to form a two-word vocabulary phrase. Then use the characters in the grey circles to read a secret question and answer it below.

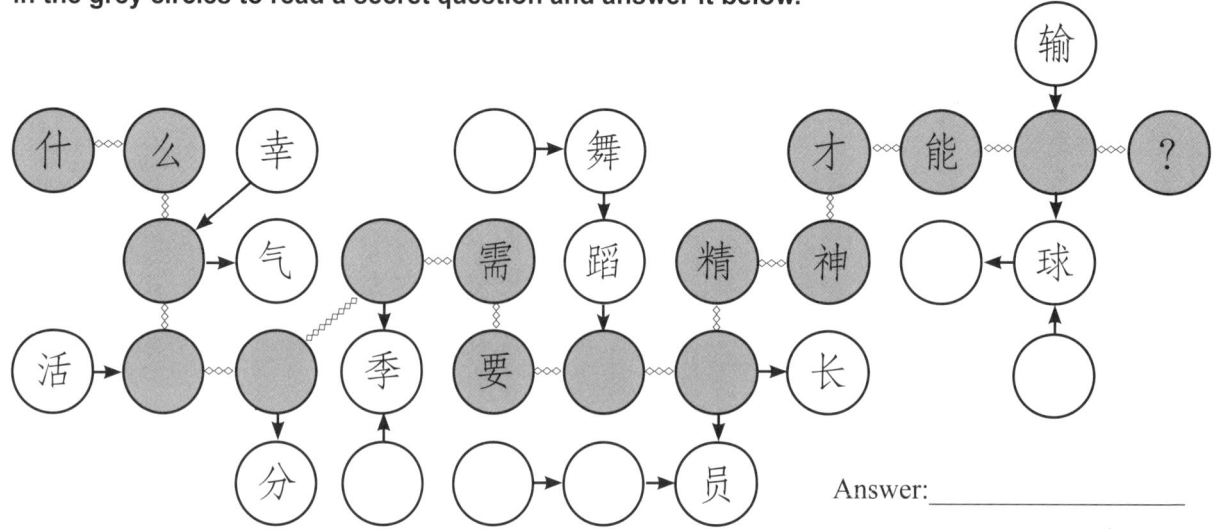

Answer:_____

II. Form characters using the components in the box below and write the pinyin.

肖	酉	亡	虫
欠	月	日	口
夫	力	弓	生
见	贝	凡	己

Example: 口 + 力 → 另 (ling)

1. ___+___→___ (_____)   4. ___+___+___→___ (_____)
2. ___+___→___ (_____)   5. ___+___+___+___+___
3. ___+___→___ (_____)   →___ (_____)

III. Complete the following sentences with the appropriate vocabulary from this lesson.

1. A: 球员犯规裁判也不吹哨。
   B: 这个裁判真不_____!

2. A: 现在山猫队对飞鼠队的比分是120比88。
   B: 山猫队一定会赢得_____!

3. A: 每个球员都非常厉害。
   B: 这个球队的实力真_____!

4. A: 山猫队的球员都配合得很好。
   B: 我想是因为教练很重视球队的_____。

5. A: 山猫队怎么可能会输球，他们不是每位都是篮球明星吗?
   B: 有时候打球除了讲实力以外也要看_____。

CHARACTER WRITING PRACTICE 5.1

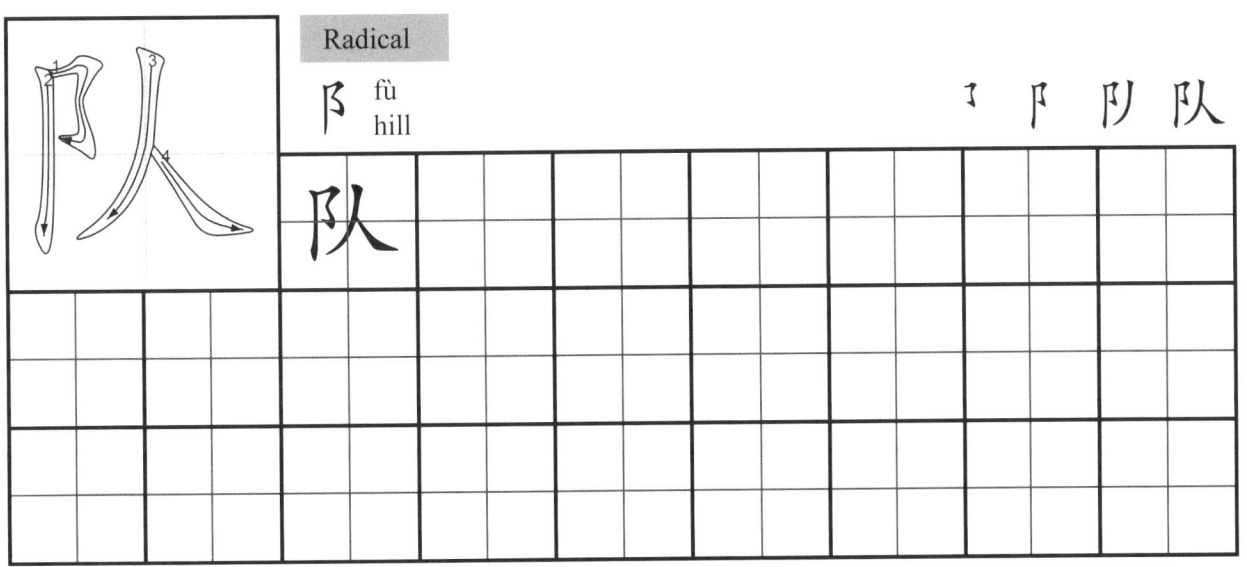

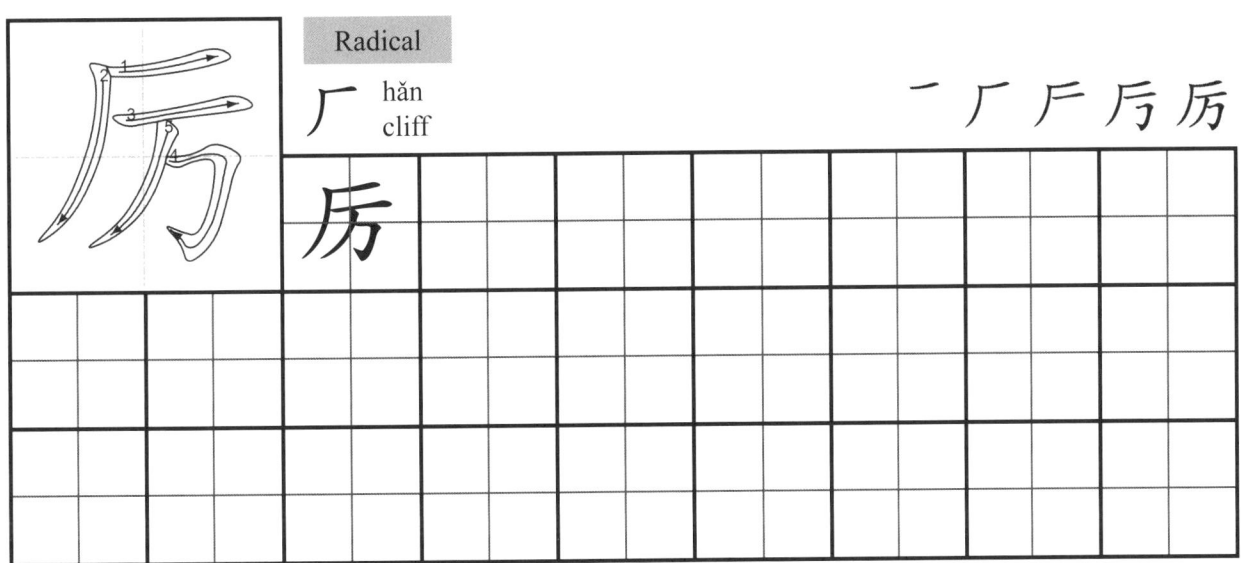

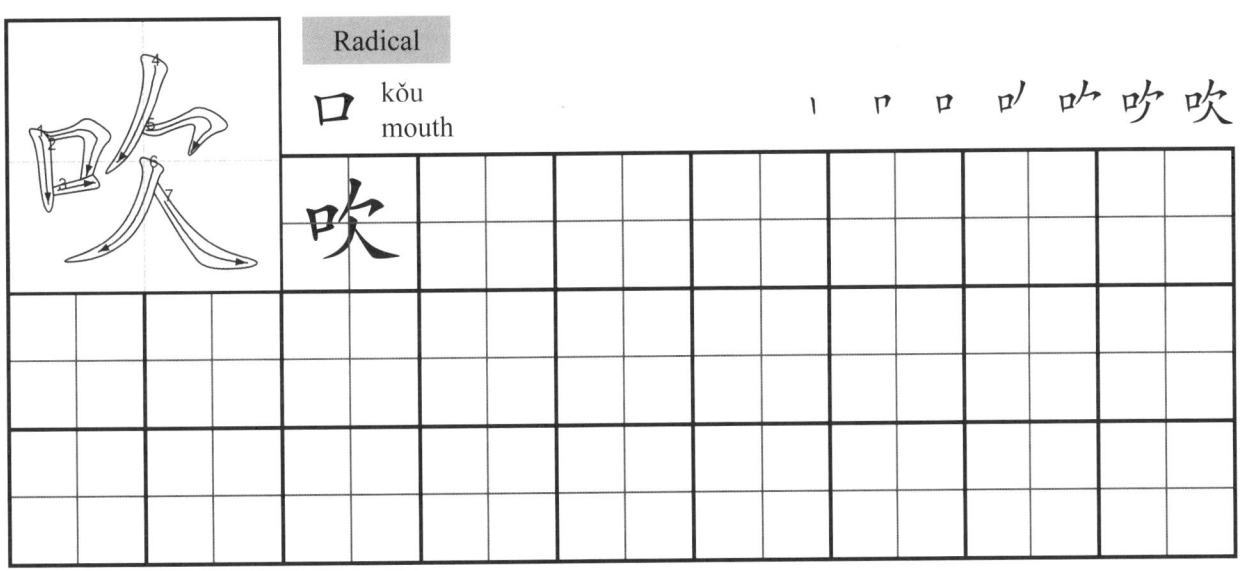

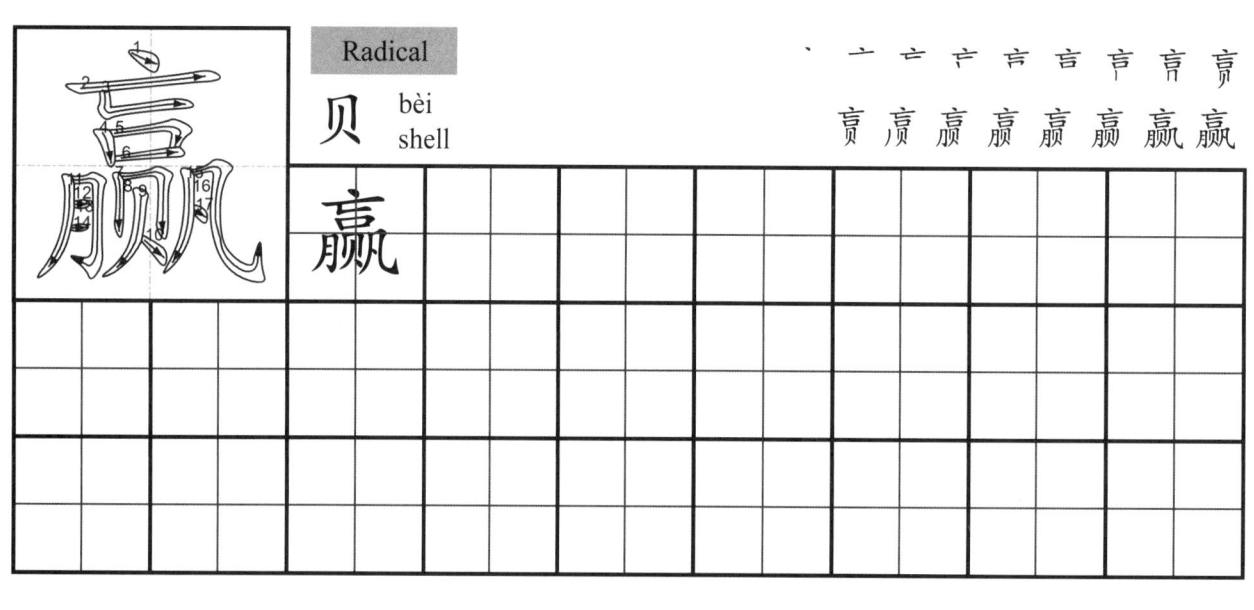

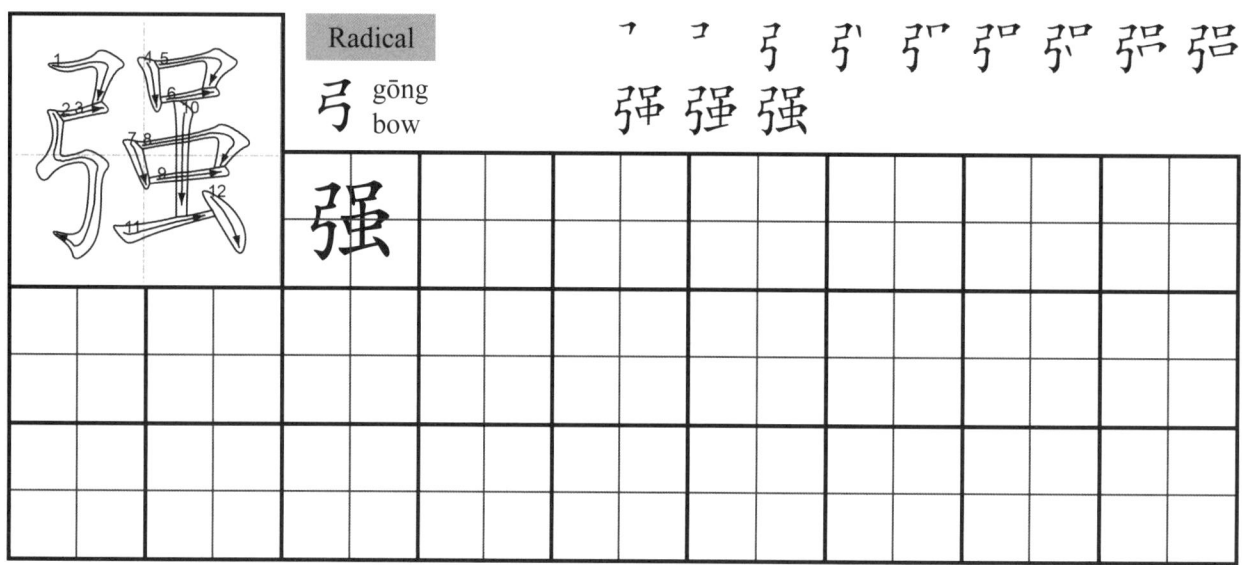

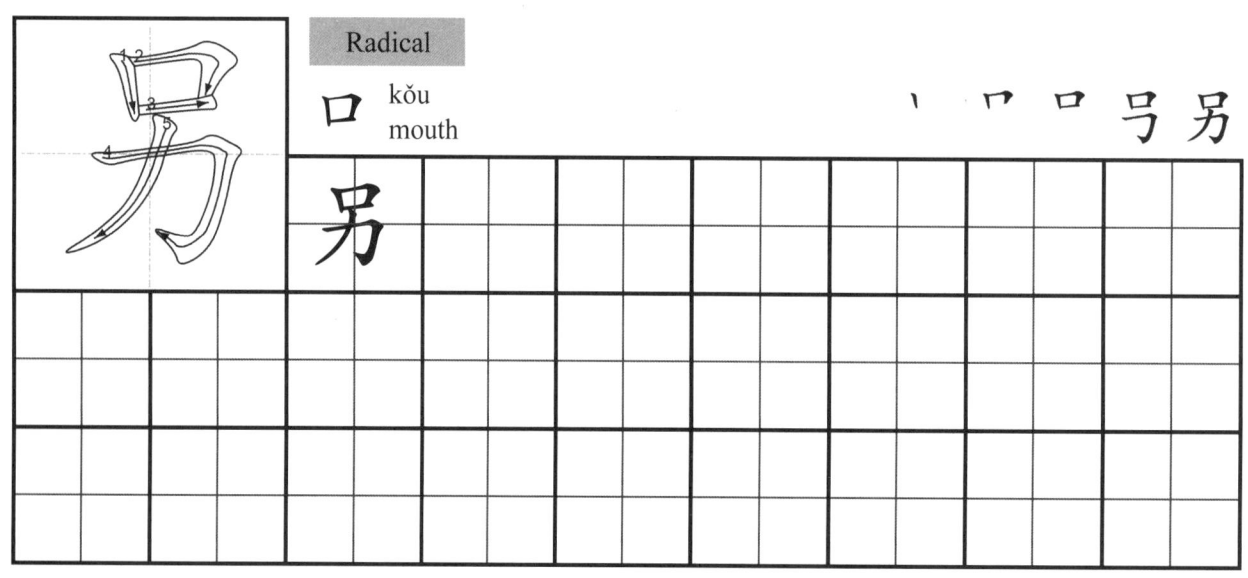

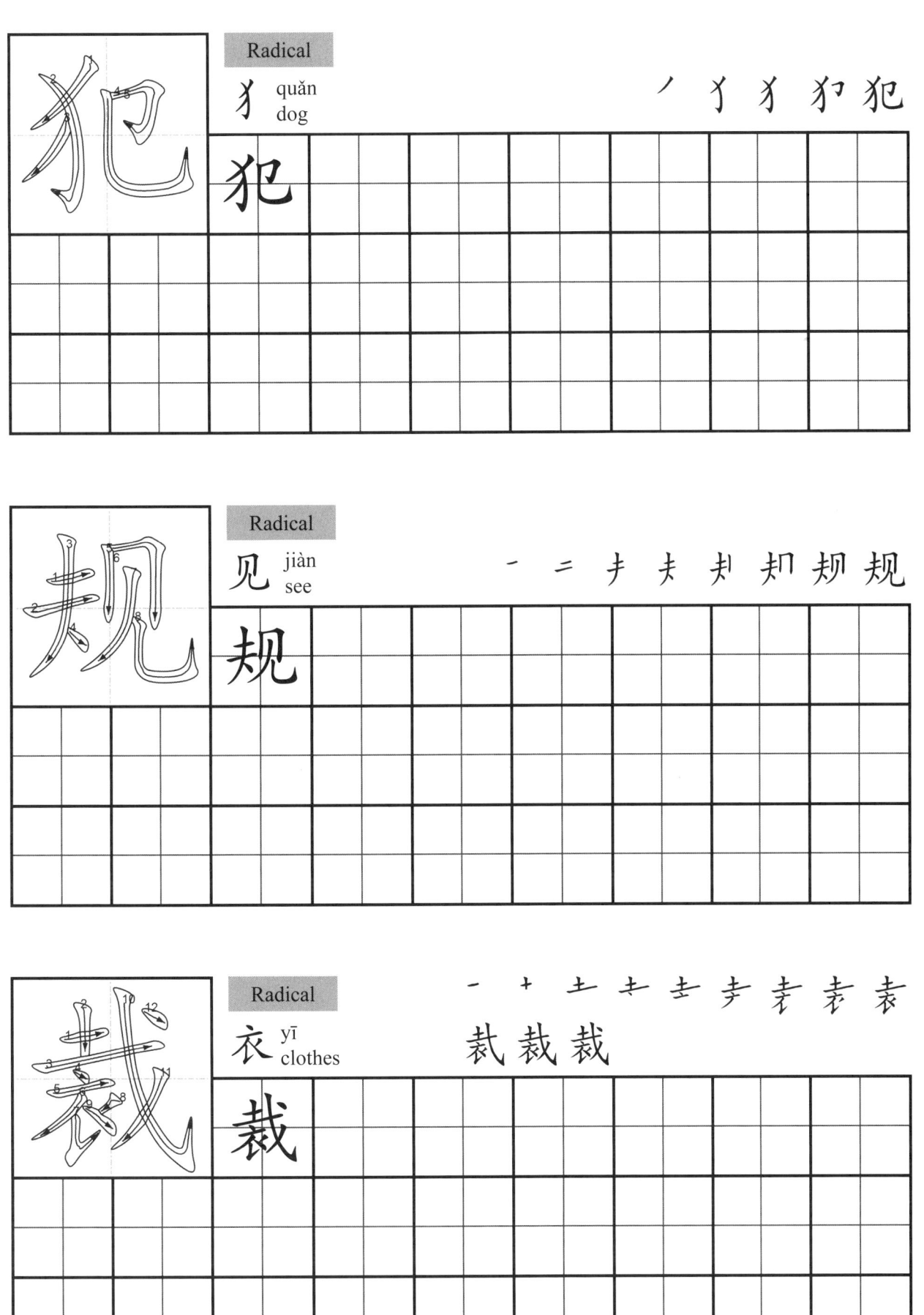

Unit 5 · Lesson 1 · Hobbies

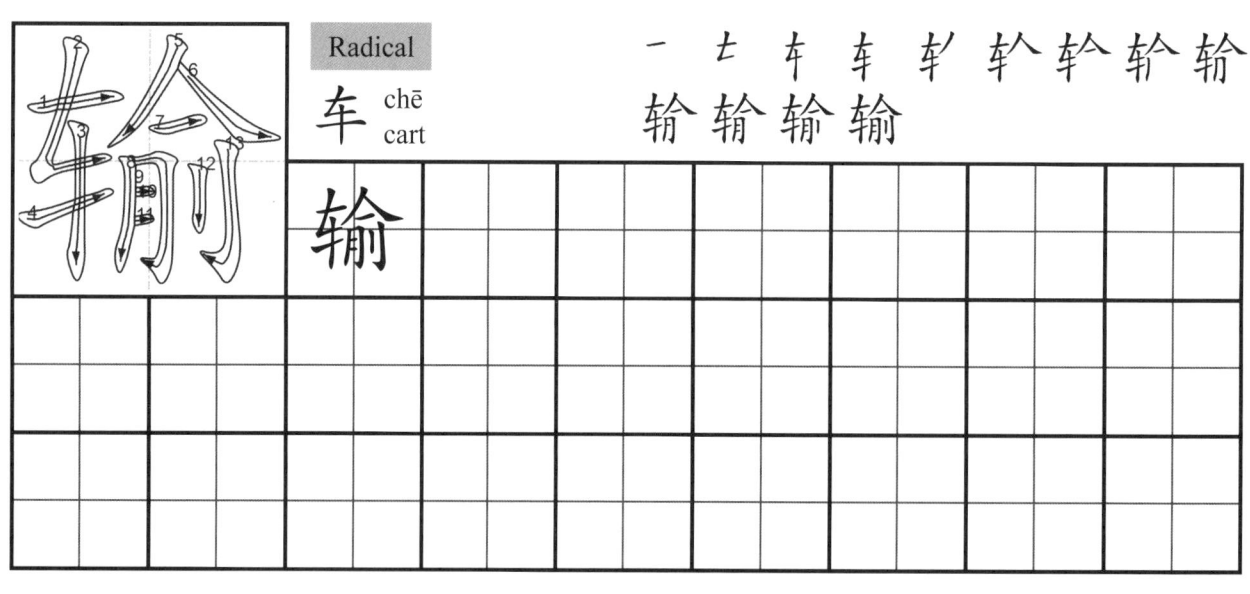

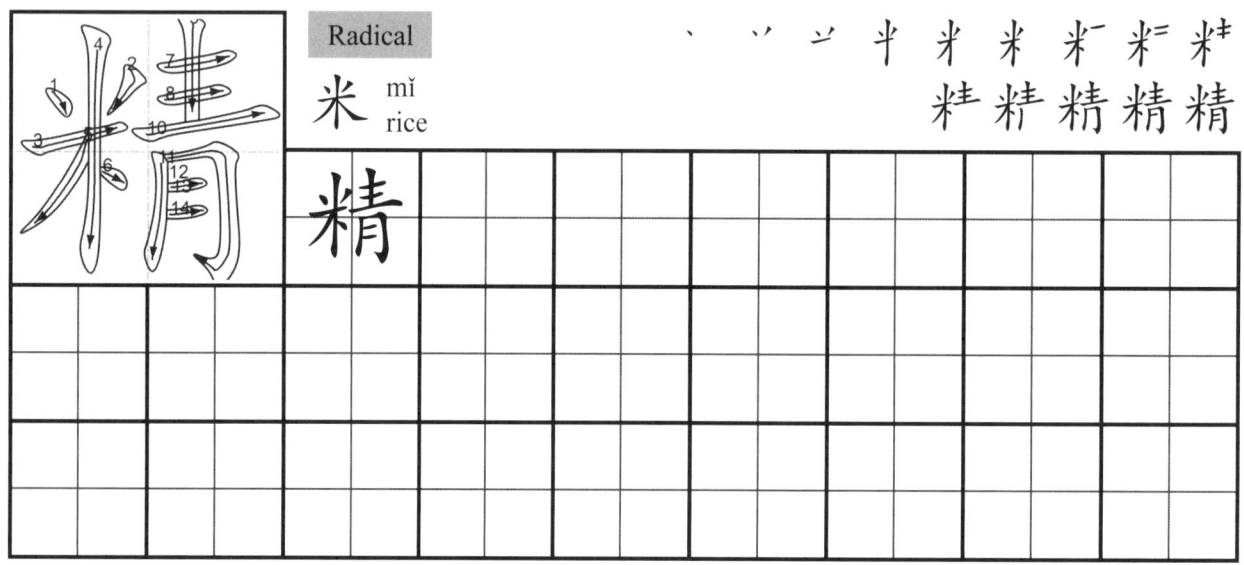

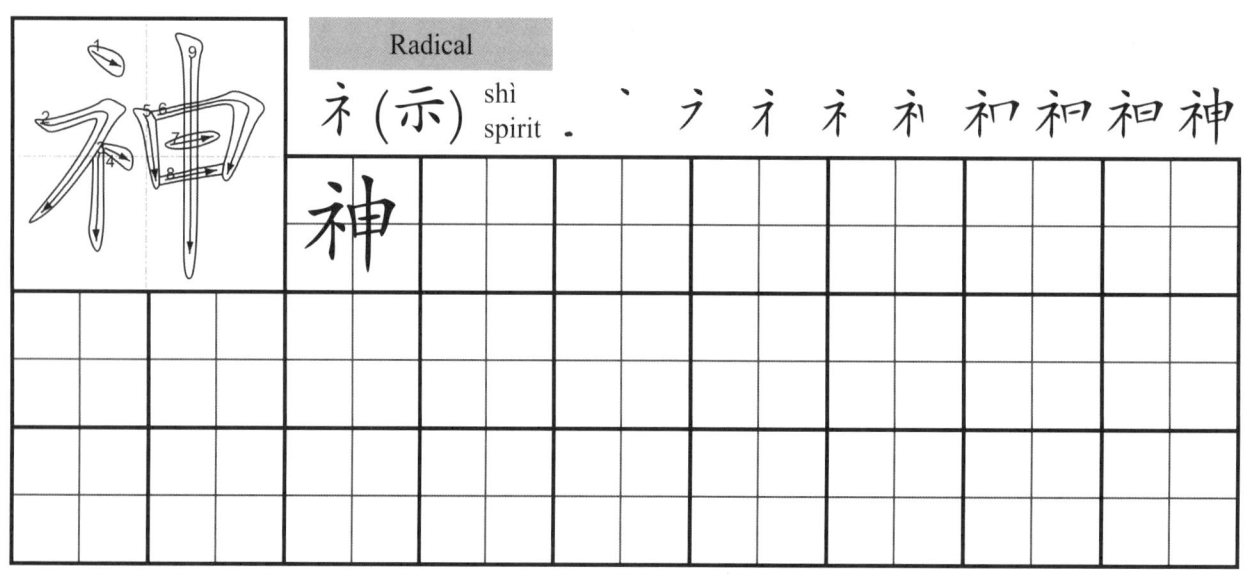

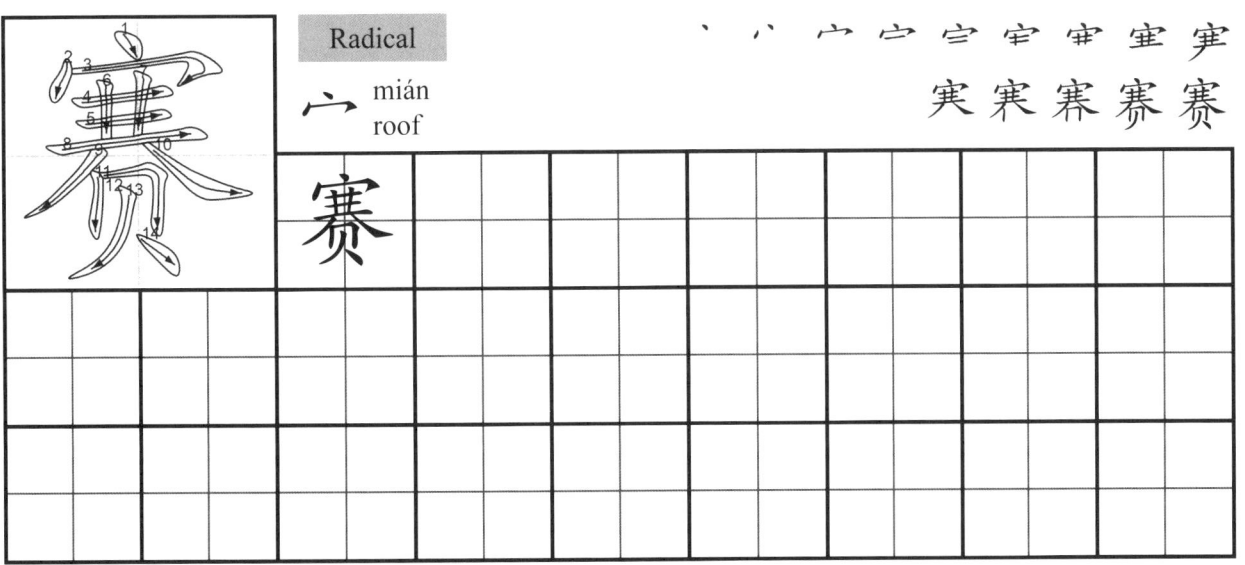

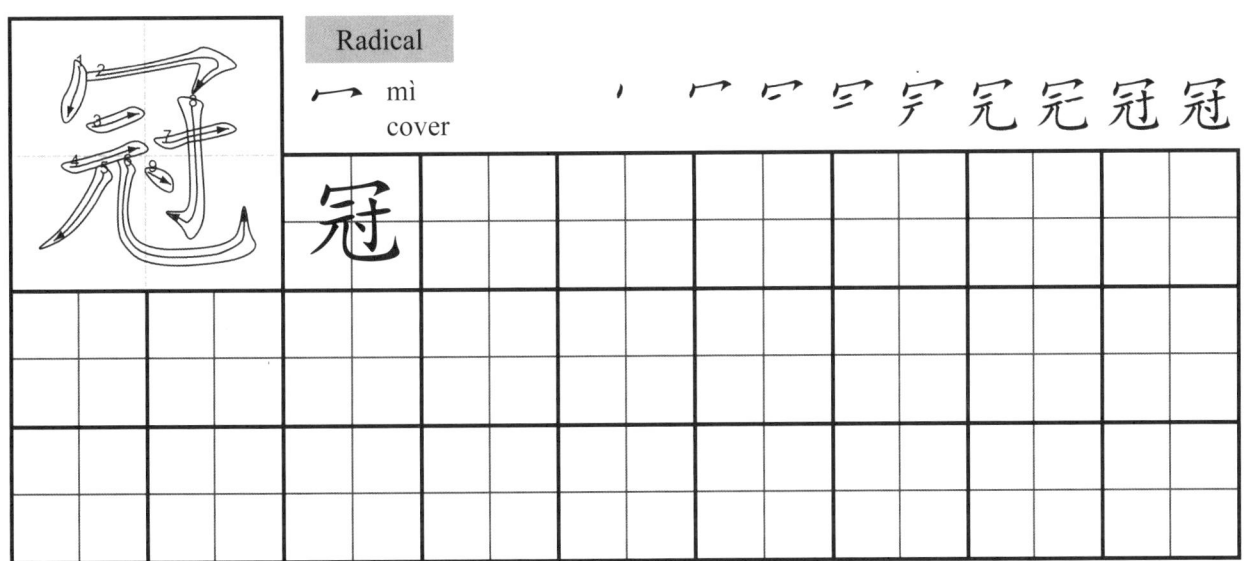

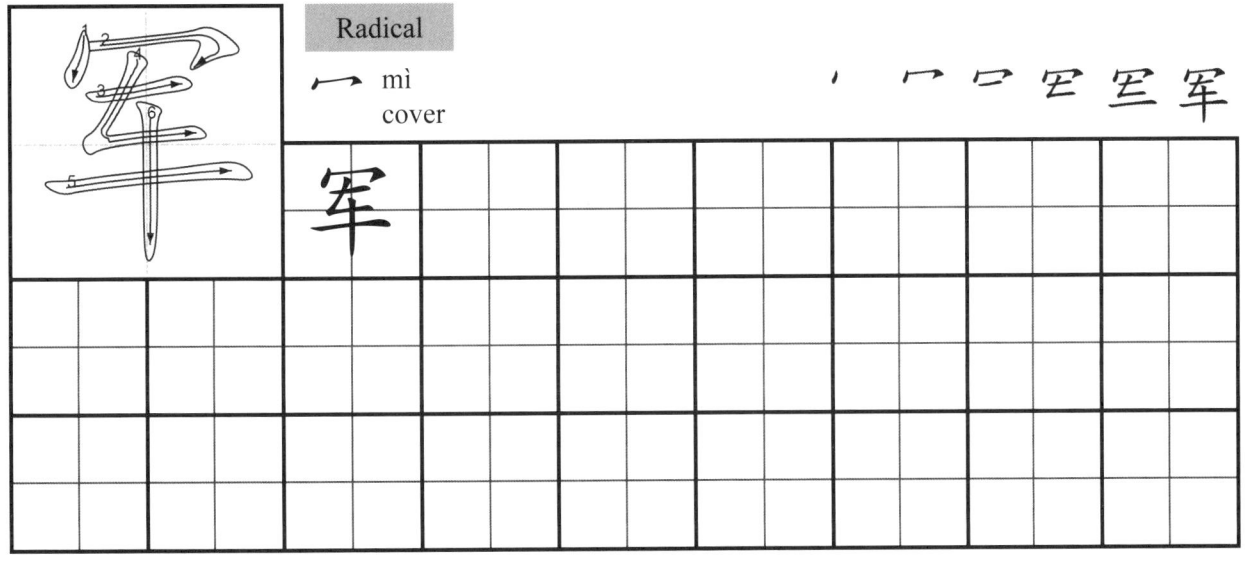

Unit 5 · Lesson 1 · Hobbies

LISTENING COMPREHENSION 5.1

I. Listen to the recording and select the best response below.

1. The woman would most likely respond with:

   A. 与其说是运气不好，倒不如说是咱们实力不强。
   B. 依我看不是裁判的问题，是配合的问题。
   C. 只不过是我们的球队里没有明星而已。
   D. 另外一个球迷也说，每次犯规裁判都吹哨了。

II. Listen to the recording and answer the following True or False questions:

1. (　) The man and the woman got a chance to watch the game together.
2. (　) The woman knows the team very well.
3. (　) According to the woman, both the team captain and the coach are very capable.
4. (　) The man believes that having team spirit is the key to winning a game.
5. (　) The woman will not treat the man to a meal today.

III. Listen to the recording and answer the questions in Chinese.

1. What was special about today's competition?

2. For what reason does Xiang'an believe he lost the match today? For what reason does the coach believe Xiang'an lost the match today?

3. The coach said that Xiang'an lost because he "输给了自己." What does this mean?

SPEAKING PRACTICE 5.1

I. You are sports fans and plan to attend an upcoming basketball game between the Black Bears and Mountain Lions. Using the chart below with some facts about each team, predict which team is likely to win and why.

黑熊	<ul><li>3个明星</li><li>跑得快，跳得高</li><li>去年的冠军</li><li>受欢迎</li><li>打了10场，赢了7场</li></ul>
山猫	<ul><li>1个明星</li><li>队长实力很强</li><li>团队精神</li><li>明星教练</li><li>打了10场，赢了9场</li></ul>

II. Select a sports team you know and make a brief introduction about this team. Be sure to include five different facts about the team.

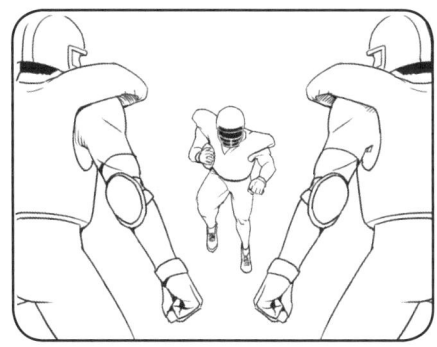

Unit 5 • Lesson 1 • Hobbies

STRUCTURE REVIEW 5.1

I. Complete the following Structure Note practice activities.

Structure Note 5.1: Use 另外 to talk about additional items

> 另外 (+ Numeral + Measure Word) + Noun / Phrase

A. Below is an ad for an electronic appliance store. Rewrite the sentences by adding 另外.

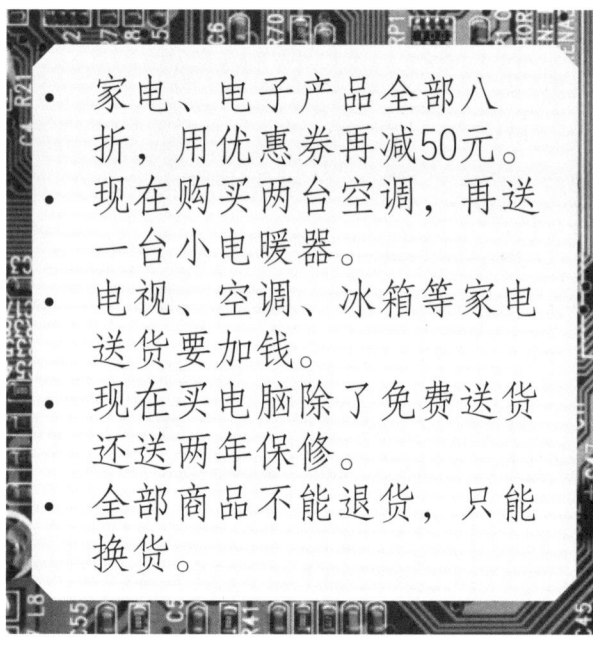
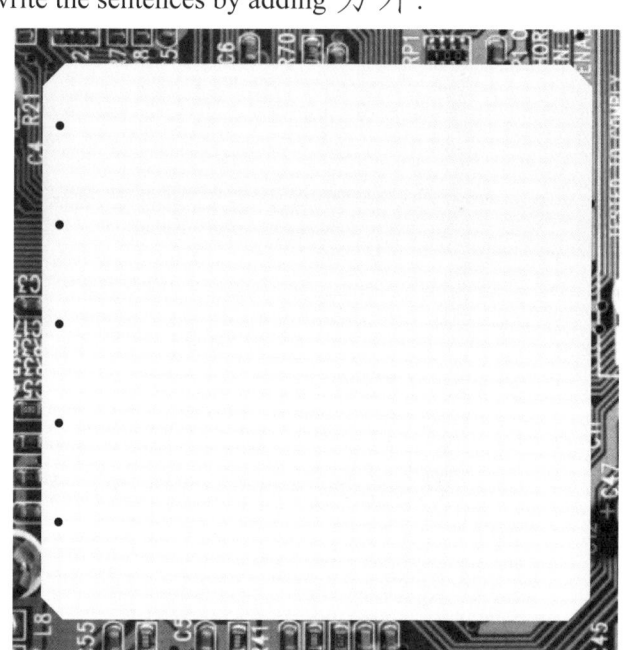

- 家电、电子产品全部八折，用优惠券再减50元。
- 现在购买两台空调，再送一台小电暖器。
- 电视、空调、冰箱等家电送货要加钱。
- 现在买电脑除了免费送货还送两年保修。
- 全部商品不能退货，只能换货。

Structure Note 5.2: Use (只)不过……而已 to minimize the significance of something.

> Subject (+只) + 不过 + Verb Phrase + 而已

B. You are the coach of a basketball team and your players have expressed some concerns below. Rewrite your responses to them by using 不过……而已.

Example: 球员："教练，山猫队的球员跑得非常快！"
教练："打篮球要像我们跳得高才有用。"
<u>山猫队的球员不过跑得非常快而已，打篮球要像我们跳得高才有用。</u>

1. 球员："教练，山猫队的队长实力非常强！"
   教练："我们球员的实力比较平均。"

2. 球员："教练，我们刚刚又被裁判吹哨了！"
   教练："我们小心不要再犯规就好了。"

   _____

3. 球员："教练，山猫队上半场运气非常好，每次都进三分球。"
   教练："我们下半场配合得好一点也是会有机会赢的。"

   _____

Structure Note 5.3: Use 与其…(倒)不如… to indicate a preferred alternative.

$$\boxed{\text{与其 + Clause, (+ 倒) 不如 + Clause}}$$

$$\boxed{\text{Subject + 与其 + Verb Phrase, (+ 倒) 不如 + Verb Phrase}}$$

C. Below is a set of options for various preferences and their alternatives. Write sentences using 与其…(倒)不如… to express your preferred choice between each pair.

	选项1	选项2
1.	考试前才复习	平时多做准备
2.	打工慢慢赚钱	自己开公司赚大钱
3.	花钱健身	花钱买药吃
4.	从书本上学习知识	出门旅游赚生活经验

1. _____

2. _____

3. _____

4. _____

Structure Note 5.4: Use 依……看 to formally express someone's opinion

$$\boxed{\text{依 + Someone + 看, Sentence}}$$

D. Below are some trends nowadays. Provide your opinion on each topic by using 依我看.

1. 你认为现代人为什么都比较晚才结婚？

2. 为什么越来越多年轻人都迷上了线上游戏？

3. 为什么明星都喜欢用名牌东西？

4. 你觉得现在的人是不是越来越重视环境保护了？

Take the challenge! 动动脑筋！

In this lesson, you learned to use 依 in the fixed pattern 依+someone+看 to introduce a person's view or opnion on a matter. The meaning of 依 in this structure is extracted from the phrase 依照 (yīzhào), which means "according to," "judging by," or "in light of." For example, "依你看，这件事该怎么办？"

Alternatively, 依 can be used in a manner to mean that someone or something must adhere or follow certain criteria, standards, or set ways, such as paying taxes according to the law, carrying out acts according to the contract, or taking action in the way that you are used to. Can you guess the meaning of the following sentence?

依这里的退货条件，特价商品不得退换。

II. You are a school advisor and a student comes to you to discuss some challenges he is facing in school. Respond by using the structure notes you learned in this lesson.

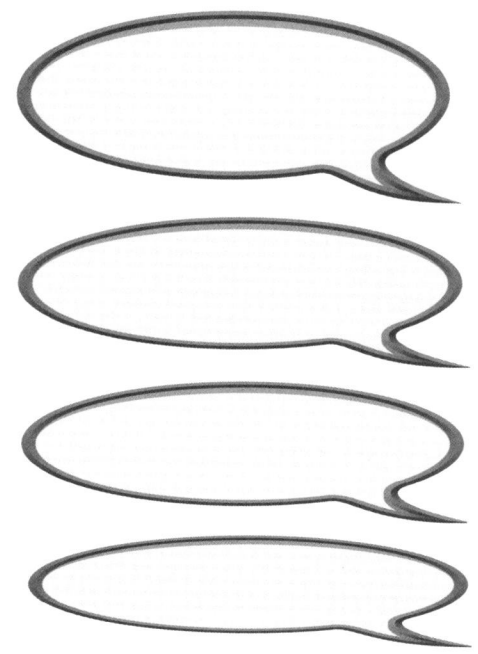

READING COMPREHENSION 5.1

I. Read the passage and answer the following True or False questions.

今天祥安看上去有点不高兴，中平和小美问他怎么了，祥安难过地说："昨天是我们篮球队这个赛季的第三场比赛。跟我们比赛的那个队实力没有我们强，我们的队里有好几个很厉害的明星球员，大家都觉得这场比赛我们赢定了！没想到最后我们输给了他们！气死我了！"

小美听祥安这么一说，笑着对祥安说："你看你，只不过是一场比赛而已，不要这么生气！"

中平问："比赛最后的比分是多少？"

祥安说："结束前一分钟我们还赢着，比分是85:80。可是因为我们队犯规，裁判吹哨，最后他们就……就反败为胜，赢了我们一分，一分啊！"

"真可惜！是谁犯规了？"中平问。

"是……是我。"

"裁判说你犯规你觉得不公平吗？"小美问。

祥安过了半天才说："是有点不公平，不过这场比赛我们确实输了。与其说是裁判不公平，倒不如说是我们运气不好。"

中平认真地告诉祥安："这个赛季才刚开始，明天不是就有另外一场比赛吗？我们大家都知道，你们这个队打球配合得好，大家都有团队精神，教练又特别棒。再说，你们的队长人长得像电影明星一样帅，球打得像NBA明星一样酷。依我看，冠军一定是你们的！"

小美也说："对，我一直是你的球迷，你是最棒的。加油加油！"

1. (　) 祥安昨天有三场篮球比赛。
2. (　) 祥安的篮球队昨天输了球，比分是85:80。
3. (　) 祥安觉得昨天比赛的裁判不太公平，而且他们的运气不好。
4. (　) 中平很了解祥安的篮球队，觉得他们实力很强。
5. (　) 中平和小美都觉得祥安篮球队的队长很棒。

Take the challenge! 动动脑筋！

半天 literally means "half a day." For example, the sentence 他今天上班上了半天就下班了 means "he only worked half a day today." However, 半天 can have different meanings depending on the situation or feeling of a sentence.

半天 can be used to describe "quite a while" or "a long time." For example, 他半天说不出话来. Sometimes, 老 is added before 半天 to create an adjective phrase meaning "a very long time." For example, 他在这里已经等了老半天了.

Another phrase using 半天 is 一天半天, which usually means "approximately half a day." For example, 这件事太难做了，不是一天半天就能做出来.

Can you guess what 半天 means in the passage above?

II. Read the following passage and answer the questions.

朱淑娟(Zhū Shū-juān)老奶奶今年七十六岁，只有一米五的个子。朱奶奶性格很开朗，她打篮球已经有二十多年了。你相信吗？她平时每天都会认真地练习投篮，而且一般最少一百遍。难怪朱奶奶投篮那么厉害，差不多是百发百中，她是很多人心中的篮球明星。她说："以前当我上学的时候，就与篮球"一见如故"。我对篮球特别有兴趣，一天到晚就喜欢看男孩子打篮球，也希望自己能跟男孩子一起打球。"可惜那时候大家都认为女孩子打球是很不合适的，所以朱奶奶一直没有机会打球。

现在的她虽然没有很多钱，但是她很快乐。她从决定开始打篮球到现在，一共有三个篮球。第一个篮球很便宜，十几块钱。但是有一天，篮球丢了，再也找不回来。为了买第二个篮球，她攒钱攒了很久，第二个球花了她三百块左右。用了几年以后，又不能用了。然后朱奶奶又开始攒钱，一个月后，她又买了一个满意的新篮球，这次要五百多块钱呢！这个篮球朱奶奶一直用到现在。

朱奶奶住在金华市(Jinhua City)。如果你正好去金华旅游，在篮球场上看到一个开心地练习投篮的老人，那说不定就是她了，我们的奶奶冠军——朱淑娟！

Notes:

奶奶 (nǎinai): *n.* granny
投篮 (tóulán): *vo.* to shoot (a basket)
攒 (zǎn): *v.* to save
百发百中 (bǎifābǎizhòng): *ie.* every shot hits the target
丢 (diū): *v.* to lose

1. 朱淑娟老奶奶……

   A. 已经七十多岁了，个子不太高。
   B. 五十岁左右开始练习打篮球。
   C. 从做学生的时候就迷上了篮球。
   D. 上面A, B 和 C都说得都对。

2. Why did she not have a chance to play basketball when she was a student?

   A. There were not any students playing basketball in her school.
   B. It was not considered appropriate for girls to play basketball at that time.
   C. She did not have money to buy basketballs.
   D. She was not good at shooting basketballs at the time.

3. 为什么我们叫朱奶奶"奶奶冠军"？

   A. 因为她实力很强，比赛的时候常常赢。
   B. 因为她投篮很厉害，也买了很多篮球。
   C. 因为她虽然七十多岁了，但是篮球还打得这么棒。
   D. 因为她是金华市篮球比赛的冠军。

Take the challenge! 动动脑筋！

中 has two pronounciations; one is zhòng, which means "to hit (a target)," In the passage above, you discovered that the 中 in 百发百中 means "every shot hits the target." Can you guess, then, what 我中了奖 means?

In *Modern Chinese* Textbook Vol. 1B, Unit 9, Lesson 1, we learned 中 can be pronounced as zhōng, which means "middle or center." However, with this pronunciation, 中 can be also used to express "in" or "among."

See the following sentences as examples:

在今天比赛中，我们学到团队精神的重要性。
In today's compeition, we learned about the importance of team spirit.

在我们三个中，只有他一个会打篮球。
"Among the three of us, only he knows how to play basketball."

In the above passage, look for the word 中. Can guess its meaning?

III. Read the following email and answer the questions.

To:	张小丽
From:	李小东
Subject:	篮球比赛门票

小丽：
　　今天是热火队对飞船队的篮球比赛**门票开售**的日子，我们现在就可以打12580**订票**了，当然也可以上网到这个网站（http://jf.10086.cn/）用信用卡的**积分**来换**门票**。今年热火队和飞船队在北京和**上海**都有比赛，时间**分别**是10月11日晚上7点和10月14日中午12点。北京离我近一点，你坐火车来应该也挺快的。票的最低价格是300元，最高是1000元。因为这次票比较紧张，很多人都想去看，我们很可能只能坐到最后面的或者是买最贵的票，1000块啊！我付不起。那样的话只能下次再去看球赛了。
　　　　　　　　　　　　　　　　　　　　　　　　　　小东

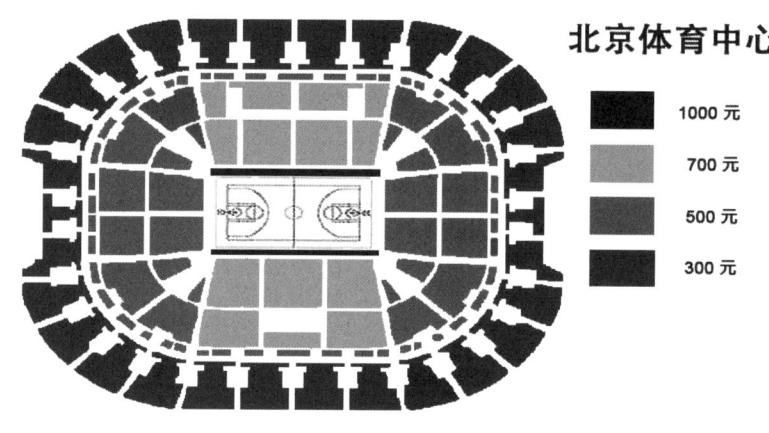

北京体育中心
- 1000 元
- 700 元
- 500 元
- 300 元

Notes:
门票 (ménpiào): *n.* entrance ticket, admission ticket
开售 (kāishòu): *v.* to go on sale
订票 (dìngpiào): *v.* to book a ticket
积分 (jīfēn): *n.* accumulate scores or points
分别 (fēnbié): *adj.* respective

Proper Noun:
上海 (Shànghǎi): *n.* Shanghai

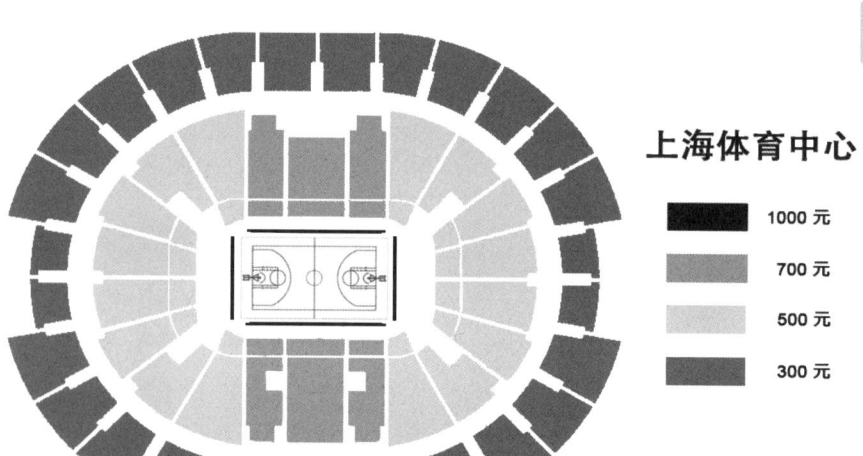

上海体育中心
- 1000 元
- 700 元
- 500 元
- 300 元

1. Briefly describe different ways for purchasing a ticket.

   _____

2. What time do the competitions in Beijing and Shanghai start?

   _____

3. If Xiaoli and Xiaodong are not able to purchase any tickets or if the only tickets left are the most expensive ones, what will they do?

   _____

4. Looking at the two seating charts from the stadiums in Beijing and Shanghai, circle the area of seats that Xiaoli and Xiaodong are likley to purchase.

   _____

WRITING PRACTICE 5.1

I. You have a pair of tickets to an upcoming soccer match between two teams that are well-matched. You want to invite your friend to go watch, however, she/he does not know much about soccer. Write an email to your friend with an invitation to the game and persuade him/her to come. Explain how you believe the game will be exciting, how the two teams compare to each other, and which team you are rooting for.

_____

_____

_____

_____

_____

_____

_____

II. Below is a sequence of images telling a story. Use the details in the images to write a short paragraph about what you think is happening in each image. Be sure to include a beginning and ending and that the story flows from one image to the next.

UNIT 5 – LESSON 2

Modern Chinese 现代中文

采访

VOCABULARY REVIEW 5.2

I. Choose at least five nouns from the word box to match each measure word.

```
乐器 碗筷 大衣 录音机 精神
记者 电影 帽子 牌子 公寓 原因
洗衣机 评委 形式 相机 京剧 手机 球员
演奏 裁判 才艺 西装 球赛 电视
观众 家具 功夫 表演 冰箱
```

1. 名 _____ 2. 套 _____

3. 种 _____ 4. 场 _____

5. 款 _____ 6. 台 _____

II. Each pair of characters are missing the same radical. Using the radicals in the box, determine which one would fit each pair and write the complete characters and pinyin.

```
刂  艹  禾  欠  讠  彡  心
```

Example: 争 <u>筝</u> (zhēng)   相 <u>箱</u> (xiāng)   1. 犾 ___ ( )   乙 ___ ( )

2. 女 ___ ( )   中 ___ ( )   3. 开 ___ ( )   页 ___ ( )

4. 平 ___ ( )   方 ___ ( )   5. 斤 ___ ( )   兼 ___ ( )

6. 亡 ___ ( )   咸 ___ ( )   7. 戈 ___ ( )   干 ___ ( )

III. Replace the underlined phrases with appropriate vocabulary words from this lesson.

昨天的大学篮球冠军赛，(1.)<u>来看比赛的人</u>差不多全部都是支持飞鸟队的。赛前飞鸟队的球员都相信自己球队可以(2.)<u>得到</u>这次大赛的冠军，可惜最后还是输了给黑熊队。记者(3.)<u>问</u>了飞鸟队的队长，他说："只不过是输了一场比赛而已，我不会因为输了就(4.)<u>不再打篮球的</u>。"他也告诉记者说他有一个(5.)<u>希望</u>，就是有一天他可以和(6.)<u>一起打球的球员们</u>参加全明星大赛。

Unit 5 · Lesson 2 · Hobbies **149**

CHARACTER WRITING PRACTICE 5.2

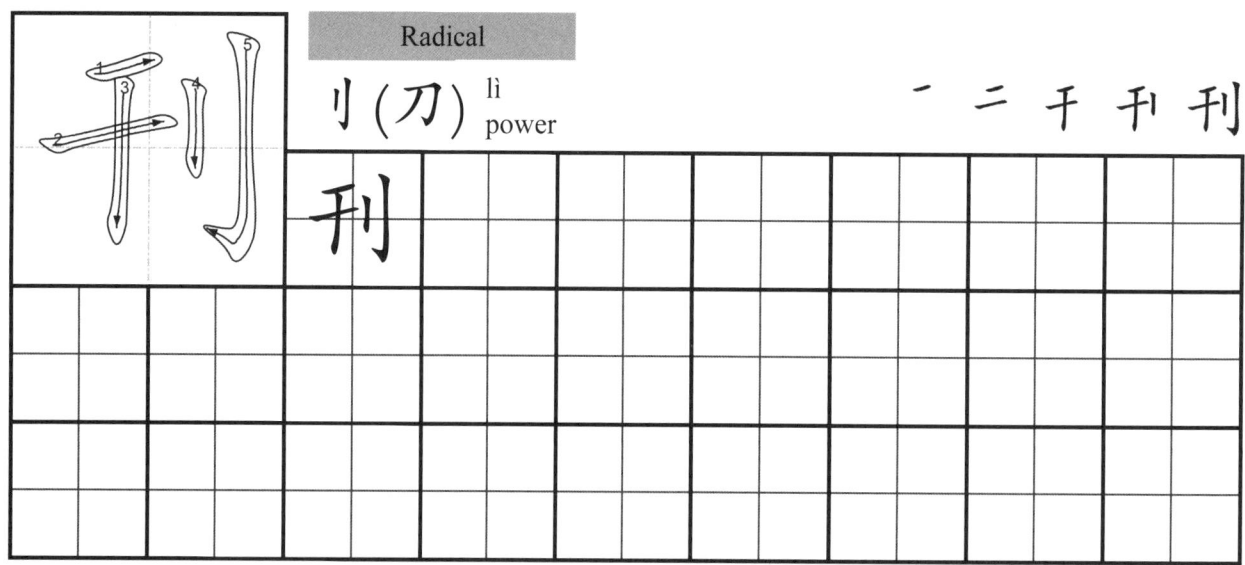

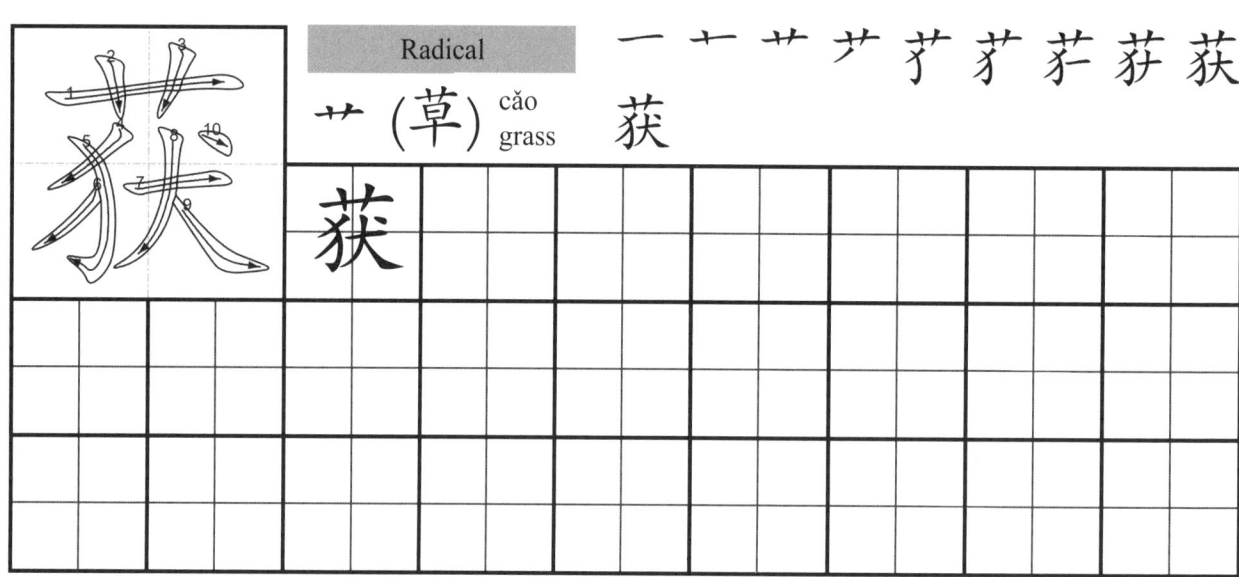

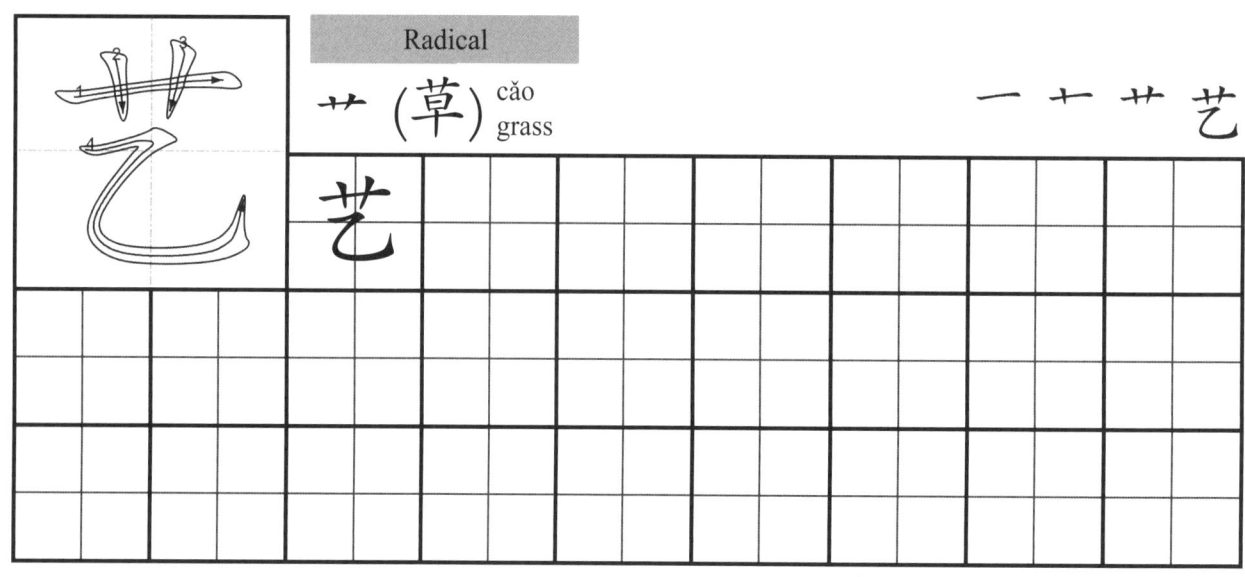

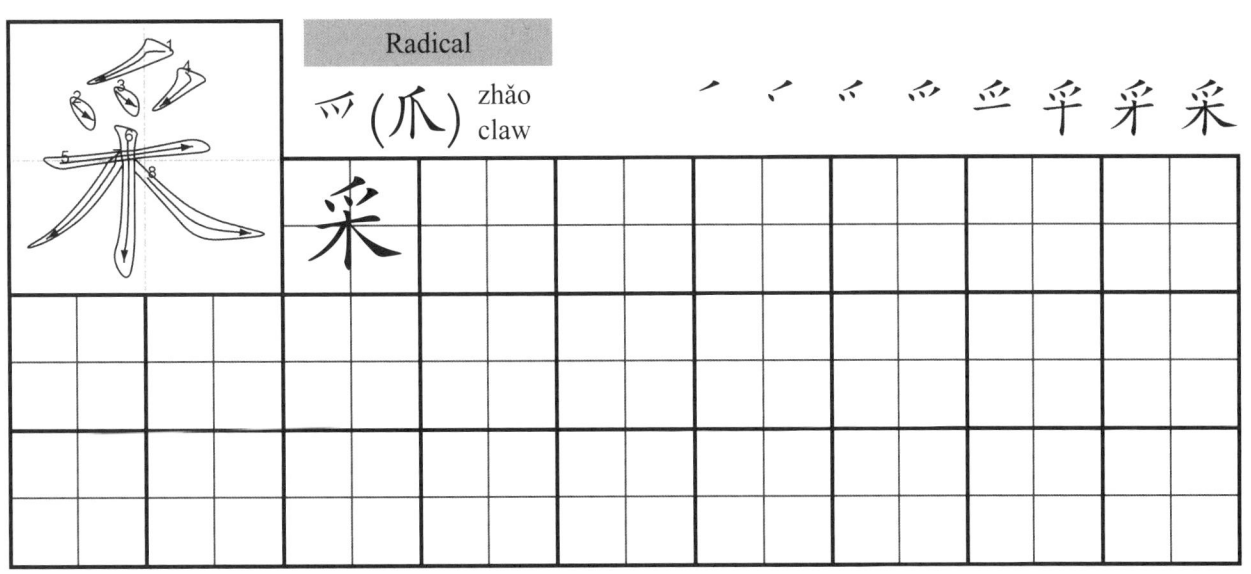

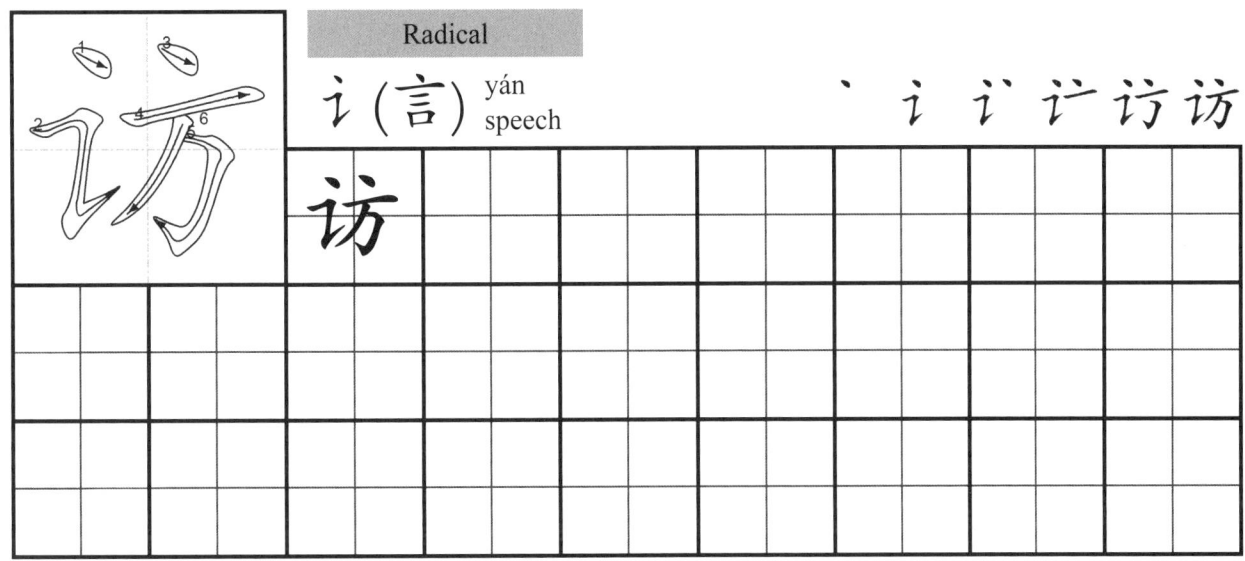

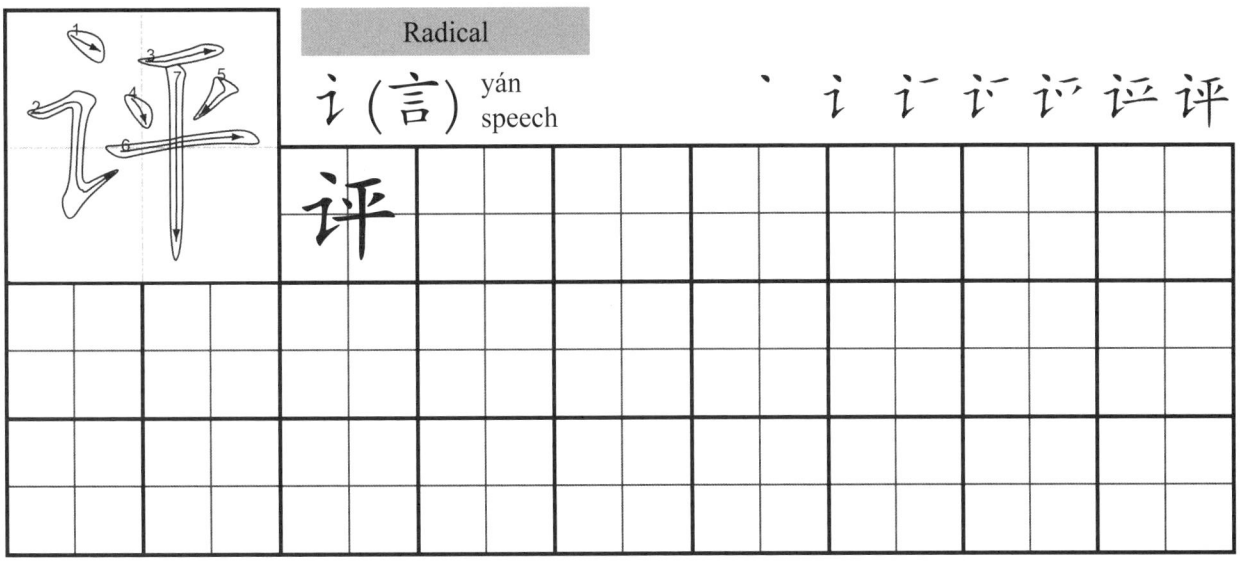

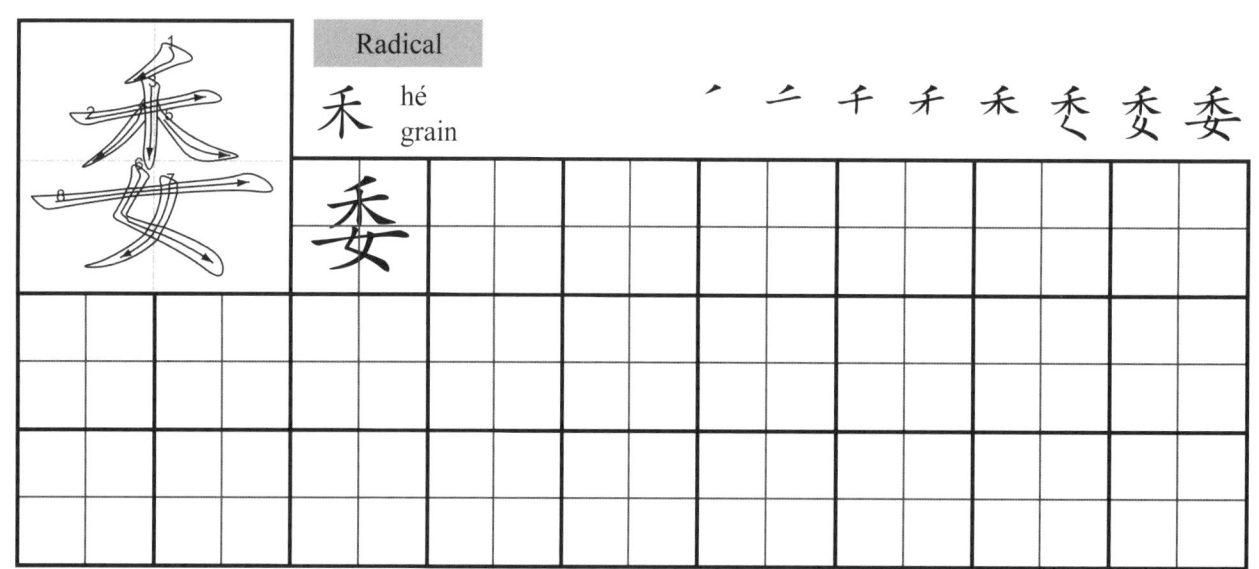

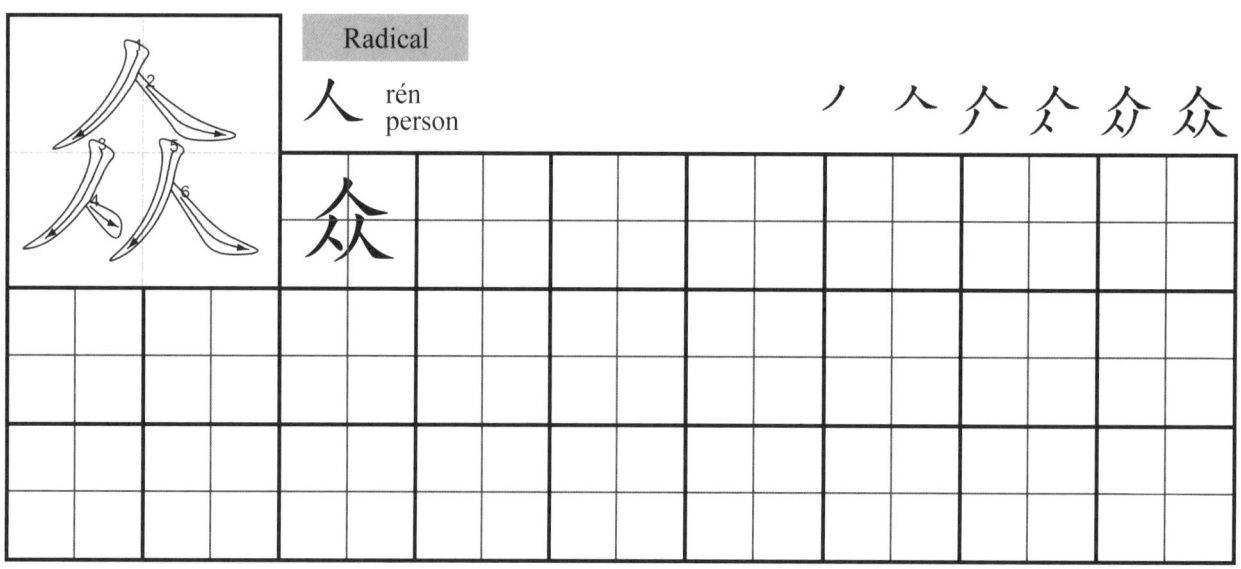

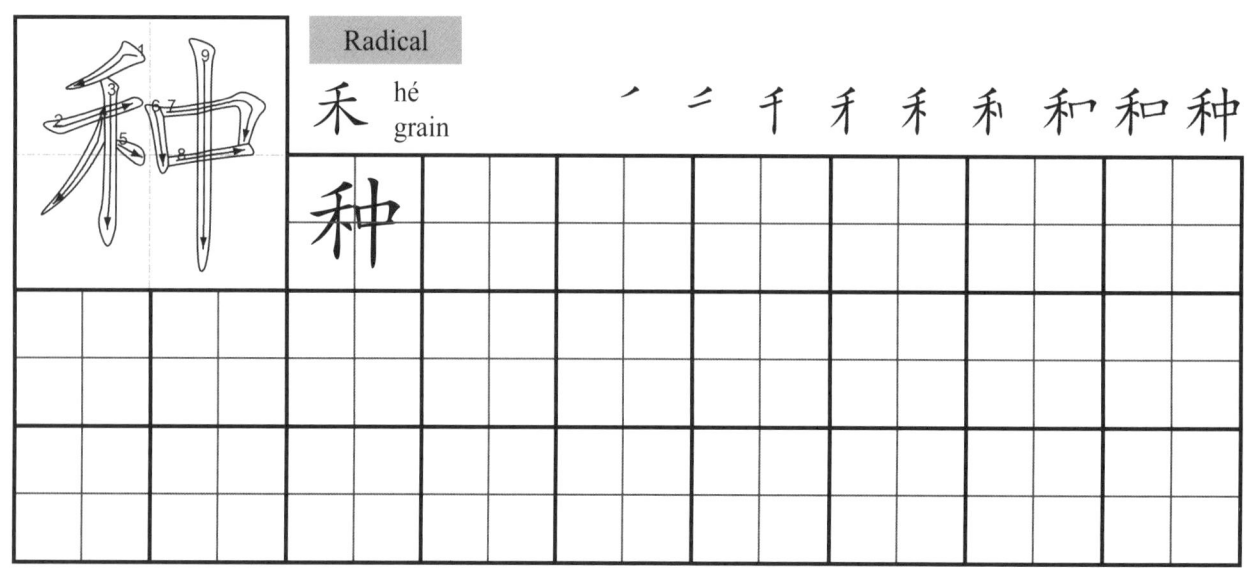

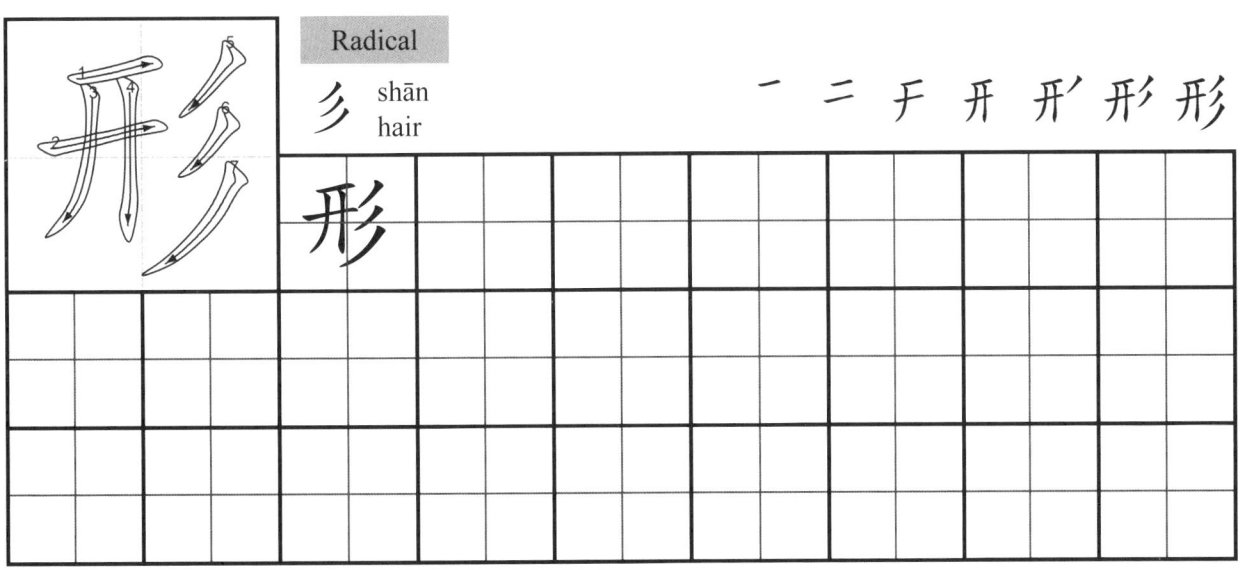

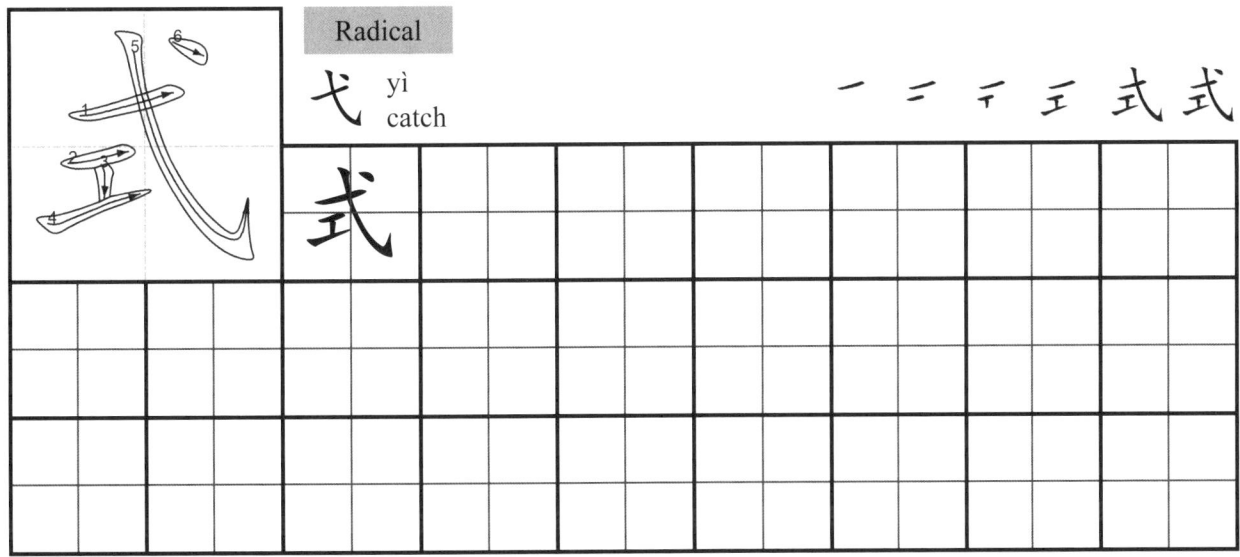

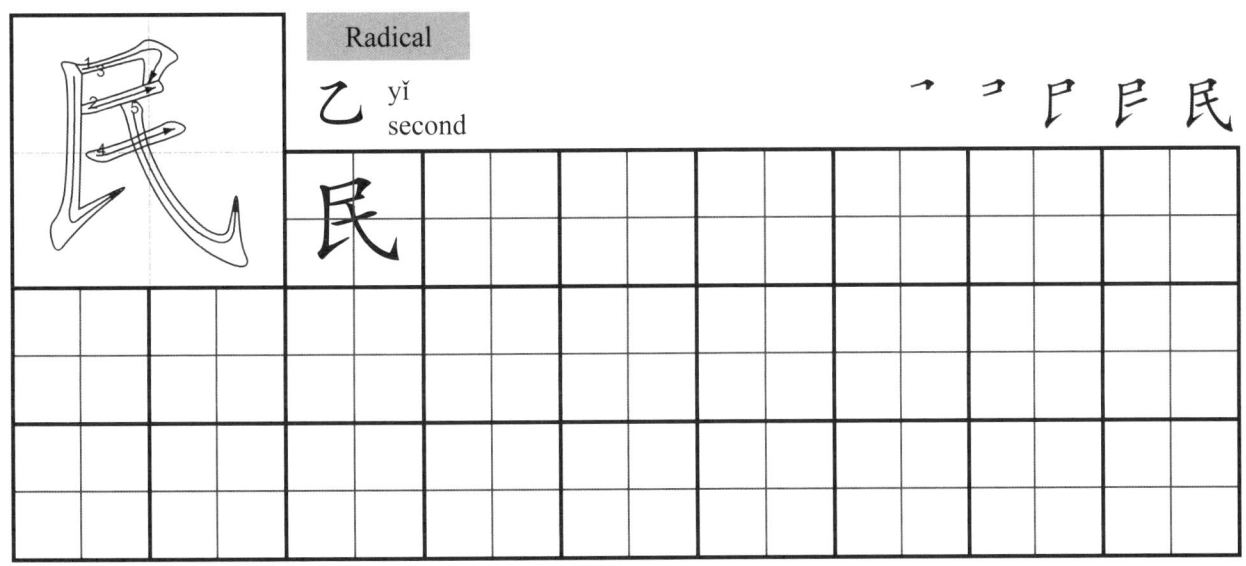

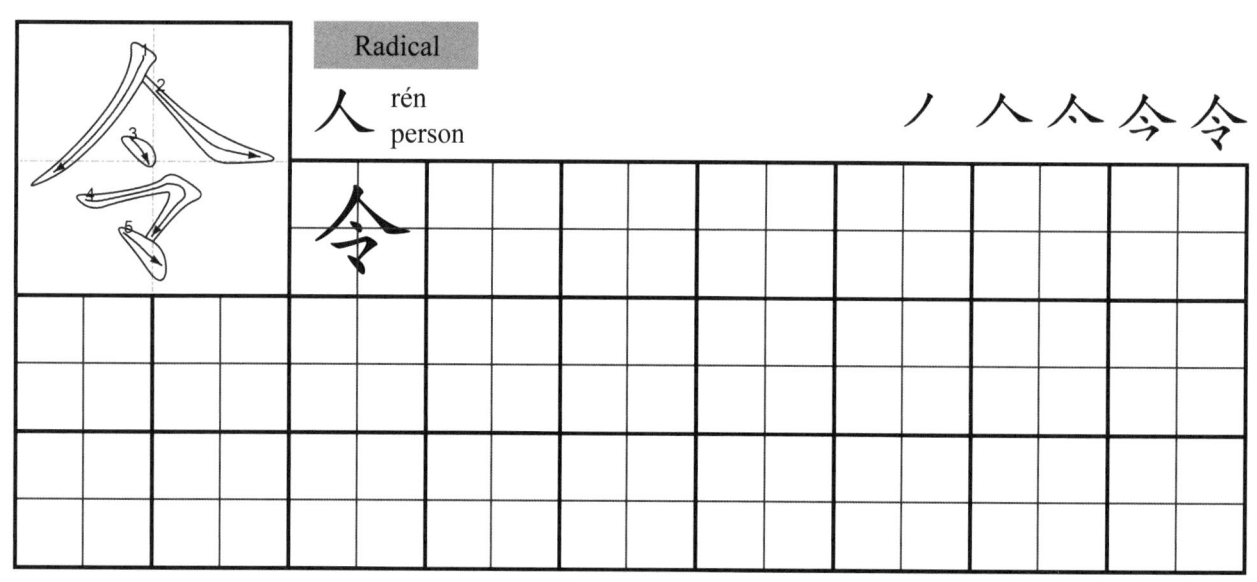

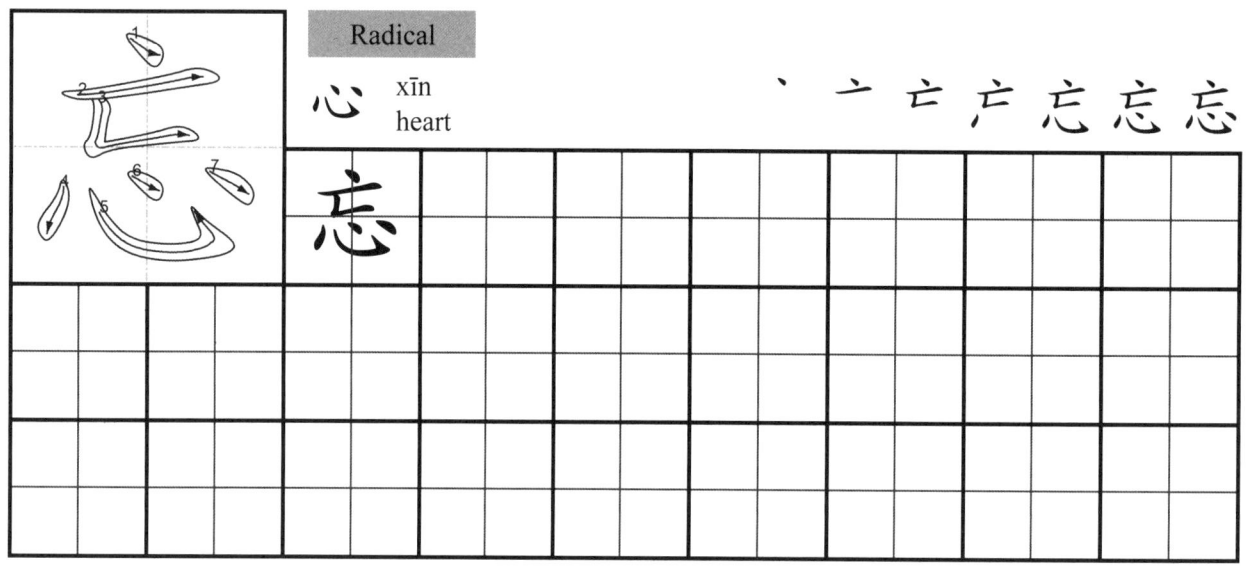

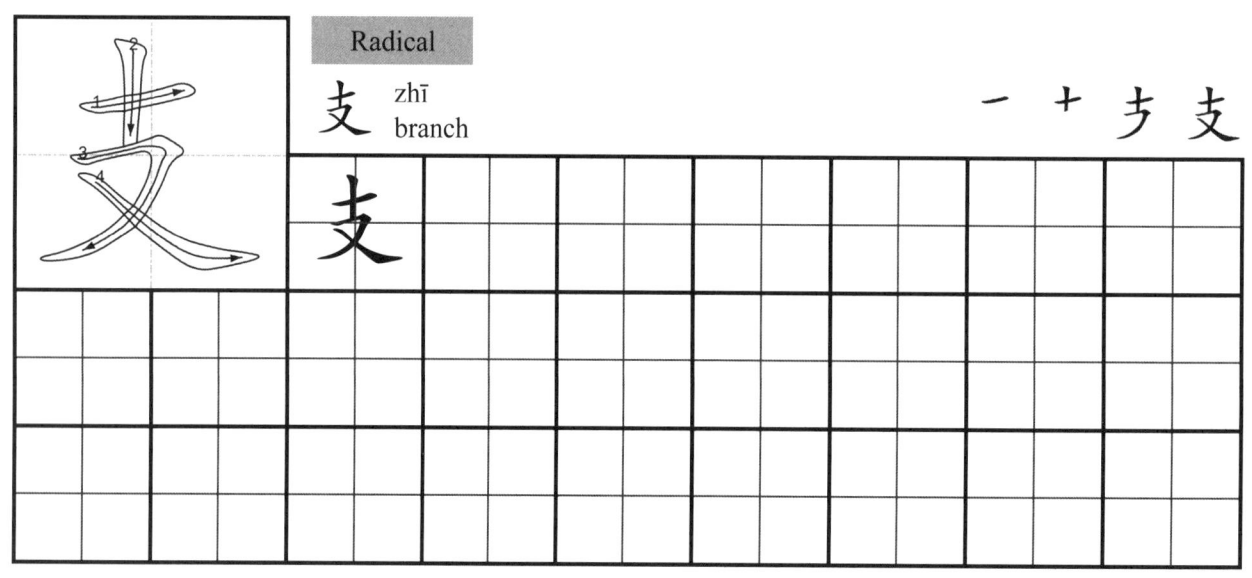

LISTENING COMPREHENSION 5.2

I. **Listen to the recording and select the best response below.**

1. The woman would most likely respond with:

   A. 像这样中西结合的演奏是很特别的，我建议你去听听。
   B. 这个乐队多才多艺，他们几个伙伴常常一起表演。
   C. 依我看，这个乐队参加才艺比赛一定能获得第一名！
   D. 上次的民乐音乐会不如这次的音乐会受观众欢迎。

II. **Listen to the recording and answer the following True or False questions.**

1. (　) Both the man and the woman went to the concert last night.
2. (　) The man really enjoyed the guzheng performance.
3. (　) The man had a chance to read a newspaper review about the concert.
4. (　) The woman agreed on the man's comments about the concert.
5. (　) The woman and the man are dating now.

III. **Listen to the recording and answer the questions in Chinese.**

1. What kind of competition did Zhongping and Mali participate in?

   _____

2. What kind of preparations did Zhongping and Mali make in order to participate in this competition?

   _____

3. Why did Zhongping give a special thank you to Mali?

   _____

SPEAKING PRACTICE 5.2

I. You are a DJ for your school's radio station. A student at your school recently won a musical competition and you want to talk about this on your radio show. Provide (A) a short recap of the event and (B) a short description about the competition winner. Use the information and list of example discussion points below to help formulate your talk.

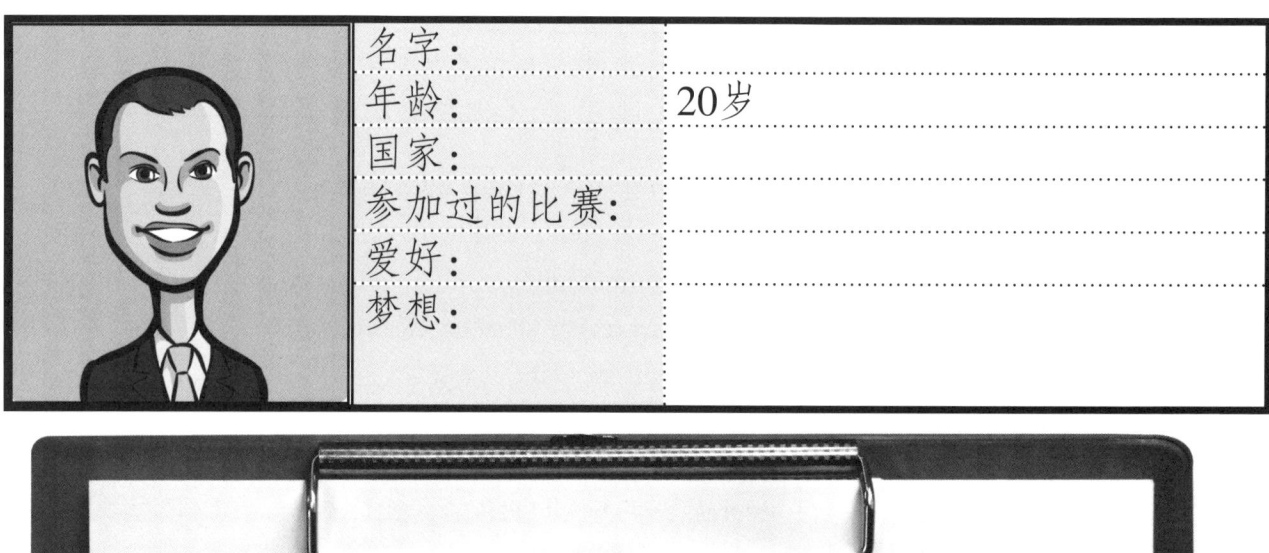

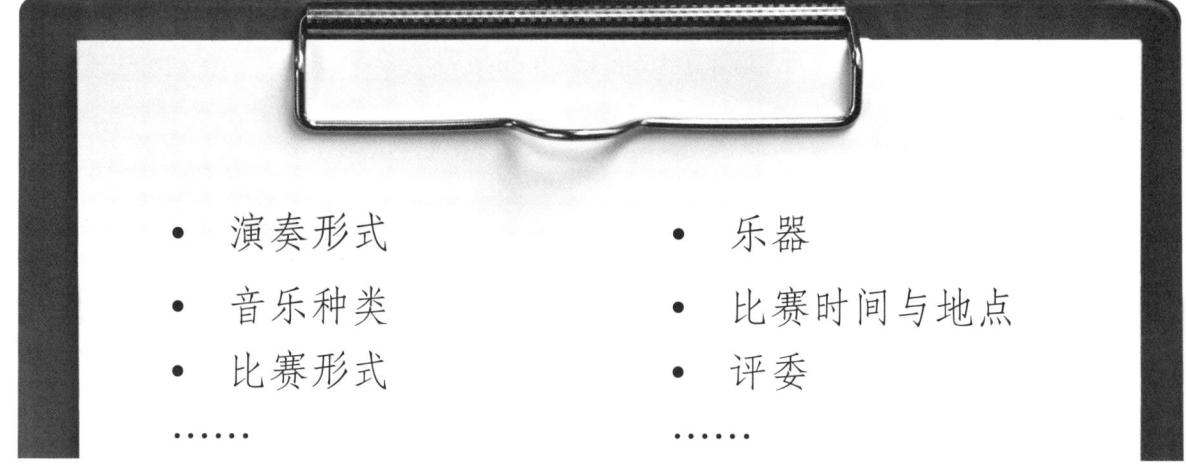

II. You have an idea for holding your own school competition. Describe your event, including the name of your competition, what kind of competition you will hold, when and where you want to have it, what prizes winners will receive, who will be the judges, etc.

STRUCTURE REVIEW 5.2

I. Complete the following Structure Note practice activities.

Structure Note 5.5: Use 来自 to indicate a place or origin.

$$\boxed{来自 + \text{Location}}$$

A. Read the following passage and answer the questions by using 来自.

> 平东是北京音乐学校的学生。这里的学生都是从中国各地来的。今年，学校请了一位非常厉害的音乐家来教音乐，他在法国非常有名，常常开演奏会。为了招募不同国家的人加入他的乐团，他常常到不同地方的学校教音乐。这次，平东和另外两位学生被他选中加入他的乐团，平东他们也获得学校的老师和学生们的支持。

1. 今年学校请到的音乐家是什么人？
   _____

2. 为什么这位音乐家常常到不同的地方教音乐？
   _____

3. 乐团的团员都是从什么国家来的？
   _____

4. 这次被选中的三位是哪个学校的学生？
   _____

Structure Note 5.6: Use 收到 to express obtaining physical objects and 受到 to indicate receiving abstract concepts.

$$\boxed{\text{Subject} + 收到 + \text{Object}}$$

$$\boxed{\text{Subject} + 受到 + \text{Object}}$$

B. The following is an interview. Fill in the blanks with 收/受.

记者：最近我们(1.)___到很多观众的来信，都是想多了解山猫队球员。我们今天很高兴请到山猫队的队长王中兴。欢迎您！

记者：首先，恭喜您获得最(2.)___欢迎篮球员，您有什么想对你球迷说的话吗？

队长：我要感谢我的球迷，我也没想到我们球队会(3.)___到那么多球迷的欢迎和喜爱。

记者：您今年换到新球队，您觉得跟以前有什么不同的地方吗？

队长：换了球队以后我觉得自己(4.)___到了重视，而且这个球队的团队精神都非常好。

记者：那现在您(5.)___到这么多球迷的注意会不习惯吗？

队长：我还是不太习惯(6.)___到这么多的礼物，我觉得球迷们来看我们的比赛我就已经很高兴了。

记者：那希望球迷们会一直支持你们。祝你们球队在全国大赛上获得冠军。

队长：谢谢！

Structure Note 5.7: Use 令 to express making someone feel a certain way.

令 + Someone + Feeling Adjective

C. Create a survey containing questions about your classmates' preferences and experiences with regards to music using 令 and the word box below.

高兴 快乐 难过 生气 烦恼 担心 喜爱 难忘 满意 羡慕

Example: 谁唱歌最令你难忘？

1. _____
2. _____
3. _____
4. _____
5. _____

Take the challenge! 动动脑筋！

"我儿子常常很晚才回家，让我每天都很担心。"
"你不让他出去玩就好啦。"
"可是我不想当一个令儿子讨厌的妈妈，也不想让儿子难过。"
"唉，那还真令人烦恼！那你再生一个不会令你担心的儿子就好了。"

Both 令 and 让 mean making someone feel a certain way. However, 让 can alternatively mean "to allow" or "to let."

While 令 is a more formal term, it can replaced by 让 in sentences. For example, "真令人烦恼！" can become "真让人烦恼！"

However, the opposite is not always true, specifically when 让 is used to express "to let" or "to allow."

Reread the passage above. Can you tell which 让 can be replaced by 令？

Structure Note 5.8: Use (在) ……上 to introduce topics

> (在 +) Topic + 上 , + Sentence

> Subject (+ 在) + Topic + 上 + Verb Phrase

D. Rewrite the billboard ad below by using 在……上.

- 比全部的百货公司都要便宜。
- 质量是全国最好的。
- 包装保证一定令您满意。
- 每个售货员都非常有礼貌，把客人放到第一位。
- 不但送三年保修期，另外还送五十元购物优惠券。

Example: 在价钱上，我们商店的货品比全部的百货公司都要便宜。

- _____
- _____
- _____
- _____

II. Teacher's Day is coming up and to celebrate, your school is holding a writing contest that you will participate in. The topic for the competition is about: The teacher you would like to thank the most. Select a teacher, past or present, and write a short paragraph, including which school the teacher was from, whether the teacher is/was popular, and in which aspect you think the teacher influenced or helped you the most. Use the structure notes you learned in this lesson to help you write your paragraph.

我最想感谢的老师是……

READING COMPREHENSION 5.2

I. Read the passage and answer the following True or False questions.

杨冰冰最近认识了一个新朋友，叫周志。他是位多才多艺的音乐家，各种乐器都演奏得很不错。他和几个喜爱音乐的伙伴常常一起练习，他们的乐队有个名字，叫"梦想"。叫这个名字的原因是因为他们很希望能实现一个理想，那就是能把现代流行音乐和传统音乐完美地结合在一起。这个乐队参加过很多的音乐比赛，也获得过冠军。

上个月他们去欧洲比赛，与来自三十多个国家的音乐家一起参赛。他们表演的是中国的传统民乐，但是用的是小提琴、钢琴，配上吉他和古筝。评委和观众都说，这种新音乐形式十分有意思，令人难忘。最后，周志和伙伴们拿到了第二名！

"梦想"乐队也常在各个大学举办周末音乐会，非常受大学生们的喜爱和支持。冰冰在上个星期的音乐会上，第一次听到他们的音乐就非常欣赏，所以表演完后冰冰就走过去认识了他们。她问周志："你们的乐队现在这么受欢迎，你最感谢谁呢？"周志说："我觉得乐队今天的成功是因为我运气好，能认识到这么好的伙伴。我们也有过很多令人头疼和烦恼的事，但是每一次我的伙伴们都告诉我不要放弃，所以我真的是从心里感谢他们。"

1. (　　) 杨冰冰和周志认识很久了，他们是在周末音乐会上认识的。
2. (　　) 周志的乐队里有很多种乐器，他们的表演很特别。
3. (　　) 除了中国的传统民乐，周志他们也会演奏西方乐器。
4. (　　) 因为比赛拿到了第二名，所以周志的乐队的名字叫梦想。
5. (　　) 周志觉得他们的乐队这么受欢迎，应该感谢乐队里的各位音乐家。

Take the challenge! 动动脑筋!

In the *Modern Chinese* Textbook Vol. 2A, Unit 5, Lesson 2, Lesson Text and the previous passage, you discovered that there are a lot of phrases to express "winning a championship." 获得 and 赢得 were both introduced in the Lesson Text. In these phrases, 得 means "get" and it can act independently as a verb too to express "obtaining." For example, 他得冠军了. Without 得, 获 and 赢 can also each act as independent verbs. As seen in the previous passage, 拿冠军 is another phrase similar to 获得 and 赢得 that means "take the championship." Apart from generally expressing "winning a championship," you will discover that these verbs can be used in many situations to express "to gain," "to achieve," "to get," or "to obtain." Look at the following examples. Can you guess what they each mean?

冠军能赢得一台电视机。

今年没有拿到奖学金。

我上星期得了感冒。

希望这次活动可以得到大家的支持。

这位音乐家获过哪些奖？

II. Read the following passage and answer the questions.

　　大家都知道，现在在中国，由于**家长**对孩子的希望越来越高，所以越来越多的孩子从很小就开始学习才艺。可是很少有人知道他们学习几种和学习哪几种才艺，所以我和几个伙伴在我们附近的几个城市做了一个**调查**，我们的**调查结果**发现：

• 三岁之内的孩子中，有10%左右什么都没有学，大部分的孩子最少学了一种才艺。

• 三至六岁时，超过60%的孩子学了一**至**三种才艺。

• 六岁**以上**的孩子，学习三种才艺**以上**的人很多，学习六种**以上**才艺的孩子超过了38%。

　　另外，三岁以后，大部分的孩子都会学习包括画画，英语和跳舞在内的才艺。特别是六岁以后，学画画与英语的孩子就更多了。在音乐上，比较多的**家长**会给孩子选钢琴，并且小提琴也很受欢迎；在体育上，很多孩子会选游泳。

还有，六岁**以上**的，20%的孩子会学习书法。

Notes:
家长 (jiāzhǎng): n. parents
调查 (diàochá): n. research
结果 (jiéguǒ): n. result
至 (zhì): prep. to
以上 (yǐshàng): n. above

1. "我"和伙伴做这个调查的原因是……

    A. 想给自己的孩子找可以学习才艺的地方。
    B. 想了解现在孩子们学习才艺的情况。
    C. 想知道孩子应该从多大开始学才艺。
    D. 想请他们做这个调查的家长越来越多。

2. Based on the information in the blog post, which statement below is true?

    A. For the kids under three years old, about 10 percent of them have learned at least one kind of "talent and skill."
    B. With regards to sports, many kids choose to play basketball.
    C. Among kids older than three years old, painting, dancing and English are the most popular skills to learn.
    D. This research is a nation-wide project.

3. 调查结果是，小学生们……

    A. 最喜欢学的才艺是画画。
    B. 希望选跳舞的比较多。
    C. 学游泳的比学书法的多得多。
    D. 除了音乐以外，还学体育、英语、画画等等。

III. Read the two notices and answer the following questions.

通知（一）

各位朋友：

　　为了迎接十一长假和丰富大家的文娱生活，十月一日（星期日）晚七点半我社区将在**社区活动中心广场**举办一场才艺比赛。只要你会表演、会乐器、会唱歌或者会跳舞，就可以参加这个比赛。另外，获得冠军的参赛者更有机会与来自上海的名乐队一起表演。有意参赛的朋友们请在九月二十日之前来社区**办公室报名**。希望大家都能**踊跃报名**！

9月1日

通知（二）

各位朋友：

　　由于最近两天天气不太好，十月一日可能会下小雨，所以才艺比赛的**场地**会**改**到**社区活动中心**里面。请大家当天前来支持本次活动，谢谢！

9月28日

Notes:

社区活动中心广场 (shèqū huódòng zhōngxīn guǎngchǎng): n. Community center square

办公室 (bàngōngshì): n. office

报名 (bàomíng): v. to sign up

踊跃 (yǒngyuè): v. to leap

场地 (chǎngdì): n. place

改 (gǎi): v. to change

1. Describe the time and place of the competition.

2. What privelege do you receive if you are the champion of this competition?

3. What is the purpose of the second notice?

4. You play the erhu and want to join the competition. Where do you sign up? Circle this information on the notice above.

WRITING PRACTICE 5.2

I. You have the opportunity to interview the competition winner from Speaking Practice Exercise 1 on p. 156. Provide a transcript of that interview, including five of your questions, such as why the winner believes he won, whom he wants to thank, and what his future plans are, and the winner's answers.

Questions:	Answers:
1.	
2.	
3.	
4.	
5.	

II. You are a journalist for your school newspaper and attended the competition described in Speaking Practice Exercise 2 on p. 156. Write an article about the competition and provide enough detail so those that were unable to attend can relive the event through your article. Be sure to also include an article headline and the opinions of those who did see the show.

News·Today

"ALL THE NEWS YOU NEED TO KNOW"

MONDAY, OCTOBER 2012
Vol. MCMXX, No. 144672

— FOUNDED 1851 —

UNIT 6 — LESSON 1

Modern Chinese 现代中文

学做中国菜

VOCABULARY REVIEW 6.1

I. The following list is a recipe for making Hot and Sour Chicken. Using the image as a guide, fill in the blanks with appropriate measure words.

酸辣鸡丁准备材料

鸡肉300___
葱10___
油500___
盐2___
糖1___
淀粉20___
料酒1___
酸辣酱1/2___

II. The characters in the box are common words found in recipes. Determine the correct radical for each character and write it under the radical.

1. 米
   _____

2. 灬
   _____

3. 皿
   _____

糖	烹	盐	醋
油	烤	糕	汁
涮	熟	盒	酒
粉	炒	炸	淀
煎	烧	煮	盘
酱	料	盛	酸

4. 火
   _____

5. 氵
   _____

6. 酉
   _____

III. Below are steps for a recipe, but they are not listed in the correct order. Fill in the blanks with appropriate vocabulary words and reorder the recipe directions.

1. _____ 把盐、料酒与淀粉加到鸡丁里后_____。

2. _____ 先将鸡肉和葱_____，然后把鸡丁放在碗里。

3. _____ 把油放进锅里，然后再加入鸡丁，用大火_____。

4. _____ 将切好的葱放在鸡丁上面，这样一_____酸辣鸡丁就做好了。

5. _____ 鸡肉熟了之后就可以放入_____的糖和酸辣酱。

CHARACTER WRITING PRACTICE 6.1

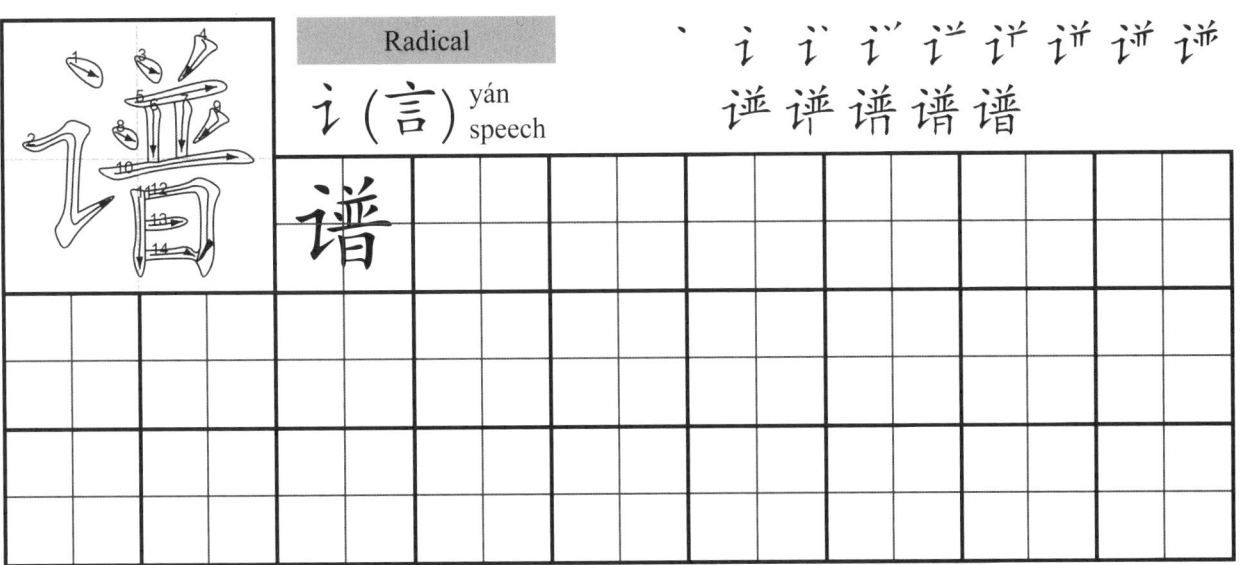

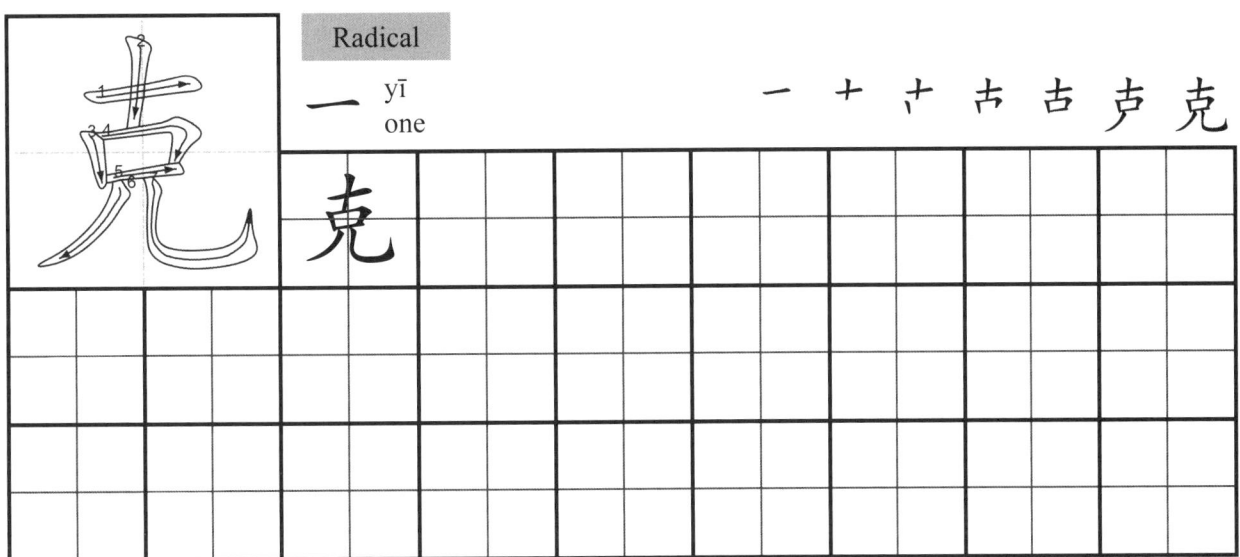

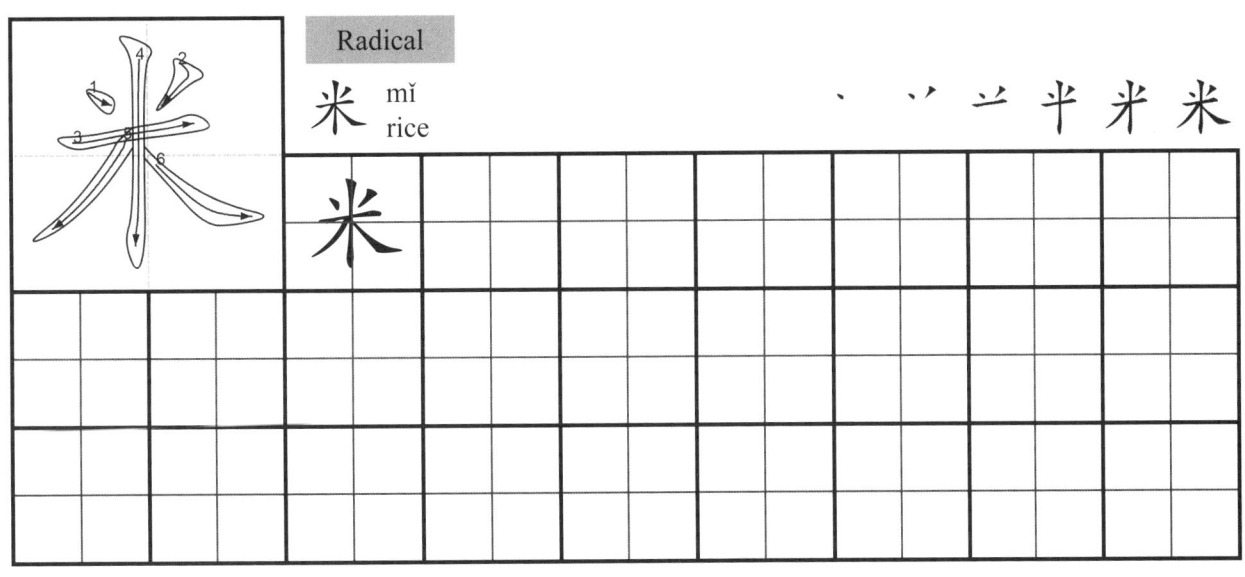

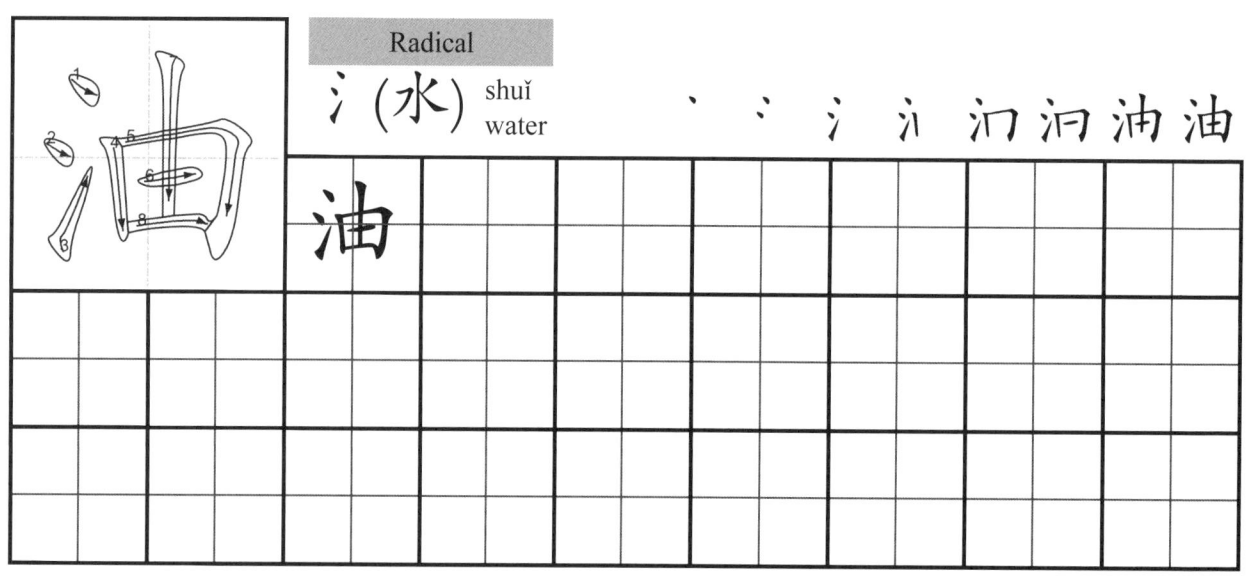

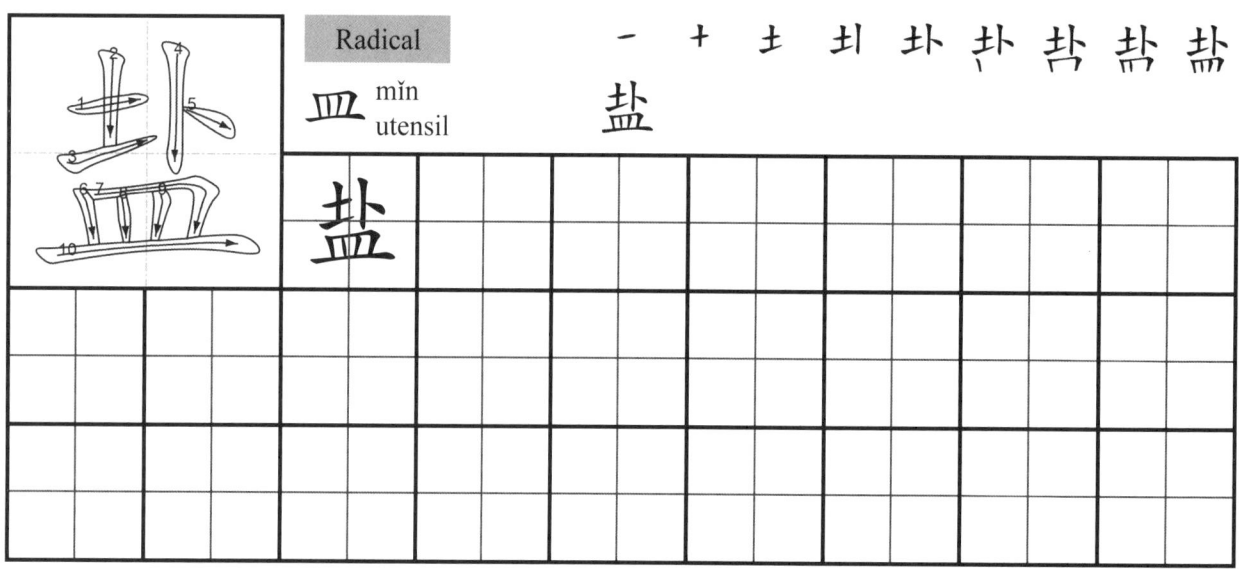

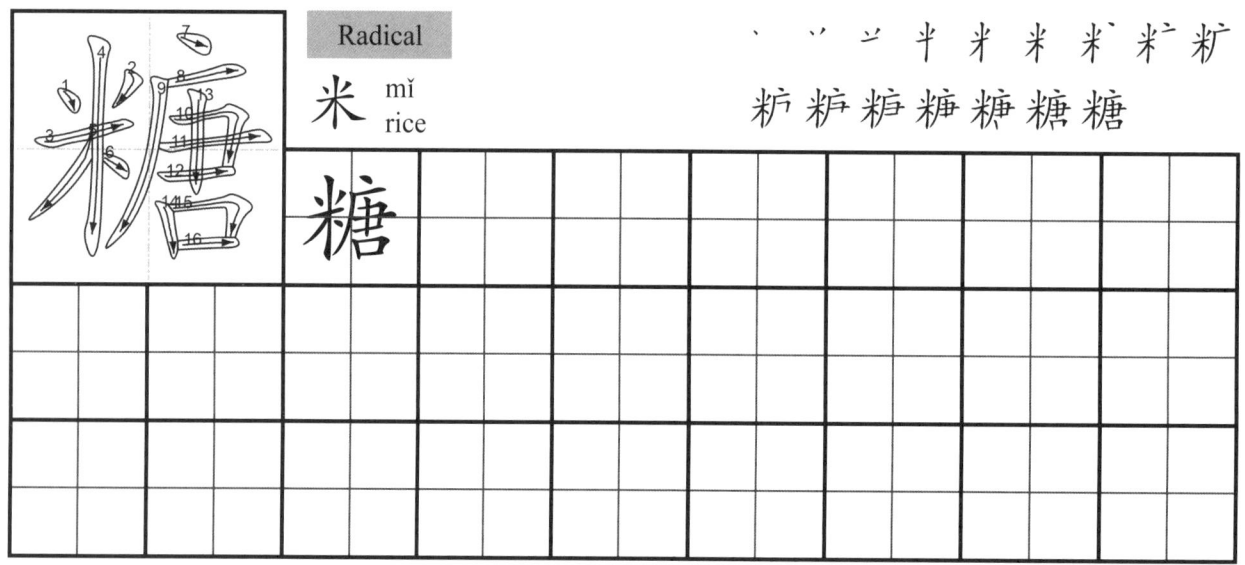

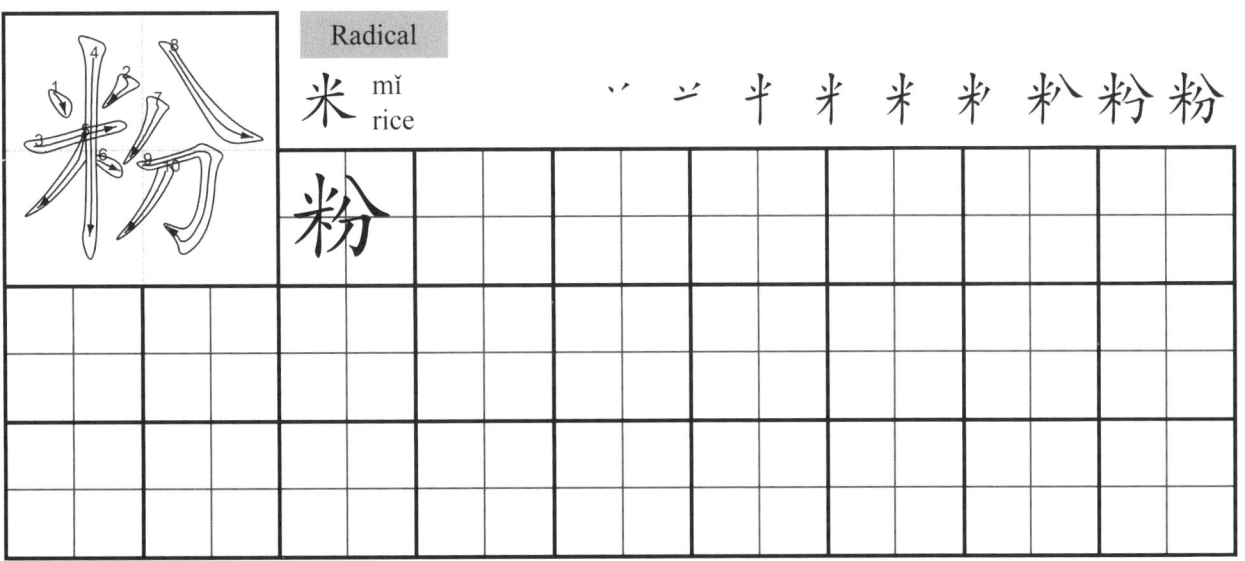

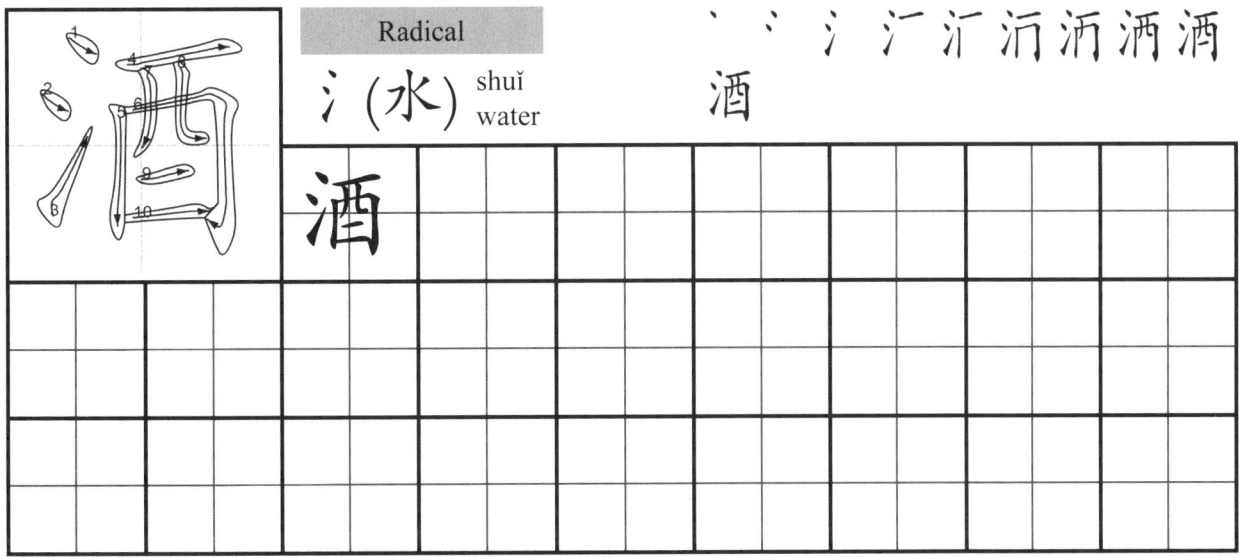

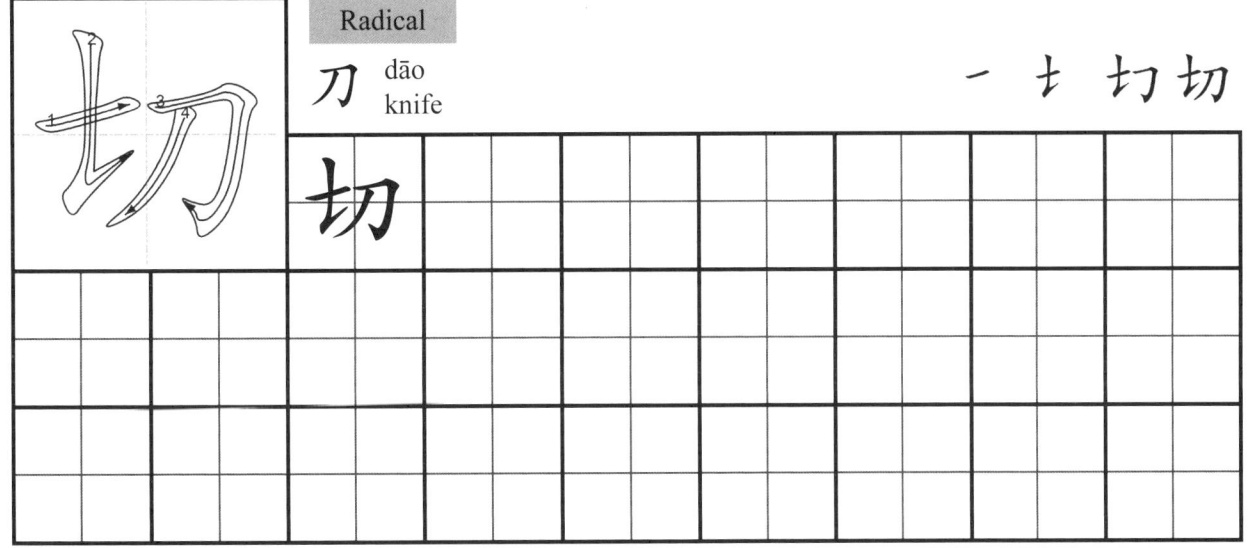

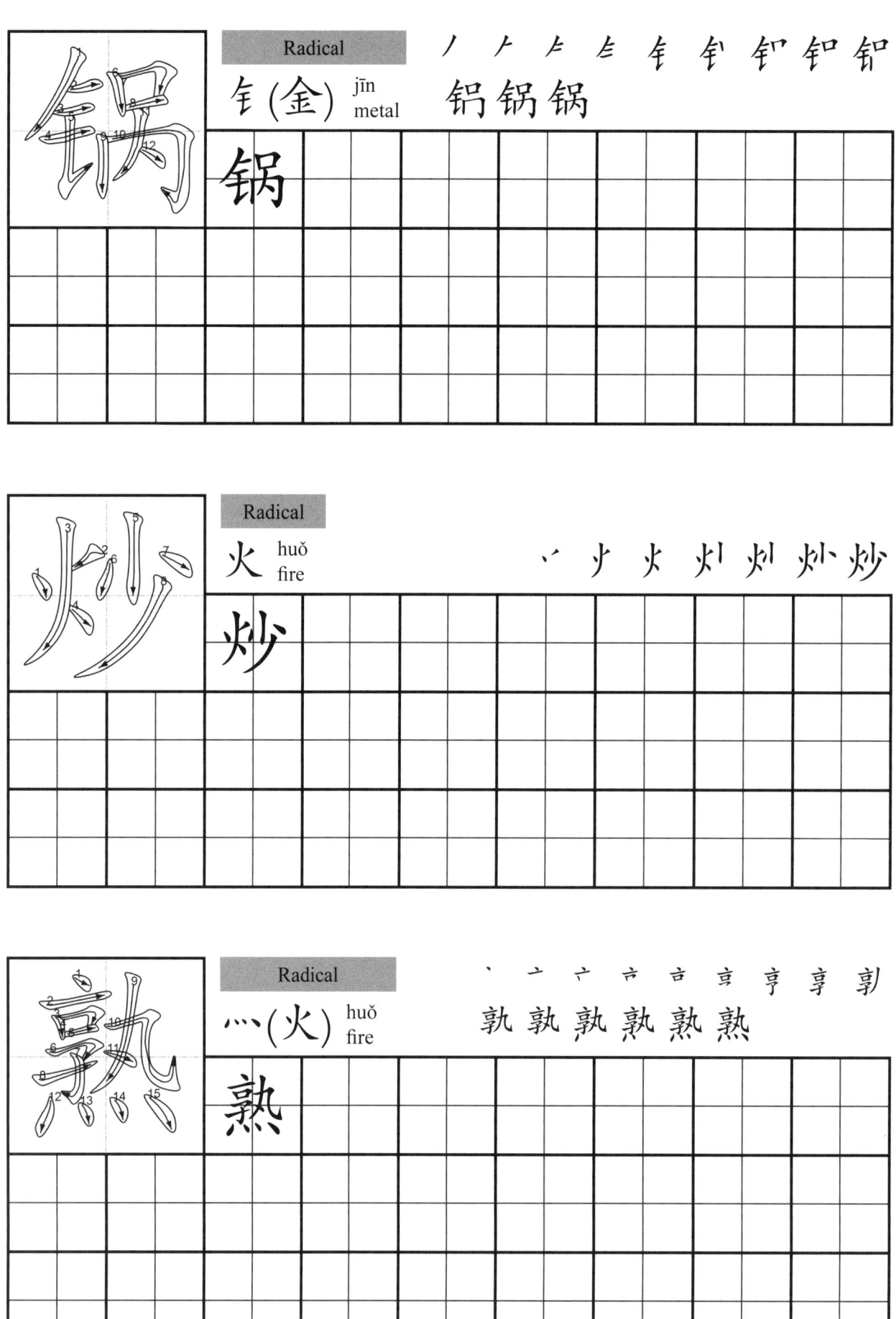

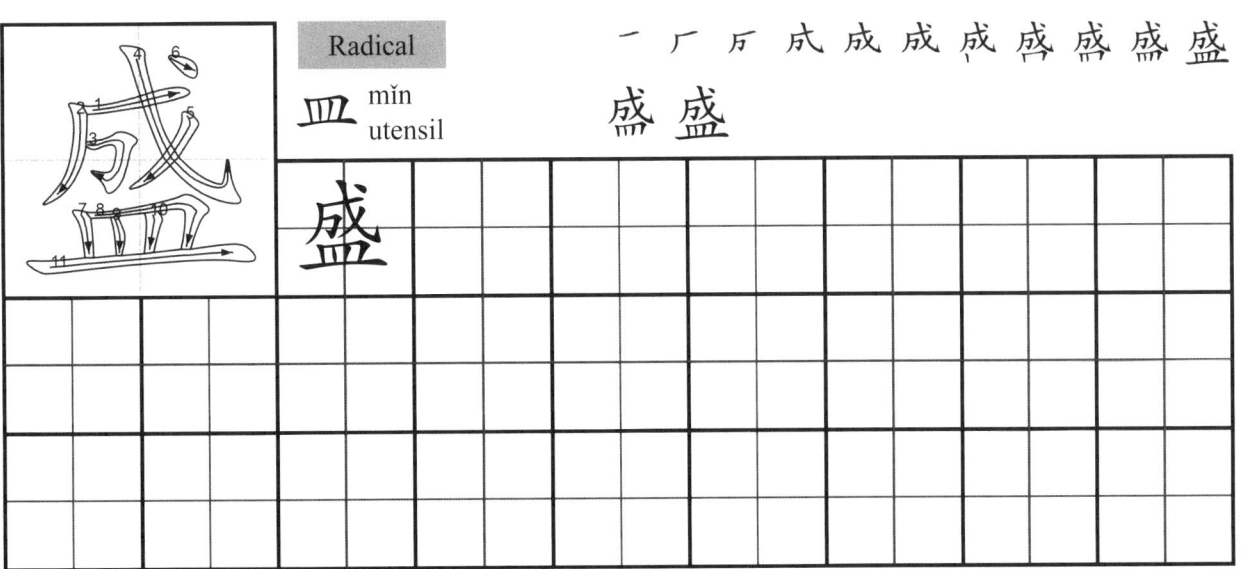

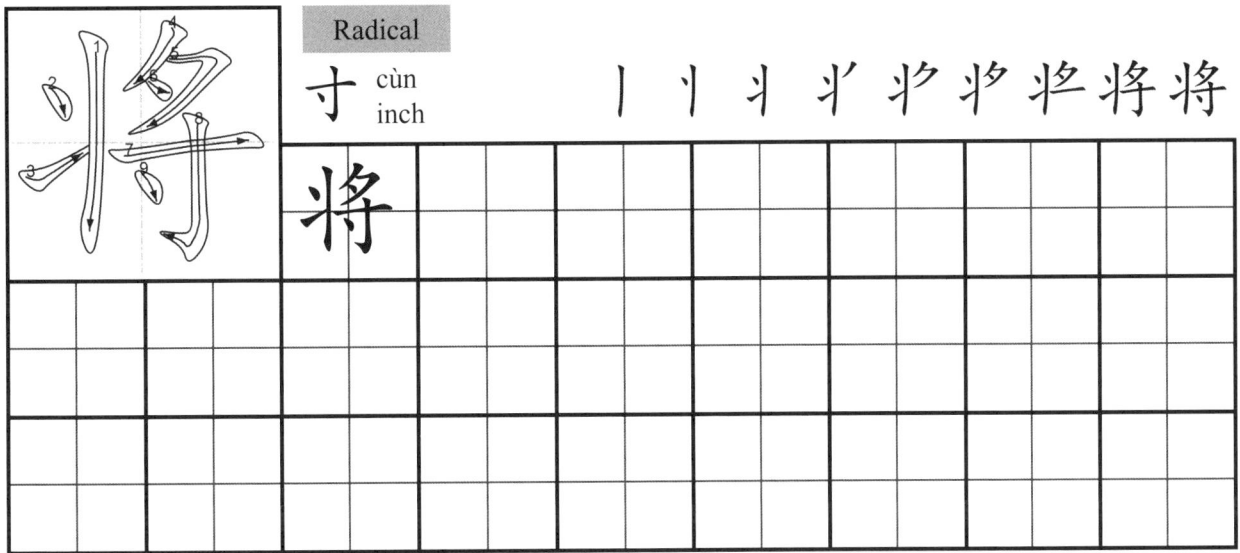

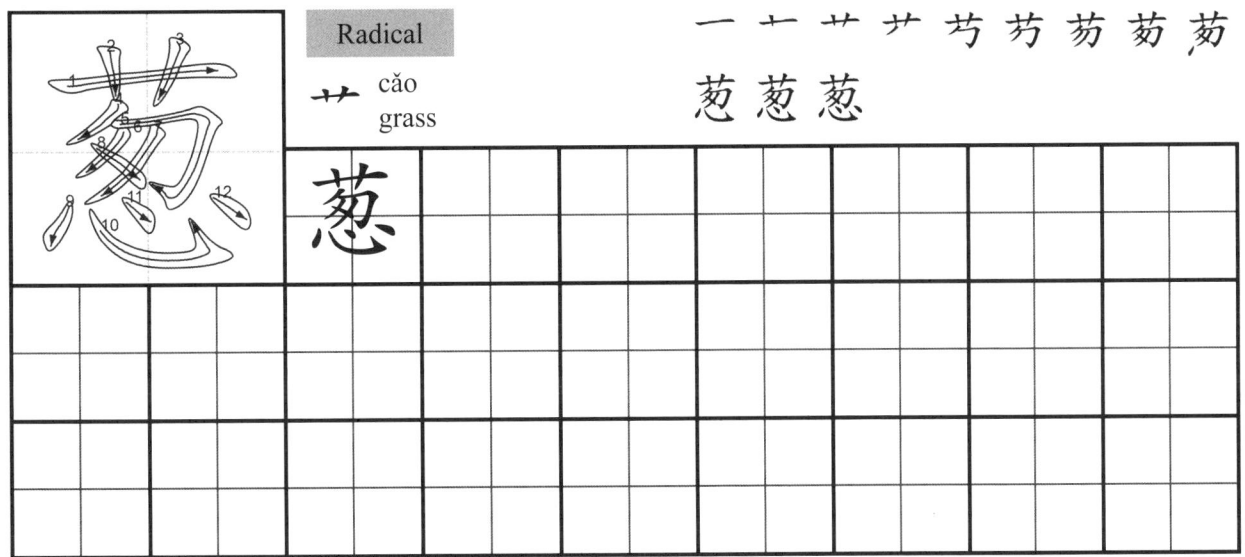

LISTENING COMPREHENSION 6.1

I. Listen to the recording and answer the question.

1. The woman would most likely respond with:

   A. 实在是太好了，谢谢你。
   B. 不好意思，我放了太多糖和盐。
   C. 你要把鸡丁、葱和辣椒切丁。
   D. 恭喜你学会做这道菜了！

II. Listen to the recording and answer the following True or False questions.

1. (　) There will be a Chinese Cooking Competition in next week.
2. (　) The woman knows how to make Drunken Chicken.
3. (　) The man thinks the dish that the woman is going to make is very easy.
4. (　) Both the woman and the man will participate in the competition.
5. (　) The dish that the man is going to make is very difficult to prepare.

III. Listen to the recording and answer the questions.

1. 小美的妈妈为什么不常做饭？

2. 妈妈做的菜好吃吗？为什么？

3. 小美的爸爸是怎么做菜的？

SPEAKING PRACTICE 6.1

I. Below are images for the steps to making Stir-fried Rice Cake. Explain what you need to do at each step.

II. After tasting the Stir-fried Rice Cake dish that your friend made, tell your mutual friends about the level of difficulty making it, how it tasted, and what changes you think you can make to the recipe to alter the dish.

Unit 6 • Lesson 1 • Food **173**

STRUCTURE REVIEW 6.1

I. Complete the following Structure Note practices.

Structure Note 6.1: Use 以为 to express mistaken belief.

$$\text{Subject} + 以为 + \text{Clause}$$

A. You went to a friend's house to have dinner and you discovered things you did not know before. Combine one sentence from the first box with the appropriate sentence from the second box to form one longer sentence.

> 我以为饺子里面一定会有肉。
> 我以为这道麻婆豆腐会很辣。
> 我以为北京烤鸭只要烤二十分钟就可以了。
> 我以为酸辣汤的材料很简单。
> 我以为做宫保鸡丁一定要放花生米。

> 原来需要那么长的时间。
> 哇！这是我第一次吃素饺子！
> 原来吃起来也不是太辣。
> 哦？这道菜的材料就只有鸡丁和辣椒？
> 没想到需要准备的材料那么多。

1. _____
2. _____
3. _____
4. _____
5. _____

Structure Note 6.2: Use 将 to indicate an action performed on a specific object in formal contexts.

> Subject + 将 + Object + Verb Phrase

B. Below are images demonstrating how to make 辣椒鸡丁. Write instructions for each step by using 将.

 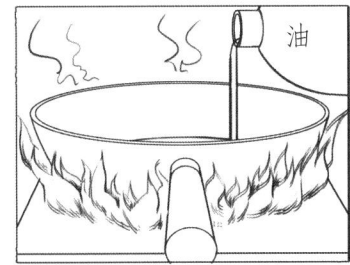 

1. _____ 2. _____ 3. _____

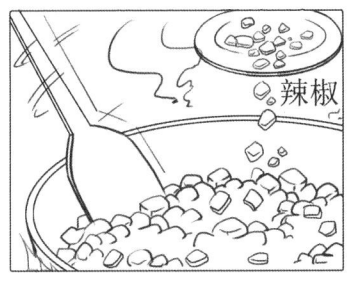 

4. _____ 5. _____

Structure Note 6.3: Use 无论⋯都 to express "no matter what" something is always the case.

> 无论 + Question / Phrase, + Subject + 都 + Verb Phrase

C. You are a fan of the Mountain Lion baskteball team and are attending one of their games with a friend. Respond to your friend's comments by using 无论⋯都⋯ to express your support for the team.

1. 这场比赛的票价非常贵!

2. 这次比赛的球场那么远!

Unit 6 · Lesson 1 · Food

3. 这次队长可能不会上场打球。

_____

4. 这次山猫队说不定会输。

_____

5. 听说山猫队的教练明年就不做了。

_____

Structure Note 6.4: Use 实在 to mean "really" and "honestly."

$$\boxed{\text{Subject} + 实在 + \text{Adjective / Verb Phrase}}$$

D. In *Modern Chinese* Textbook Vol. 2A, Unit 3, Lesson 1, we learned to use 确实 to emphasize a speaker's confidence that his/her assessment of a sitiuation is correct. Read the following dialogue between a customer and salesperson. Fill in the blanks using 实在 to indicate "really" or using 确实 to indicate affirmation.

A: 你们店的手机质量(1.)_____太不好了,手机买回去第一天就坏掉。

B: 我们店是不会骗人的,你在买之前试用过吗?

A: 有,买之前还好好的,可是回家以后手机(2.)_____用不了,我要退货。

B: (3.)_____非常抱歉,你买之前我们的店员(4.)_____已经跟你讲好不能退货的。

A: 你们的售后服务(5.)_____是太差了,我要投诉你们。

B: 我们(6.)_____没有做错,如果你要投诉的话就请打电话到我们公司吧。

Take the challenge! 动动脑筋!

"这件事情是谁对谁错?你最实在,你说!"
"说实在的,这件事情我也实在是看不下去了,依我看我还是先走好了。"

In this lesson, we learned to use 实在 as an adverb to express "really," which is similar to 真的。实在 and 真的 are interchangeable when you want to say "to be honest..." or "honestly." However, this is not the case when 实在 is used as an adjective to describe something as "concrete" or "particular," such as 实在的建议, "concrete suggestion." As an adjective, 实在 can also be used to describe someone who is "earnest and realistic." Can you determine what each 实在 means in the passage above?

II. You are a food blogger and many people leave comments on your message board. Respond to the questions using the structure notes you learned in this lesson.

做宫保鸡丁一定要放花生米吗？因为我弟弟不能吃花生。请问不加花生米的宫保鸡丁会一样好吃吗？

1. _____

我想做宫保鸡丁，但是不知道应该先炒鸡肉还是先炒辣椒，你知道地道的做法是怎样吗？

2. _____

听说做宫保鸡丁辣椒放得越多越好吃，真的是这样吗？

3. _____

我看了宫保鸡丁的食谱，觉得做起来应该挺简单的。我想试试做给男朋友吃，他是云南人，你觉得他会喜欢吃吗？

4. _____

READING COMPREHENSION 6.1

I. Read the following passage and answer the following questions.

> 小美一直以为中国菜很难做，不过看了玛丽在邮件里介绍做宫保鸡丁的食谱之后，小美觉得做中国菜看起来也不是那么难。小美马上在网上查了一下别的中国家常菜，发现除了宫保鸡丁以外，辣椒炒鸡丁也很容易做。她在查食谱的时候，正好大中来找她，小美就津津有味地跟大中讲起了怎么做这道菜。做辣椒炒鸡丁的材料也不复杂：鸡肉两百克、辣椒两克、盐一克、酱油一小匙、淀粉十克、料酒一大匙、葱五克、花生油四十克。材料都准备好之后，就可以开始做菜了：首先把鸡肉和辣椒切丁，之后鸡丁放盐和淀粉拌匀，最后将材料放进锅里，大火炒熟以后盛出来。如果喜欢吃甜的，还可以放少许糖。这样，地道的辣椒炒鸡丁就做好了。看起来无论是味道还是颜色都很棒，再说做法实在非常简单。小美告诉大中，说不定以后她也会试试做这道菜。大中说："你一定要试一试！到时候你来做菜，我来做评委！"

1. 小美在网上又找了什么家常菜？

2. 这道菜怎么做？

3. 你觉得这道菜的做法难吗？为什么？

Take the challenge! 动动脑筋！

In *Modern Chinese* Textbook Vol. 2A, Unit 6, Lesson 1, Lesson Text, we were introduced to 切丁, meaning "to cut into small cubes." When you read a Chinese recipe, you can see a lot of phrases related to cutting. Looking at the following Chinese phrases, can you match each to its correct English definition?

切块　　切条　　切片　　切丝　　切碎

to cut into slices　to cut into pieces　to cut into strips　to cut into long thin strips　to chop into very small pieces

II. Read the news article and answer the following True or False questions.

宫保鸡丁— 最受外国人欢迎的中国菜

虽然宫保鸡丁是中国的传统名菜，但是这道菜的材料和做法都不复杂：用鸡肉、辣椒和花生米就可以做出这道名菜。由于宫保鸡丁的味道很特别，又香又辣，非常受人欢迎。宫保鸡丁不但是中国人饭桌上常常见到的家常菜，也是外国人很喜欢的一道中国菜。在英美等西方国家，这道菜变成了中国菜的**代名词**，**中餐馆**的菜单上都有这道菜。有人在美国加州做了**统计**，美国人最喜欢吃的外国菜是**墨西哥**菜，第二喜欢吃的就是中国菜。在中国菜里，宫保鸡丁是最受欢迎的。关于这道菜还有一个有意思的**故事**，你可以自己去找找看。

Notes:
代名词 (dàimíngcí): *n.* pronoun
中餐馆 (Zhōng cānguǎn): *n.* Chinese restaurant
统计 (tǒngjì): *n.* statistics
墨西哥 (Mòxīgē): *n.* Mexico
故事 (gùshi): *n.* story, tale

1. 下面哪一个不是做宫保鸡丁的材料？
   A. 鸡肉
   B. 辣椒
   C. 酱油
   D. 花生米

2. Based on the statistics, which of the following foreign cuisine is the most popular in California?
   A. British food
   B. Chinese food
   C. American food
   D. Mexican food

3. 下面哪一个说法是不对的？
   A. 中国人不太喜欢吃宫保鸡丁。
   B. 美国人很喜欢吃中国菜。
   C. 宫保鸡丁这道菜很有名。
   D. 宫保鸡丁的做法不难。

III. Read the following passage and answer the questions.

To:	李华
From:	陈大中
Subject:	麻婆豆腐食谱

李华：
你不是一直想吃麻婆豆腐吗？我在网上找到了麻婆豆腐的做法，发给你看看。
主料：豆腐 肉末 豆瓣酱 辣椒酱
辅料：葱 蒜 酱油 淀粉
做法：
一. 把豆腐切成块，葱和蒜切成丁。
二. 锅里放油，把肉末炒熟后盛出来。
三. 锅里再放一点油，放入豆瓣酱、辣椒酱、葱和蒜，翻炒一会儿后放入豆腐和炒好的肉末继续翻炒。加入一些酱油和水。
四. 起锅前加入淀粉勾芡。一道又香又辣的麻婆豆腐就做好了！
怎么样？是不是很容易？明天我们就做这道菜吧！
大中

Notes:
肉末 (ròumò): *n.* ground meat
豆瓣酱 (dòubàn jiàng): *n.* thick, spicy broad-bean sauce
勾芡 (gōuqiàn): *vo.* to thicken soup/dishes with cooking starch

1. How many different types of ingredients do you need to make Mapo Tofu?

_____

2. Why did Dazhong e-mail Li Hua the recipe for making Mapo Tofu?

_____

3. The images on the next page show the steps for making Mapo Tofu. However, they are currently out of order. Number the images in the correct order according to the recipe instructions in Dazhong's e-mail.

_____

WRITING PRACTICE 6.1

I. You are inviting five friends over for dinner. Create a menu of at least five Chinese dishes, including a soup, that you are going to serve. In addition to the soup, be sure you have a seafood dish, meat dish (chicken, pork, beef, lamb), vegetable dish, and a dessert.

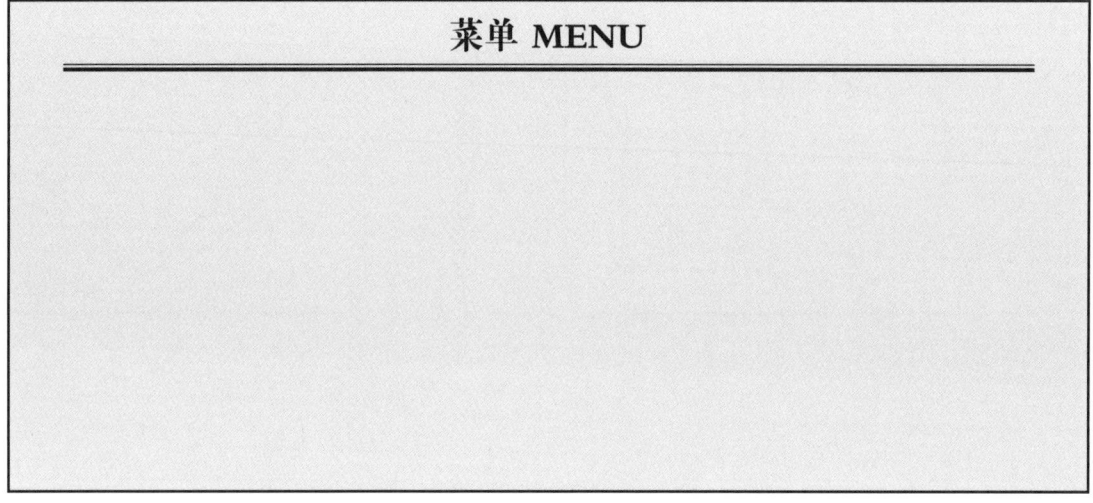

II. You are entering a cooking competition and are given the ingredients below. Select at least five ingredients, determine what you can make, and describe the steps to making your dish. Be sure to also give your dish a name and describe how it tastes.

   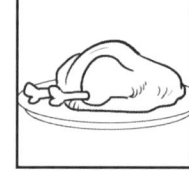 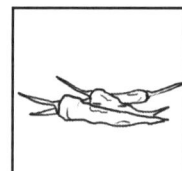 

  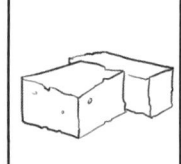   

UNIT 6 — LESSON 2

逛超市

Modern Chinese 现代中文

VOCABULARY REVIEW 6.2

I. Below is a menu with both Chinese and English. Fill in the missing information on the menu.

```
菜单 MENU
★ 香辣豆腐汤 1._____
★ 2._____ Seafood Beancurd Soup
★ 葱油鸡 Chicken with Scallion in Hot Oil
★ 3._____ Chicken with Soy Sauce
★ 4._____ Roasted Duck
★ 蒜香烤牛肉 5._____
★ 6._____ Fried Pork with Vegetables
```

```
菜单 MENU
★ 7._____ Hot and Sour Fish
★ 蒜香海鲜炒饭 Fried Rice with Seafood and Garlic
★ 猪肉炒年糕 8._____
★ 特色菜饭 Special Vegetable Rice
★ 海鲜火锅 Seafood Hotpot
★ 牛肉火锅 9._____
```

II. Use the following clues to determine the radical. Add the radical to the characters to form a new character and write the pinyin.

A: The radical related to food is _____.

Example: 壬   任   (rèn)
2. 欠 _____
4. 反 _____

1. 包 _____
3. 我 _____
5. 交 _____

B: The radical related to grass is _____.

1. 忽 _____
3. 监 _____
5. 疏 _____

2. 采 _____
4. 示 _____
6. 化 _____

III. Replace the bolded words with vocabulary you learned in this lesson.

1. 我从来没有吃过这么**好吃**的麻婆豆腐。

2. 宫保鸡丁是这家店厨师**最会做的**菜。

3. 这道香辣豆腐让人**想继续吃东西**。

4. 你吃过北京烤鸭吗？没有的话就**试试**看吧。

CHARACTER WRITING PRACTICE 6.2

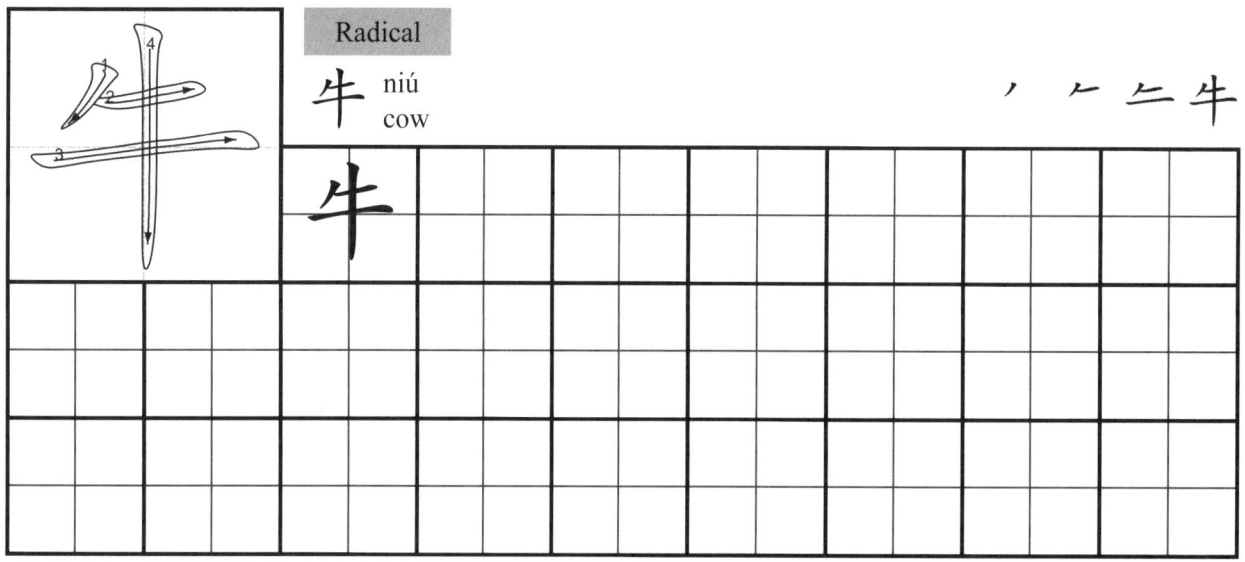

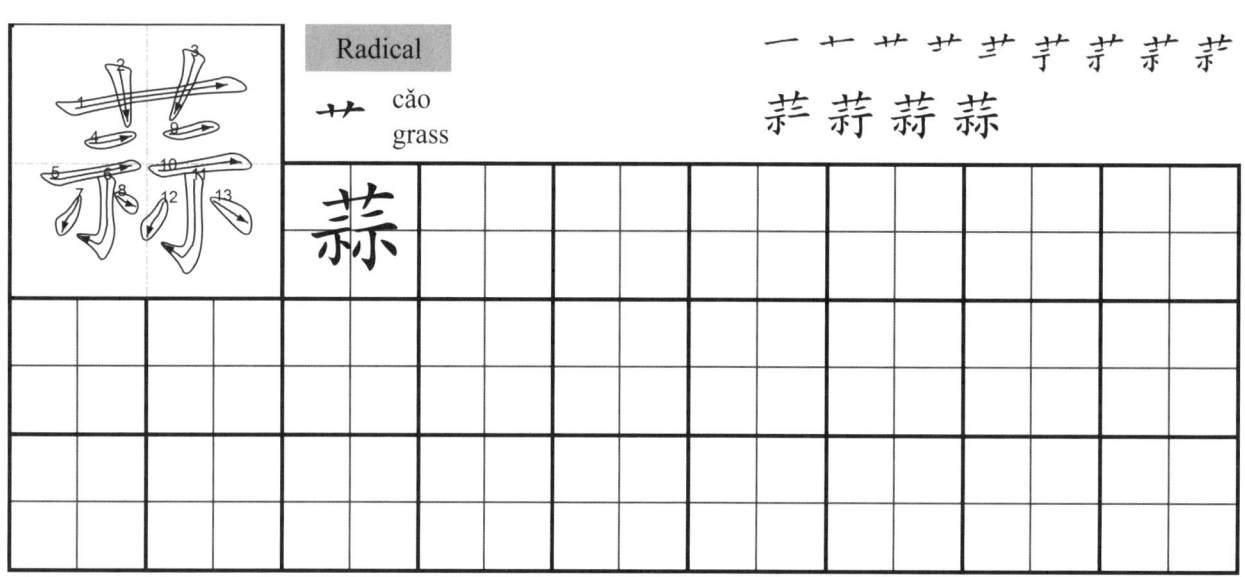

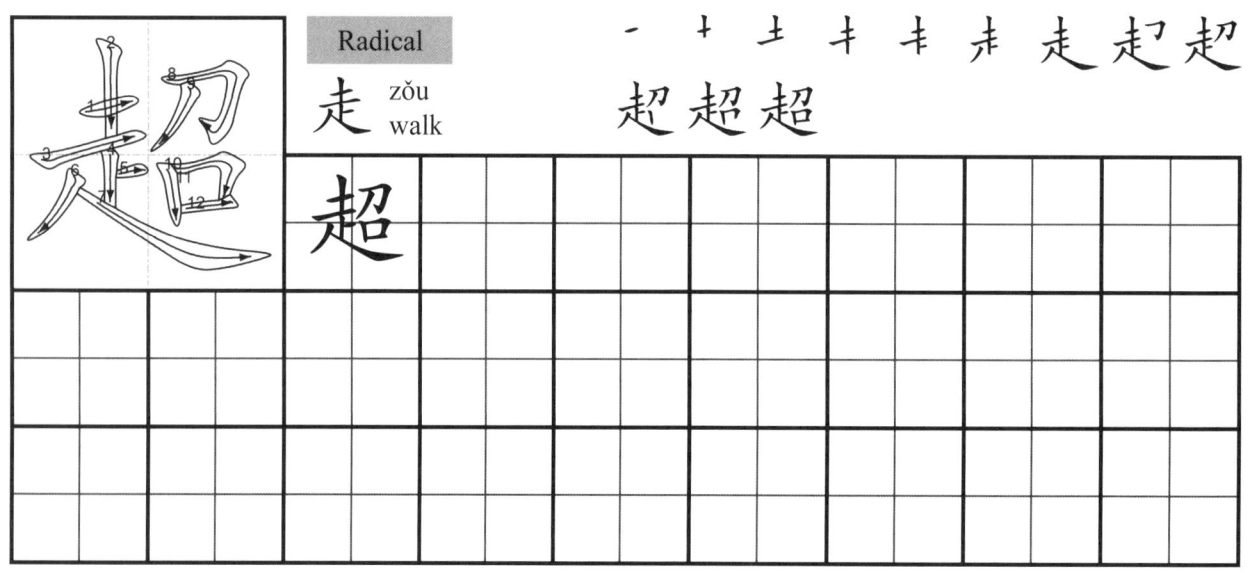

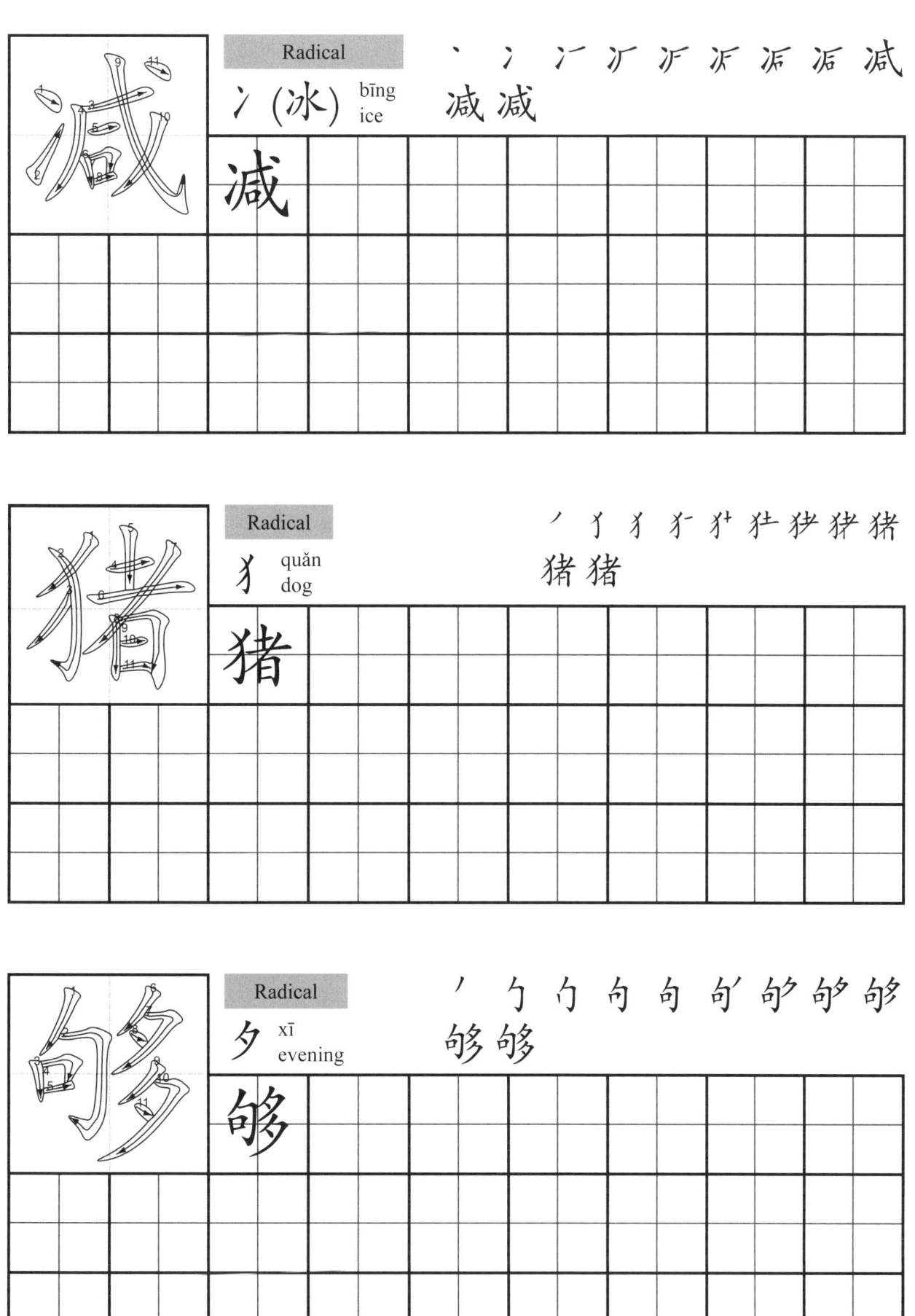

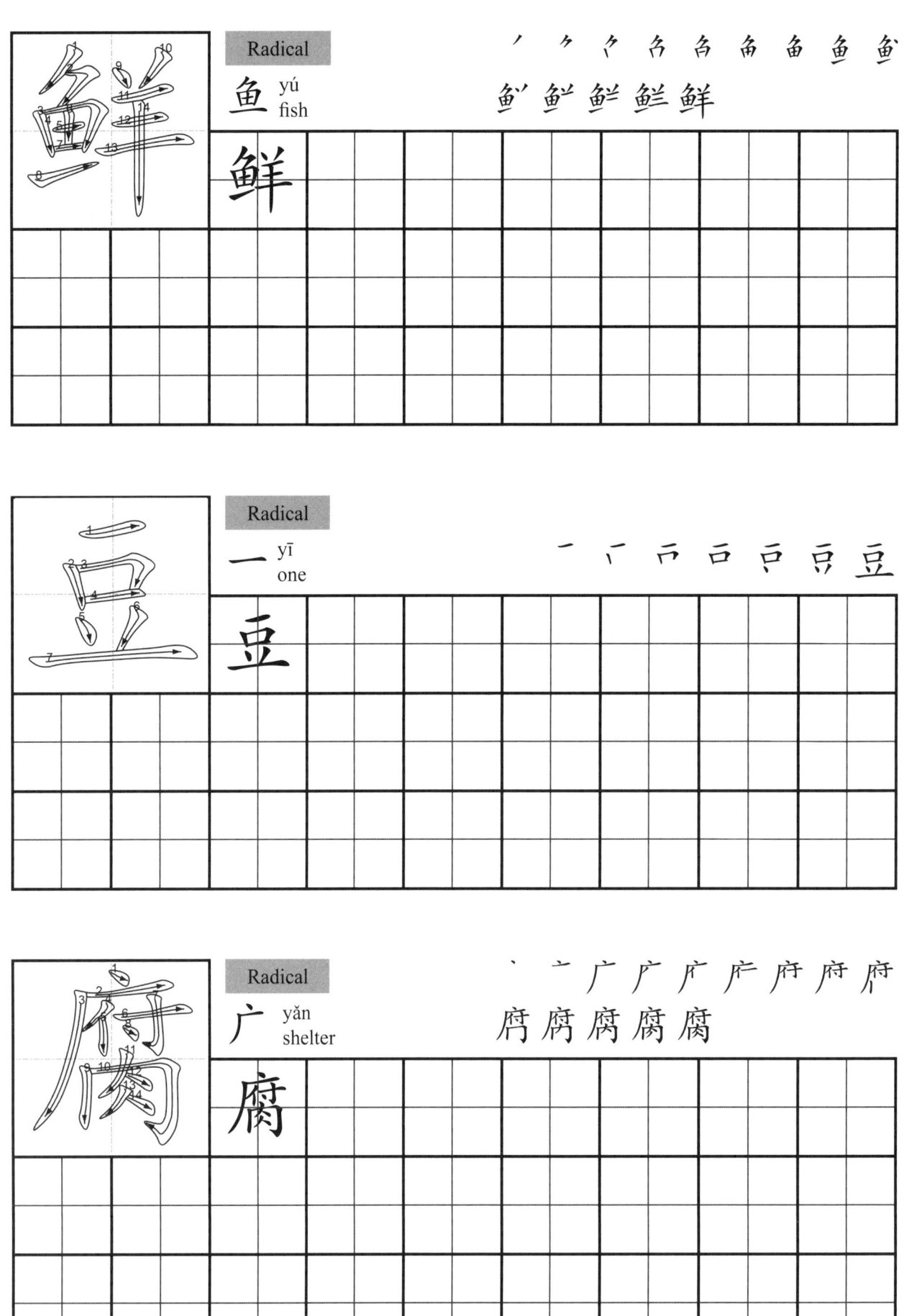

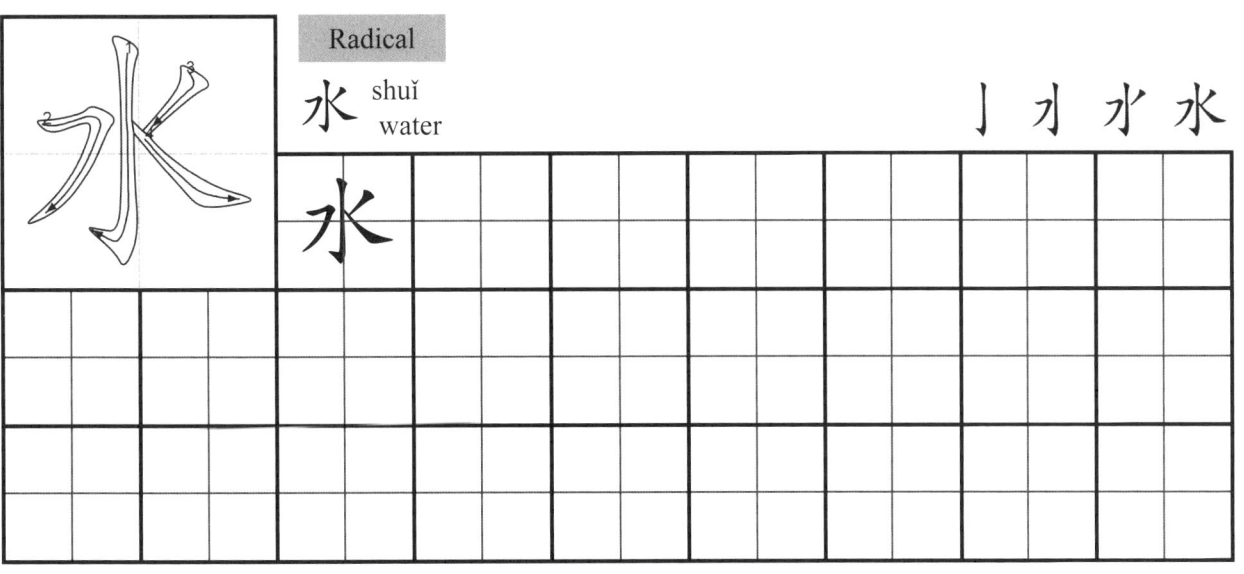

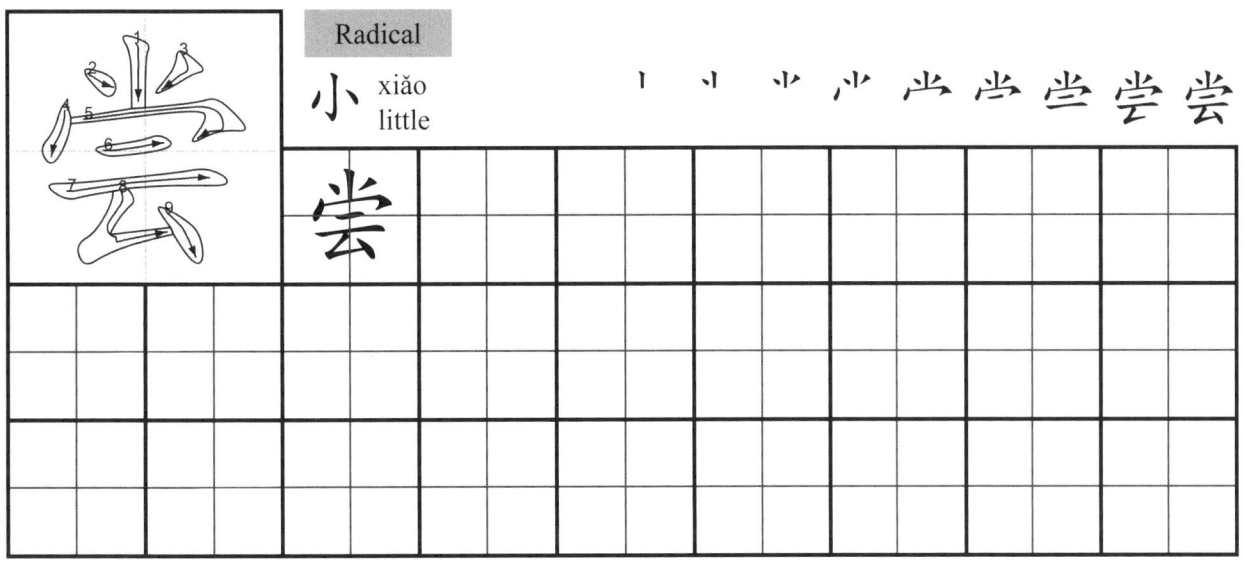

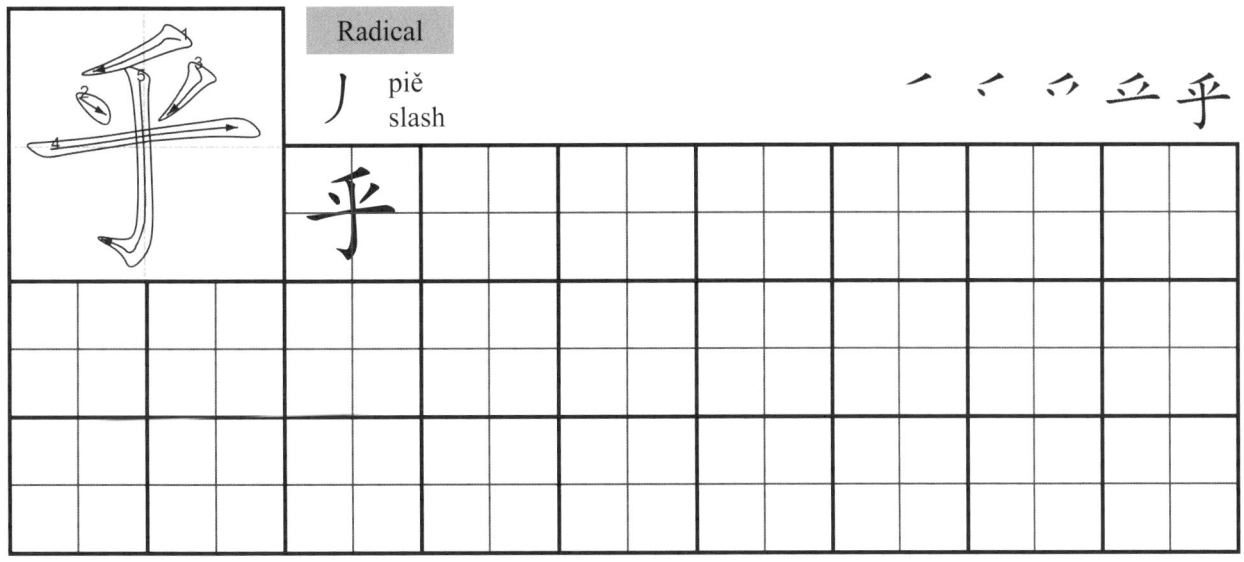

Unit 6 · Lesson 2 · Food

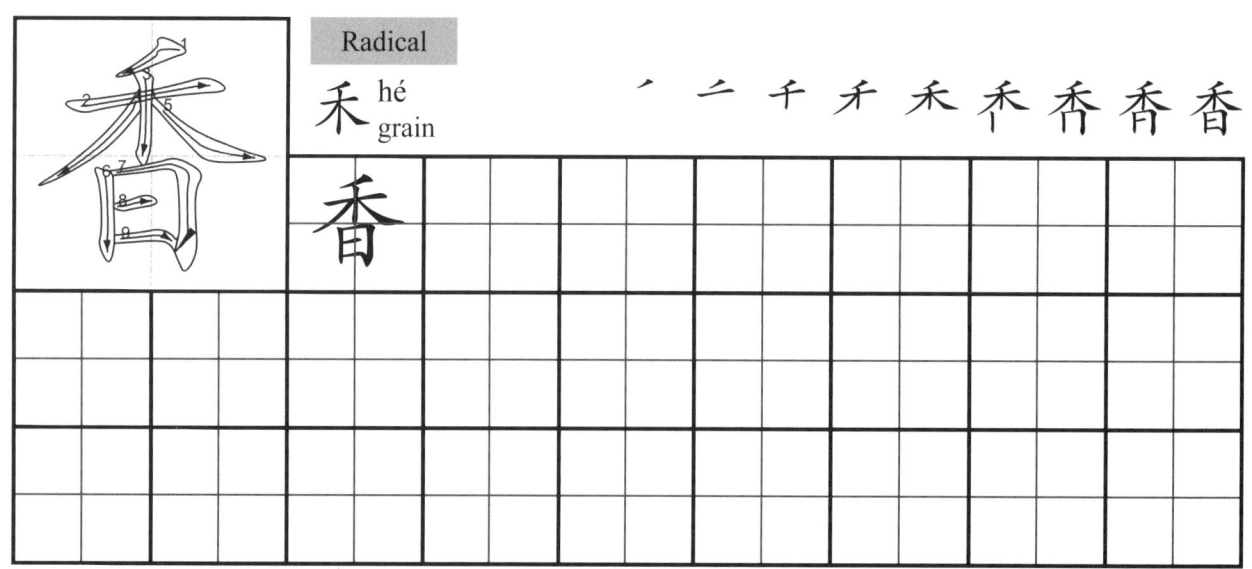

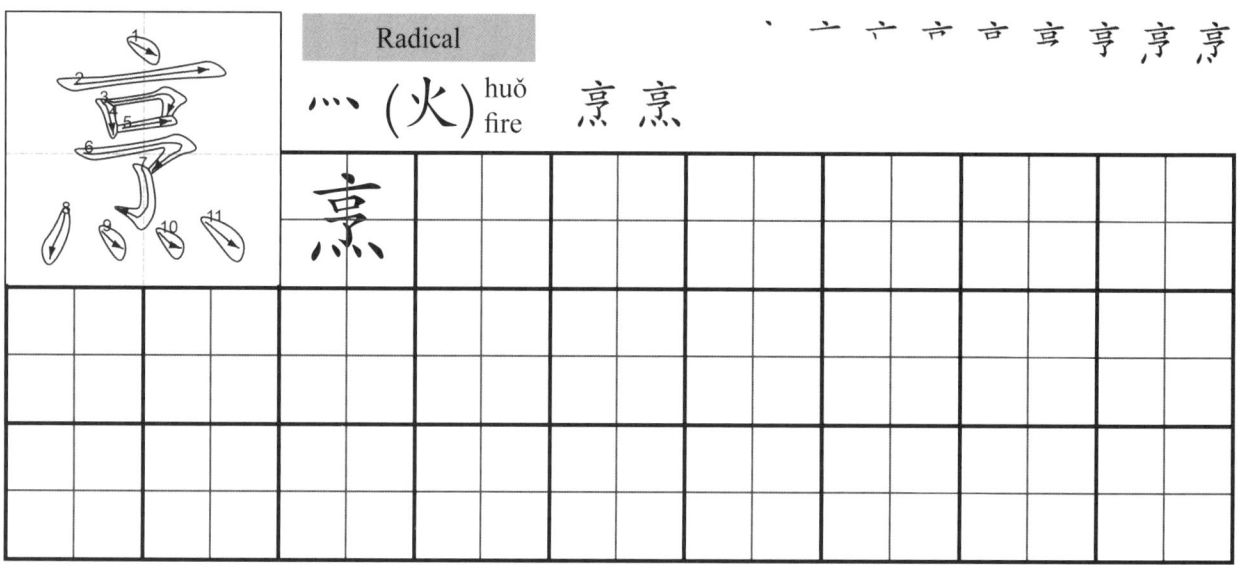

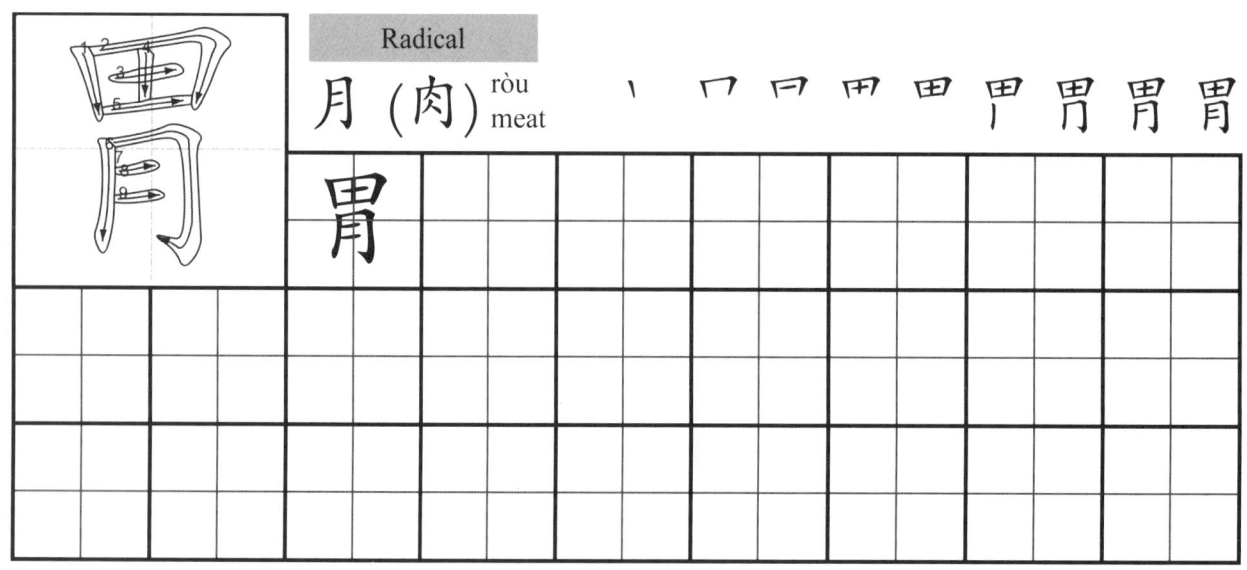

LISTENING COMPREHENSION 6.2

I. Listen to the recording and answer the question.

1. The woman would most likely respond with:

    A. 这道特色菜果然很美味。
    B. 你难得会去超市买菜啊!
    C. 谢谢,你真为我着想。
    D. 我们还差蒜没买。

II. Listen to the recording and answer the following True or False questions.

1. (　　) The man wants to go to the supermarket.
2. (　　) The woman thinks the man does not like shopping at the supermarket.
3. (　　) The woman is going to buy a cookbook.
4. (　　) The man lost the cookbook.
5. (　　) The man wants to go to the supermarket to buy ingredients.

III. Listen to the recording and answer the questions.

1. Why does the speaker go to the supermarket?

   _____

2. Why did the speaker return home so quickly from the supermarket?

   _____

3. What items did the speaker purchase at the supermarket?

   _____

SPEAKING PRACTICE 6.2

I. Below are advertisements from two different supermarkets. The items listed for each are the same but both have different promotions. You will be making Mapo Tofu and need to buy the ingredients for this dish. Describe which market you would choose to go to and why.

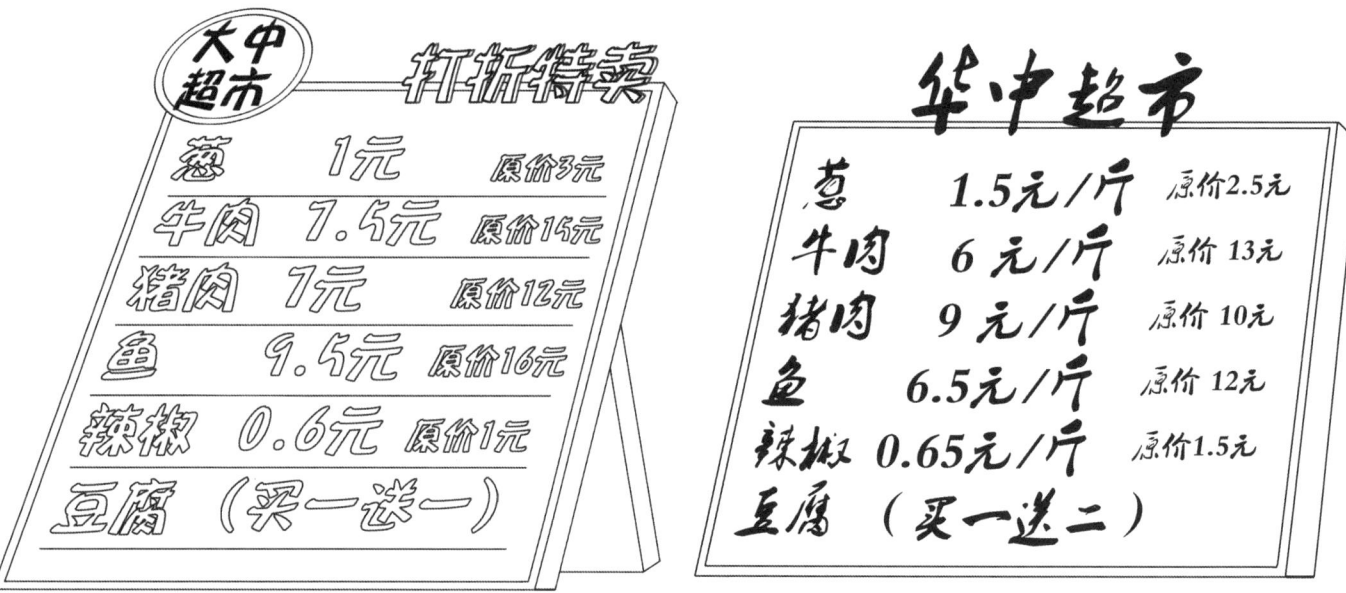

II. You went to the market and bought ingredients for making Mapo Tofu. When you get home, you realized you forgot a few items. You call your friend, who is at a supermarket, to ask him/her to purchase your missing ingredients. Explain why you did not buy your ingredients when you went shopping at the market.

STRUCTURE REVIEW 6.2

I. Complete the following Structure Note practices.

Structure Note 6.5: Use 于是 to say "hence" or "thus."

> Condition clause + 于是 + Result clause

A. Looking at the pictures below, write a short description with complete sentences using 于是 to explain what is happening in each scene.

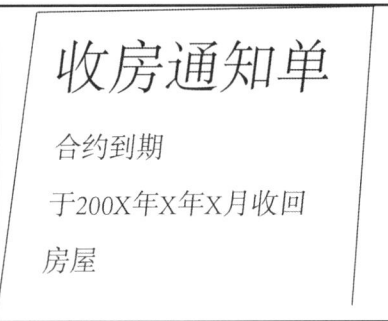

1. _____   2. _____

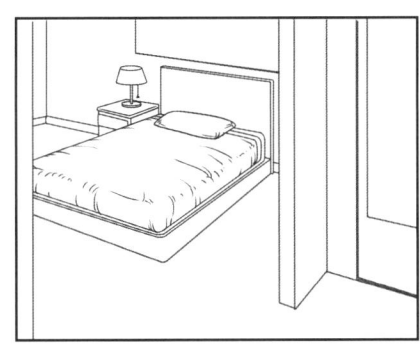

3. _____   4. _____

Structure Note 6.6: Use 几乎 to say "nearly."

> 几乎 + Verb / Noun / Adjective Phrase

B. Read the following passage. Fill in the blanks using 差不多 to express "about" or "roughly" or using 几乎 to express "nearly."

十多年后……

今天我约了以前的小学同学在车站见面。早上我(1.)_____没吃什么就出门了，饿着肚子走到车站等。等了(2.)_____十分钟那位同学也没到。于是我打电话问他，他说他还在忙，要晚点儿到。我看(3.)_____到午饭时间了，就走到附近一家餐厅吃点东西。当我正想点菜，一位服务员走过来说："不是约在车站见面的吗？"原来他就是我的小学同学！"哦！(4.)_____十多年没见面，我(5.)_____认不出你来。"我说。"都过了十多年了，但是你的个子怎么(6.)_____都没变？"

Take the challenge! 动动脑筋！

In *Modern Chinese* Textbook Vol. 1A, Unit 3, Lesson 1, we learned 差不多 expresses "about" or "roughly." 几乎, a similar expression, is introduced in this lesson to express "almost" or "nearly." While similar, there are subtle differences in what each implies.

As in the practice above, you will find that 差不多 is always used in a description where you do not have exact numbers and can only provide a general approximation. In English, you can also say "sort of" or "pretty much" in addition to "about" or "roughly" to express 差不多. For example, "哥哥和弟弟差不多一样高" means you think two brothers are pretty much the same height, but you are not positive. However, saying "哥哥和弟弟几乎一样高" means you know they are almost the same height and implies that one is perhaps slightly taller than the other. Another similar adverb is 大概 meaning "approximately" or "probably." For example, "哥哥和弟弟大概一样高" indicates that you think two brothers are probably the same height, but you are not quite sure. Can you guess what each of the examples below implies?

来看比赛的差不多都是山猫队的球迷。　　他差不多每天都会上网。
来看比赛的几乎都是山猫队的球迷。　　　他几乎每天都会上网。
来看比赛的大概都是山猫队的球迷。　　　他大概每天都会上网。

Structure Note 6.7: Use 果然 to indicate that something happened as expected.

果然 + Sentence

Subject + 果然 + Adjective / Verb Phrase

C. You go to a supermarket bringing the following ad with you. Use 果然 to create five sentences to indicate the sales you see in the supermarket is as expected according to the ad.

宜美超市

调味料　　名牌电器
全部半价　　买一送一

保证海鲜新鲜美味

免费试吃麻婆豆腐

买满￥300
送20优惠券

1. _____

2. _____

3. _____

4. _____

5. _____

Structure Note 6.8: Use 难得 to describe rare situations and opportunities.

(Subject +) 难得 + Verb Phrase

D. Use 难得 to write sentences suggesting what you should do if you have the opportunity to travel to China and to travel within your home country.

中国	我的国家
Example: 难得来到北京，当然要尝尝北京最有名的北京烤鸭。	

Unit 6 • Lesson 2 • Food　**193**

Take the challenge! 动动脑筋!

In this lesson, 难得 is used as an adverb to express "rarely" and used before a verb phrase to descibe a rare opportunity. 难得 can also act as an adjective to describe someone, something, or a situation that is rare. For example, "这位大学生是难得的人才" or "他那么年轻就能这么成功，实在是非常难得."

"难得一见" is a common expression. Can you guess what it means? You can use the passage below to help decipher the meaning.

"难得来到黄山，怎么可以一天到晚都留在旅馆睡觉！"
"黄山确实是难得一见的美景，可是现在也是我难得的假期啊，就让我休息休息吧！"

II. Below is 小安's travel journal. Using the first photo caption as example, help him create the captions for the other two pictures.

Example: 我们去了一家烤鸭店，里面的客人几乎都是外国人，这家店果然非常有名。难得来到北京，我们一定要尝尝地道的美食，于是我们点了两只北京烤鸭，好吃极了！

1.

2.

READING COMPREHENSION 6.2

I. Read the passage and answer the following questions.

> 平时我和妈妈都很忙，上个星期天，难得我俩都有空。听说我家附近新开了一家超市，于是我和妈妈就决定去那家超市逛逛。这家超市很大，购物的人很多。你能想得到的商品，这里几乎都可以找到，而且很多商品在减价。超市正在举办试吃活动，放了不少美味的特色食物请大家试吃。像我最喜欢吃的麻婆豆腐就可以免费试吃，看得我口水都要流出来了。我和妈妈尝了一下，果然是又香又辣，吃得我胃口大开。在超市工作的人告诉妈妈，这些麻婆豆腐是用一种调味料做的，所以妈妈就买了那种调味料，说要回家试做一下。看到这里的东西种类很多，也很新鲜，妈妈顺便也买了一些猪肉和蔬菜，准备回家做几道拿手菜给我吃。我看了一下妈妈买的东西，告诉她我们还差辣椒和花生米。妈妈不明白，我说今天晚上我也要做一道宫保鸡丁请妈妈尝尝。妈妈笑着告诉我："来超市除了能买到烹饪材料，还能学到烹饪知识。依我看，与其说超市是个买东西的地方，倒不如说是个烹饪学校。"

1. 这个超市怎么样？

2. 妈妈买了什么？为什么？

3. 为什么妈妈说超市就像烹饪学校？

Take the challenge! 动动脑筋！

In the above passage, 胃口大开 literally means "the appetite is widely opened," which is equivalent to the *Modern Chinese* Textbook Vol. 2A, Unit 6, Lesson 2, Lesson Text "有胃口," meaning "to have a good appetite." Another similar expression is 好胃口. The opposite is 倒胃口, meaning "losing one's appetite." Moreover, if you want to say this dish is very much to your taste, you can say "这道菜很合/对我的胃口." Apart from describing appetite, 合胃口 can also be use to express liking an object, while 倒胃口 can be used to express being sick of something. Can you guess the meaning of the following sentences?

这件衣服不合我的胃口。 这部电视剧真让人倒胃口。

II. **Read the blog post and answer the following True or False questions.**

超市购物**如何**省钱

　　去超市买东西有一些地方要注意，我**总结**了一些超市购物经验与大家分享。

　　一．首先要注意看广告。超市常常会有一些减价促销广告，这些**促销**的产品价格很低，但是一定要选自己需要的东西，不要只因为便宜就买。

　　二．另外，**收集**各种优惠券。现在网上就有很多优惠券，超市门口也可能找到优惠券，用优惠券买东西可以省很多钱。

　　三．还有，**促销**的东西一定要注意日期，超市有时候会把快到期的产品打折卖。如果产品快过期，或者不新鲜了，就一定不要买。要为自己的身体着想，身体健康比什么都重要！

　　四．还有，碰到免费试吃的机会不要**错过**。要先尝再买，一定是自己喜欢吃的才买。

　　五．最后，一定要留好收据，有问题可以退换。

Notes:
如何 (rúhé): *adv.* how
总结 (zǒngjié): *v.* to summarize
促销 (cùxiāo): *adj.* promotional, on sale promotion
收集 (shōují): *v.* to collect, to gather
错过 (cuòguò): *v.* to miss, to let slip

1. ( ) 作者总结了五条经验和大家分享。
2. ( ) 作者认为促销广告上的商品很便宜，可以多买。
3. ( ) 到网上收集优惠券是省钱的好办法。
4. ( ) 快到期的产品最好不要买。
5. ( ) 如果遇到自己不需要的东西在打折也可以买下来。

III. Read the receipt and note and then answer the following questions.

货号	品名	数量	金额
987665	鸡肉 500g/盒	1	12.4元
765443	三全牌速冻饺子	2	48.6元
878873	青菜 500g/盒	1	4.9元
879963	辣椒 100g/盒	1	7.5元
879233	葱 200g	1	6.8元
234156	牙膏	2	10.4元
789943	糖果	1	5.6元
235908	洗衣粉（买一送一）	2	18元
			−9元

购买总件数：11
应付总额：105.6
使用优惠券 满100减5元
付款方式：现金
实付总额：101
找零：0.4

丽丽，等你起床后帮我去超市买一些东西。晚饭我想做宫保鸡丁，需要鸡肉、葱和辣椒。如果有新鲜的青菜也可以买一些。另外家里的牙膏和洗衣粉都快用完了。你自己想吃什么可以再买一些。桌子上有一张超市优惠券，别忘了拿。
妈妈

Notes:
洗衣粉 (xǐyīfěn): *n.* washing powder, laundry detergent
总额 (zǒng'é): *n.* gross amount
找零 (zhǎolíng): *v.* to return charge

1. (　) 今天晚上丽丽家会吃宫保鸡丁。
2. (　) 丽丽买了洗衣粉，因为洗衣粉在打折。
3. (　) 丽丽的妈妈晚上想做饺子。
4. (　) 丽丽自己想吃糖果。
5. (　) 用优惠券省了五块钱。
6. Circle on the receipt that the money 丽丽 paid to the counter.

WRITING PRACTICE 6.2

I. Below are images of an event that happened on March 3 while shopping for an item at a supermarket. Describe what occurred in each scene.

1.

2.

3.

4.

II. Describe shopping at a local mom and pop market and discuss the pros and cons.

UNIT 7 — LESSON 1

交通意外

VOCABULARY REVIEW 7.1

I. Each of the underlined phrases below are vocabulary words you have learned. However, a character taken from each pair make up a new phrase — shown within the circle. Guess the correct meaning for each within the circle.

1.
   (A) insurance fee
   (B) violation fee
   (C) compensation fee
   (D) medical fee

2.
   (A) to be injured
   (B) to go to a doctor
   (C) to cure wound
   (D) to be worried

3.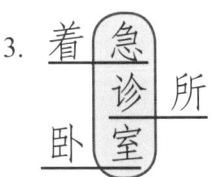
   (A) clinic
   (B) police station
   (C) emergency room
   (D) ambulance

4.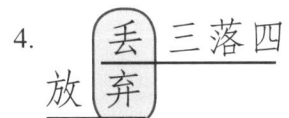
   (A) to lose
   (B) to be missing
   (C) to put
   (D) to abandon

II. Find two characters you have learned that have approximately the same pronunciation as the provided character and write down the words and pinyin.

Pronunciation   Characters: Pronunciation   Characters:

Example: 户 (hù)   护 (hù)   沪 (hù)   1. 竟 _____   _____

2. 两 _____   _____   3. 古 _____   _____

4. 加 _____   _____   5. 每 _____   _____

III. Fill in the blanks with the word in the box below that best completes the phrases.

> 倒霉 辆 马路 轻 意外 落 着急 闯

李强是个丢三落四的人。考试那天，他到公车站的时候才发现他把钱包_____在家里了。没有钱坐公车，时间又不够回家拿钱包，他开始_____起来了。后来他看到对面的饭馆停了一_____自行车，就问老板借了骑到学校。在_____上他看到每天坐的那辆公车发生了_____，还好车上的人都只是_____伤而已。李强觉得自己今天其实也并不是那么_____。回到学校，他紧张地_____进教室，但发现一个人也没有。原来他记错了考试时间，同学们已经考完试走了。

CHARACTER WRITING PRACTICE 7.1

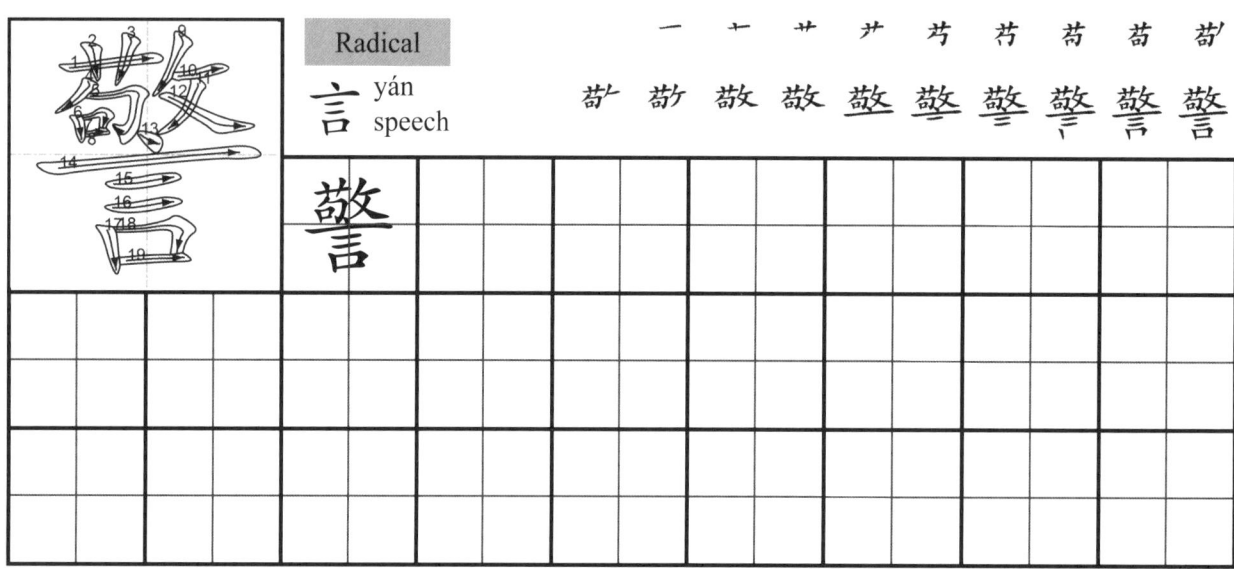

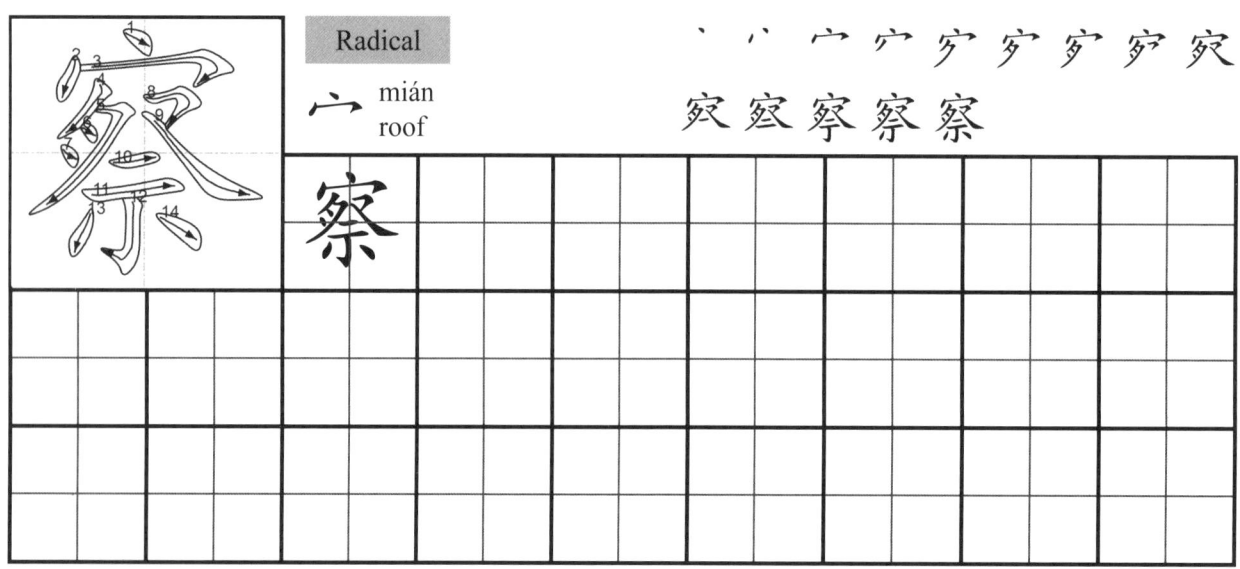

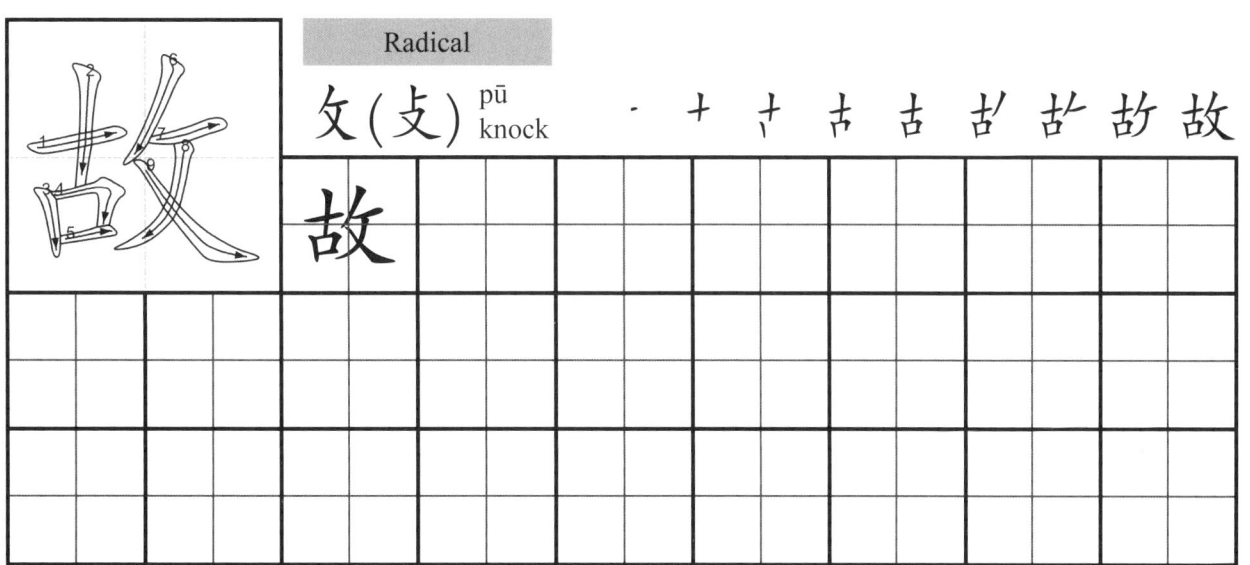

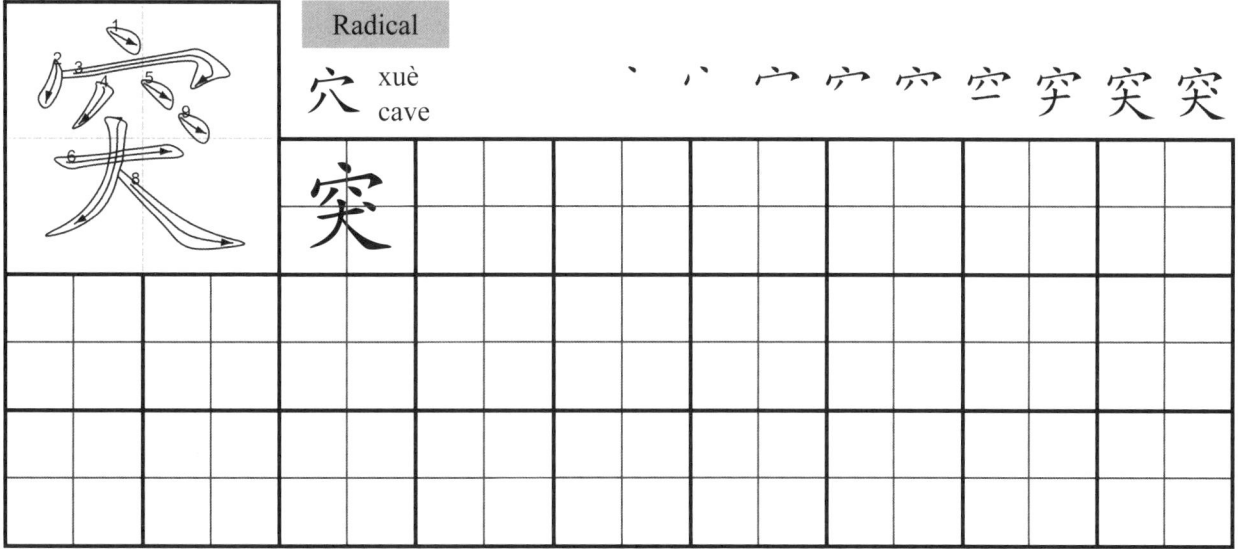

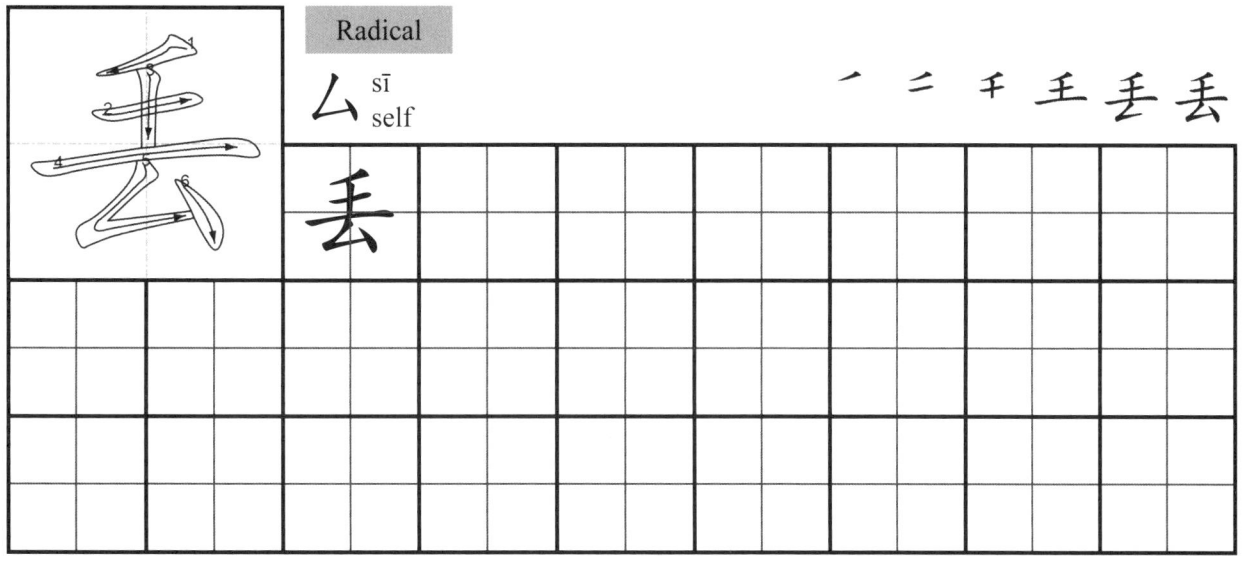

Unit 7 · Lesson 1 · Emergencies

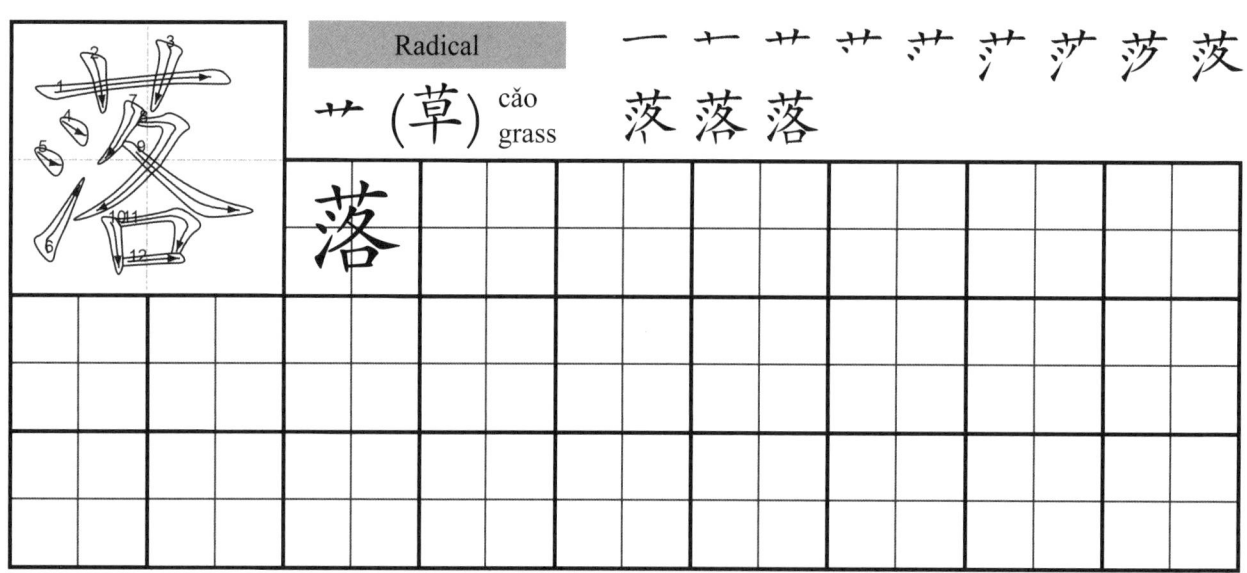

Radical 艹(草) cǎo grass

一 艹 艹 艹 艹 艹 莎 莎 茖 茖 落 落

落

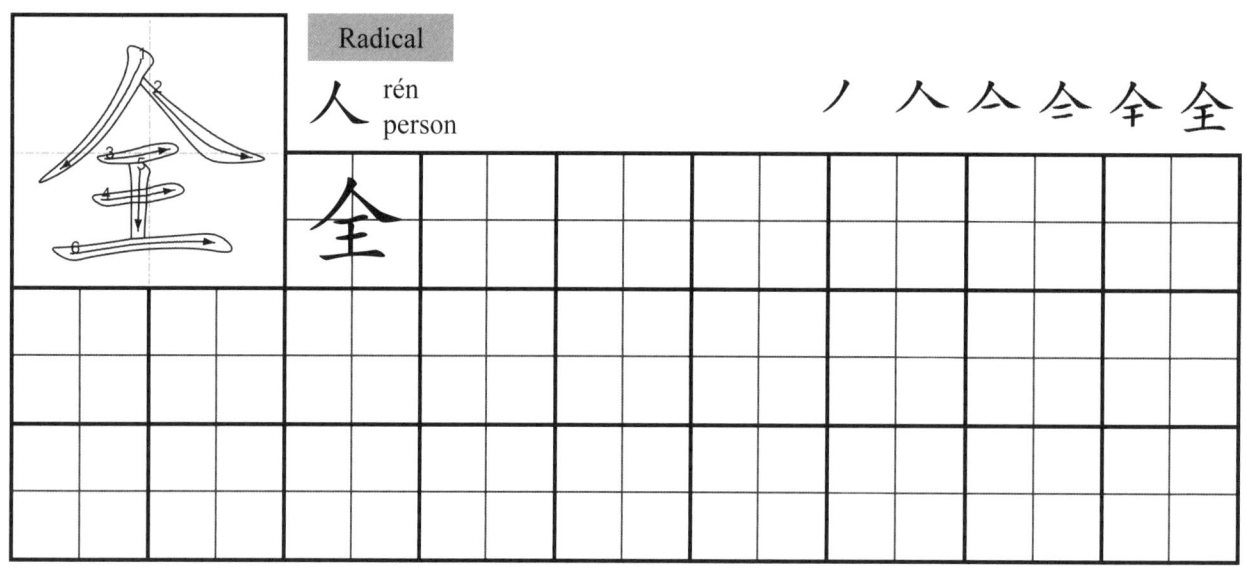

Radical 人 rén person

丿 人 人 仐 仝 全

全

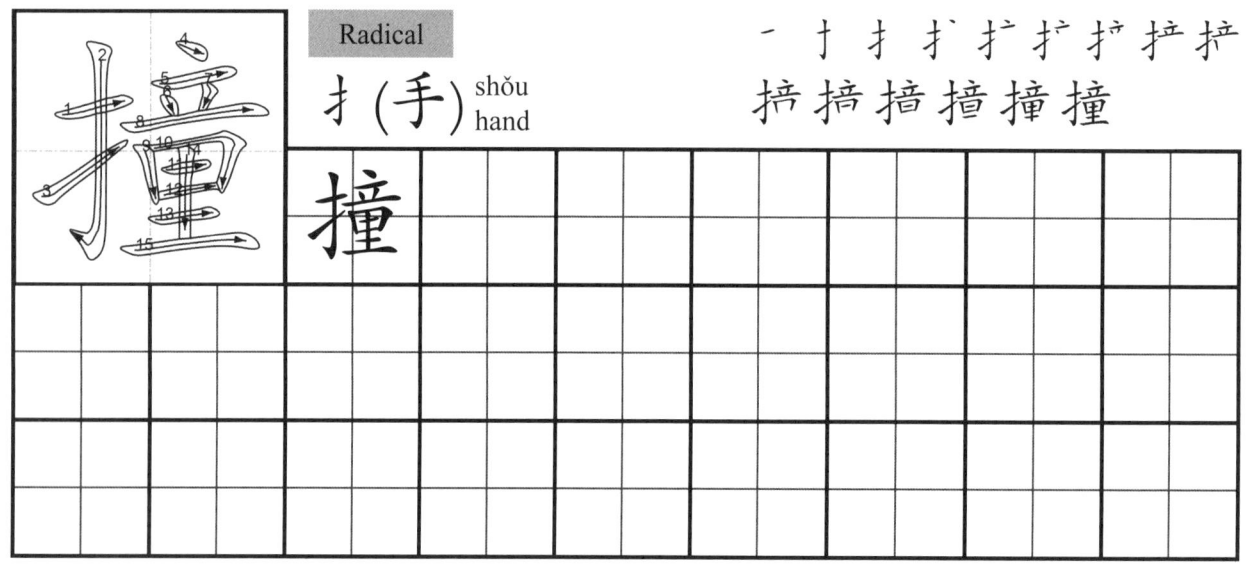

Radical 扌(手) shǒu hand

一 十 扌 扌 扩 扩 扩 护 护 挡 挡 挡 撞 撞 撞

撞

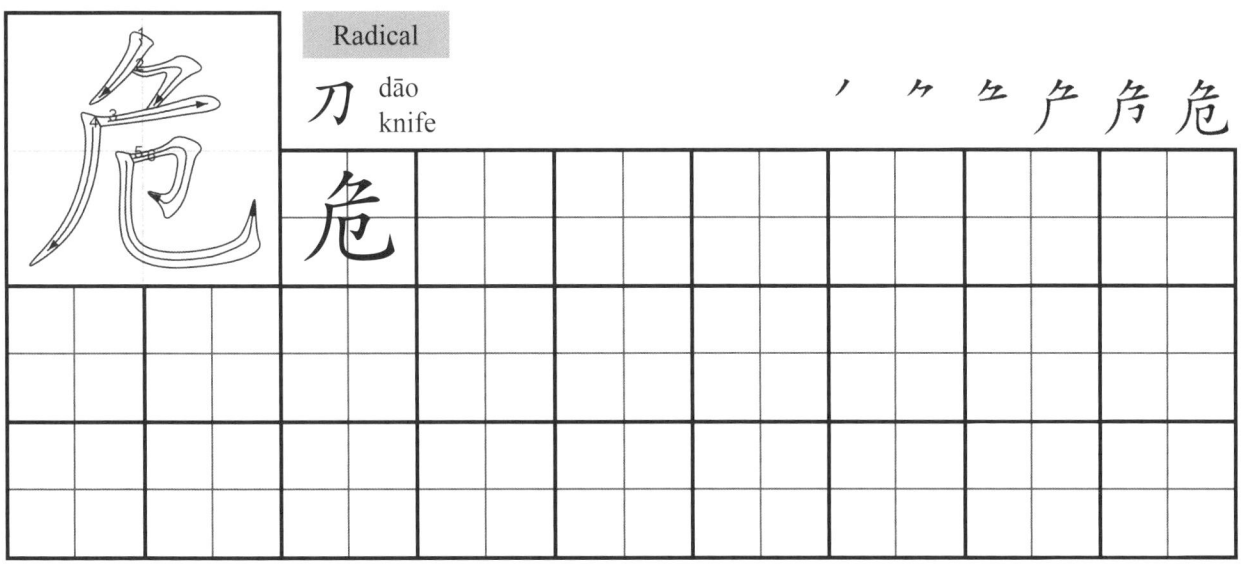

Radical 刀 dāo knife

丿 ㇈ ⺈ 产 产 危

危

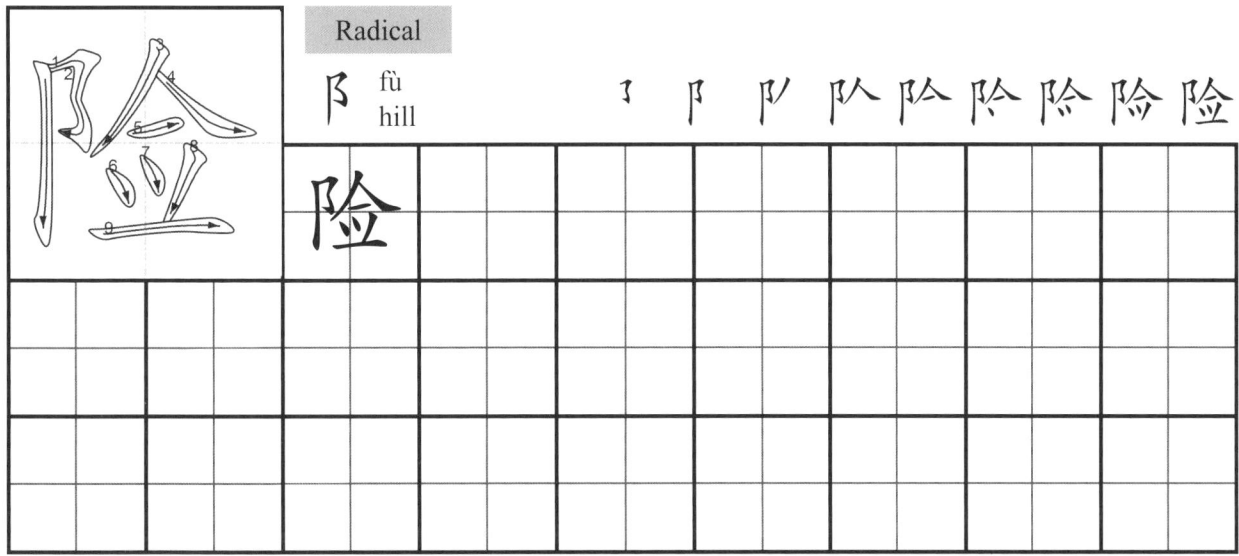

Radical 阝 fù hill

丨 卩 阝 队 阼 阷 险 险

险

Radical 示 shì spirit

一 十 オ 木 朩 村 材 林 林
埜 埜 禁 禁

禁

Unit 7 · Lesson 1 · Emergencies

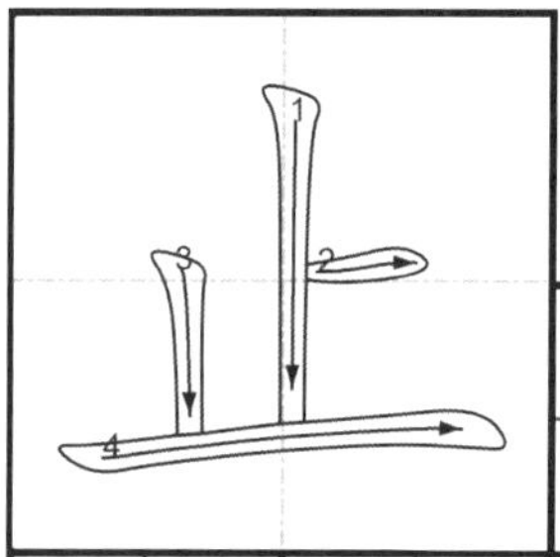

Radical

止 zhǐ stop　　　丨 卜 止 止

止

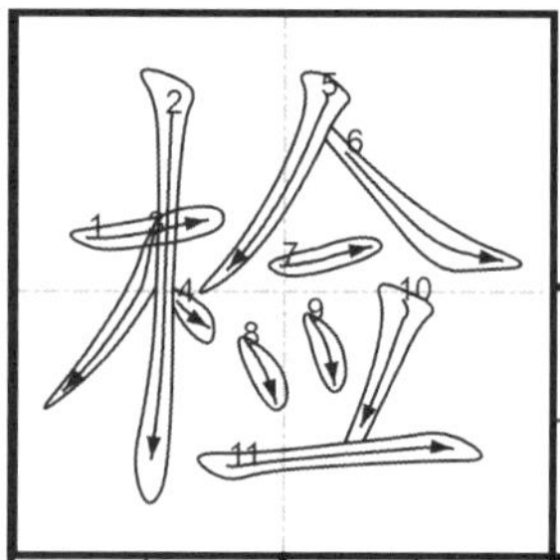

Radical

木 mù wood　　　一 十 才 オ 木 朴 朴 检 检 检 检

检

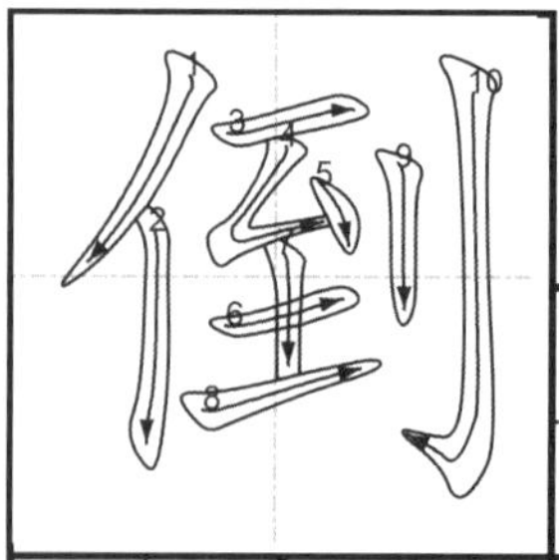

Radical

亻(人) rén person　　　ノ 亻 亻 亻 仁 仵 伜 侄 倒 倒

倒

LISTENING COMPREHENSION 7.1

I. Listen to the recording and answer the question.

1. The woman would most likely respond with:

    A. 警察先生给我开了一张罚单。
    B. 糟糕，我忘了带身份证！我这个人常常丢三落四的。
    C. 我帮你叫救护车吧！
    D. 这辆三轮车突然撞了过来。

II. Listen to the recording and answer the following True or False questions.

1. (　) The man is a police officer.
2. (　) The man asked the woman for her ID.
3. (　) The woman said she lost her driver's license.
4. (　) The man is going to issue a ticket to the woman.
5. (　) The weather caused the accident.

III. Listen to the recording and answer the questions.

1. How was the speaker yesterday?

    A. The speaker was very happy.
    B. Everything was going very smoothly for the speaker.
    C. Something bad happened to the speaker.
    D. It was an ordinary day for the speaker.

2. What did the speaker's friend tell the police office?

    A. The driver was not carrying his driver's license.
    B. The driver did not run the red light.
    C. When my friend and I crossed the road, we did not see the red light.
    D. The driver ran the red light.

3. What did the police officer say?

    A. The driver should drive more carefully from now on.
    B. The driver did nothing wrong.
    C. The police office will write the driver a ticket.
    D. Neither the speaker nor the driver did anything wrong.

SPEAKING PRACTICE 7.1

I. You were a witness to an automobile accident where two drivers hit each other. Each driver argues that it was the other person's fault. A police officer arrives on the scene and asks you what you saw. Use the image below to describe how the accident happened.

II. You recently got a traffic ticket and had to go to traffic school for a day. Talk about at least five things you learned in class about how to be a better and safer driver.

STRUCTURE REVIEW 7.1

I. Complete the following Structure Note practices.

Structure Note 7.1: Use 完全 to say "completely."

$$\boxed{完全 + \text{Adjective / Verb Phrase}}$$

A. Read the following passage about a student from China and use 完全 to answer the questions below.

> 杨艺是从中国来的留学生，他记得刚刚来美国的时候，别人对他说英语他一点都听不懂，他也不知道怎样和他的美国室友相处。杨艺发现美国人和中国人的生活习惯非常不同，于是为了多了解他的室友，杨艺常常跑到他的室友房间里看，又喜欢问他室友比较隐私的问题。后来他的室友受不了，就申请换宿舍了。杨艺这时候才发现原来中西文化有很多不同的地方。

1. 杨艺刚来美国的时候会英语吗？

   _____

2. 杨艺和他的室友相处得好吗？

   _____

3. 杨艺和室友的生活习惯一样吗？

   _____

4. 你觉得那时候的杨艺对美国文化了解吗？为什么？

   _____

Structure Note 7.2: Use 并 to emphasize a negative contrast.

$$\boxed{\text{Subject} + 并 + \text{Verb Phrase}}$$

B. Your friend is asking you about something related to China. Answer the questions using 并 to express a negative sense or to negate something.

1. 昆明的冬天像北京一样冷吗？

   _____

2. 孔子和庄子的思想相同吗?

3. 中国人新年的时候都会吃饺子吗?

4. "对不起"和"不好意思"是一样的意思吗?

Take the challenge! 动动脑筋!

In this lesson, we learned 并 acts as a particle before a negative phrase to emphasize the negative tone of voice and indicate that something has happened contrary to expectation. 并 can also be used as a conjunction, in formal contexts only, to connect two things to indicate that they are on par, a continuation, or a step futher. For example, 他看书的时候遇到不会的生词会马上查字典,并写在本子上。According to the passage below, can you determine what each usage of 并 means?

他看到前面的交通警察突然停下来,于是他紧张地把车停下,并把驾照拿出来。之后他才知道警察并不是要开他罚单,原来这位警察的车只不过是坏了而已。

Structure Note 7.3: Use 因此 to say "therefore."

因此 + Sentence

C. Complete the sentences below by talking about your own city and using 因此.

1. 在我的城市,宠物是不可以带上公共汽车的……

2. 在我的城市,所有博物馆都是免费入场的……

3. 在我的城市,想考驾照就一定要到驾驶学校学开车……

4. 在我的城市，叫救护车的费用非常贵……

_____

5. 在我的城市……

_____

Structure Note 7.4: Use 再也 (不 / 没) to emphatically state "never ever again."

$$\boxed{\text{Subject} + 再也不 / 没 + \text{Verb Phrase}}$$

D. You are telling your friend about your experiences walking and driving on public roads. Complete each sentence by telling what happened and what you learned by using 再也不/没.

1. 有一次我过马路的时候没看红绿灯……

_____

2. 平时开车的时候我会用手机发电邮……

_____

3. 上个月警察突然走过来要检查我的驾照……

_____

4. 昨天开车我闯了红灯……

_____

5. 上一次我因为走了禁止通行的路……

_____

II. You bought a camera online, but after you received it, you discovered it did not work. You returned the camera by shipping it back to the store. However, the store did not send you a new one. Fill in the customer complaint form below, explaining the reasons for your complaint and proposed actions in detail using the structure notes you learned in this lesson.

顾客投诉表格

顾客姓名 (Name of Customer) _____

收到投诉日期 (Date Received) _____

产品 (Product) _____ 数量 (Quantity) _____

投诉原因 (Reasons of complaint)

_____
_____
_____

建议 (Proposed action)

_____
_____
_____
_____

签字 (Signature)

_____

日期 (Date)

_____

READING COMPREHENSION 7.1

I. Read the passage and answer the following True or False questions.

> 玛丽出了交通事故之后，虽然她被撞得并不厉害，但是周信还是很着急，带她去诊所检查。医生说她的伤不严重，给她开了一些药，告诉她不要担心，但要多喝水、多休息才能好得快。交了医疗费之后，周信问玛丽会不会因为发生了交通事故就生那位师傅的气。玛丽说她并不生气，也不能完全怪那位闯红灯的司机。其实她也有错，她过马路的时候没有看到路上还有没停下来的三轮车，因此那辆出租车突然开过来的时候她也不知道。玛丽说其实那位师傅也挺倒霉的，今天不但被警察开了罚单，而且因为这次的意外，他的车好像也出了点小问题。玛丽又说，以后过马路的时候要特别小心，再也不要一看到绿灯就马上过马路。无论怎么样，都要先等一等，看看路上的车是不是都已经停下来了再走。周信听完玛丽说的话之后，笑着说："依我看，坏事变成了好事，这次的车祸就当做给我们大家都上了一堂课吧。"

1. (　) 医生说玛丽的伤不严重。
2. (　) 周信要玛丽多喝水、多休息。
3. (　) 玛丽还是很生气，觉得是出租车师傅的错。
4. (　) 玛丽说过马路的时候看到绿灯就可以走了。
5. (　) 玛丽觉得以后过马路要特别小心。

Take the challenge! 动动脑筋！

In the Chinese language, some verbs are made up of two characters, such as the verb-object compounds 睡觉, 帮忙, 洗澡, and 游泳. The characters in these separable verbs can still function even if split apart to form a a longer phrase. For example, although the verb 生气 in the sentence "生那位师傅的气" from the passage is separated, it still means "angry" in the context of Zhou Xin asking Mali whether she is angry with the driver. Be careful when forming sentences with separable verbs as they cannot be followed by an object. For example, it is wrong to say "我生气那位师傅。" Can you tell which of the following sentences are correct? Circle ✓ for correct and X for incorrect.

(1.) 有件事情想请你帮忙。　✓ X　(2.) 这个忙我没办法帮你。　✓ X
(3.) 老师帮了我一个大忙。　✓ X　(4.) 这次玛丽帮忙我很多。　✓ X

II. Read the following passage and answer the questions.

发生交通事故怎么办？

开车在路上谁都不想发生事故，但如果发生了事故，要怎么办？下面是一些老司机的经验：

首先，要**保持冷静**。你应该马上停车，放好**警告标志**。发生事故后有的人会非常紧张，坐在车里打电话**报警**，但是**千万**不要这样子做，因为这是很危险的。后面的车如果没有看到前面的事故，就会非常容易发生二次事故。放好**警告标志**以后，可以下车看看有没有人受伤、受伤是不是严重。如果有人伤得比较严重，你不要**挪动**他，最好等救护车来。除了打电话**报警**以外，你也可以用手机或照相机拍下事故的照片。警察来了以后，可以把你拍的照片给警察看，并且告诉警察事故是怎么发生的。

无论是遇到小意外还是严重的车祸，都要报告给警察。**千万**不要因为怕麻烦或者怕被开罚单就离开事故发生的地点。

Notes:
保持冷静 (bǎochí lěngjìng): *v.* to keep calm
警告标志 (jǐnggào biāozhì): *n.* warning sign
报警 (bàojǐng): *vo.* to report to the police
千万 (qiānwàn): *adv.* by all means, absolutely
挪动 (nuódòng): *v.* to move

1. 发生交通事故以后应该先做什么？

   _____

2. 为什么说发生事故后坐在车里打电话报警很危险？

   _____

3. "二次事故"是什么意思？

   _____

4. 如果有人受伤很严重，你应该怎么做？

III. Read the following text messages and answer the questions.

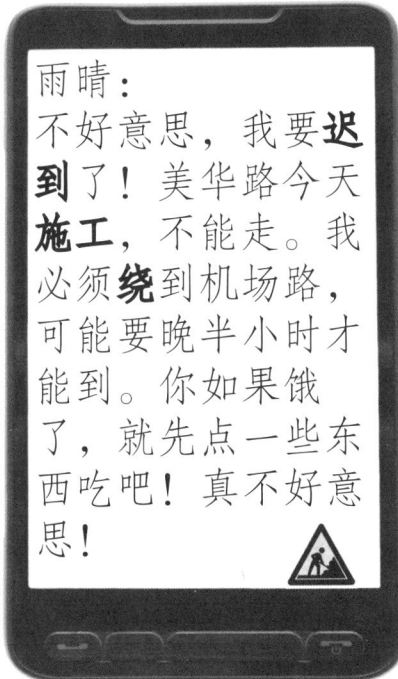

雨晴：
不好意思，我要**迟到**了！美华路今天**施工**，不能走。我必须**绕**到机场路，可能要晚半小时才能到。你如果饿了，就先点一些东西吃吧！真不好意思！

建新：
我刚才听**广播**，好像机场路上发生了事故，车很多。我建议你不要走机场路，走京华路，那条路车比较少。你不要着急，我会等你。

1. 建新为什么迟到了？

   A. 起床晚了
   B. 路上发生了交通事故
   C. 他要走的路施工
   D. 他走错路了

2. 雨晴为什么建议建新不要走机场路？

   A. 机场路有事故
   B. 机场路也在施工
   C. 机场路太远了
   D. 机场路要收费

3. 他们约在哪里见面？

   A. 电影院
   B. 餐厅
   C. 机场
   D. 学校

Notes:
迟到 (chídào): *v.* to be late
施工 (shīgōng): *vo.* to construct
绕 (rào): *v.* to make a detour
广播 (guǎngbō): *n.* broadcast

4. 建新在施工的路上也看到这个标示，你知道是什么意思吗？

WRITING PRACTICE 7.1

I. You were biking to school in the morning, and a car accidentally hit you while you were walking your bike through a crosswalk. It was not a major accident, but you hurt your leg and have a headache. You need to go see a doctor and cannot make it to class. Write an e-mail to your professor explaining what happened.

To:
From:
Subject:

II. In your area, there has been an increase in traffic accidents. You want to help curb this alarming trend, so you write an email to your local representative to offer suggestions for new driving laws that they should consider. In your e-mail, provide two suggestions of what new driving laws should be implemented and why. Support your ideas with a personal experience.

To:
From:
Subject:

UNIT 7 — LESSON 2

Modern Chinese 现代中文

自然灾害

VOCABULARY REVIEW 7.2

I. The following characters have more than one pronunciation. Write the pinyin and an alternate pinyin for each character and form a vocabulary or phrase for each one.

Example: 匙 (chí) 一匙盐   (shi) 钥匙

1. 和 _____ _____   2. 长 _____ _____
3. 得 _____ _____   4. 场 _____ _____
5. 行 _____ _____   6. 处 _____ _____
7. 假 _____ _____   8. 划 _____ _____

II. Below are riddles each describing a different character. Figure out what the character is and use it to form a vocabulary term.

Example:
把冬天吃到嘴巴里： 图 （图片）   1. 家里着火了： _____

2. 大雨落在横山上： _____   3. 很小的土地： _____

4. 有雷但不下雨： _____   5. 水边就是少了水： _____

III. Rewrite each sentence by substituting the bolded words with appropriate vocabulary words from this lesson.

1. 听说王大中上个月被车撞了，他现在**好**了吗？

   _____

2. 因为暴雨的关系，我们下午要**坐的飞机**延误了。

   _____

3. 由于最近干天气干燥，我们的国家公园发生了多**次**火灾。

   _____

4. 我们平时应该**特别注意**我们城市环境质量的工作。

   _____

5. 现在很多年轻人迷上了上网，叫他们**不要用**网络实在是不容易。

   _____

CHARACTER WRITING PRACTICE 7.2

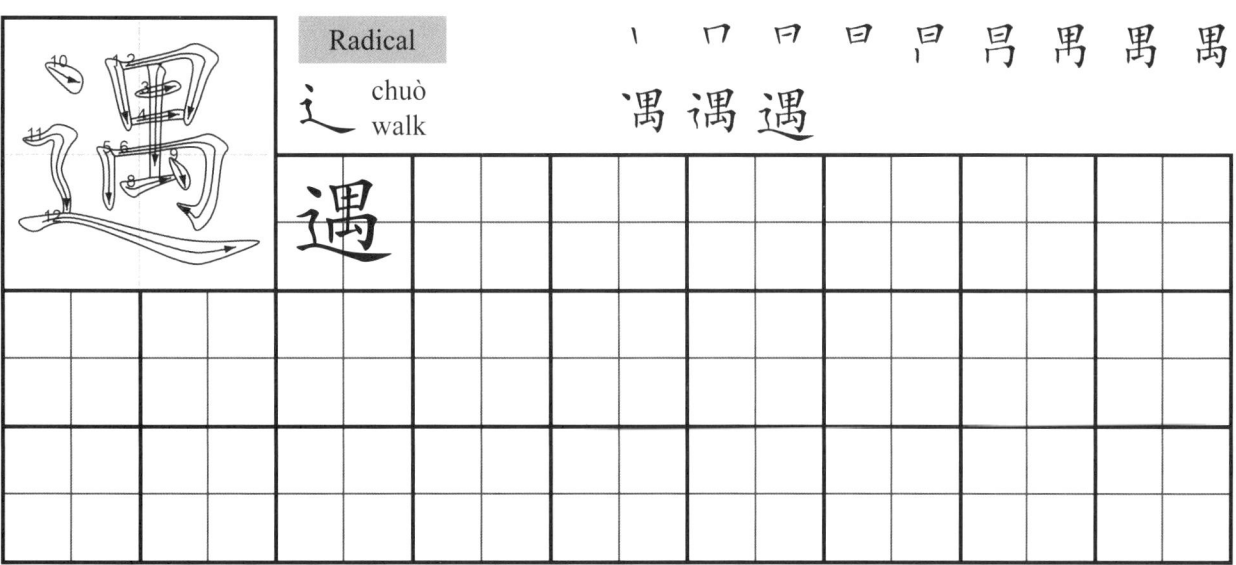

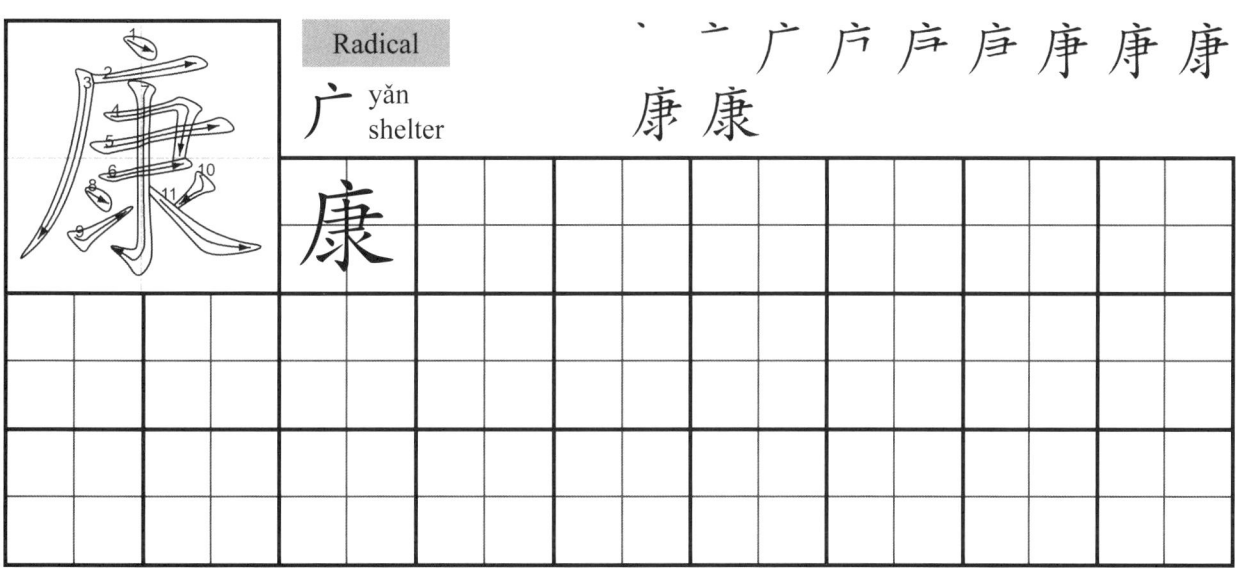

Unit 7 • Lesson 2 • Emergencies

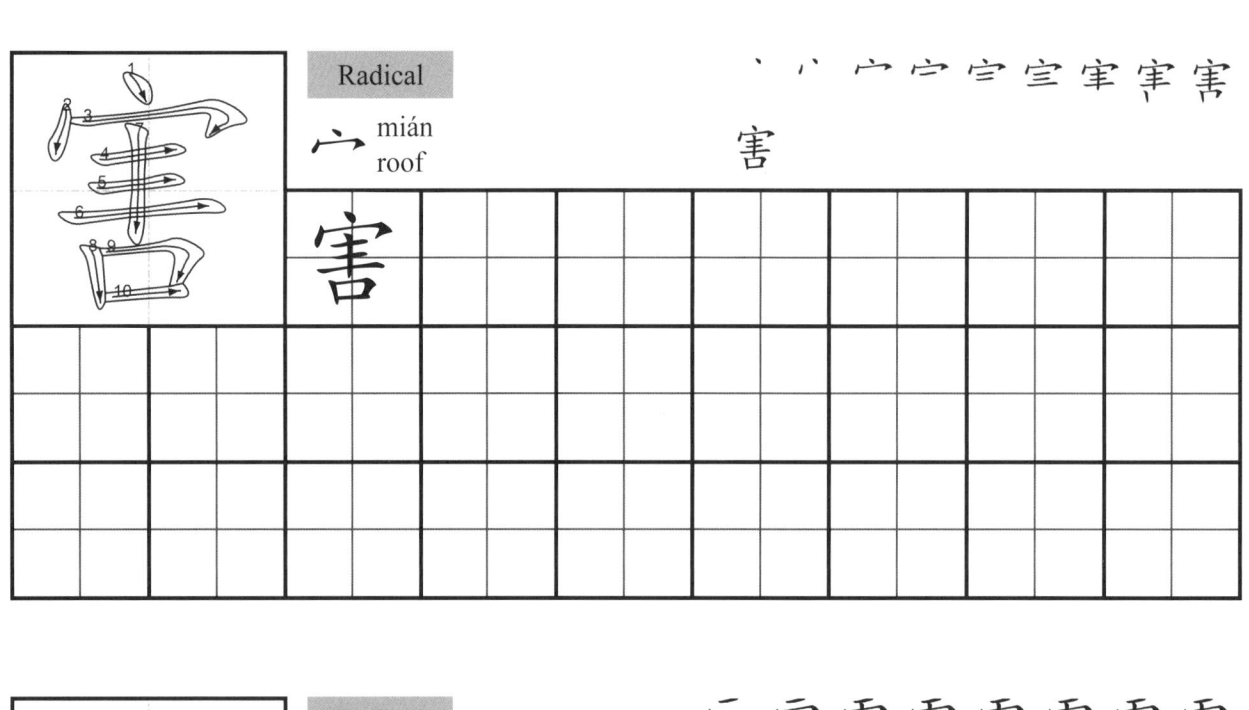

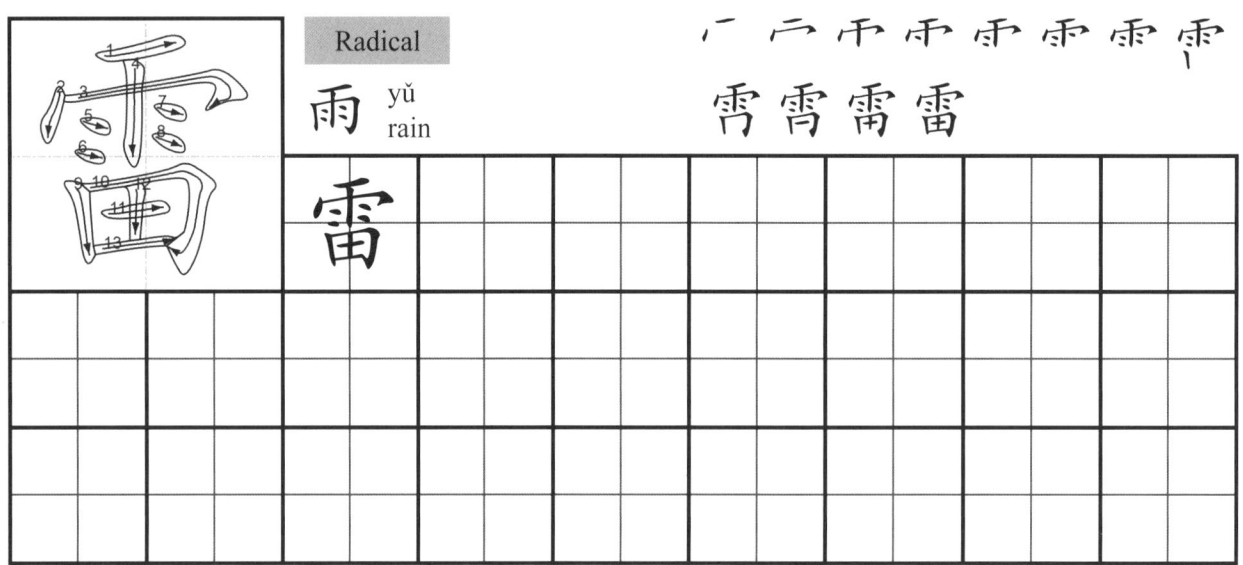

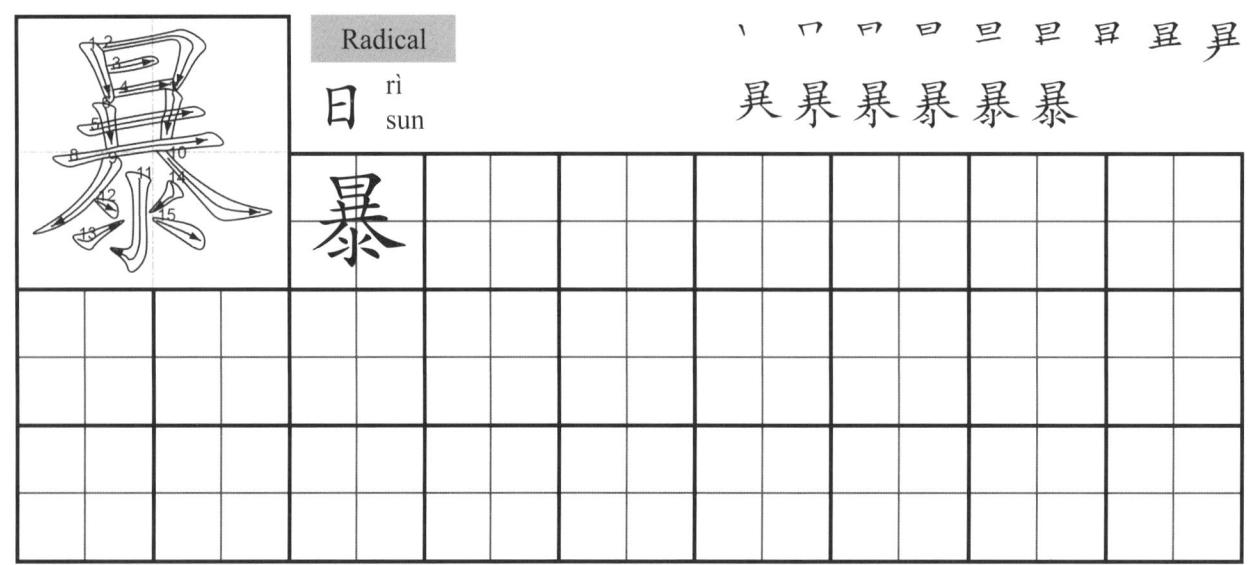

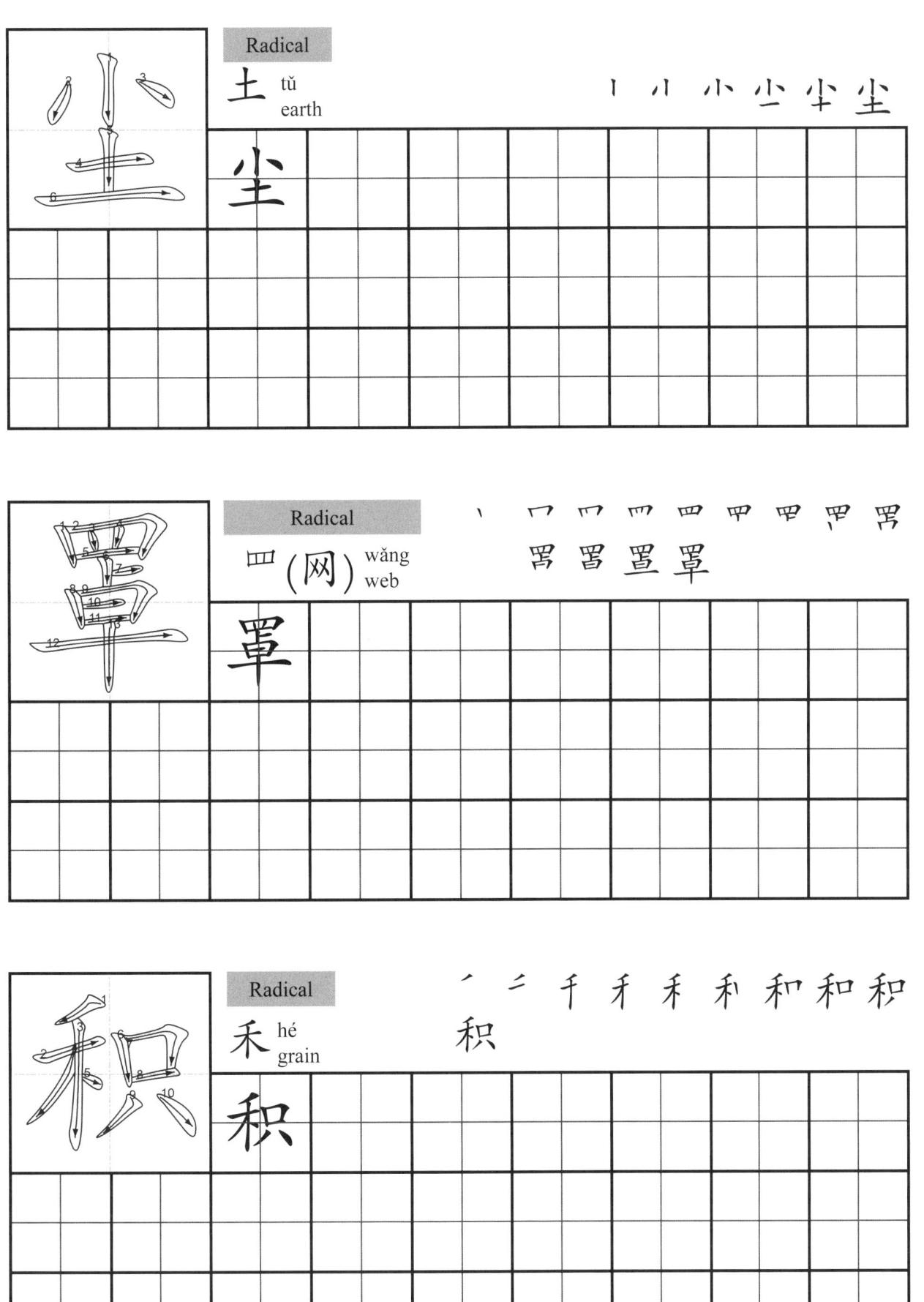

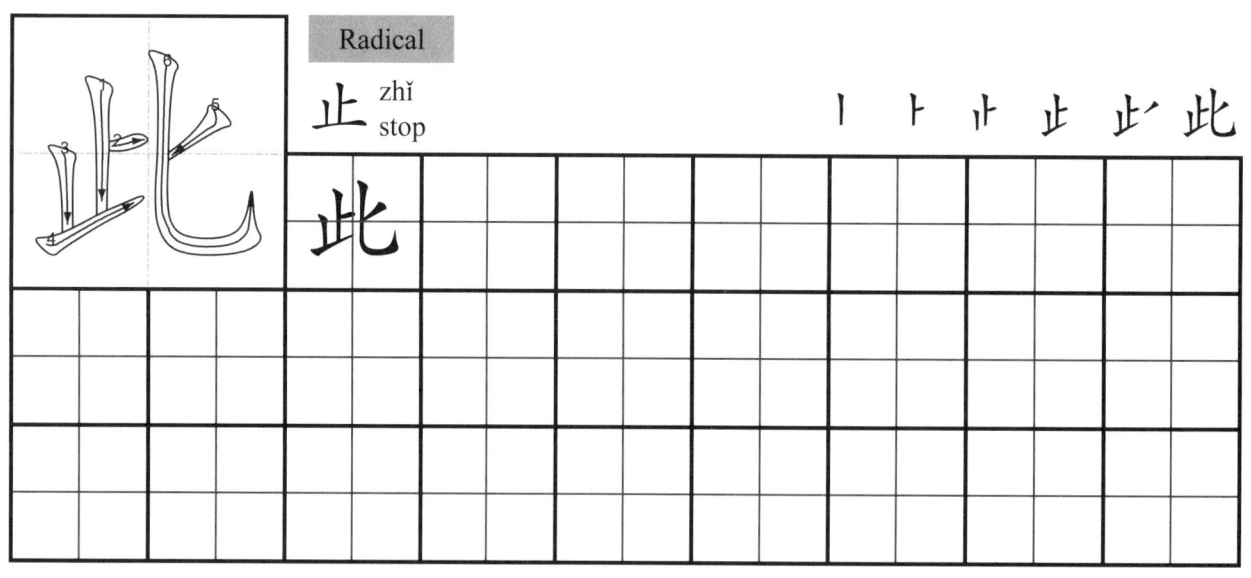

Radical 止 zhǐ stop
丨 ⺊ ⺌ 止 此 此
此

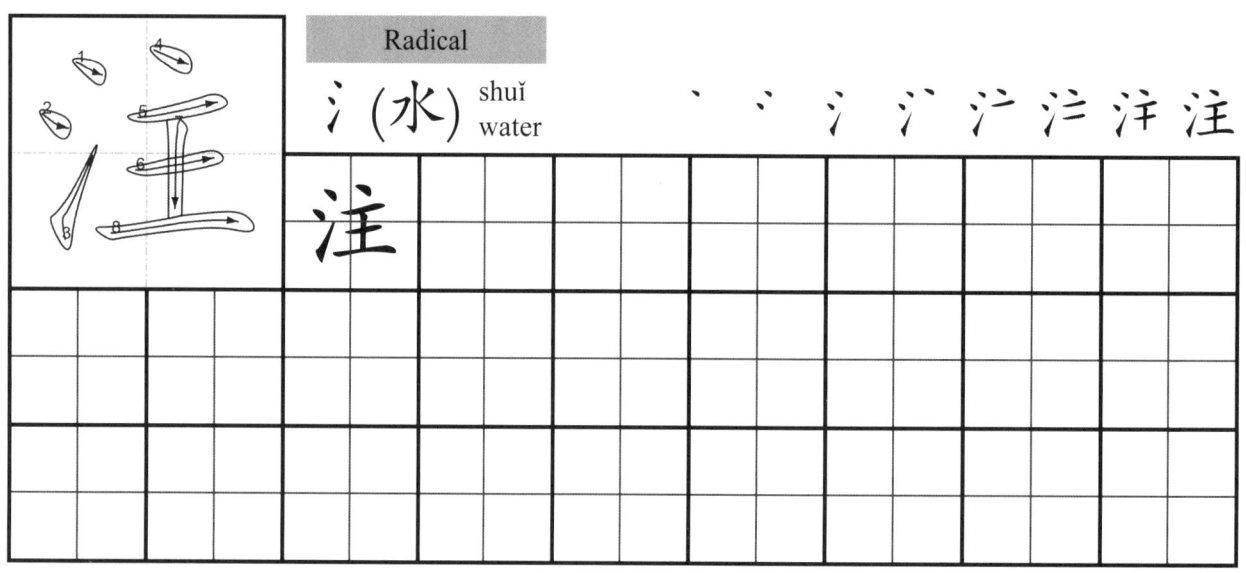

Radical 氵(水) shuǐ water
丶 丶 氵 氵 汀 汁 泮 注
注

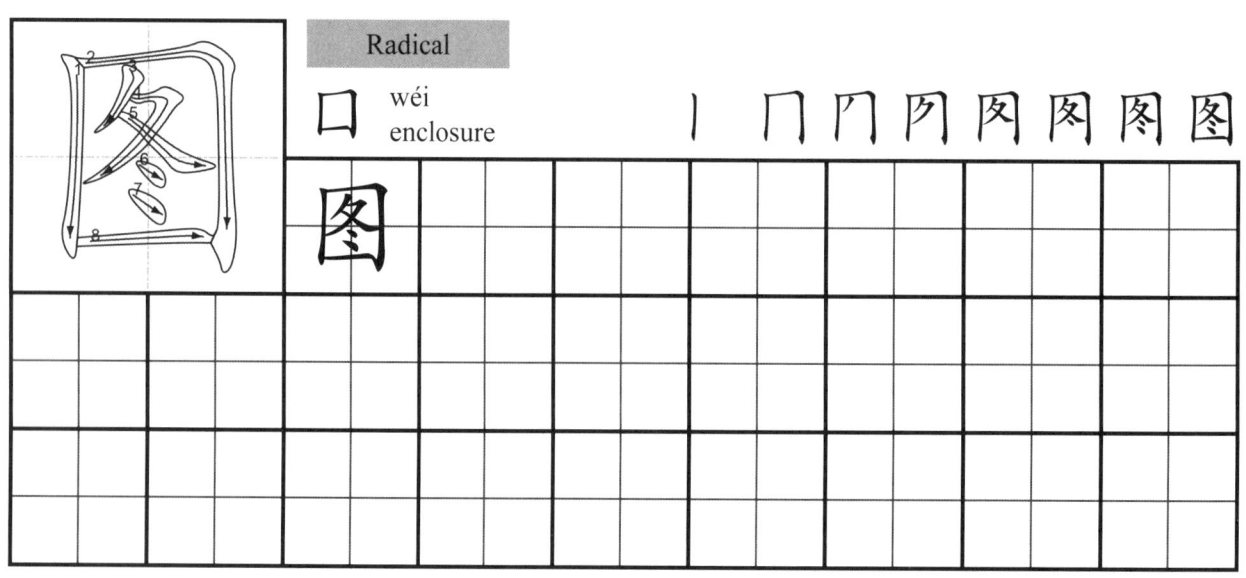

Radical 囗 wéi enclosure
丨 冂 冂 冈 図 图 图 图
图

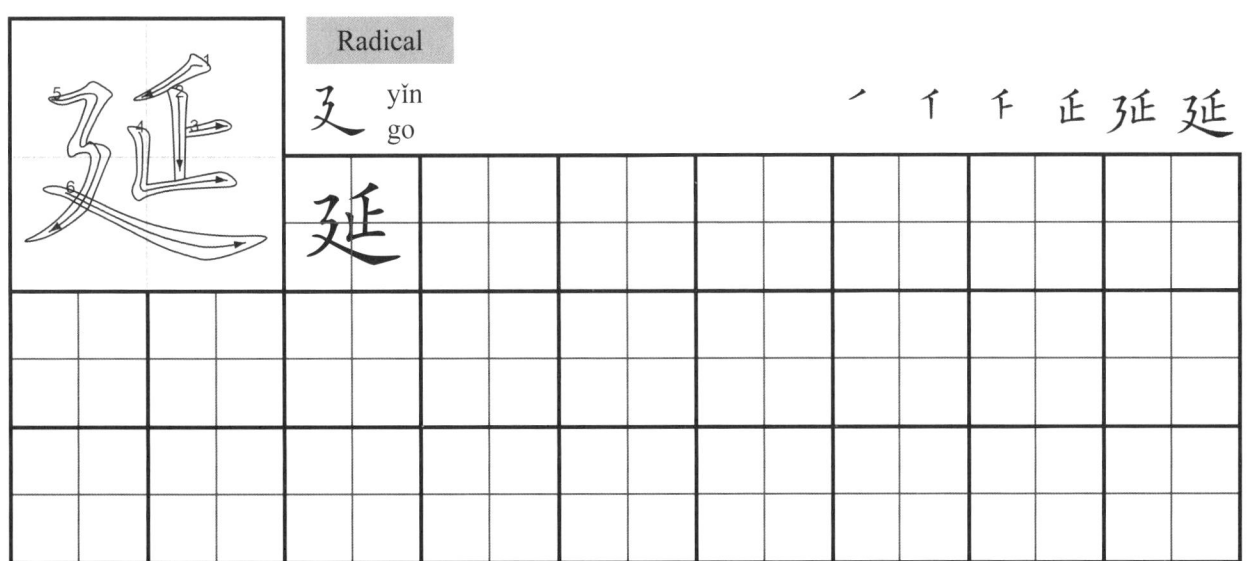

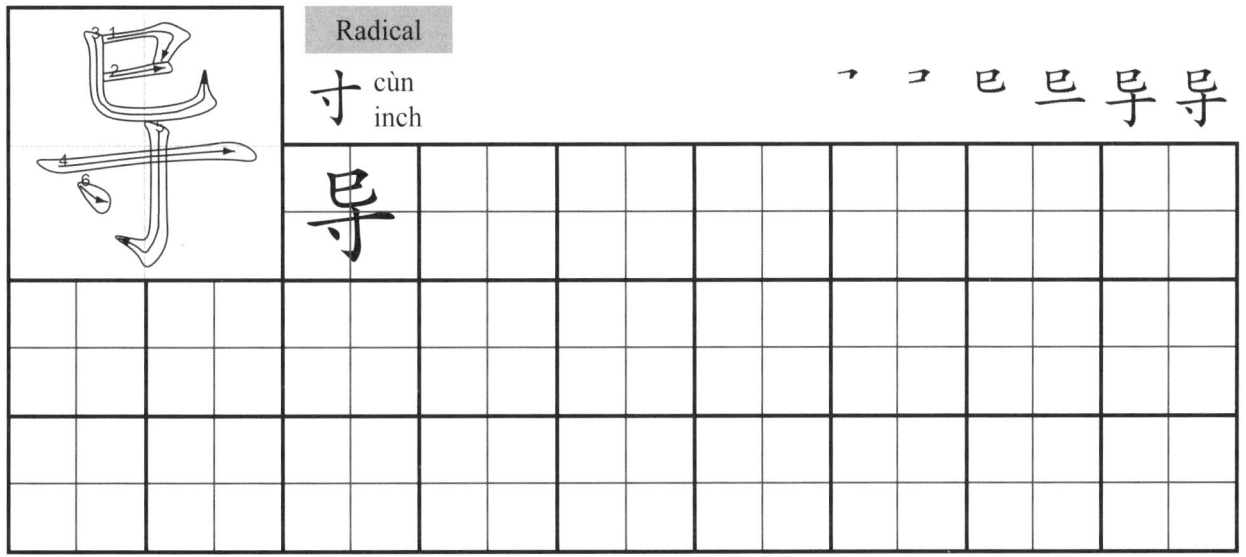

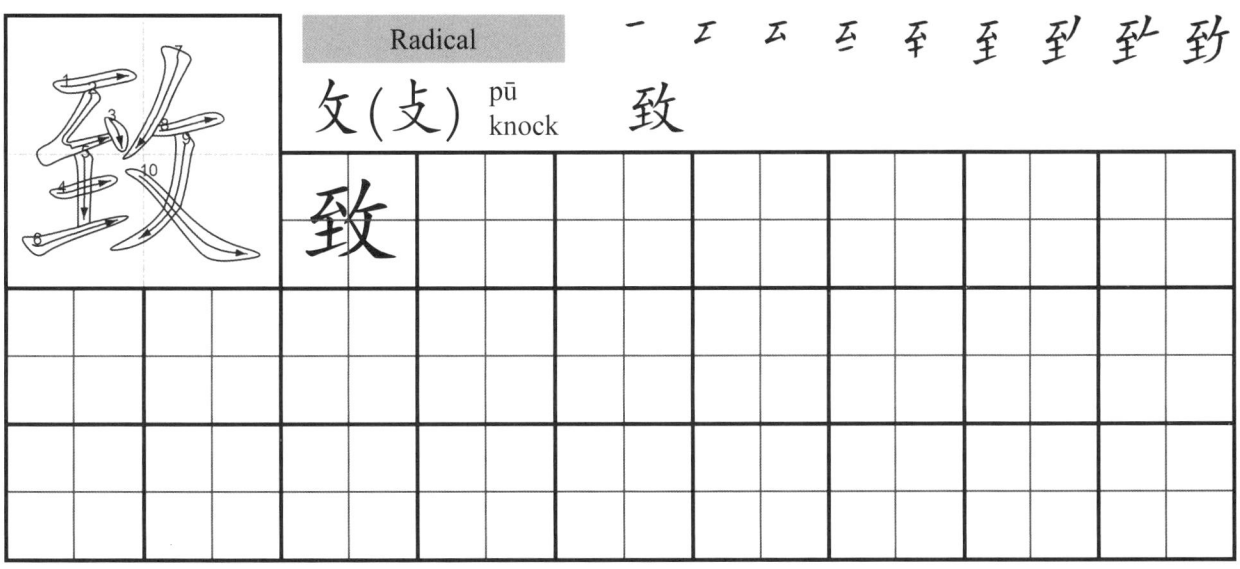

Unit 7 · Lesson 2 · Emergencies

LISTENING COMPREHENSION 7.2

I   Listen to the recording and answer the question.

1. The man would most likely respond with:

   A. 沙尘暴一般发生在春天。
   B. 最好不要出门，要是外出的话要带上口罩和眼镜。
   C. 要找安全的地方蹲下。
   D. 会让多个航班延误。

II. Listen to the recordings and answer the following True or False questions.

1. (   ) The man experienced an earthquake before.
2. (   ) The man said someone was injured during his earthquake experience.
3. (   ) The woman disagreed with the idea that people should hide under tables during an earthquake.
4. (   ) The man always pays attention to natural disaster reports.
5. (   ) The woman let the man borrow her natural disaster report.

III. Listen to the recordings and answer the questions.

1. Why do many people not pay close attention to natural disasters and how can you best protect yourself?

   _____

2. What should you do when a rainstorm occurs?

   _____

3. Why should you pay close attention to various natural disaster reports?

   _____

SPEAKING PRACTICE 7.2

I. Recently, there was a major rainstorm in your region that caused numerous problems. You are a news reporter for your school's student-run TV station. Using the images below, give a news report about what happened and how it affected everyone in your area.

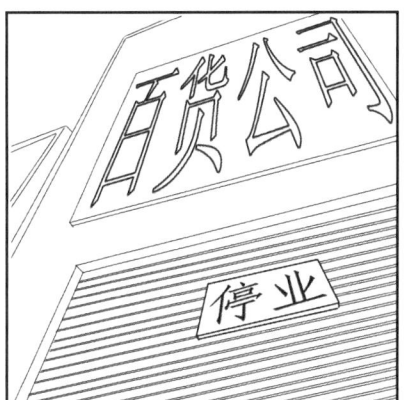

II. A major natural disaster occurred in another area outside of where you live, and you went to volunteer to help with the relief efforts. Describe what happened, what you saw, and what you did in your volunteer work.

Unit 7 ▪ Lesson 2 ▪ Emergencies

STRUCTURE REVIEW 7.2

I. Complete the following Structure Note practices.

Structure Note 7.5: Use 关于 to say "with regard to" a topic.

$$关于 + \text{Topic} + 的 + \text{Noun}$$

A. Below is a list of Xiang'an's preferences regarding his interests. Use 关于 to describe his preferences.

> 最喜欢上的课：英国文学
> 最近看过的一本书：《中国近代历史》
> 最喜欢看的电影：《功夫熊猫》
> 最常看的杂志：《宠爱宠物》
> 最喜欢看的博客：美食在欧洲

Example: 祥安最喜欢上关于文学的课。

1. _____
2. _____
3. _____
4. _____

Take the challenge! 动动脑筋！

关于 is a preposition that means "about" or "on." For example, 他写了一本关于美食的书, meaning "he wrote a book about gourmet food." In *Modern Chinese* Textbook, Vol. 1, Unit 13, Lesson 2, we learned 有关 acts as a verb to indicate that a noun is relevant or related to a particular topic. For example, 一本有关美食的书 and 一本跟美食有关的书 both indicate that a book has information related to gourmet food. They can also imply that the book is not necessary all about gourmet food.

这本关于中国文化的书只有几页是跟书法有关的。

Read the above sentence and determine which of the following statements is true.

这本书跟文化有关。(T/F)

这本书是关于书法的。 (T/F)

这是一本有关书法的书。 (T/F)

这本书有几页是关于书法的。 (T/F)

Structure Note 7.6: Use 此外 to introduce additional points.

$$\boxed{\text{此外 + Sentence}}$$

B. Use the vocabulary in the word bank to complete the following sentences.

> 减少 增加 外出 开车 室内 室外 伤者 蹲下
> 大型 物品 关注 口罩 关掉 积水 安全 远离 高
> 危险 严重 电器 检查 打电话 报警

1. 地震的时候，_____
2. 遇到暴雨时，_____
3. 遇到沙尘暴的时候，_____
4. 发生交通意外后，_____

Structure Note 7.7: Use 以 to indicate the purpose of an action.

$$\boxed{\text{Subject + Action + 以 + Purpose}}$$

C. Below are some problems and suggestions. Use 以 to connect a clause from "problems" column with a clause from the "suggestions" column to create one sentence.

建议

减少医院对病人收的医疗费
增加闯红灯的罚款
增加发展环保的项目
多开一些图书馆

问题

很多人都付不起看病的费用
最近的交通事故越来越多
关注自然环境的人不多
很多孩子没机会看课本以外的书

Example: 我建议减少医院对病人收的医疗费，以保证每个人都能付得起看病的费用。

1. _____
2. _____
3. _____
4. (create your own sentence) _____

Structure Note 7.8: Use (从)……以来 to indicate "ever since" a certain time in the past.

> (从 +) Time + 以来, + Clause

> Subject + (从 +) Time + 以来 + Verb Phrase

D. Below are records of various weather conditions. Use (从)……以来 to describe how long it has been since the last occurrence of each weather condition.

Weather Condition	Previous Record	Latest Record
Rainstorm	2003-7-30	2013-8-23
Sandstorm	2012-5-14	2013-4-6
Earthquake	1998-2-15	2013-1-12
Low temperature	2013-11-11	2013-12-15
Snowstorm	2013-1-2	2013-12-28

Example: 二零一三年八月二十三日的暴雨是十年以来最严重的一次。

1. _____
2. _____
3. _____
4. _____

II. Below is a news report about a traffic accident. Rewrite the underlined sentences in this article or add new ones using the structure notes you learned in this lesson.

减少交通意外发生
你我都有责任

今天发生了最近两年最严重的一起交通事故。事故的原因是一位出租车司机开车时不小心睡着，导致与另外两辆校车发生碰撞。事故里有四十多名学生受伤，伤者大部分都是五到十二岁的小学生。警察提醒司机，如果开车的时候太累的话，就应该把车停在安全的地方休息。开车的时候每时每刻都要注意马路情况。警察也建议司机多关注交通安全的报告和知识，这样才能减少交通意外发生。

READING COMPREHENSION 7.2

I. Read the passage and answer the following questions.

　　小美只在电影里见过沙尘暴，她想多了解一些关于沙尘暴的知识，所以她上网去查了一些资料。沙尘暴是北京常见的自然灾害，一般多出现在春天（3月-5月）。因为北京的春天经常刮大风，下雨又比较少，所以大风常常带起很多地上的沙尘。

　　在2000年左右，北京的沙尘天气比较多。2000-2002年一共发生沙尘天气51次：2000年11次、2001年21次、2002年19次。这几年沙尘天气少了一些，一般一年不超过10天。沙尘天气有四级，最严重的是四级——强沙尘暴。

　　强沙尘暴时，航班常常会被延误或者停飞。北京的沙尘天气一般是一级或二级，不会非常严重，不过还是得减少室外活动，必须外出的时候一定要记得戴上口罩，注意眼睛和鼻子不要进沙尘。

　　小美看了这些资料后，增加了对于沙尘暴的了解，也就不觉得那么怕沙尘天气了。

1. 北京的沙尘天气一般会出现在什么季节？

2. 为什么会在这个季节？

3. 近20年里，北京哪年的沙尘天气最多？

4. 沙尘暴分几级？最强的是几级？

5. 北京的沙尘天气一般是几级？

II. Read the passage and answer the following True or False and question/answer questions.

北京昨天发生61年以来最大暴雨

昨天，北京发生暴雨，到7月22日0点，全市平均**降雨量**达到164mm，是61年以来最大的一场暴雨。昨天上午10点左右，部分地区开始**降雨**。**降雨量**增加得很快，到中午十二点左右，全市开始强**降雨**。昨天气象台一共**发布**了4次暴雨**预警**。早上9点30分，**发布**第一次蓝色**预警**，到下午2点，全市发生强**降雨**后，暴雨**预警提高**到黄色。下午3点30分，**气象台**继续**发布**黄色**预警**。到18:30分，暴雨**预警**再次**提高**，到橙色**预警**。这是从北京2005年开始气象**预警**以来第一个橙色暴雨**预警**。这场大暴雨导致了好几起事故。除了几场车祸以外，另外一起事故是一位六岁的小孩在暴雨发生的时候正好在室外，没想到飞来横祸，挂在旁边公寓楼上面的广告掉了下来打到了他。幸运的是伤并不是太严重。孩子的父母表示现在他已经没有危险，正在康复中。各位父母都应该告诉自己的孩子，当灾害出现时，一定要注意远离大型物品。

Notes:
降雨量 (jiàngyǔliàng): *n.* rainfall
降雨 (jiàngyǔ): *vo.* to rain
发布 (fābù): *v.* to issue
预警 (yùjǐng): *n.* advance warning
提高 (tígāo): *v.* to raise
气象台 (qìxiàngtái): *n.* observatory

1. (　) 暴雨发生在7月22日。
2. (　) 这是61年以来最大的暴雨。
3. (　) 降雨最早出现在上午9点半。
4. (　) 昨天发布了暴雨红色预警。
5. (　) 2005年以前北京没有气象预警。

6. 昨天一共发布了几次暴雨预警？分别在几点，是什么级别？

_____

7. 那位小孩遇到了什么事故？是怎么发生的？现在的情况怎么样？

_____

III. Below is a daily advice index that is seen on the official Chinese weather website. On a scale of 1 - 5, with 1 being the most suitable and 5 being the least suitable, the index provides a rating on the suitability of doing various activities, depending on the weather. Read the index and the text message and answer the following questions.

明天的生活指数

空气质量：4
明天可能会出现沙尘天气，空气质量非常不好。

穿衣指数：2
明天不冷不热，适合穿长衣长裤。

洗车指数：3
最近一周都不会下雨，但明天可能会有沙尘天气，不太适合洗车。

交通指数：3
明天可能会出现沙尘天气，能见度较低，车辆应缓慢行驶。

旅游指数：4
明天可能会出现沙尘天气，不适合旅游。

运动指数：4
明天空气质量不好，不适合室外运动。

小文：
你看天气预报了吗？明天可能会有沙尘天气，**空气**质量非常不好。我刚刚在网上查了明天的生活**指数**，明天既不**适合**旅游也不**适合**运动。我觉得我们还是不要去爬山了，你说呢？

Notes:
空气 (kōngqì): *n.* air
指数 (zhǐshù): *n.* index
适合 (shìhé): *adj.* suitable

1. What will the weather be like tomorrow?

2. What did Xiaowen and his friend plan to do tomorrow?

3. What would you recommend Xiaowen and his friend do tomorrow? Why?

WRITING PRACTICE 7.2

I. You are at the airport waiting for your flight home to spend Christmas with your family when suddenly an earthquake occurs. This causes your flight to be delayed. You want to reassure your family that you are okay, so you text message them and describe what happened and that you are not hurt. In your text, also let them know that you are bringing gifts for your family members and cannot wait to see them.

II. You have a travel blog for your city. The holidays are coming up and many tourists are expected to visit your city. Write a blog post introducing what kind of weather and natural disasters they can expect during this season, and what items they should bring in preparation.

UNIT 8 — LESSON 1

Modern Chinese 现代中文

在机场

VOCABULARY REVIEW 8.1

I. Match the verbs with the nouns and then write the English meaning for each phrase.

1. 办 •
2. 订 •
3. 赶 •
4. 靠 •
5. 登 •

• 时间
• 公共汽车
• 机票
• 走道
• 驾照
• 长城
• 计划
• 签证
• 机
• 自己

_____
_____
_____
_____
_____
_____
_____
_____

II. Write the meaning of each radical. Then write two characters containing the radicals and form a vocabulary phrase with each one that is related to the meaning of the radical.

Example: 足 (foot, leg)   踢球 舞蹈 道路 跑步 跌倒 跳跃

1. 车 _____ _____   2. 舟 _____ _____
3. 广 _____ _____   4. 户 _____ _____

III. In each of the following sentences, fill in the blank by circling the correct vocabulary term.

1. 今年夏天的最高气温大大 _____ 了去年，你知道是什么原因吗？
   (A) 超   (B) 超过   (C) 赶   (D) 不如

2. 这辆出租车突然停在马路 _____，导致多辆汽车从后撞上。
   (A) 中   (B) 中间   (C) 上   (D) 上面

3. 这家医院里的医护 _____ 每天最少要工作一十二个小时。
   (A) 人   (B) 员   (C) 人员   (D) 者

4. 弟弟一岁的时候就有十二 _____，比我小时候重多了。
   (A) 米   (B) 磅   (C) 斤   (D) 公斤

232 第八单元 · 第一课 · 行

CHARACTER WRITING PRACTICE 8.1

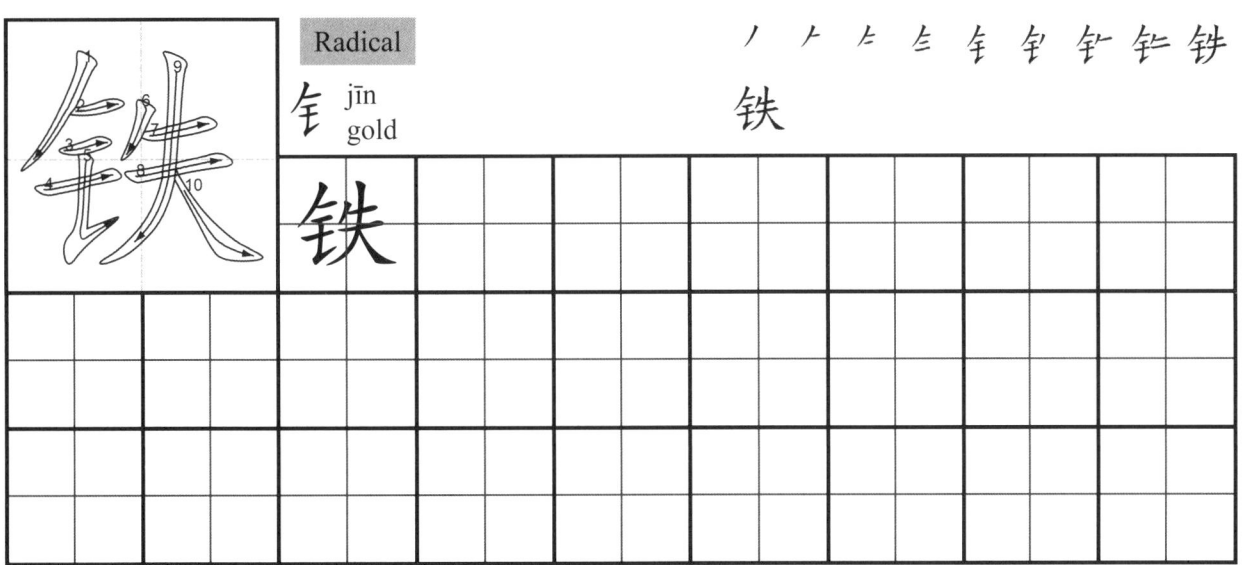

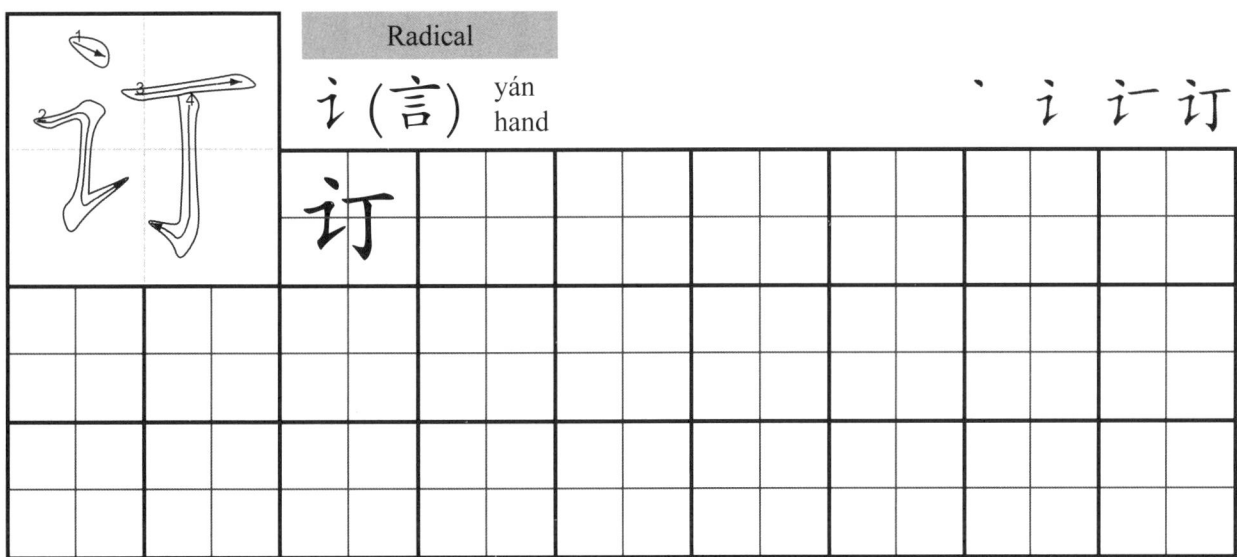

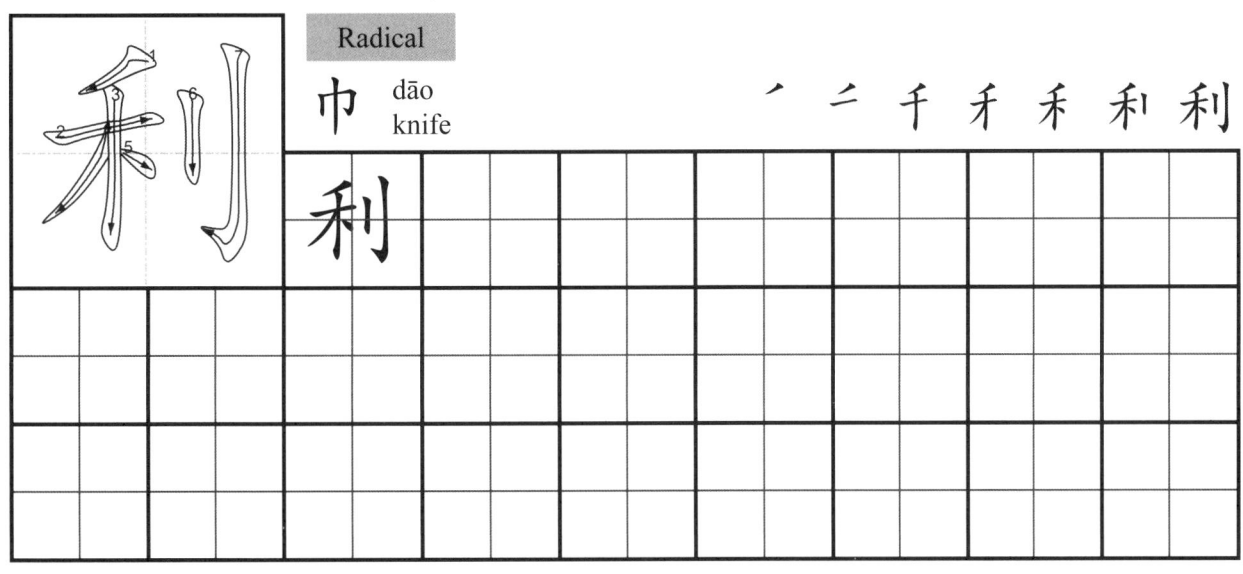

Unit 8 • Lesson 1 • Travel

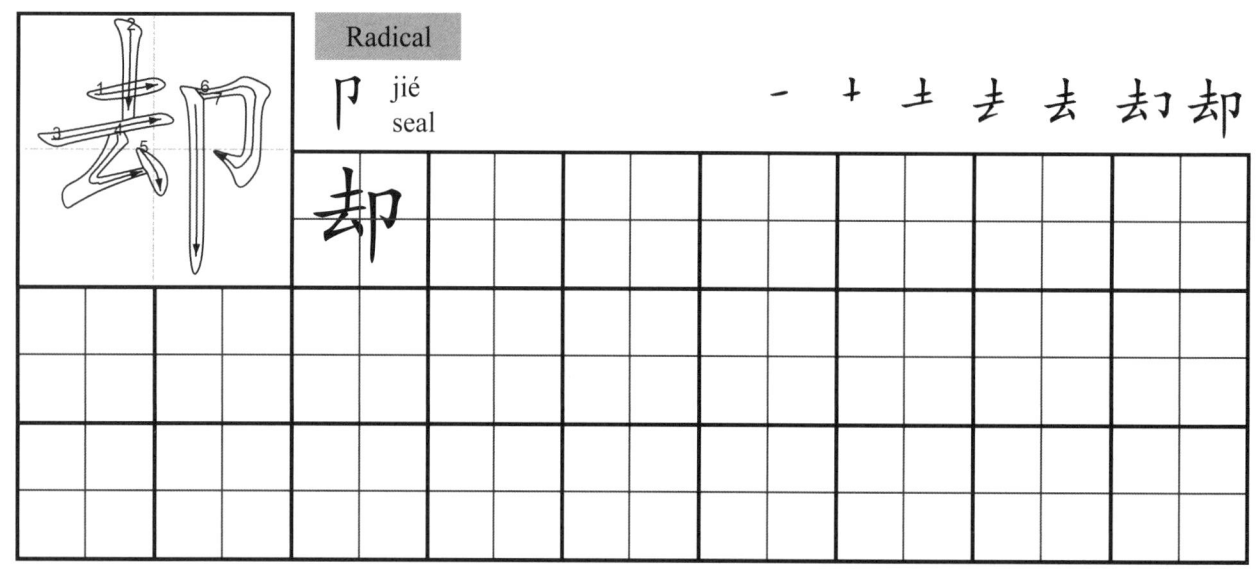

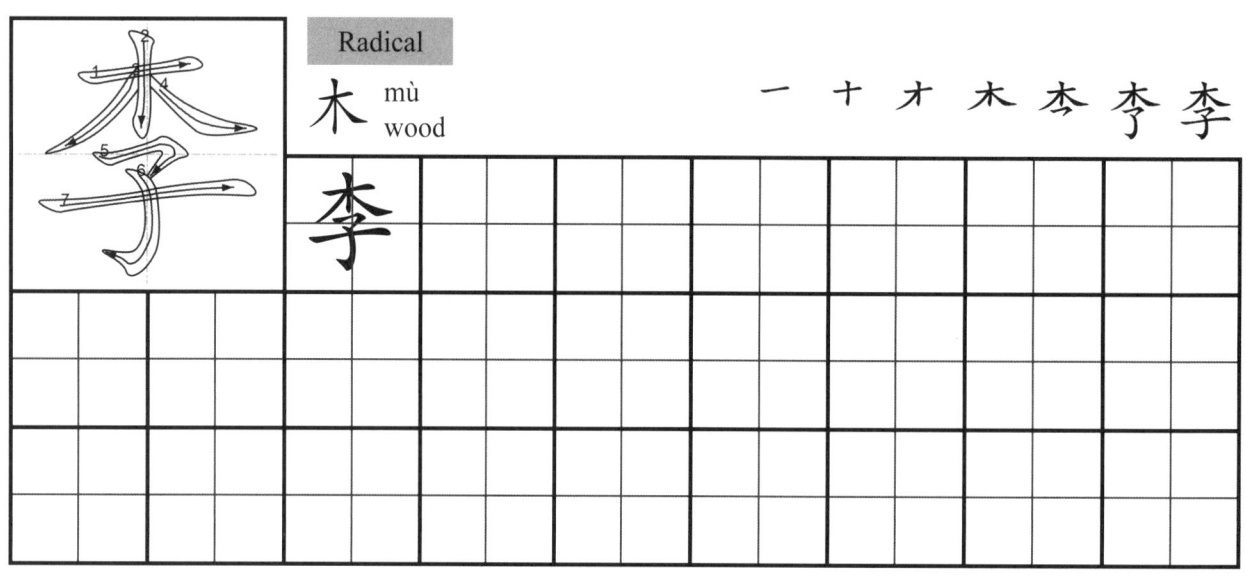

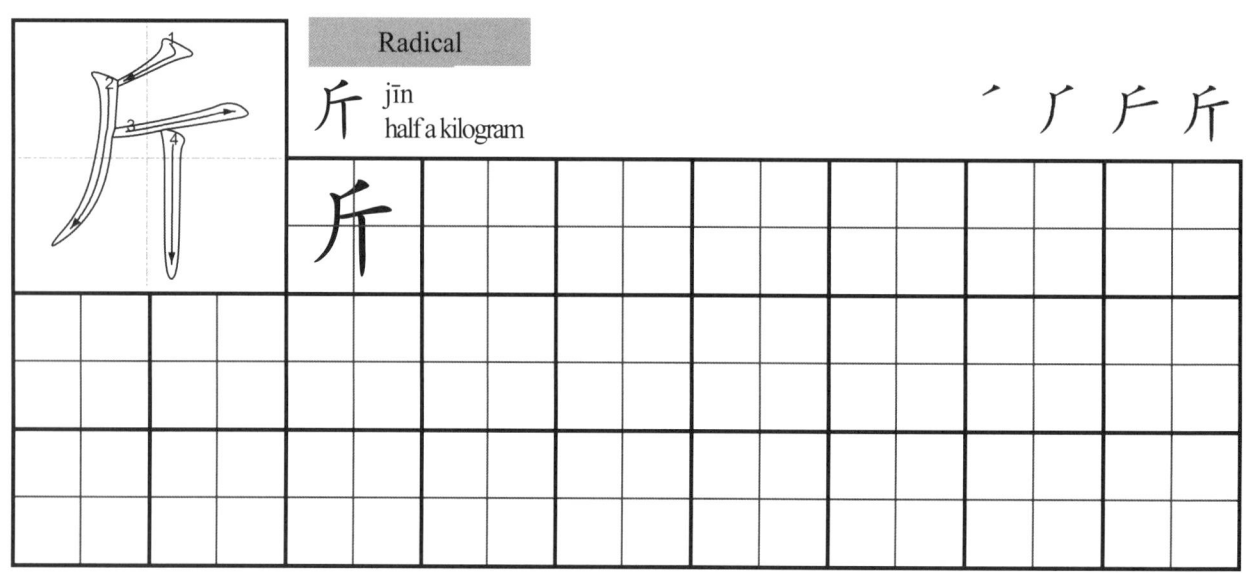

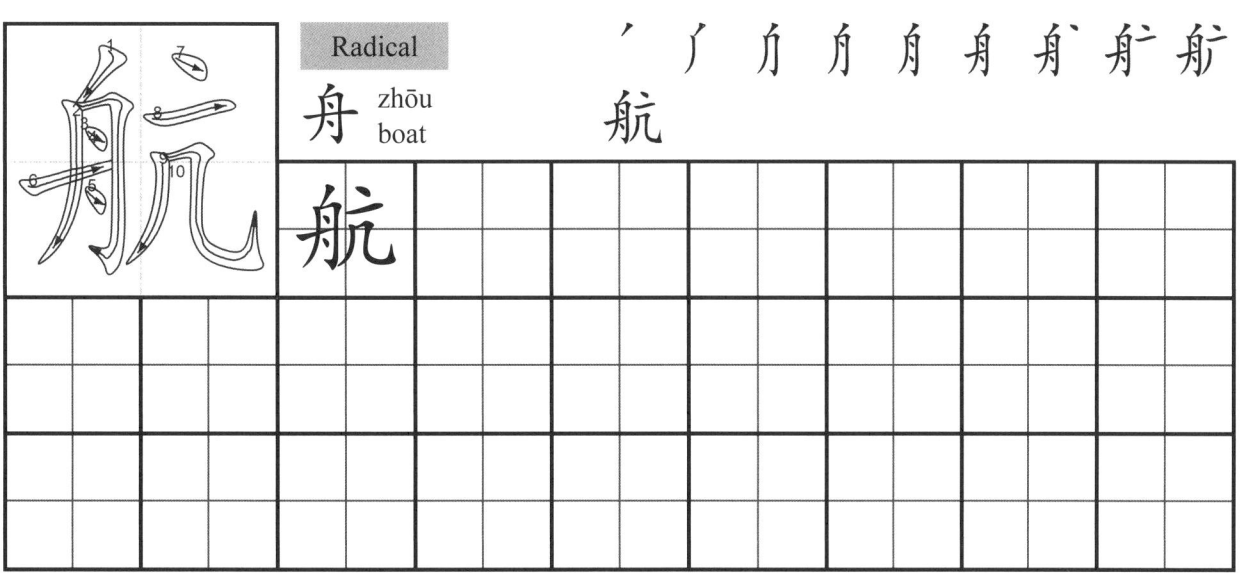

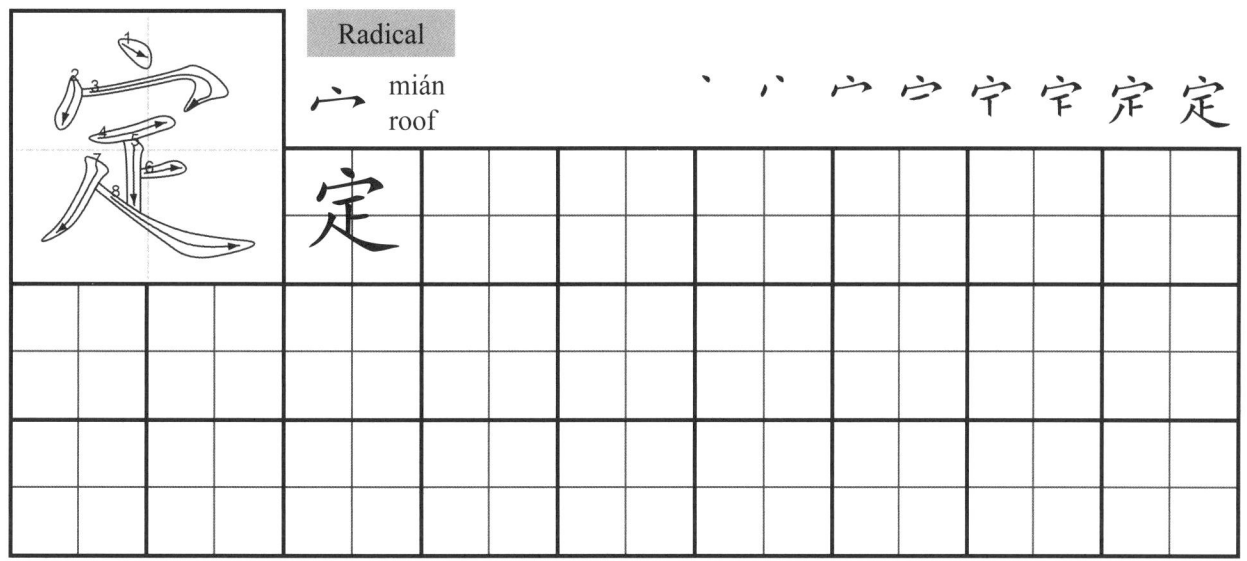

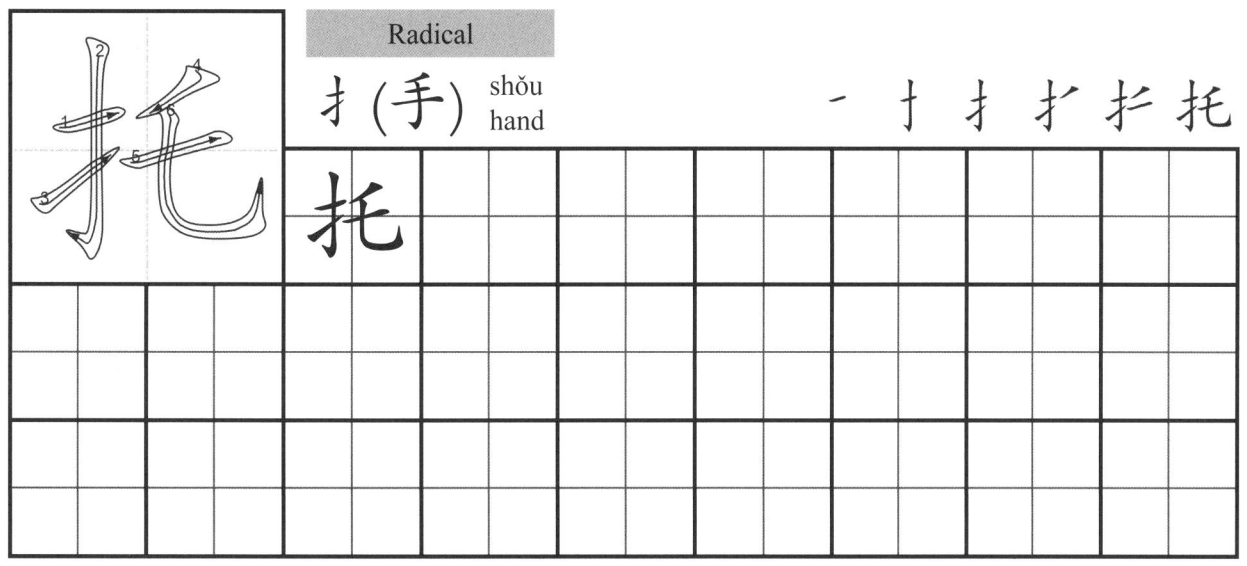

Unit 8 · Lesson 1 · Travel

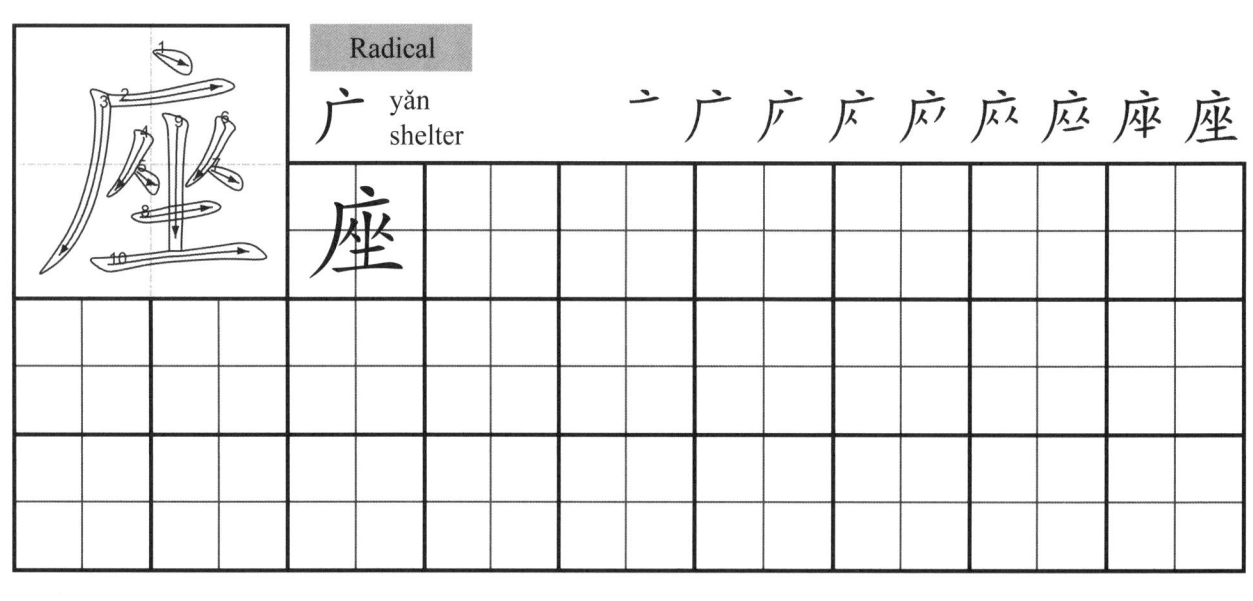

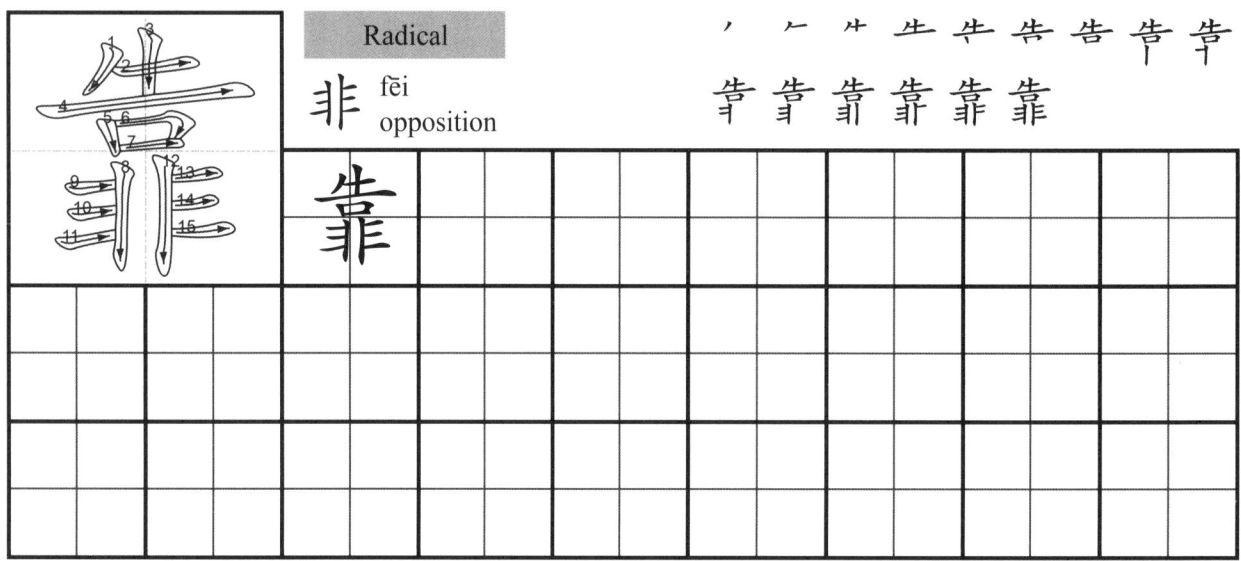

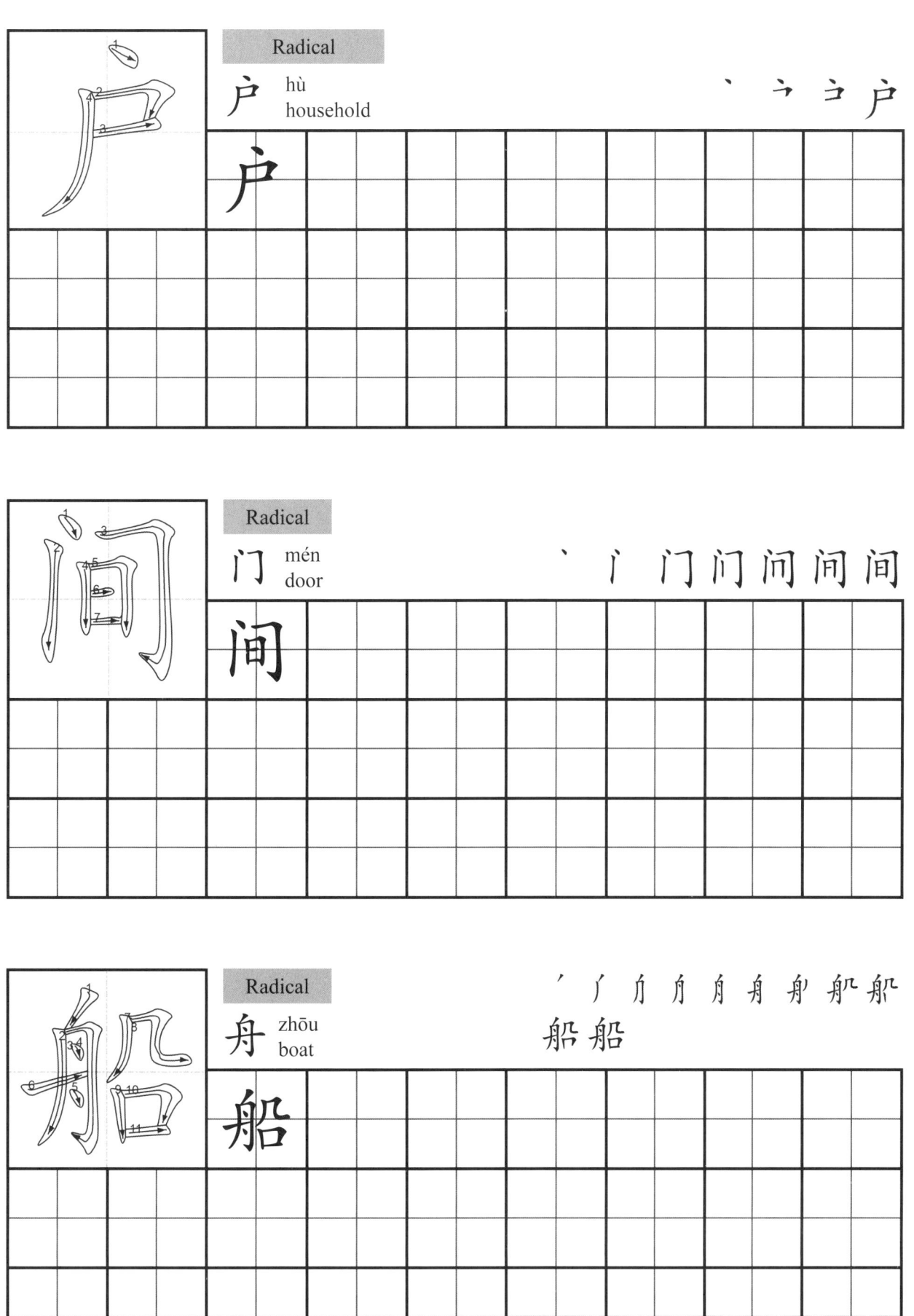

LISTENING COMPREHENSION 8.1

I. Listen to the recording and answer the question.

1. The man would most likely respond with:

    A. 这是航空公司的规定，您必须付超重费，要不然是不能托运的。
    B. 办签证和订机票其实很容易。
    C. 可以，但只能带一个小箱子登机。
    D. 不好意思，我们只剩下中间的座位了。

II. Listen to the recording and answer the following True or False questions.

1. (　) The man and woman are having a conversation at the airport.
2. (　) The man and woman are talking about the overweight baggage fee.
3. (　) The man prefers an aisle seat.
4. (　) The woman thinks it is convenient to sit on the aisle seat.
5. (　) The man likes having the opportunity to exercise on the airplane.

III. Listen to the recording and answer the questions.

1. How many hours before the departure did the family arrive at the airport?

2. Where did the family end up finding the passport?

3. Why did the speaker feel like she caused a lot of trouble for her mother and father?

SPEAKING PRACTICE 8.1

I. You and your family members — grandma, mom, dad, older brother, baby sister — are at the airport to catch a flight to Paris. At the check-in counter, the airline staff tells you that you are not all sitting together. Looking at the flight seating chart below, ask the staff member to change seats so that certain members are sitting together or sitting in certain types of seats, and explain why.

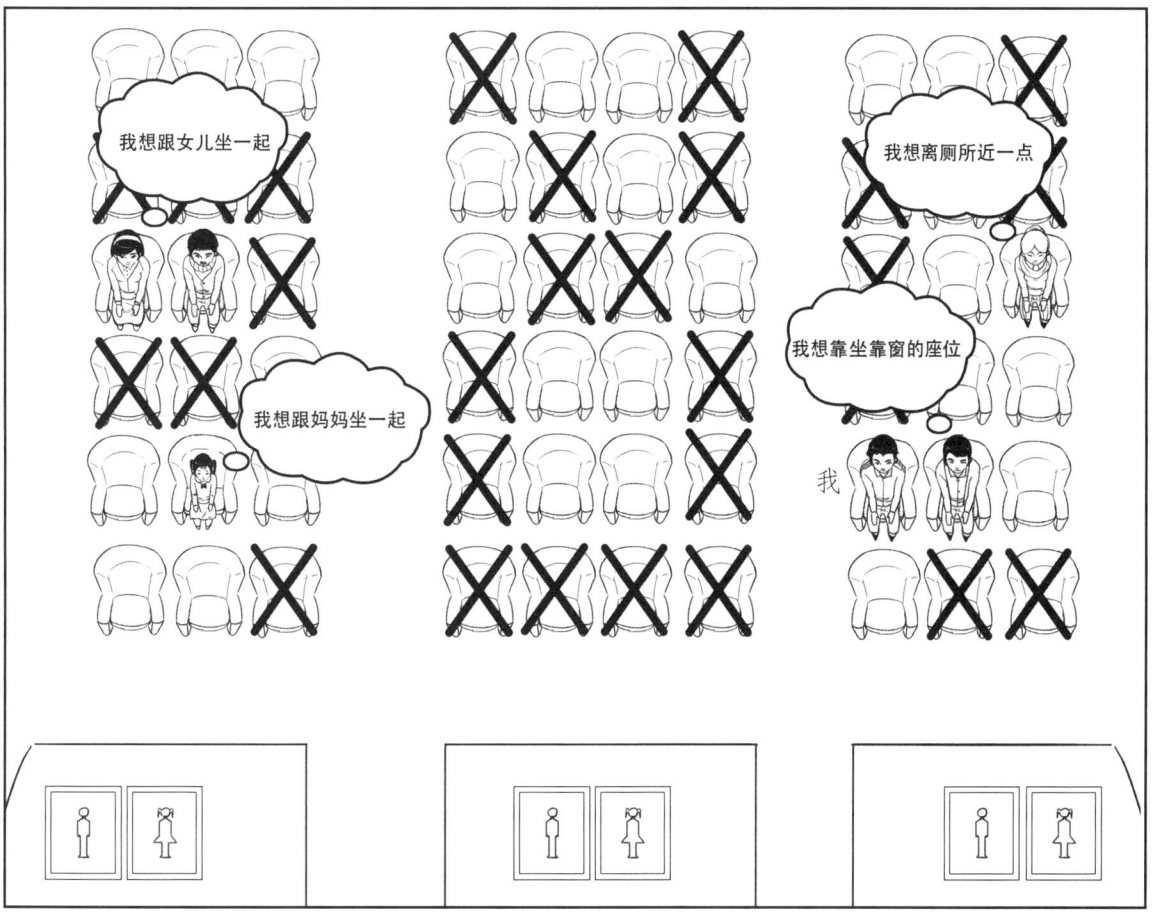

II. Your friend is traveling overseas for the first time and heading to England, where it often rains. Tell your friend what documents she needs to bring to the airport and what items she may need while on the plane and while traveling through England. Make sure to remind her to check the airline policy regarding luggage and food options.

Unit 8 · Lesson 1 · Travel

STRUCTURE REVIEW 8.1

I. Complete the following Structure Note practices.

Structure Note 8.1: Use 将 (要 / 会) to describe future events in formal contexts.

> Subject + 将 (+ 要 / 会) + Verb Phrase

A. Read the poster and create five sentences by using 将(要/会) and the information from the poster.

学校书画比赛

日期：五月十五日
地点：文化中心
评委：两位来自中国的
　　　书画大师

*第一名可以获得数码相机一台

1. _____
2. _____
3. _____
4. _____
5. _____

Structure Note 8.2: Use 却 to indicate a reversal or contrast.

> Subject + 却 + Verb Phrase

B. The images below show the difficulties that Xiao Wang ran into on the day of his departure at the airport. Describe each picture using 却.

1. _____

2. _____

3. _____

_____

4. _____

_____

Structure Note 8.3: Use 除非⋯要不然⋯ to make "unless" statements.

> 除非 + Condition, + 要不然+ Result

C. You are going to visit your friend who lives overseas. He e-mails you some tips about visiting his country. Rewrite the tips using 除非⋯要不然⋯.

- 一定要早点在网上订火车票，到时候才在车站买票就可能没好的座位了。
- 没有签证不能留在这里超过三个月。
- 不会开车的话会很麻烦，因为这里的公共汽车和地铁站不多。
- 这里大部分的商店都只收现金。
- 这里饭馆的菜味道都是比较辣的，不吃辣的人可能会不太习惯。

1. _____

2. _____

3. _____

4. _____

5. _____

Take the challenge! 动动脑筋！

In this lesson, we learned that the structure 除非…要不然 expresses "unless A happens, otherwise B will happen." For example, 除非现在就走，要不然我们会赶不上飞机的. Other than 要不然, 除非 can be also followed by 才 to express "unless A happens, only then can B happen." For example, 除非现在就走，我们才能赶上飞机的. 否则 is another formal phrase that you can use with 除非 to make "unless" statements. Can you create a sentence using the the examples above using 否则? You can also use the dictionary to help.

Structure Note 8.4: Use 刚才 to talk about events or situations that have just occured.

> Subject + 刚才 + Verb Phrase

> 刚才 + Subject + Verb Phrase

> 刚才 + 的 + Noun

D. Read the following passage and fill in the blanks with 刚, 刚刚, or 刚才.

考试_____结束，李阳就马上把_____王静借他的笔记本还给她。

王静："_____的考试考得怎么样？"

李阳："你笔记本上写的东西真的全都在_____的考试里面出现呢！"

王静："那你这次考试一定能考得高分！"

李阳："这也说不定，因为考试_____开始我肚子就痛起来，然后上完洗手间回来考试就刚刚好结束了。"

Take the challenge! 动动脑筋！

Although you have learned all the different usages of 刚, 刚刚, and 刚才 from the *Modern Chinese* Textbook lessons, you may have noticed that the 刚刚 that appears in the last sentence in the above reading passage does not have the meaning "just" or "just now." This is because 刚刚 can also mean "to just reach a certain point or level."

For example, 他今年刚十九岁, meaning "he just turned 19 years old this year."

Can you guess the meaning of 刚刚好 in the following sentence? 这双鞋子大小刚刚好。

II. You join a travel tour to Africa and the travel agency send you a text message with some reminders. Read the message and use the structure notes you learned in this lesson to rewrite some of the sentences or add new ones.

亲爱的团友：

　　我们下星期六要出发到南非了，你已经准备好你的行李了吗？有一位团友问我有关托运行李的费用，我打电话查过了，我们乘坐的航空公司会收两百块的行李托运费。所以如果你不是带很多东西，我们建议你最好用可以带上飞机的箱子。关于箱子大小的规定，请团友们自己到航空公司的网站查看。还有，去南非需要办签证，办好了签证还没发给我们的团友，请您在这个星期之前发到我们公司的电邮。

　　感谢大家对我们旅行社的支持！

小李

READING COMPREHENSION 8.1

I. Read the passage and answer the following True or False questions.

　　将去留学前的一天晚上，中平还在认真地准备留学的事情。中平检查飞机票、签证和护照有没有带上，信用卡和支票有没有放好，衣服是不是都带够了，必需的药有没有买，去机场的出租车订了没有等等。东西都准备得差不多了之后，中平的箱子里还是有一些空的地方。中平想北京的冬天会比较冷，所以顺便往行李里多放了一些衣服。之后他觉得还可以给玛丽带一些礼物，所以就又多加了很多东西。中平以为东西都带好了，明天就不会有什么问题了。

　　第二天一早出租车到了中平的公寓来接他，没想到到了机场之后，航空公司的工作人员却告诉他行李超重了两磅。虽然只是超了一点，但因为是航空公司的规定，除非交超重费，要不然他的行李是不能托运的。中平觉得把箱子打开，再把一些放好的东西拿出来实在是太麻烦了，所以最后他决定付超重费了。

　　之后，中平看了看登机牌，是他最不喜欢坐的中间座位。糟糕！他还发现这次他的座位旁边无论是靠窗户的还是靠走道的，都是不认识的人。幸运的是大东就坐在他的后面。虽然刚才登机的时候不太顺利，但一想到很快就能去中国了，一下飞机就能见到玛丽了，中平还是十分开心的。

1. (　　) 留学前一晚上中平已经准备好了留学的事情。
2. (　　) 中平觉得带的衣服太多了，就拿出来了一些。
3. (　　) 出发的那一天，中平不太顺利。
4. (　　) 朋友们都没有坐中平旁边。
5. (　　) 出发的那一天中平还是很高兴的。

II. Read the passage and answer the following questions.

春节坐飞机需注意

春节快到了，很多人会坐飞机回老家。春节前坐飞机有哪些需要注意的问题呢？记者采访了一家航空公司的工作人员，他给了一些建议。

首先，最好**提前**订机票。因为离春节越近，机票就越紧张，价格也越高，而且一些**热门**城市的机票可能很早就订完了。另外，由于春节前来机场坐飞机的乘客增加很多，最好提前2-3小时到机场办登机**手续**。

中国人喜欢在回家时给家人和朋友带很多礼物，但一定要注意行李不要超重，行李超重的费用是很高的。此外，一些危险物品，如刀子、烟火都是不能带上飞机的。春节前后一两个月，机场的人会很多，需要帮助的人也很多，所以乘客一定要和航空公司的工作人员互相**理解**，这样很多问题就能得到**解决**。

Notes:
提前 (tíqián): *adv.* in advance, beforehand
热门 (rèmén): *n.* popular, in great demand
手续 (shǒuxù): *n.* procedure
理解 (lǐjiě): *v.* to understand
解决 (jiějué): *v.* to resolve

1. 提前订机票有哪些好处？

   _____

2. 为什么春节前乘客的行李特别容易超重？

   _____

3. 如果你觉得航空公司的工作人员的服务不够好，你会怎么做？

   _____

Take the challenge! 动动脑筋！

紧张 can mean "to not have a relaxed mind or be in a relaxed mood," "to be keyed up or nervous," or a relationship that is "intense, urgent, or in a state of crisis." More often 紧张 is used to describe things like work, a competition, a situation, etc. For example, 这场篮球比赛很紧张. However, in the above passage, 离春节越近，机票就越紧张 does not mean that the air ticket is nervous. Rather, 紧张 is used to describe that the demands for materials and rental housing are high, or in short supply. Can you guess the meaning of the following sentences?

最近来云南旅游的人多得很，旅馆房间都非常紧张。

III. Read the following e-mail and itinerary and answer the questions.

To:	李平
From:	王月
Subject:	可以去机场接我们吗？

李平：

　　我和孙华昨天已经买了11月4号去北京的机票，你4号有空吗？可不可以去机场接我们一下？因为你喜欢吃南方的水果，我们**特意**在广州给你买了很多水果，所以我们的行李有点重。我们的航班号是CZ3101，上午8点起飞，要是不**误点**的话，飞机11点左右到北京。好**期待**在北京见到你！

王月

Notes:

特意 (tèyì): adv. deliberately
误点 (wùdiǎn): v. to be behind schdule
期待 (qīdài): v. to await

1. What is the main purpose of Wang Yue's e-mail to Li Ping?

2. According to the itinerary, what is the maximum luggage weight limit?

3. According to the e-mail, fill in the missing information in the itinerary receipt e-ticket, including the name of traveler, place of departure and arrival, carrier and flight number, and time.

WRITING PRACTICE 8.1

I. Below are images of Xiaowen's recent trip to the airport. Write a short description for each picture, explaining what is happening in the scene.

1. _____
_____
_____
_____

2. _____
_____
_____
_____

3. _____
_____
_____
_____

4. _____
_____
_____
_____

II. You recently had a very bad experience at the airport waiting for a flight to head home after doing volunteer work in another city. Write an e-mail to the airline complaining about three things that went wrong. In your e-mail, also ask for compensation in the form of a coupon or free flight voucher.

To:
From:
Subject:

UNIT 8 — LESSON 2

Modern Chinese 现代中文

中国游

VOCABULARY REVIEW 8.2

I. Combine each character with other characters to form at least five different phrases.

Example: 心	1. 票	2. 客	3. 记	4. 馆	5. 游
安心 开心 细心 心急 担心 心烦 心疼					

II. Match the radicals on the left with the components on the right to form a new character. Place the newly formed character into the correct box according to the pinyin.

木	足	竹
火	水	金
门	人	走
阝	草	心

+

每	办	示
龙	谷	各
汤	耳	参
木	昔	咸

→

林 (lín)	(wén)	(sū)
(jì)	(gǎn)	(chèn)
(hǎi)	(sú)	(cuò)
(lù)	(lóng)	(tàng)

III. Provide the Chinese phrases for each item in the list below for your friend who is going on a trip with you.

Items you need to prepare: 准备事项：

1. plan itinerary	
2. apply for a visa	
3. book an air ticket through travel agency	
4. call to book a hotel	
5. book tourist spot entrance tickets online	
6. sign up for a one-day travel tour	
7. contact the tour guide	

第八单元 · 第二课 · 行

CHARACTER WRITING PRACTICE 8.2

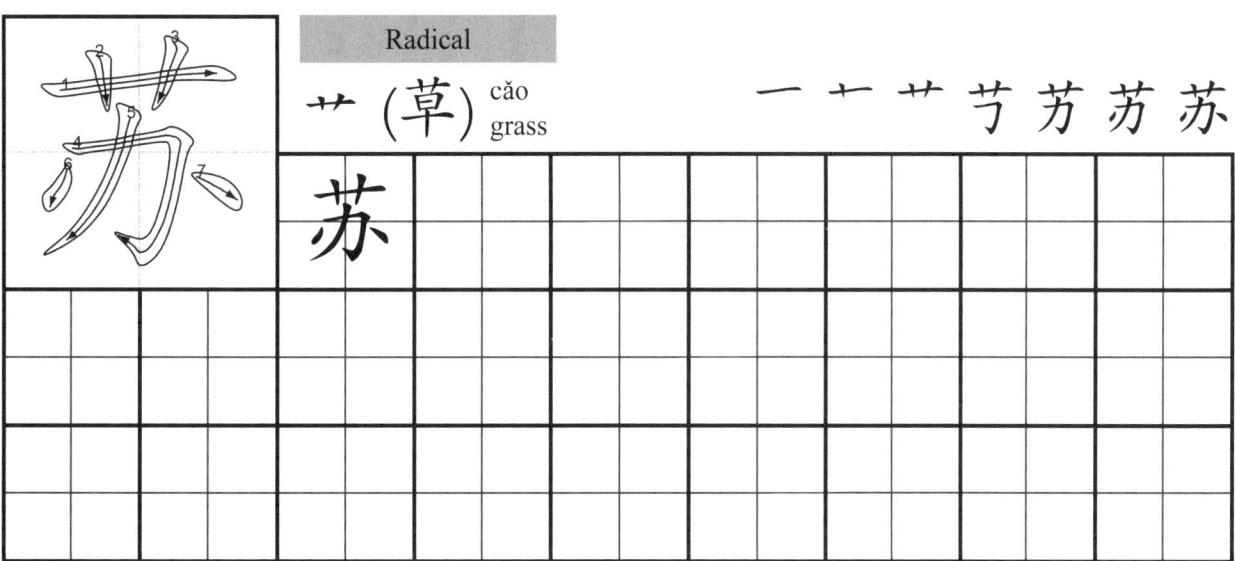

Unit 8 • Lesson 2 • Travel

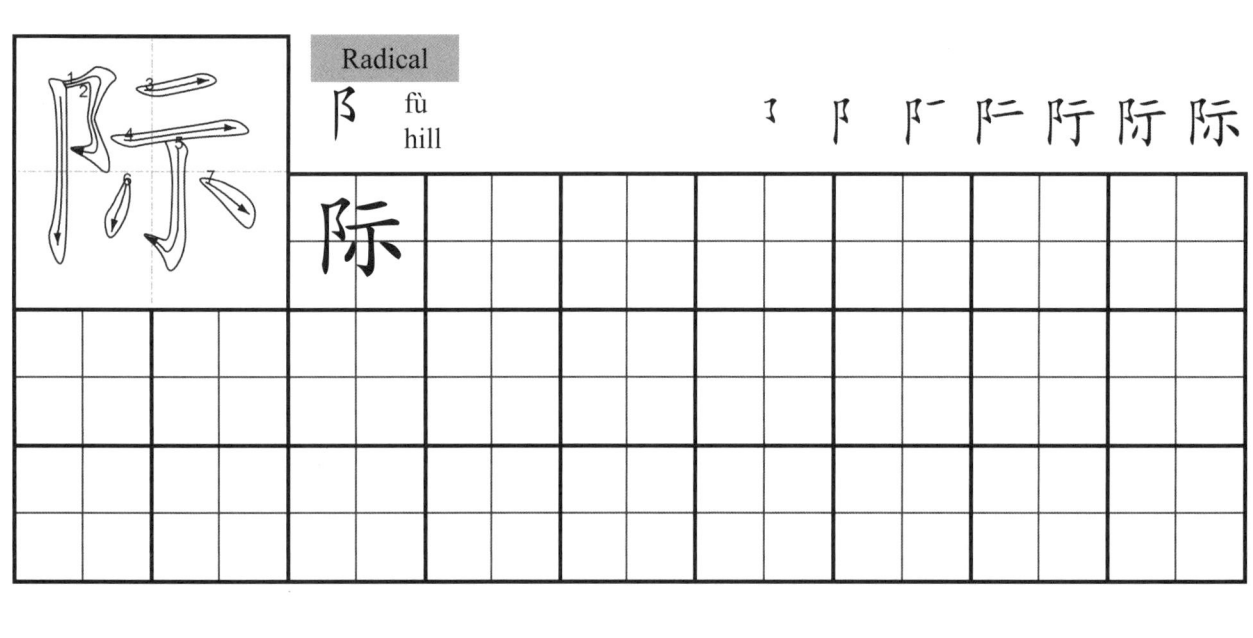

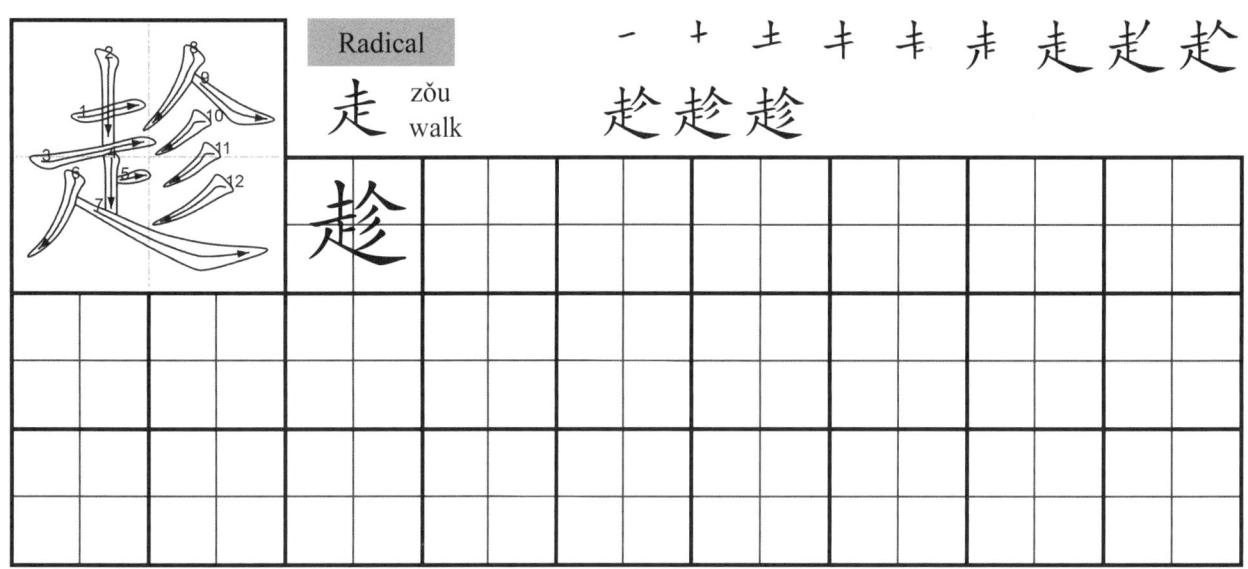

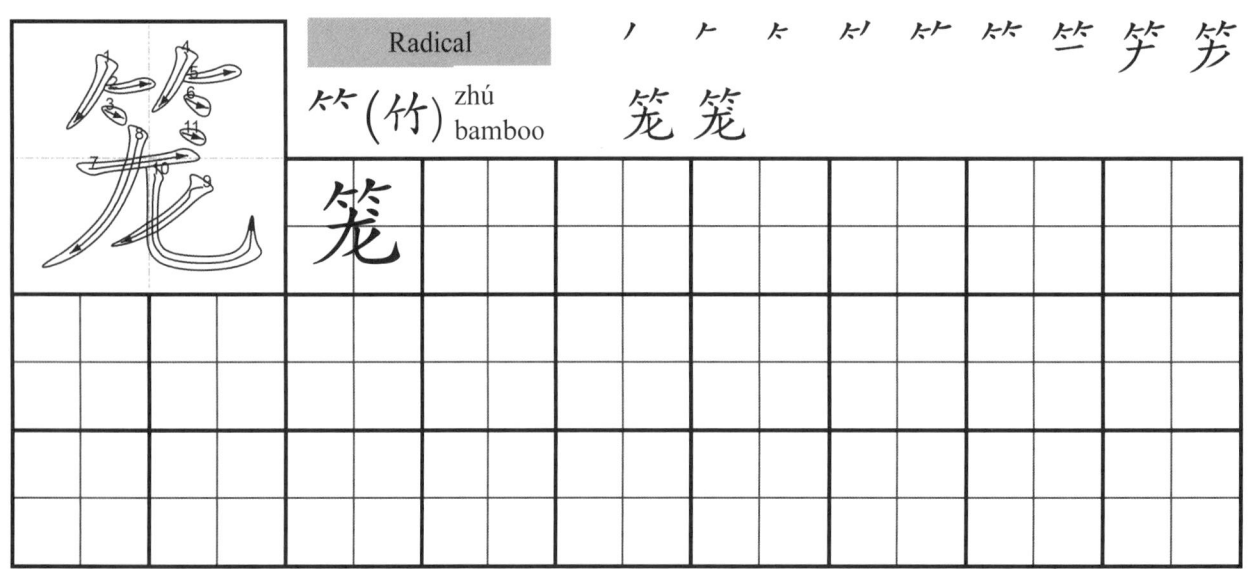

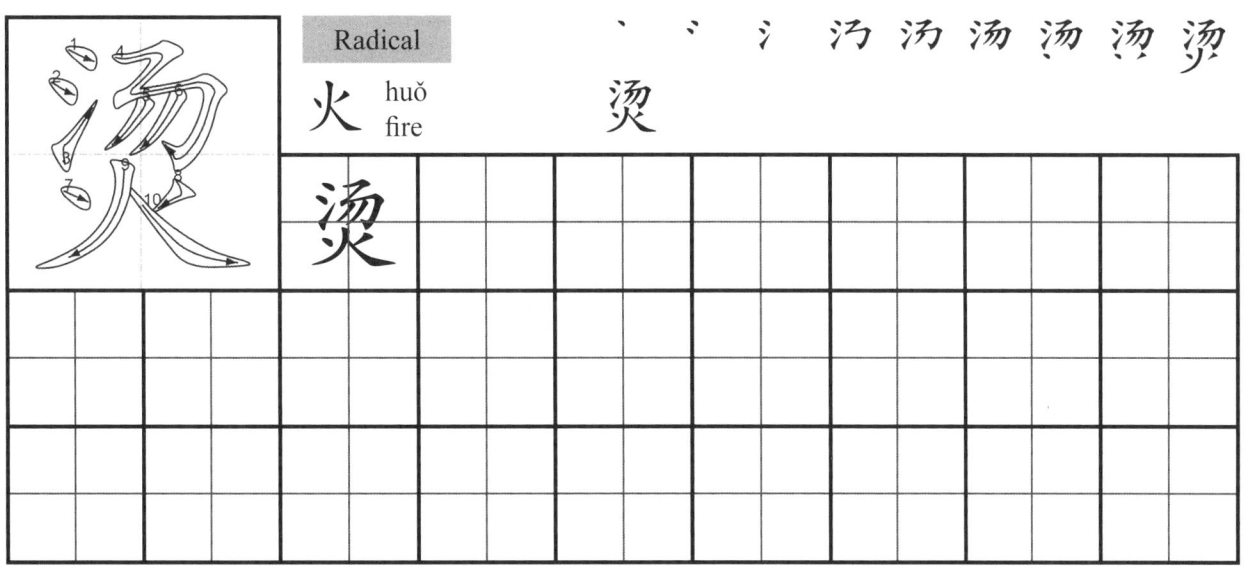

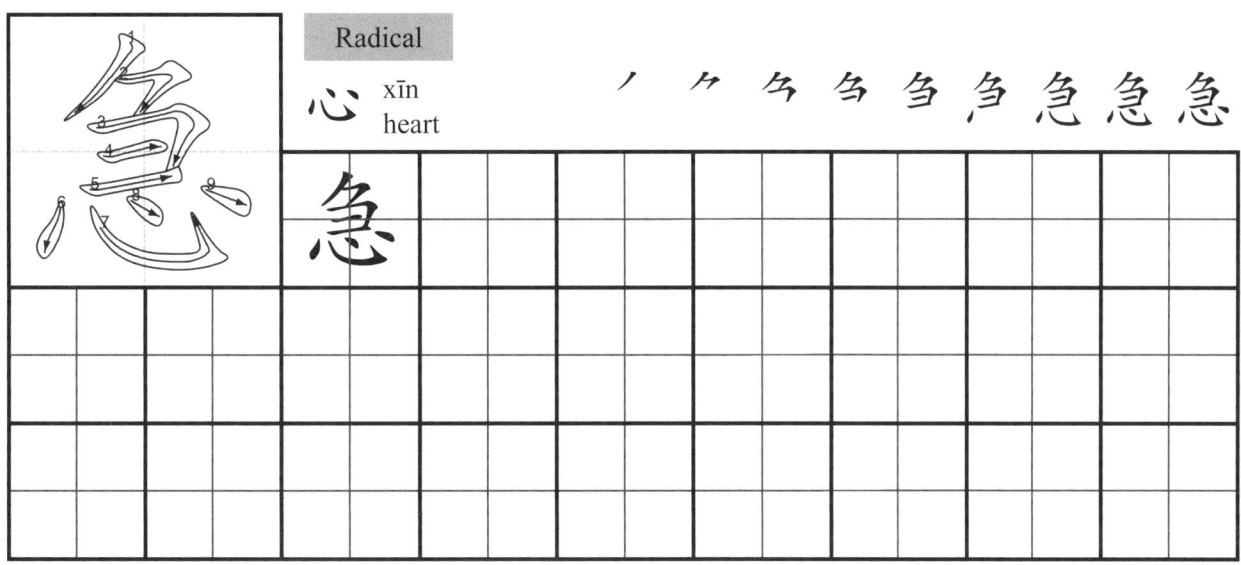

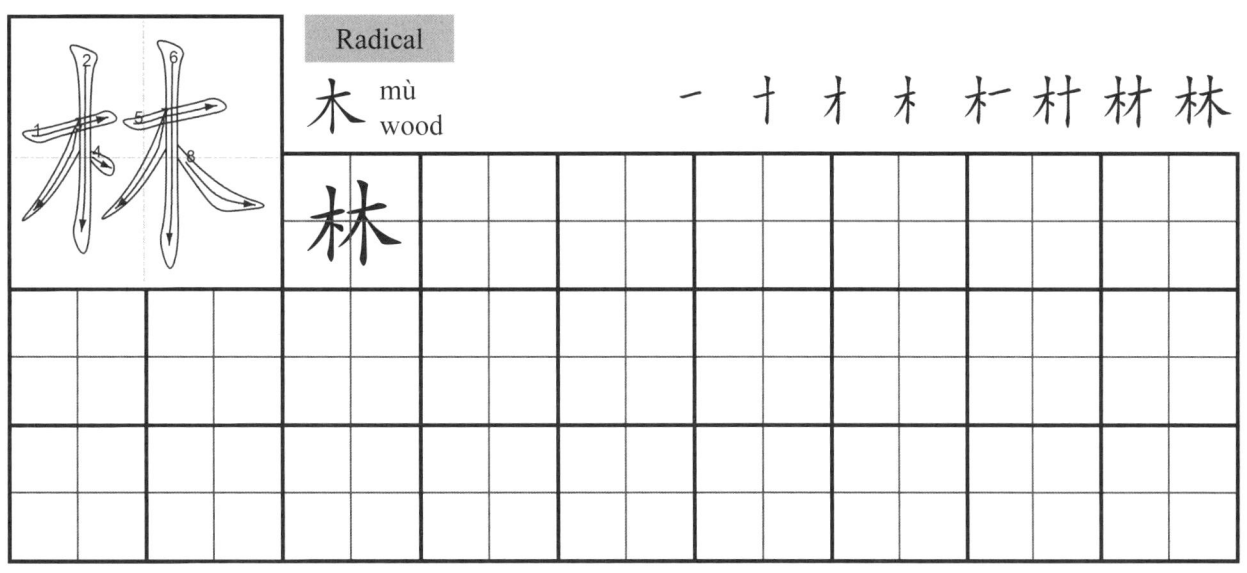

Unit 8 • Lesson 2 • Travel

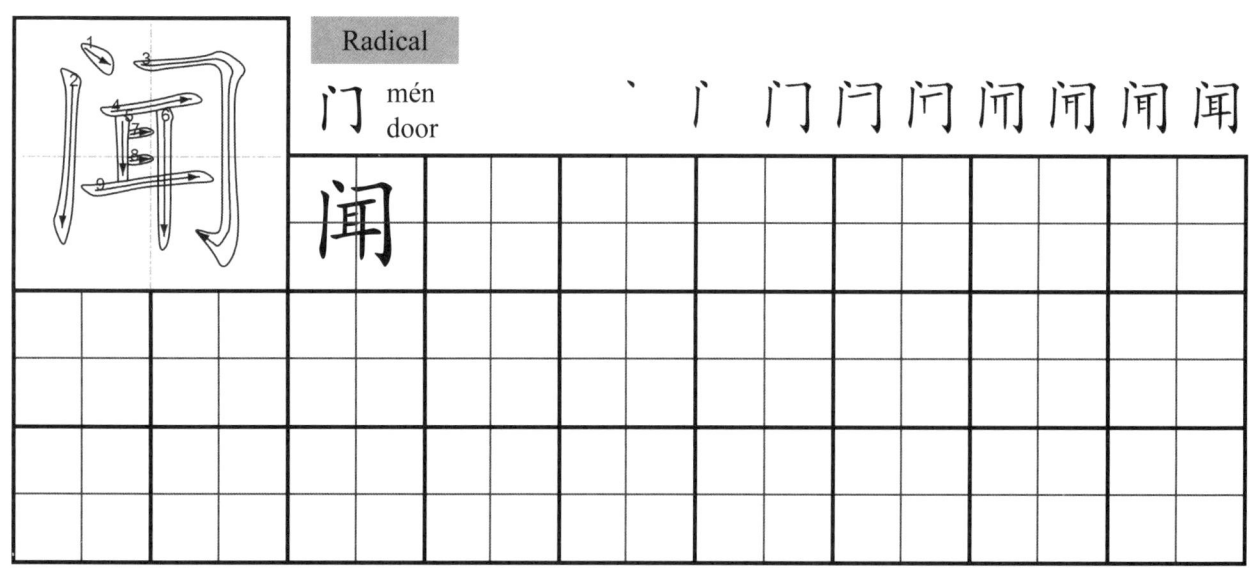

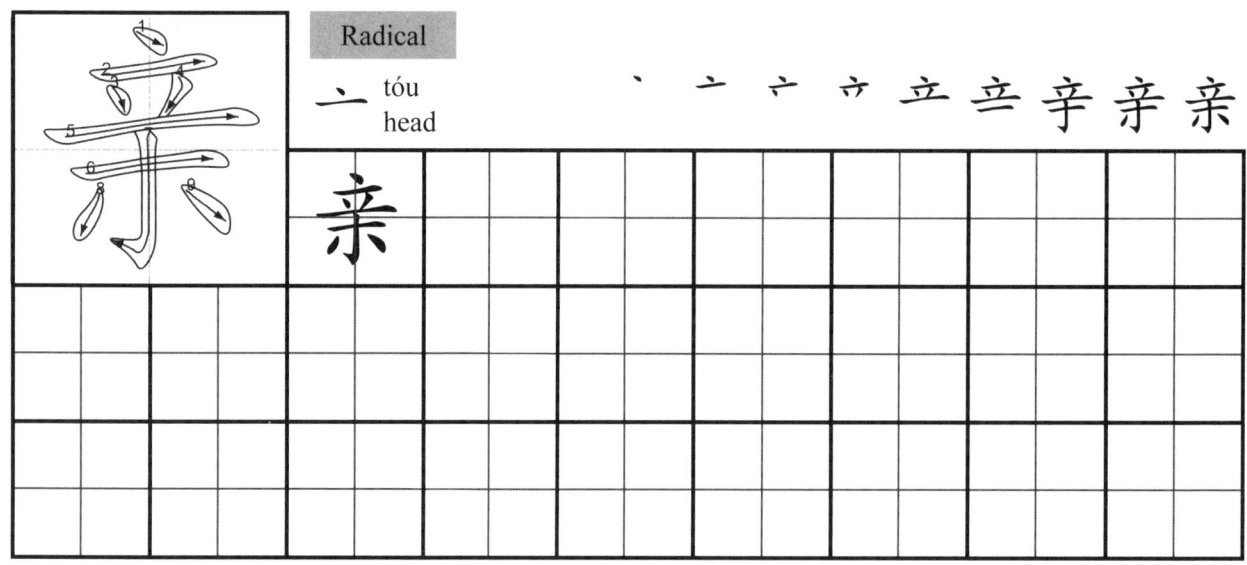

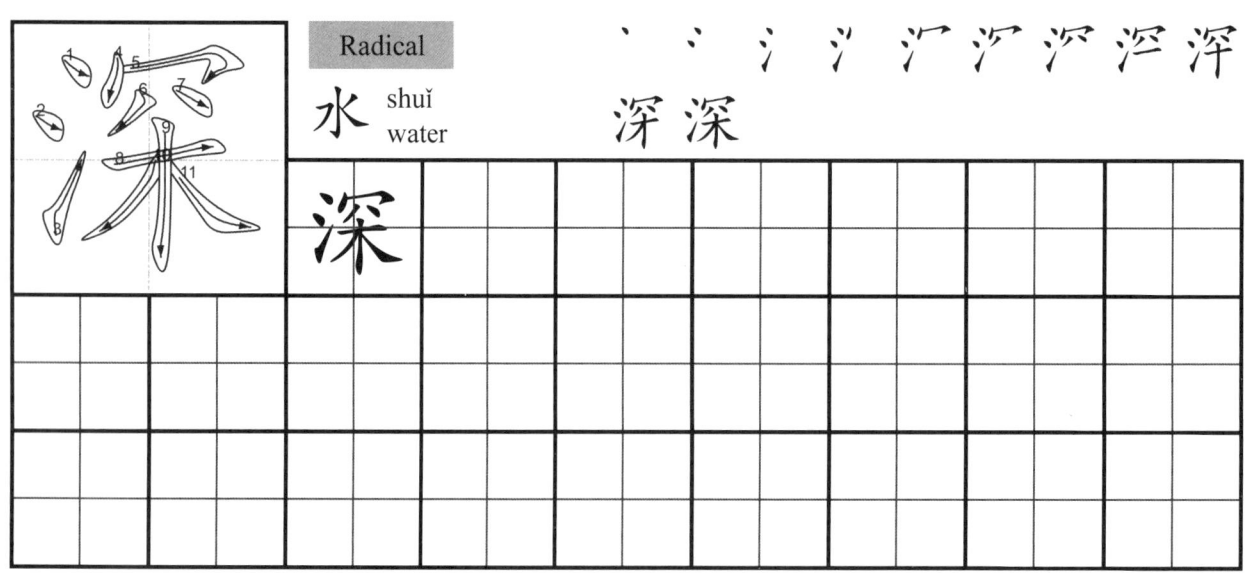

	Radical		
俗	亻(人) rén person	ノ 亻 亻 亻` 亻^ 伀 伀 俗 俗	
	俗		

	Radical		
改	攵(攴) pū knock	フ 己 己 己′ 己^ 改 改	
	改		

	Radical		
变	又 yòu again	丶 一 亠 亣 亦 亦 亦 变 变	
	变		

Unit 8 • Lesson 2 • Travel

LISTENING COMPREHENSION 8.2

I. Listen to the recording and answer the following True/False questions.

1. The woman would most likely respond with:

   A. 只有亲自去故宫才有意思。
   B. 我们趁去上海的时候吃小笼包吧。
   C. 别担心，我们带上地图，或者请一个导游就可以了。
   D. 故宫的门票一点儿也不贵。

II. Listen to the recording and answer the following True or False questions.

1. (   ) The man and the woman are talking about traveling to China together.
2. (   ) The man does not recommend taking a tour group in China.
3. (   ) The man thinks taking a tour group can enable you to learn more about a place.
4. (   ) The woman is not always satisfied with a tour groups's itinerary.
5. (   ) The woman decided to sign up with a tour group in China

III. Listen to the recording and answer the questions.

1. Why does the speaker travel often?

   _____

2. What was the one thing that left the speaker with the strongest impression about Suzhou when she visited the area?

   _____

3. Why does the speaker like to travel?

   _____

SPEAKING PRACTICE 8.2

I. Below are two ads for different tours. Review each and explain which one you would like to join and why.

北京文化历史二日游

行程：

第一天：

早上：中国历史博物馆

下午：长城

晚上：逛胡同。包晚饭（吃北京烤鸭）

第二天：

早上：中国国家博物馆

下午：故宫

晚上：秀水街-买东西，包晚饭（吃饺子）

价格：￥200（包车费，晚餐费，导游服务，门票），十岁以下￥100

发团时间：天天发团

丽山旅游社

上海艺术美食二日游

行程：

第一天：

早上：于上海火车站集合发车（包小笼包，素菜包）

下午：到南京路逛百货公司（包午餐-上海炒年糕，牛肉汤，葱油面）

晚上：东方艺术中心听中国民乐演奏（包晚餐-醉鸡，上海菜饭）

第二天：

早上：参观复旦大学，同济大学（品尝大学生食堂的饭菜，自费）

下午：多伦路文化街体验现代艺术（小吃街-午餐自费）

晚上：新天地（自费）

价格：￥440（包车费，导游服务）

十岁以下￥220

发团时间：周五

喜越旅游社

II. Foreign exchange students from China are coming to visit your school next week. You have been chosen to be their tour guide for a week. Prepare a speech introducing yourself and talk about the itinerary. Explain the on-campus and off-campus activities you are arranging for them, including your plans for visiting scenic spots, accommodations, meals, and transportation, and the reasons for your plans. Be sure to also mention some cultural differences and things they need to pay special attention to while visiting your country.

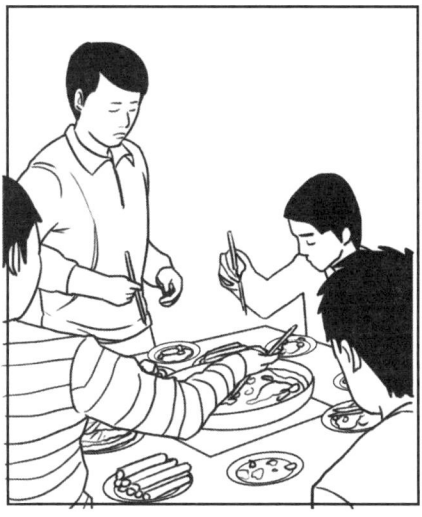

STRUCTURE REVIEW 8.2

I. Complete the following Structure Note practices.

Structure Note 8.5: Use 不是 A 而是 B to emphasize a contrast between A and B.

> Subject + 不是 + Noun Phrase / Verb Phrase + 而是 + Noun Phrase / Verb Phrase

> 不是 + Sentence + 而是 + Sentence

A. In the sentences below, your friend makes some factual mistakes about Beijing and Shanghai. Correct his statements by using 不是⋯而是⋯.

1. 北京最有名的美食是小笼包。

   _____

2. 上海在北京的北方。

   _____

3. 在北京最常见的自然灾害是地震。

   _____

4. 北京假日最多游客去的旅游景点是故宫。

   _____

5. 大部分人从北京到上海都会选坐地铁去。

   _____

Structure Note 8.6: Use 实际上 to explain how things really are.

> 实际上, + Sentence

> Subject + 实际上 + Verb / Adjective Phrase

B. After moving into an apartment, you realize that some of the amenities and the environment are different from what you were led to believe. Complete the sentences below by using 实际上 to explain how things actually are.

1. 我以为这家公寓会包水电费⋯⋯

   _____

2. 广告上写"家具全新"……

_____

3. 房东说公寓里会有冰箱、空调等家电……

_____

4. 有些同学说那家公寓离学校很近……

_____

5. 听说公寓附近有一个大型的百货公司……

_____

Structure Note 8.7: Use 趁(着) to take advantage of a situation.

$$\text{Subject} + 趁(着) + \text{Noun Phrase} + \text{Verb}$$

C. Below is an ad for a summer tour in China. Write five sentences using 趁(着) to pursuade your friend to join you on the tour.

> 我们知道现在的年轻人都喜欢出国亲自体会别的国家的风俗和文化,所以今年我们举办了一个名叫"暑假游北京"的旅游活动。只需要一个暑假,我们保证学生们都能学到一口地道的汉语。我们还会带学生到北京各个博物馆参观,现在只要出示学生证,门票都会有5折优惠。而且,七月十五日到八月十日是旅游购物节,很多百货公司都会有减价活动。喜欢文化又喜欢购物的您,一定要赶快报名!

1. _____

2. _____

3. _____

4. _____

Structure Note 8.8: Use 只有…才… to describe necessary conditions for a condition to occur.

$$只有 + \text{Condition Clause, } (+ \text{Subject}) + 才 + \text{Verb Phrase}$$

$$\text{Subject} + 只有 + \text{Verb Phrase, } + 才 + \text{Verb Phrase}$$

D. Rewrite the following sentences using 只有⋯才⋯.

只要学生能认真地学习，成绩一定会有进步。

1. _____

如果每个球员都能配合得好，这场比赛就一定会赢。

2. _____

在我们公司每个人都要做好自己负责的工作，这样我们公司才会成功。

_____

想要拍出好的照片，一定要先用心感受这个城市的美好。

3. _____

虽然每天练习让我非常累，但是为了实现梦想我是不会放弃的。

4. _____

Take the challenge! 动动脑筋！

只要⋯就 and 只有⋯才 are both structures that express one condition is dependent on another. In *Modern Chinese* Textbook, Vol. 2A, Unit 2, Lesson 1, we learned 只要A，就B to indicate that as long as A exists, B will happen. For example, the sentence 只要常运动，身体就会健康 implies that exercising will be sufficient enough to be healthy, but exercising is not the only condition that can elicit this result. On the other hand, changing the sentence into 只有常运动，身体才会健康 implies that only by exercising often will you healthy. In other words, in this 只有A，才B pattern, if A does not happen, B will not occur either. Below is a conversation between a boss and staff member using both structures. Can you understand what they are saying?

A: "老板，只要有钱，这件事就不是问题了。不，我觉得只有用钱才可以把这件事情办好。"

B: "我们公司不是没钱，但我相信只要有心，这件事一定不会是个问题。不，你们只有用心，这件事情才能办好。"

II. Below is part of a report about students' opinions toward the pros and cons of joining a tour group. Rewrite some of the sentences by using the structure notes you learned in this lesson.

参加旅游团的好处与坏处

王同学：我认为旅行团的费用挺划算的，不但路线已经帮你计划好了，一天三餐也不用自己烦恼，省掉很多麻烦。

李同学：有些人喜欢报旅行社，觉得很方便。但其实很多年轻人都不喜欢参加旅游团，因为他们比较喜欢自己计划行程。

周同学：我觉得参加旅游团的最大好处不是费用便宜，是自己不用花时间计划行程，省心又省力。

林同学：很多人都希望可以用旅游的机会用最少的时间去最多的地方，所以有些旅行团会保证在数天内走遍所有有名的景点。而且有些景点是旅游团带你才能去参观的。

陈同学：导游带我们去逛一些景点，说是为了让大家更好地欣赏风景、感受和体会风俗，但我觉得他是为了让旅客去商店买东西！

杨同学：我比较喜欢自己去旅游，因为我希望假期可以好好休息，不想像参加旅游团要赶行程那样累。

READING COMPREHENSION 8.2

I. Read the passage and answer the following True or False questions.

中平和朋友们从到中国的那天起就打算去各地旅游。他们研究了以后，决定趁新学期开始以前，去上海和苏州玩几天。而且他们打算不找旅游团，不找导游，自己订票，自己找住的地方，亲自好好感受和体会一下中国人的生活。决定好旅游路线之后，他们就讨论怎么去。大家都认为坐火车最省钱。大家一起决定的行程是坐火车从北京到上海，玩两天，之后去苏州玩一天，游遍各个苏州园林，然后坐飞机回北京。

于是，中平第二天一大早就去帮大家买火车票，就坐地铁去了火车站。火车站上车下车的游客很多，人山人海，中平等得很心急，等了很久才买到票。可是回到家他才发现票买错了！他买的不是从北京去上海的票，而是买了从上海回北京的票。虽然周信帮他把票换了，但中平还是很不好意思，不太开心。玛丽见了，告诉中平其实他做的挺好的，而且中文很好，刚来中国就能自己买票了。她还告诉中平，以后买票不用亲自去火车站，实际上不管是火车票还是旅游的门票，都可以在网上购票，票还可以寄到家里，省心又省力。

1. (　) 大家觉得坐火车比坐飞机便宜。
2. (　) 中平去火车站买到了火车票，但是火车站的售票员给错了票。
3. (　) 玛丽说中平的中文不太好，来中国以后得多练习。
4. (　) 中平以后可以在网上买火车票。
5. (　) 在网上买火车票的好处是会便宜一点。

Take the challenge! 动动脑筋！

We have learned how to say morning, 早, and night, 夜, in Chinese but never learned how to describe early in the morning and late at night. To indicate the former, we will say 一大早. However, if we want to say late at night, we will not add 一大 in front of night 夜. Instead, we will say 半夜, which means "midnight" or "in the middle of night," and 深夜, which means "late at night," or "deep into the night." In the above passage, can you find the sentence that uses 一大早 and correctly translate the sentence into English?

II. **Read the passage and answer the following True or False questions.**

豆腐脑与豌豆黄

今天是我来北京的第一天，我的朋友小王带我去吃了北京小吃。那家小吃店很受欢迎，里面人山人海，我们点了包括"豆腐脑"和"豌豆黄"在内的五六种小吃。给我印象最深的是豆腐脑，因为北京的豆腐脑不是甜的，而是咸的。和我在南方吃的非常不一样，那里的豆腐脑是甜的。但是咸的豆腐脑味道也不错，我吃了一大碗。

另外一种叫"豌豆黄"的小吃我也很喜欢。它是用豌豆做的，因为颜色是黄色的，所以叫"豌豆黄"。豌豆黄这么受北京人欢迎的原因是它的味道香甜，软软的，凉凉的，非常好吃。小王还告诉我，豌豆黄是传统的北京小吃，依北京的习俗，每年春天都要吃豌豆黄。可惜今天我忘了给美食拍照，不能和大家分享照片了。明天小王会带我吃更多的北京美食，我一定会拍很多照片跟你们分享！

Notes:

豆腐脑 (dòufunǎo): *n.* bean curd jelly
豌豆 (wāndòu): *n.* garden pea
印象 (yìnxiàng): *n.* impression
软 (ruǎn): *adj.* soft
习俗 (xísú): *n.* custom

1. (　　) 作者没有去过除了北京以外的其他中国城市。
2. (　　) 作者不喜欢吃北京的豆腐脑，因为味道太咸了。
3. (　　) 北京人喜欢吃豌豆黄是因为只有春天才能吃豌豆黄。
4. (　　) 作者今天没有拍到北京美食的照片。
5. (　　) 作者明天还会在北京旅游。

III. Read the blog post and train information below and answer the following questions.

车次	始发站/终点站	出发时间	到达时间	运行时间	预订火车票
G101 详情 高速动车	始 北京南 终 上海虹桥	07:00 当天	12:23 当天	5小时23分 1318公里	订购
G105 详情 高速动车	始 北京南 终 上海虹桥	07:32 当天	13:07 当天	5小时35分 1318公里	订购
G11 详情 高速动车	始 北京南 终 上海虹桥	08:00 当天	12:55 当天	4小时55分 1318公里	订购
G31 详情 高速动车	始 北京南 终 上海虹桥	08:05 当天	13:29 当天	5小时24分 1318公里	订购
G107 详情 高速动车	始 北京南 终 上海虹桥	08:10 当天	13:40 当天	5小时30分 1318公里	订购

昨天，我第一次坐高铁（**高速铁路**）从北京到上海，真的太方便了！从北京到上海只用了5个多小时。要知道，坐飞机到上海也要2个小时呢！我经常去上海**出差**，以前我都是坐飞机。但是我家离机场很远，开车去机场就要1个多小时。现在有了**高速铁路**，就方便多了。因为我家旁边就是火车站。我7点20分出门，坐8点10分的火车，中午1点40就到上海了。如果是坐8点的飞机，我早上5点就要起床。下次去上海，我还要坐高铁。

Notes:

车次 (chēcì): *n.* train number

到达 (dàodá): *v.* to arrive

高速铁路 (gāosù tiělù): *n.* high speed railway

当天 (dàngtiān): *n.* the same day

出差 (chūchāi): *v.* to go away on a business

1. Why does the author believe that traveling by high speed rail is better than traveling by air?

2. Which train did the author take to Shanghai?

3. According to the train schedule, which train heading to Shanghai take the least amount of time?

WRITING PRACTICE 8.2

I. Your cousin e-mailed you asking for your suggestions about going to China. She likes shopping and at the same time she also likes nature. She is debating whether to go to Shanghai or Yunnan this summer. Based on her preferences, write her an e-mail back to help her select destination and provide your reasoning.

To:
From:
Subject: RE: 暑假去中国玩!

II. Your cousin is going to China during her ten-day holiday break over Chinese New Year and needs your help creating a travel itinerary. Provide detailed information about where to go, what to do, how to get there, what to eat, where to stay, and what method of transportation to take. Your cousin has a budget of $1500-2000 (air ticket not included).